P9-DCW-132

THE REAL WALLIS SIMPSON

ALSO BY ANNA PASTERNAK

Lara: The Untold Love Story and the Inspiration for "Doctor Zhivago"

Princess in Love

THE REAL WALLIS SIMPSON

A New History of the American Divorcée Who Became the Duchess of Windsor

ANNA PASTERNAK

ATRIA BOOKS

New York London Toronto Sydney New Delhi

An Imprint of Simon & Schuster, Inc.
1230 Avenue of the Americas
New York, NY 10020

First Atria Books hardcover edition March 2019

Manufactured in the United States of America

10 9 8 7 6 5 4 3 2 1

Library of Congress Cataloging-in-Publication Data

Names: Pasternak, Anna, 1967– author.
Title: The real Wallis Simpson : a new history of the American divorcee who became the Duchess of Windsor / Anna Pasternak.
Other titles: New history of the American divorcee who became the Duchess of Windsor
Description: New York : Atria, [2019] | Includes bibliographical references and index. |
Identifiers: LCCN 2018049232 (print) | LCCN 2018049536 (ebook) | ISBN 9781501198465 (eBook) | ISBN 9781501198441 (hardcover) | ISBN 9781501198458 (pbk.)
Subjects: LCSH: Windsor, Wallis Warfield, Duchess of, 1896-1986. | Windsor, Edward, Duke of, 1894–1972—Marriage. | Nobility—Great Britain—Biography. | Marriages of royalty and nobility—Great Britain—History—20th century.
Classification: LCC DA581.W5 (ebook) | LCC DA581.W5 P37 2019 (print) | DDC 941.084092 [B] —dc23
LC record available at https://urldefense.proofpoint.com/v2/url?u=https-3A__lccn.loc.gov_2018049232&d=DwIFAg&c=jGUuvAdBXp_VqQ6toyah2g&r=Lq-ns-jcESvYUdATgkcNbvMOlNoGVprXLxKfNLoNW2jIXd1mrwshf3RFabPay8c9&m=pAddWf4SEL5QY6TlgnH_St-7H1MXLhIdo9KOIsVwuY4&s=AqMFZ9G5qbGtjYlwd9cbbLbCsolgBhn9HvJxGq_i8co&e=

ISBN 978-1-5011-9844-1
ISBN 978-1-5011-9846-5 (ebook)

To Wallis,
"Her Royal Highness" the Duchess of Windsor

I who had sought no place in history would now be assured of one—an appalling one, carved out by blind prejudice.

—The Duchess of Windsor

The fault lay not in my stars but in my genes.

—HRH the Duke of Windsor

CONTENTS

Wallis Simpson's family

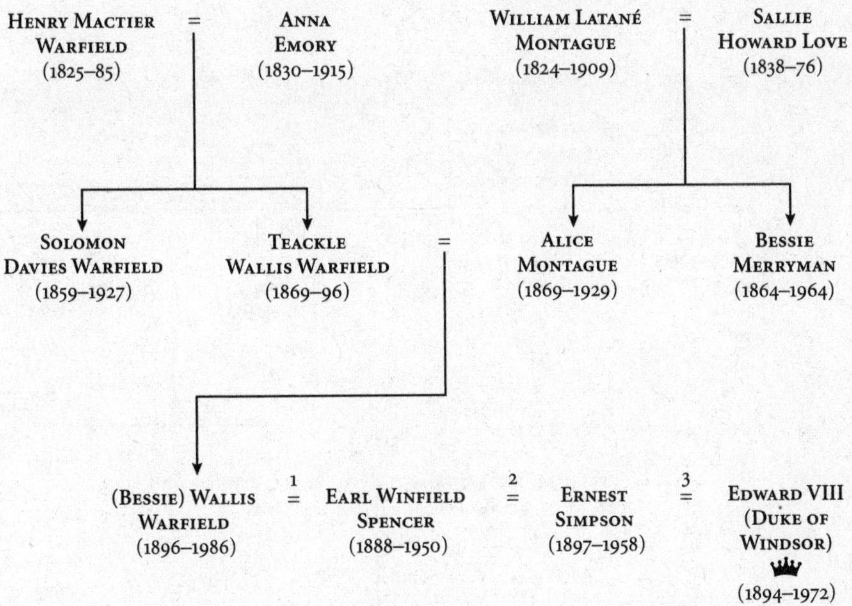
Henry Mactier Warfield (1825–85)
=
Anna Emory (1830–1915)
William Latané Montague (1824–1909)
=
Sallie Howard Love (1838–76)
Solomon Davies Warfield (1859–1927)
Teackle Wallis Warfield (1869–96)
=
Alice Montague (1869–1929)
Bessie Merryman (1864–1964)
(Bessie) Wallis Warfield (1896–1986)
1 =
Earl Winfield Spencer (1888–1950)
2 =
Ernest Simpson (1897–1958)
3 =
Edward VIII (Duke of Windsor) (1894–1972)

British royal family

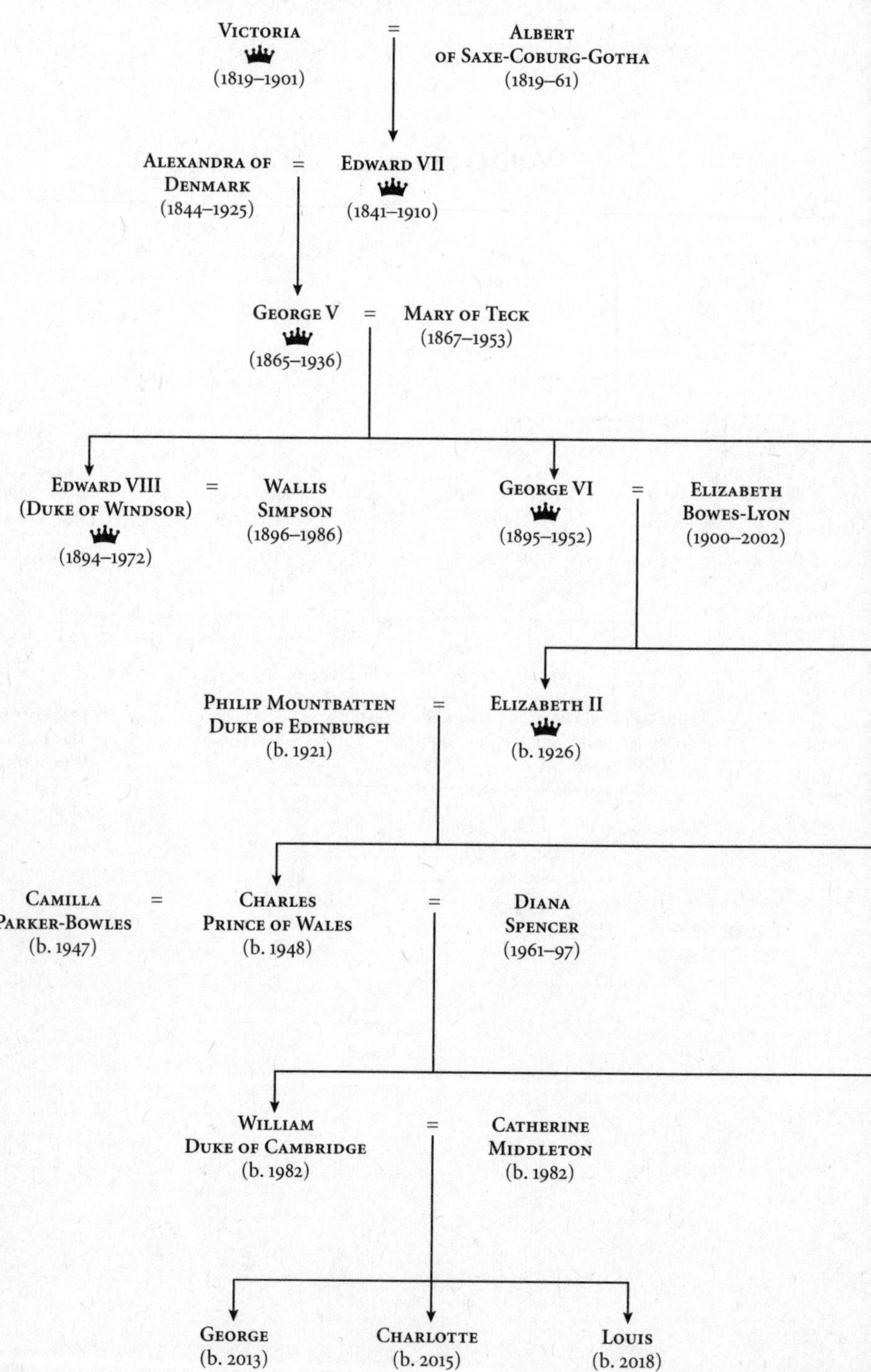

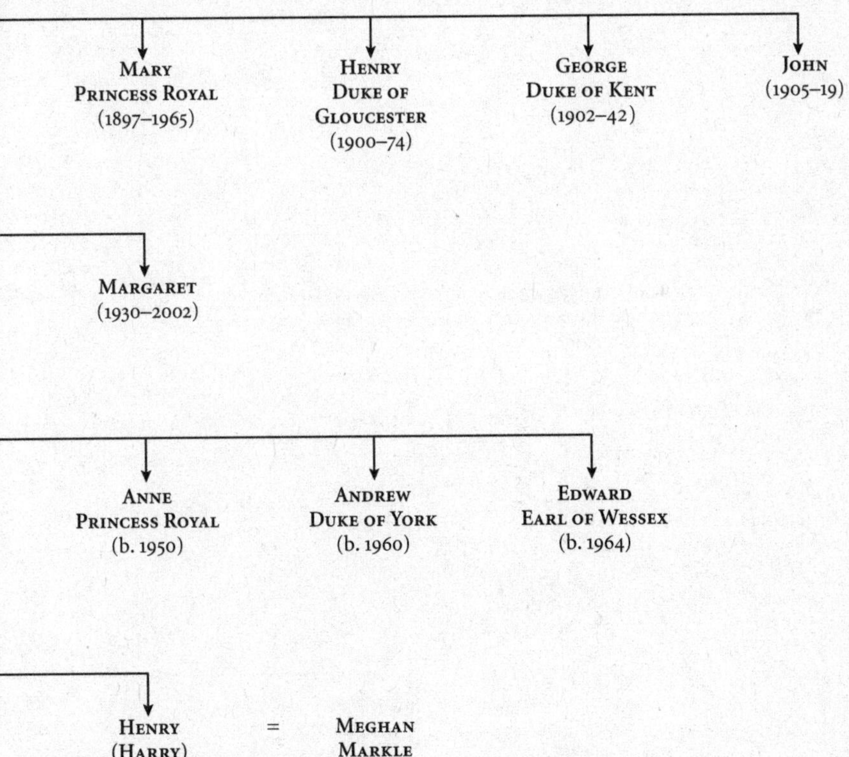
Mary
Princess Royal
(1897–1965)
Henry
Duke of
Gloucester
(1900–74)
George
Duke of Kent
(1902–42)
John
(1905–19)
Margaret
(1930–2002)
Anne
Princess Royal
(b. 1950)
Andrew
Duke of York
(b. 1960)
Edward
Earl of Wessex
(b. 1964)
Henry
(Harry)
Duke of Sussex
(b. 1984)
=
Meghan
Markle
(b. 1981)

PROLOGUE

The Heart Has Its Reasons

Once upon a time, there was a charming, handsome prince. Whenever he visited even the farthest reaches of his kingdom, his people flocked to see him. He was adored the world over. Everyone expected him to marry a pretty, well-bred English virgin who would one day become Queen of England and its vast empire. But, when the prince was thirty-seven years old—having previously shown no sign of wanting to get married—he fell in love with an odd-looking, twice-divorced American. No one thought that the affair would last, so everyone close to him kept quiet about it. When the prince's father, the king, died five years later, the prince inherited the Crown. Courtiers assumed that the new king would find a suitable young bride. To their horror, he said that he could not continue to be king without the American woman he loved by his side and that he intended to marry her. Everyone in the royal palaces, the prime minister, the government, the Church, were shocked. They accused the wicked witch–divorcée of being a sorceress who had cast a spell over their poor, gentle prince in order to become queen. The king's ministers told him that if he married this terrible woman, he would have to surrender the Crown.

But instead of renouncing his love, the king sacrificed his whole realm—an empire of over five hundred million people—to be with her. He only ruled for 326 days, making his reign one of the shortest in his country's history. His devoted subjects were heartbroken. They blamed the ugly witch for taking their beloved sovereign away from them. His family banished him from the land, leaving him free to marry the woman he loved. Denied royal status, the couple spent the rest of their lives in exile, roaming the world aimlessly, sad that they could not return to the king's homeland and to the little castle that he adored. The world, meanwhile, imagined that this was the Greatest Love Story Ever Told and that husband and wife went on to live Happily Ever After.

The story of the abdication of King Edward VIII and his marriage to Wallis Simpson has been told so many times that it has taken on the character of a fairy tale. Like fairy tales, much of what we are repeatedly told is in fact make-believe. The most scandalous love affair of the twentieth century may have softened into a romantic legend with time, but dark myths still endure. The dashing young prince, whose charisma and glamour ensured him the status of a movie star, gave up "the greatest throne in history," as Churchill called it, to marry his one true love, an American divorcée. Surely there can be no greater act of sacrifice than to give up such power, privilege and adoration for love? And for a woman whose appeal was such a mystery to most.

Edward Albert Christian George Andrew Patrick David Windsor was considered the world's most eligible bachelor. Society hostess Elsa Maxwell first met the Prince of Wales in the early 1920s "at Mrs. Cuckoo Belleville's house in Manchester Square. He was a gay, golden-haired, blue-eyed, debonair Prince Charming, the most famous celebrity in the world, who seemed a Raphael angel grown up. He projected an aura of glamour that was as unmistakable as it was authentic."[1] To the fashion editor Diana Vreeland, "he *was* the Golden Prince. You must understand that to be a woman of my generation in London—*any* woman—was to be in love with the Prince of Wales."[2]

Men were equally beguiled. Even the senior palace courtier, Alan Lascelles, known in royal circles as "Tommy" and later a fierce critic of the former king, gushed in 1921 that the heir to the throne was "the most attractive man I ever met."[3] Piers "Joey" Legh, an equerry who remained in the prince's service for twenty years, accompanying him into exile, said of Edward a decade after the abdication: his "charm was so great that I would thrill with emotion if the duke entered the room just now."[4]

When news of Wallis Simpson's affair with Edward broke from under a media blackout in 1936, what seemed unfathomable was why, when the Prince of Wales could have had any beauty he desired, he was smitten with an unconventional, severe-looking American two years his junior with two living husbands. So much gossip and innuendo have been leveled at Wallis that it has become near impossible to discern the real woman or to hear her authentic voice amid the cacophony of condemnation. As her friend Herman Rogers said of her in 1936, "much of what is being said concerns a woman who does not exist and never did exist."[5] Lady Monckton, a close friend of the Windsors, later concurred: "People were always being nasty about Wallis. You must remember how jealous people felt when the Prince of Wales fell in love with her."[6]

Ever since, we have been overfed a diet of fantastical slander: that Wallis was really a man; that she had a perverse psychosexual hold over the prince; that she used manipulation and feminine wiles to lure him into abdicating; that she was a ruthless, cold, ambitious bitch who schemed from the outset to be Queen of England. The well-worn view is that she alone was responsible for almost bringing down the British monarchy, triggering a constitutional crisis caused by her determination to marry the heir apparent. We have experienced her so fully as Machiavellian through others' projections and prejudices, through misogynistic memoirs, biographies and unflattering portrayals, that she has become a caricature of villainous womanhood. Devoid of warmth, emotional complexity and a beating heart, she remains the brittle victim of salacious chatter and brutal character assassination many decades after her pitiful death.

Instead of simply belittling Wallis and defaming her reputation, we might try to understand this modern, intelligent, remarkable woman and the impossible situation she was placed in. She was, in fact, very warm, funny, irresistibly charming, loyal and dignified to the end. Adored by her many friends, she was written off by a cunning, powerful British establishment that sought to destroy and diminish her; men like Tommy Lascelles—who famously dismissed Wallis as "shop-soiled" with "a voice like a rusty saw"—the British prime minister Stanley Baldwin; and Cosmo Lang, the archbishop of Canterbury.

However, far from being the villain of the abdication, Wallis was the victim. Instead of pushing for Edward to leave the throne, she had tried to prevent it. What most of her detractors fail to acknowledge is that she never wanted to marry Edward. Naturally she was initially flattered by his attention; as an American woman living in London, surrounded by society hostesses and social climbers, she felt giddy to be included in His Royal Highness's elegant and rarefied circle. What woman would not have been beguiled by the prince's "unmistakable aura of power and authority?"[7] According to Wallis: "His slightest wish seemed always to be translated instantly into the most impressive kind of reality. Trains were held; yachts materialized; the best suites in the finest hotels were flung open; aeroplanes stood waiting."[8] Wallis made no secret of her open-mouthed delight, but she also believed Edward's interest in her was transitory. She never expected his infatuation to last. In 1935 she wrote to her beloved aunt, Bessie Merryman, in Wallis's hometown of Baltimore: "What a bump I'll get when a young beauty appears and plucks the Prince from me. Anyway, I am prepared."[9]

The real tragedy for Wallis is that she could never have been prepared for what was to come, for the speed with which events spun so quickly out of her control. Though worldly, she would find herself painfully out of her depth. Unable to juggle her settled, second marriage to Ernest Simpson with the overwhelming and incessant demands of a besotted prince—whom she and Ernest nicknamed "Peter Pan"—Wallis became the perfect pawn. She did not bargain for Edward's self-absorbed, possessive and stubborn love for her and his absolute refusal to give her up. Although she valiantly tried to break off the relationship prior to the abdication, it would become impossible for Wallis to ever leave his side.

Probably the biggest lie in this fable is that Wallis lured Edward from his destiny. Her detractors claim that if she had never divorced Ernest

Simpson, the abdication would not have occurred. Yet the truth is that she had had no intention of divorcing Ernest. It was Edward, then king, who forced her into this untenable position. In the name of his needy love, Wallis paid the ultimate price: entrapment by a childish narcissist who threw the largest tantrum in history when he could not have the two things he wanted most in the world: Wallis and the throne.

When I began my research, keen to strip away decades of grotesque caricature in an attempt to find the real Wallis, I feared that doors might close. The opposite happened: people were keen to talk with me and I found that those close to the story did not hold Wallis in contempt. Many powerful, key players who had led the charge against Mrs. Simpson were now dead. The late Queen Mother, then Elizabeth, Duchess of York, for one, was furious that Edward's abdication might force her highly strung and physically weak husband, Bertie, onto the throne and dehumanized Wallis as "that woman" and "the lowest of the low." The spite meted out to Wallis by certain members of the royal family was staggering. Those of Wallis's friends who are still alive seem to finally feel freer to speak about the injustice they witnessed. Sitting in elegant drawing rooms in London, Paris, Gstaad and Marbella, interviewing those who knew Wallis, I heard the same sentiments echoed: that she was witty and diverting company; that the duke was self-absorbed and less engaging. That Wallis, possessed of perfect manners, behaved with laudable inner strength and dignity, despite the terrible slurs and insults hurled at her. "The world adored *him*," Hugo Vickers said of the Duke of Windsor, "yet the people who knew him and worked for him had reservations about him. The world hated *her* but the people who knew her and worked for her absolutely adored her."[10]

None of those with whom I spoke recognized the wicked Wallis of the history books. Repeatedly, I heard of her kindliness, sense of fun and depth of friendship, which contradicted the public image of a hard-nosed, shallow woman. The closer I got to Wallis's true character, the greater my incredulity and mounting fury that the world has judged her unfairly and unkindly. She certainly was no saint, but she was far from the sinister manipulator depicted in many accounts. Her friends noted in their diaries and memoirs their warmth and respect for Wallis, yet these tender recollections never seemed to gain sufficient attention. "She was so affectionate, a loving sort of friend—very rare you know," wrote Diana Vreeland. "Women are rarely that sort of friend to each other."[11] Wallis was similarly loyal to male friends. The Conservative MP Sir Henry "Chips" Channon said: "She has always shown me friendship, understanding and even affection, and I have known her to do a hundred kindnesses and never a mean act."[12]

Wallis was viciously derided at the time of Edward's abdication and then kept at a distance, denied the opportunity to change public mistrust and misgivings about her. When the scandal broke in the press, she was, understandably, devastated. "The enormity of the hatred I had aroused and the distorted image of me that seemed to be forming in minds everywhere went far beyond anything I had anticipated even in my most depressed moments," she later wrote. "I became obsessed by the notion that, in a manner impossible for me to comprehend, a calculated and organized effort to discredit me had been set afoot."[13]

She was right. So sensational were the press reports and fevered gossip in 1936—Mrs. Simpson was a "gold digger," "a whore," "a sorceress," "a Nazi spy"—that many of the British and European aristocracy, meeting her for the first time, were taken aback. The woman they encountered was nothing like her vulgar fictional persona. "I was absolutely flabbergasted when I first met the duchess," recalled Count Rudolf von Schönburg. "She was the complete opposite of everything we had heard about her."[14]

Count Rudi became a close friend of the Windsors after meeting them in the early sixties in Marbella, where he ran a fashionable hotel. "The story of the abdication was so shocking," he recalled, "but the duchess was so much more ladylike than anything we had been led to believe. It was all 'this loud, twice-divorced *American*' . . . yet here was this charming, dignified woman, always well dressed but never overdoing it. Maybe sometimes she laughed too loudly but that was it. I liked her very much and we spent many days and evenings with the couple, so had the opportunity to be treated like close friends and almost family. I have always considered that her position in history is factually incorrect and very unfair."[15]

The Duke of Fragnito had similar preconceptions when he met the duchess in Palm Beach in the early 1960s. "I didn't want to like her because of everything I had heard about her," he admitted. "But I was taken aback by her grace and impeccable manners. To my great surprise she behaved like a real royal. She was just as captivating as the duke. They both had this ability to produce an electric charm which I have never forgotten."[16]

Vogue editor Diana Vreeland noted of Wallis: "There was something about her that made you look twice."[17] The duchess's private secretary, Joanna Schultz, accompanied Wallis to New York by boat shortly after the duke died. The duchess did not put her name on the passenger list and usually ate in her room. Occasionally, she would enter the dining room to keep Miss Schultz company. "Some people recognized her, others didn't, but they knew she was special," said Hugo Vickers. "She was somebody. She had a hypnotic effect."[18]

"I can't say that she was sexy but she was sassy," remembered Nicky Haslam. "She walked into the room and it took off. The only other person I knew who had that quality was Frank Sinatra."[19] Haslam, an interior designer who met Wallis in New York in 1962, said: "Wallis had innate American style. But to be an American was against her then, almost more than the divorce."[20] Wallis described the archaic snobbery she encountered when living in London: "The British seemed to cherish a sentiment of settled disapproval towards things American."[21]

I was sitting with Nicholas Haslam in a Chelsea restaurant when he produced an envelope, saying that he had something special to show me. It was a handwritten letter from Wallis to her friend Elsie de Wolfe. Elsie, who became Lady Mendl in 1926 on her marriage to Sir Charles Mendl, a press attaché to the British embassy in Paris, was an eccentric who practiced yoga and underwent plastic surgeries years before both became de rigueur. Credited with inventing the profession of interior decorating, she was famed for her elaborate parties, and in particular the Circus Ball at the Villa Trianon in Versailles in 1939. Attended by over seven hundred guests, including the duke and duchess, the ball was held in a green-and-white dance pavilion and featured a fabulously jeweled elephant.

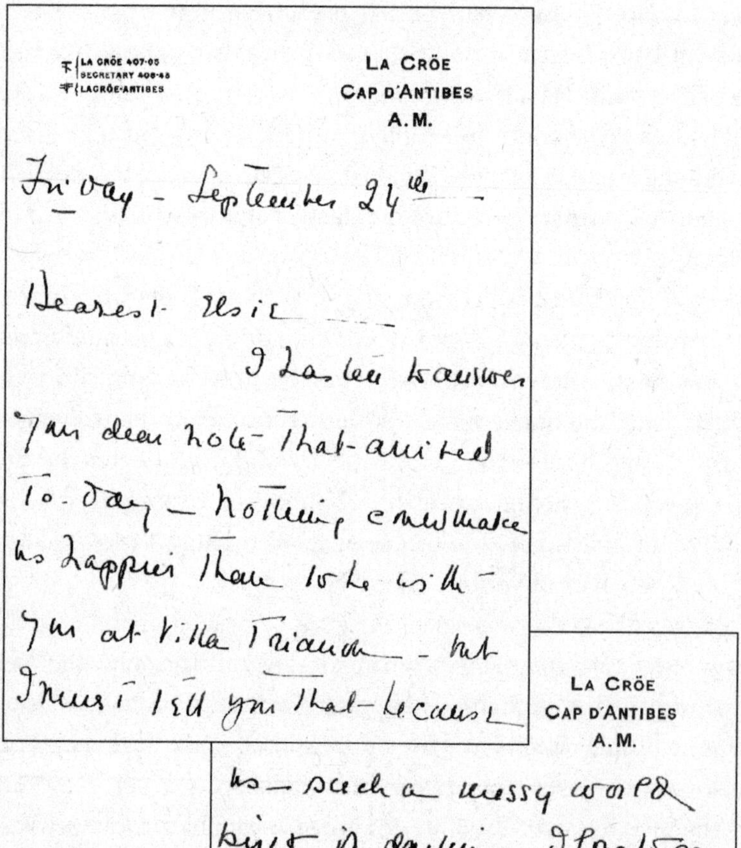

LA CRÖE 407-05
SECRETARY 408-45
LACRÖE-ANTIBES

LA CRÖE
CAP D'ANTIBES
A.M.

Friday – September 24th –

Dearest Elsie —

I have been to answer your dear note that arrived to-day — nothing could make us happier than to be with you at Villa Trianon — but I must tell you that because

LA CRÖE
CAP D'ANTIBES
A.M.

us — such a messy world isn't it darling. I long to see your elephant again and sit in the tent with the blackamoors, look at you and the things you have created. I do wish I could come sooner to do all this —

My great and deep affection as always Wallis

Circumstances would force Wallis to adopt Elsie's favorite motto, embroidered on taffeta cushions strewn throughout the Villa Trianon: "Never Complain, Never Explain."

Turning the letter over in my hand, I admired Wallis's chic stationery, the thick envelope lined with forest-green tissue paper and the simple address on crisp cream-colored paper, "La Croë, Cap d'Antibes," the duke and duchess's villa in the south of France. The letter, written in 1948, and dated Friday, September 24, reveals Wallis's loose, looping handwriting in black ink: open and hurried in style and pace, there are endearing crossings out and insertions as her thoughts race across the page with barely any punctuation. She asks Elsie if she and Edward can come to stay with her at the Villa Trianon on their way back to Paris, and shares details of her day-to-day life: "I swam this A.M and tonight I go to Cap d'Ail to play Oklahoma [a card game] with Winston Churchill who is stopping with Max Beaverbrook—we are great rivals and play every other night . . ."[22]

The letter is full of warmth and love. Wallis reveals herself to be a genuine, open friend. She tells Elsie how difficult it is packing up and leaving La Croë, which she and the duke had leased for the previous decade. Her loneliness and tension are tangible; she details her desire to be alone, relaxing with Elsie, whom she misses: "I long to see your elephant again and sit in the tent with the blackamoors, look at you and the things you have created," Wallis wrote. "I do wish I could come sooner to do all this. My great and deep affection, as always, Wallis."[23]

When I contemplated the duke and duchess's empty, peripatetic life after abdication and exile, I felt a profound sadness. What was their purpose from that point on? To live a life together to prove that it had not all been for nought? To be happy? To appear to be happy? There must have been an element of continuous silent strain for them both, a seam of guilt they dared not plunder. "I have a theory that when men let women down, they feel awful," Hugo Vickers told me. "The duke turned Wallis into the most hated woman in the world, then he couldn't get her what he promised her: the HRH title, or his family to accept her. So he must have spent his whole life feeling guilty. I saw him once at

Princess Marina's* funeral and I have never seen a man with sadder eyes."[24]

Over three decades into their post-abdication existence, just a few years before the duke's death, the Windsors were interviewed on live television, on the BBC, by the broadcaster Kenneth Harris. The program was watched by twelve million viewers. Wallis comes across effortlessly; she is witty and warm. The duke, with his hangdog eyes, appears less comfortable in his own skin, constantly looking down at his hands, studying his nails, fidgeting. The interviewer asks the couple if they have any regrets. The duchess, elegant in cream silk with a pale-blue scarf, laughs nervously: "About certain things. I wish it could have been different. Naturally, we've had some hard times. Who hasn't? But we've been very happy." The duke awkwardly grabs her hand in confirmation.[25]

The main aim of this book is to look beneath this convenient illusion and give Wallis a voice: to peel back the layers of prejudice and examine the wider motives for the enduring propaganda against her. For Edward, the relationship started as a thrilling *coup de foudre*; for Wallis, it would soon feel like a Faustian pact. Did a genuine love emerge between them as they surmounted the abdication together, or was the monumental sacrifice on both their parts a tragedy of Shakespearean proportions? Wallis, quietly stoical, rarely sought pity or openly complained about her suffering. She was always incredibly dignified, generously concluding in her memoirs: "Any woman who has been loved as I have been loved, and who, too, has loved, has experienced life in its fullness."[26]

* Princess Marina, Duchess of Kent (1906–68), was born Princess Marina of Greece and Denmark. She was married to Prince George, Duke of Kent, Edward's favorite brother.

1

The Prince's Girl

As the train hurtled north from St. Pancras to Melton Mowbray in Leicestershire, Wallis Simpson stood in the aisle of a compartment, practicing her curtsy—no mean feat, given the lurch and sway of the carriage. She was being instructed that the trick was to put her left leg well back behind her right one. Wallis's balance was further challenged due to a streaming cold; her head was bunged up, while a voice rasped in her ears as she tried to master an elegant swoop down, then up. This comical scene was being watched by her husband, Ernest Simpson—always gently encouraging—and their friend Benjamin Thaw Jr., who was delivering the etiquette tutorial. Benjamin, known as Benny, first secretary at the United States embassy, was married to Consuelo Morgan, whose glamorous American half sisters were Thelma, Viscountess Furness, and Gloria Vanderbilt.

Benny and Connie Thaw had become close friends of the Simpsons in London. Wallis and Ernest mixed in society circles thanks to the introductions of his sister, Maud Kerr-Smiley. Maud had married Peter Kerr-Smiley in 1905. He became a prominent member of Parliament and it was the Kerr-Smileys who facilitated the Simpsons' entrée into the upper echelons of the aristocracy. It was through Consuelo that Wallis first met Thelma Furness. Consuelo had told her sister that Wallis was fun, promising Thelma that she would like her. In the autumn of 1930, she took Wallis to her sister's Grosvenor Square house for cocktails. "Consuelo was right," said Thelma. "Wallis Simpson was 'fun,' and I did like her."[1] "She was not beautiful; in fact, she was not even pretty," she recalled of thirty-four-year-old Wallis—who was accustomed to an ever-present scrutiny of her looks—"but she had a distinct charm and a sharp sense of humour. Her dark hair was parted in the middle. Her eyes, alert and eloquent, were her best feature."[2] Wallis was blessed with riveting sapphire-blue eyes.

That November Wallis received a tantalizing invitation. Connie Thaw asked her if she and Ernest would act as chaperones to Thelma and the Prince of Wales at a weekend house party in Leicestershire. Connie had to leave for the Continent at the last minute, due to a family illness, and wondered if Wallis and Ernest would accompany Ambassador Thaw to Burrough Court, Viscount Furness's country house, instead. The Simpsons had heard the rumors that Thelma Furness was "the Prince's Girl," having stolen the *maîtresse en titre* role from his previous lover, Mrs. Freda Dudley Ward. The prince's pet name for Thelma was "Toodles," and she was said to be madly in love with him.[3] It was an open secret in society circles that Thelma was unhappily married to Marmaduke, the 1st Viscount Furness. Known as the "fiery Furness," he had red hair and a temper.[4]

Wallis's first reaction to the invitation was "a mixture of pleasure and horror. . . . Like everybody else, I was dying to meet the Prince of Wales," she said, "but my knowledge of royalty, except for what I had read, had until then been limited to glimpses at a distance of King George V in his State Coach on his way to Parliament."[5] Though unsure of royal etiquette, she was at least confident of looking the part, having been on a shopping spree in Molyneux in Paris, a few months earlier. Her attractive blue-grey tweed dress, with a matching fur-edged cape, "would meet the most exacting requirements of both a horsy and princely setting."[6]

It was past five o'clock on Saturday afternoon when Thaw and the Simpsons arrived at Melton Mowbray, in the heart of fox-hunting country. A thick fog choked the county. Burrough Court was a spacious, comfortable hunting lodge full of traditional mahogany furniture and lively chintz. Thelma's stepdaughter, Averill, greeted the guests, informing them that the rest of the party had been delayed out hunting on the road, due to the fog. Taken into the drawing room, where tea had been laid out on a round table in front of the fire, Wallis could feel her skin burning. Suspecting she had a slight temperature, she hankered to go to bed. Instead, they were forced to wait a further two hours until the royal party arrived.

After what seemed an age, voices were heard in the hallway, and Thelma appeared with two princes: Edward, Prince of Wales, and his younger (favorite) brother, Prince George. To her surprise, Wallis's curtsy to each prince came off well, to the Simpsons' shared amusement. Thelma led everyone back to the table in front of the fire, and they had tea all over again.

Like many who meet celebrities in the flesh for the first time, Wallis was taken aback; she was surprised by how small the Prince of Wales was. She was five foot five, and Edward less than two inches taller. Prince George was "considerably taller," she noted, "with neatly brushed brown hair, aquiline features, and dark-blue eyes. He gave an impression of gaiety and joie de vivre."[7] Facially, Edward was immediately recognizable. "I remember thinking, as I studied the Prince of Wales, how much like his pictures he really was," she recollected. "The slightly wind-rumpled golden hair, the turned-up nose, and a strange, wistful, almost sad look about the eyes when his expression was in repose."[8]

At eight o'clock Prince George's friends arrived and took him to another house party. Finally, the Simpsons could retire upstairs to change. Wallis had a much-longed-for hot bath and took two aspirin, while Ernest—from America but naturalized British—remarked on the charm of the two royal brothers and how they instantly put everyone at their ease. "I have come to the conclusion," he added, "that you Americans lost something that is very good and quite irreplaceable when you decided to dispense with the British Monarchy."[9]

The dinner party that night for thirty guests went late even by European standards, past ten o'clock. Ernest and Wallis knew no one and were at a conversational loss, as they had no knowledge of, or curiosity about, hunting—a fact not lost on the prince. "Mrs. Simpson did not ride and obviously had no interest in horses, hounds, or hunting in general," Edward later wrote. "She was also plainly in misery from a bad cold in the head."[10] Discovering that she was American, the prince kicked off conversation by observing that she must miss central heating, of which there was a lamentable lack in British country houses and an abundance in American homes. Wallis's response astonished him: "On the contrary. I like the cold houses of Great Britain," she replied. According to the prince, "a mocking look came into her eyes," and she replied: "I am sorry, Sir, but you have disappointed me."

"In what way?" said Edward.

"Every American woman who comes to your country is always asked the same question. I had hoped for something more original from the Prince of Wales."[11]

Wallis, born Bessie Wallis Warfield on June 19, 1896, took pride in coming from old southern stock. "Wallis's family was very old by American standards," said her friend Lady Diana Mosley, approvingly.[12] Wallis's mother, Alice, gave birth to her in a holiday cottage in Blue Ridge Summit in Pennsylvania, where she had gone with her consumptive husband, named Teackle, to escape the heat of his native Baltimore. Alice and Teackle, both twenty-six years old, were fleeing their disapproving parents. Wallis wrote that her mother and father had married in June 1895: "without taking their parents into their confidence, they slipped away." Records show that they actually married on November 19, seven months before her birth, in a quiet ceremony with no family present.[13] Wallis was conceived out of wedlock, a fact she tried to blur in later accounts of her life. She recalled how she once asked her mother for the date and time of her birth, "and she answered impatiently that she had been far too busy at the time to consult the calendar let alone the clock."[14] Wallis learned early the benefits of discretion.

Her mother was a Montague from Virginia. They were famous for their good looks and sharp tongues. When Wallis was growing up, if she made one of her familiar wisecracks, friends would exclaim: "Oh, the Montagueity of it!"[15] Perhaps it was a Montagueism that caused Wallis as a young child to drop the first name Bessie and say that she wished to be known simply as "Wallis." She was "very quick and funny," remembers Nicky Haslam. "She could be cutting too. She put people's backs up amid the British aristocracy in the sense of being too bright and witty."[16] On meeting Wallis, Chips Channon declared: "Mrs. Simpson is a woman of great wit," she has "sense, balance and her reserve and discretion are famous."[17] "Her talent was for people," said Diana Mosley. "Witty herself, she had the capacity to draw the best out of others, making even the dull feel quite pleased with themselves."[18]

From a young age, realizing that she was not conventionally attractive and could not rely on the flimsy currency of her looks, Wallis developed an inner resilience and astute insight. "My endowments were definitely on the scanty side," she later recalled. "Nobody ever called me beautiful or even pretty. I was thin in an era when a certain plumpness was a girl's ideal. My jaw was clearly too big and too pointed to be classic. My hair was straight where the laws of compensation might at least have produced curls."[19]

Wallis's father died from tuberculosis when Wallis was five months old, leaving her mother penniless. The Warfields supported Alice and their granddaughter, affording Wallis a happy childhood. An only child, she plainly adored her mother, who summoned up "reserves of will and fortitude" to surmount her single-mother status. Wallis admired her mother for never "showing a trace of self-pity or despair"—characteristics that she inherited and would employ throughout her own life with similar aplomb. Alice urged Wallis never to be afraid of loneliness. "Loneliness has its purposes," she counseled her daughter. "It teaches us to think."[20]

Wallis and her mother were so close that Wallis described their relationship as "more like sisters" in terms of their "comradeship."[21] Alice Warfield was both loving and strict. If Wallis swore, she would be marched to the bathroom to have her tongue scrubbed with a nailbrush. When Wallis was apprehensive about learning to swim, her mother simply carried her to the deep end of a swimming pool and dropped her in. "Then and there I learned to swim, and the thought occurs that I've been striking out that way ever since," Wallis wrote years after Edward VIII's abdication.[22]

When Alice first met Ernest Simpson, she warned her future son-in-law: "You must remember that Wallis is an only child. Like explosives, she needs to be handled with care. There are times when I have been too afraid of having put too much of myself into her—too much of the heart, that is, and not enough of the head."[23] Alice sent Wallis to a fashionable day school in Baltimore, where Wallis was a diligent student. "No one has ever accused me of being intellectual. Though in my school days I was capable of good marks," she said.[24] As a young girl, Wallis was already tiring of her unsettled life and "desperately wanted to stay put."[25] This desire to find a stable home would become a constant theme in her life, heightened when forced into exile with the Duke of Windsor. For a few years, Wallis and her mother lived with her Warfield grandmother, then with her Aunt Bessie, until Alice, craving a place of her own, took a small apartment when her daughter was seven. Wallis loved her grandmother's Baltimore house: "a red brick affair, trimmed with white with the typical Baltimore hall-mark, white marble steps leading down to the side-walk."[26] Here her grandmother lived with her last unmarried son, S. Davies Warfield—"Uncle Sol" to Wallis. "For a long and impressionable period he was the nearest thing to a father in my uncertain world," Wallis recalled. "But an odd kind of father—reserved, unbending, silent. I was always a little afraid of Uncle Sol."[27]

A successful banker, Sol paid the school fees until Wallis's mother married again. Alice's new husband was John Freeman Rasin, who was prominent in politics and fairly wealthy. While offering financial security, he took Alice to live part-time in Atlanta, which was a wrench for Wallis. In 1912 she was sent to boarding school—Oldfields—where the school motto, pasted on the door of every dormitory, was "Gentleness and Courtesy are expected of the Girls at all Times." Wallis's best friend at Oldfields was Mary Kirk, who was later to play an astonishing part in her life.

In 1913 Wallis and her mother suffered another shock. Freeman Rasin died of Bright's disease, a failure of the kidneys. Wallis was heartbroken to see her mother so distressed. "It was the first time I had ever seen her dispirited." Wallis would never forget her mother whispering to her: "I had not thought it possible to be so hurt so much so soon." Alice had been with her second husband for less than five years.[28]

Wallis left Oldfields in 1914, signing her name in the school book with the bold and rebellious "ALL IS LOVE," and made her debut as part of the jeunesse dorée at the Bachelor's Cotillion, a ball in Baltimore, on December 24. (To be presented at the ball was "a life-and-death matter for Baltimore girls in those days," maintained Wallis.[29]) The Great War had begun in Europe in August, and the US daily newspapers were "black with headlines of frightful battles."[30] Baltimore's sentiments were firmly on the side of the Allies, and the thirty-four debutantes attending the ball were instructed to sign a public pledge to observe, for the duration of the war, "an absence of rivalry in elegance in respective social functions."[31] This was, according to Wallis, an attempt to set an example of how young American women should conduct themselves at a time when other friendly nations were in extremity.[32]

Unable to afford to buy her ball gown from Fuechsl's, Baltimore's most fashionable shop, like most other debutantes, Wallis designed her own dress. White satin with a white chiffon tunic and bordered with seed pearls, it was made by "a local Negro seamstress called Ellen." Wallis's mother permitted her for the first time a brush of rouge on her cheeks, even though rouge "was considered a little fast."[33] Wallis's love of couture would become legendary; as the Duchess of Windsor, she became an icon of style and an arbiter of meticulous taste. She regularly featured in the best-dressed lists of the world. Her sharp eye for fashionable detail burgeoned early. According to Aunt Bessie, Wallis created a "foot-stamping scene" at one of the first parties she ever attended as a little girl, when she wanted to substitute a blue sash her mother wanted her to wear with a red one. "I remember exactly what you said," Aunt Bessie later told Wallis. "You told your mother you wanted a red sash so the boys would notice you."[34] Wallis told a fashion journalist in 1966: "Whatever look I evolved came from working with a little dressmaker around the corner years and years ago, who used to make all my clothes. I began with my own personal ideas about style and I've never felt correct in anything but the severe look I developed then."[35]

As the Duchess of Windsor, she created an eternal signature style, which became her personal armor. Her dedication to appearance defined her as a southern woman, hailing from an era when a woman dressed to please her man. "She was chic but never casual," said the French aristocrat and designer Jacqueline de Ribes, who similarly topped the best-dressed lists. "Other American society women, like Babe Paley, could be chic in blue jeans. The duchess was a different generation."[36] Elsa Maxwell observed: "The Duchess has impeccable taste and she spends more money on her wardrobe than any woman I've ever known. Her clothes are beautiful and chic, but though she invests them with elegance, she wears them with such rigidity, such neatness, that she destroys the impression of ease and casualness. She is too meticulous."[37] Diana Vreeland, later of *Harper's Bazaar* and editor of *Vogue*, described Wallis's style as "*soignée*, not *dégagée*"—polished but not relaxed.

Wallis learned to distil every outfit to its essence, later asking Parisian couturiers, including Hubert de Givenchy and Christian Dior's Marc Bohan, to dispense with pockets. Yet in her choice of nightwear she was the essence of soft, traditionally feminine sensuality. Vreeland, who had an exclusive lingerie boutique off Berkeley Square in London in the mid-1930s, recalled that when Wallis shopped, "she knew *exactly* what she wanted." One day in autumn 1936, just before the king's abdication, Wallis ordered three exquisite nightgowns to be made in three weeks. "First, there was one in white satin copied from Vionnet, all on the bias, that you just pulled down over your head," said Vreeland. "Then there was one I'd bought the original of in Paris from a marvelous Russian woman. The whole neck of this nightgown was made of petals, which was too extraordinary, because they were put in on the bias, and when you moved they rippled. Then the third nightgown was a wonderful pale blue crêpe de Chine."[38]

Years after the abdication, Elsa Maxwell asked Wallis why she devoted so much time and attention to her clothes. Was it not a frivolous pursuit when she had so many other responsibilities and her extravagance merely invited criticism? Wallis replied candidly: "My husband gave up everything for me. I'm not a beautiful woman. I'm nothing to look at, so the only thing I can do is to try and dress better than anyone else. If everyone looks at me when I enter a room, my husband can feel proud of me. That's my chief responsibility."[39]

"Wallis was a much more artistic creature than people thought," said Nicky Haslam. "She liked beautiful things and had a keen eye."[40] Haslam, who worked on American *Vogue* in the 1960s, was introduced to Wallis in New York by the magazine's social editor, Margaret Case. "We were seated at a booth at the back of the Colony restaurant in New York, on the best banquette, and in walked the duchess," he recalled. "Every single head turned to look at her and cutlery literally dropped. She was wearing an impossibly wide pink angora Chanel tweed with a black grosgrain bow at her nape. At the end of a wonderful lunch, she took a discreet peek at her watch, which was tied to her bag by a delicate chain. It was Fulco di Verdura* who told her that it was common for women to wear a watch."[41]

Having the sartorial edge hugely increased Wallis's confidence. Of her first meeting with the Prince of Wales at Melton Mowbray, she said her clothes would give her "the added assurance that came from the knowledge that in the dress was a little white satin label bearing the word Molyneux."[42]

It was her sister-in-law, Maud, who suggested that Wallis should be presented at court on June 10, 1931. Ernest Simpson's rank as a captain with the Coldstream Guards gave him the requisite social status, but Wallis was reluctant to go. Once again, as for her debutante ball in her youth, she did not have the funds to buy the splendid clothes the occasion demanded. However, Wallis's friends persuaded her that she would be foolish to turn down the generous offer of her girlfriend Mildred Anderson,

---

* Fulco di Verdura was an influential Italian jeweller who designed for the duchess. His career took off when he was introduced to Coco Chanel by Cole Porter.

to present her. "Determined to get through the ceremony in the most economical manner," she wore the dress that Connie Thaw herself had worn to be presented, while Thelma Furness lent her the train, feathers and fan. She treated herself to a large aquamarine cross and white kid three-quarter-length gloves,[43] writing to her Aunt Bessie that her aquamarine jewelery "looked really lovely on the white dress."[44]

Of the magnificent pageantry of the event, what impressed Wallis "to the point of awe" was the grandeur that invested King George V and Queen Mary, sitting side by side in full regalia on identical gilt thrones on their red dais.[45] Standing behind the two thrones were the Prince of Wales and his uncle, the Duke of Connaught. Ernest Simpson, in his uniform of the Coldstream Guards, looked on proudly as Wallis and Mildred performed deep curtsies to the sovereign, then to the queen. The Prince of Wales later recalled of Wallis: "When her turn came to curtsy, first to my father and then to my mother, I was struck by the grace of her carriage and the natural dignity of her movements."[46] After the ceremony, Wallis was standing with Ernest in the adjoining state apartment, in the front row, watching as the king and queen walked slowly by, followed by other members of the royal family. As the Prince of Wales passed her, Wallis overheard him say to his uncle: "Uncle Arthur, something ought to be done about the lights. They make all the women look ghastly."[47]

That evening, at a party hosted by Thelma Furness, Wallis met the Prince of Wales again. Over a glass of champagne, he complimented Wallis on her gown. " 'But, Sir,' she responded with a straight face, 'I understood that you thought we all looked ghastly.' " The prince "was startled," Wallis noted with some satisfaction. "Then he smiled. 'I had no idea my voice carried so far.' "[48]

The prince was captivated. No British woman would have dreamed of speaking to him in such a direct and provocative way. "In character, Wallis was, and still remains, complex and elusive," he wrote of that encounter. "From the first I looked upon her as the most independent woman I had ever met."[49]

* * *

Prince Edward
Park, the home c
ordinary prophe
Queen Victoria, tl
year of her reign.
Commons to shatt
he hollered: "This b
the score and will be
in due course . . . he
rumours of a morgan
that the country will
Edward's royal destin

Baptized by the arc
water from the River J
as his family always ca ... strict, unhappy and
largely loveless childho... His mother showed little maternal warmth to her six children, while her husband, who in 1910 became King George V, was even more severe. A dogged disciplinarian, with rigid rules on dress and protocol, he ensured that any errant childish behavior was bullied and beaten out of his offspring. "My father was the most *terrible father*, most *terrible father* you can imagine," Edward's brother Prince Henry later said.[51] "He believed in God, in the invincibility of the Royal Navy, and the essential rightness of whatever was British," said Edward.[52] Handwritten on his father's desk were the words that Edward was made to memorize as a young boy: "I shall pass through this world but once. Any good thing, therefore, that I can do or any kindness that I can show any human being, let me do it now. Let me not defer nor neglect it for I shall not pass this way again." These were the lines of an early-nineteenth-century American Quaker Stephen Grellet.

As a sense of duty and responsibility cleaved through every aspect of his royal bearing, the Duke of York made Edward fully aware of the influence of his great-grandmother Queen Victoria. Her children and grandchildren ruled the courts of Europe. Her eldest daughter, Victoria, was the Dowager Empress of Germany; Kaiser Wilhelm II was the

ia, Nicholas II, was her grandson
n Queen Victoria ruled was the most
aced a quarter of the earth's surface and
pulation. On her death in 1901, this empire
n, Edward VII, and then to George—an empire
inherit, albeit briefly.

ater wrote of his childhood: "For better or worse, royalty
from the more settled forms of domesticity. . . . The mere
stances of my father's position interposed an impalpable barrier
inhibited the closer continuing intimacy of conventional family
life."[53] Despite having five siblings and being particularly close to Bertie and later, George, his younger brother by eight years, Edward recalled that "We were lonely in a curious way."[54] Denied association with other children their own age and home educated by uninspiring tutors, behind the turreted facades of the royal households, there was emotional sterility. "Christmas at Sandringham," Edward reflected, "was Dickens in a Cartier setting."[55] The writer James Pope-Hennessy described Sandringham as "a hideous house with a horrible atmosphere in parts, and in others no atmosphere at all. It was like a visit to a morgue."[56] The Honorable Margaret Wyndham, who served as Woman of the Bedchamber to Queen Mary from 1938, recalled: "At Sandringham if the king were present they put on Garter ribbons, tiaras and diamonds for every family dinner even without guests."[57] Freda Dudley Ward later said of the prince's childhood: "If his life was a bit of a mess, his parents were to blame. They made him what he was. The duke hated his father. The king was horrible to him. His mother was horrible to him, too. . . . The duke loved his mother but his mother wouldn't let him love her. She always took the king's side against him."[58]

In 1907 twelve-year-old Edward was dispatched, in tears, to the Royal Naval College at Osborne on the Isle of Wight with the bizarre assurance from his father that "I am your best friend." Edward quickly settled in as a cadet. His letters home were full of boyish excitement: he wrote to his parents of meeting the explorers Sir Ernest Shackleton and Captain Robert Falcon Scott, and he performed in a pantomime.[59] Instead of inheriting his father's unassailable sense of duty, a duty that was "drilled into" him, Edward, burdened by his regal inheritance, longed to break free. Even as a young boy, he said, he "never had the sense that the days belonged to me alone."[60] Edward progressed to officer training at Dartmouth Royal Naval College, where he struggled academically—he came bottom of his year—but proudly reported to his parents that he was "top in German." Perhaps the only thing he excelled in as a boy was German, learning first from his German nursemaid and then from Professor Eugene Oswald, an elderly master who had previously taught his father the language. "I liked German and studied diligently," he said, "and profited from the hours I spent with the professor."[61]

The death of King Edward VII on May 6, 1910, after a reign of nine years, interrupted Edward's summer term at Dartmouth for three weeks. Now heir apparent, he was called home to Windsor for his sixteenth birthday. His father informed him that he was going to make him Prince of Wales (the king's eldest son does not automatically become Prince of Wales; he is anointed by the monarch when deemed appropriate). Edward returned to Dartmouth with a new title, the Duke of Cornwall, and considerable wealth from the Duchy of Cornwall estate. For the first time, he had an independent income. "I do not recall that this new wealth gave rise to any particular satisfaction at the time," he said.[62]

In his last term at Dartmouth, both Edward and Bertie (who had followed his brother's trajectory from Osborne to Dartmouth, where Edward had "assumed an older brother's responsibility for him") caught severe cases of mumps, followed by measles. Two-thirds of the cadets were hospitalized in this epidemic. It is believed that Edward then developed orchitis, a complication of mumps that left him sterile. The knowledge that Edward would not be able to produce an heir may have been significant later, in the establishment's push to have brother Bertie (George VI) as king.

The coronation of George V in June 1911 thwarted Edward's "first serious ambition." He was forced to forgo the goal of his officer-cadet life and miss a training cruise in North American waters. After completing his naval training, Edward underwent a "finishing" program in preparation for his future full-time role as Prince of Wales. Assumed to be studying for Oxford while his parents traveled to India for the coronation durbar, Edward instead opted to play cards with his grandmother Queen Alexandra, and helped her with jigsaw puzzles.[63] Nevertheless, Edward went up to Magdalen College, Oxford, in October 1912. Befitting the future king, he had a special suite of rooms installed for him, including his own bath in the first private undergraduate bathroom.

Missing the camaraderie of his Royal Navy friends, he was "acutely lonely" and "under the added disadvantage of being something of a celebrity."[64] He soon realized that the skills he had acquired in the navy, which included an ability to "box a compass, read naval signals, run a picket boat, and make cocoa for the officer of the watch," held little sway with learned Oxford dons.[65] The prince was tutored by the most eminent scholars, including Magdalen's esteemed president, Sir Herbert Warren, but Oxford did nothing academically for him. Personally, he seemed uncertain of himself, encouraging familiarity from fellow undergraduates, then swiftly acting with regal hauteur. He found himself happiest on the playing fields, discovering at Oxford a love of sport; he played football, cricket and squash. He beagled with the New College, Magdalen and Trinity packs, took riding lessons—progressing to become a fearless horseman. He punted, gambled, smoked, drank to excess and even smashed glasses and furniture as part of the high jinks of the Bullingdon Club—a club which, the *New York Times* explained to its readers, represented "the acme of exclusiveness at Oxford; it is the club of the sons of nobility, the sons of great wealth; its membership represents the 'young bloods' of the university."[66]

Like Wallis, Edward displayed a strong early interest in fashion, developing his own flamboyant style. Rather than starchy formal garb, he preferred an eccentric mix of sports coats, loud "Prince of Wales checks" (named after his grandfather, but popularized by Edward), bright tartans, baggy golfing plus fours and boyish Fair Isle sweaters. This was to become a source of conflict with his sartorial stickler of a father. When Edward entered the breakfast room at Buckingham Palace one morning, proudly sporting a suit with the new style of trouser turnups, the king bellowed: "Is it raining in *here*?"[67]

"Edward was completely different to any of the rest of the family," recalled John Julius Norwich, who, as a young man, knew both Edward and Wallis. "George V was very stiff and regal yet here was his son, a boy in a peaked cap, smoking and winking."[68] The young prince "was dandyish and out to shock," said David Maude-Roxby-Montalto di Fragnito. "He wanted to break tradition. He wore his signet ring in the continental way, just to be different. The British wear it facing inward, to use on seals, whereas the Europeans wear it facing out. It was very arriviste of the prince to wear his continental style as no British gentleman would ever have done this."[69]

During his Easter and summer vacations in 1913, Edward went to visit his German relatives. "The purpose of these trips was to improve my German and to teach me something about these vigorous people whose blood flows so strongly in my veins. For I was related in one way or another to most of the many Royal houses that reigned in Germany in those days,"[70] Edward wrote. Later in life, "the duke loved to sit with my wife and speak perfect German (with a slight English accent) for hours with her," recalled Count Rudolf von Schönburg, husband of Princess Marie Louise of Prussia, who was related to Edward through Queen Victoria. "Nothing made him happier than speaking at length about his German relations, to whom he was very close. He was very pro-German and would have liked to avoid a war between the two countries."[71]

"Later in his life, the prince lived in France for over fifteen years, yet he never spoke a word of French," said John Julius Norwich. "He would start a conversation with a Frenchman in German. As you can imagine, his fluent German did not go down well in 1946 in France. To him, there was English and there was 'foreign,' and his 'foreign' was German. The prince really was incredibly stupid."[72]

Edward left Oxford before taking his finals and seemingly without the slightest intellectual curiosity, claiming: "I have always preferred outdoor exercise to reading."[73] He was now fully confirmed as the playboy bachelor prince. Painfully thin, he subjected himself to punishing physical regimes throughout his twenties and thirties. He liked to sweat a lot—he wore five layers to exercise[74]—then party into the early hours, existing on minimal sleep and even less food. According to Lord Claud Hamilton, the Prince of Wales's equerry from 1919 to 1922, Edward took after his mother, who, "frightened of becoming fat, ate almost nothing at all."[75] Her ladies-in-waiting regularly went hungry as meals consisted of tiny slivers of roast chicken, no potatoes, and a morsel of vegetables, followed by a wafer.

Edward loathed Buckingham Palace so much, with its "curious musty odour,"[76] that he refused to take meals there and only ate an orange for lunch. This became his daily routine. "His amazing energy makes him indulge frantically in exercise or stay up all night," observed Chips Channon.[77] Boyish and hyperenergetic, Edward never had to shave and preferred nightclubs to formal society. Like a more sophisticated Bertie Wooster, he even took up the banjulele. His favorite question to courtiers was the decidedly unroyal, rebellious teenage riposte: "Can I get away with it?"

"The late king and queen are not without blame," Chips Channon wrote at the time of Edward's abdication in 1936. "For the twenty-six years of their reign, they practically saw no one except their old courtiers, and they made no social background whatever for any of their children. Naturally, their children had to find outlets and fun elsewhere, and the two most high-spirited, the late king (Edward) and the fascinating Duke of Kent (George) drank deeply from life."[78] Edward partied his way through the last London season before the outbreak of the Great War with gusto. With his angelic looks, electric charm and personality dedicated to pleasure, not pomp, he infuriated his parents with his dilettante behavior.

Yet when Britain declared war on Germany on August 4, 1914, Edward was desperate to unveil his courage and serve his country. Commissioned into the Grenadier Guards, he was vexed to find himself denied a combat role. It was a bitter blow—"'the worst in my life,"[79] he said later. Sent to France in 1914, he was kept well behind enemy lines at general headquarters, reduced to conducting basic royal duties such as visits and meeting and greeting dignitaries. Complaining he was the one unemployed man in northern France, he did eventually manage to get into the battle zone, where he observed the horrors of trench warfare. The fighting on the Somme, he wrote in a letter home, was "the nearest approach to hell imaginable." In 1915 a shell killed his personal chauffeur.[80]

"Manifestly I was being kept, so to speak, on ice, against the day that death would claim my father," Edward wrote, expressing his mounting frustration. "I found it hard to accept this unique dispensation. My generation had a rendezvous with history, and my whole being insisted that I share the common destiny, whatever it might be."[81] When he was promoted to captain and awarded the Military Cross, Edward's feelings of unworthiness and self-loathing spiraled. He wrote to his father on September 22, 1915: "I feel so ashamed to wear medals which I only have because of my position, when there are so many thousands of gallant officers who lead a terrible existence in the trenches who have not been decorated."[82]

By the end of the war, which saw the collapse of the Romanov, Hohenzollern, Habsburg and Ottoman dynasties, the Prince of Wales seemed ordained to protect the House of Windsor.[83] It was during the Great War that King George decided that, due to anti-German sentiment in Britain (according to the popular press, even dachshunds were being pelted in the streets of London), the royal family must change its Germanic-sounding surname. Saxe-Coburg-Gotha became Windsor.

From the war years onwards, throughout his twenties and early thirties, Edward did his duty, dazzling the world as the fairy-tale prince. He visited forty-five countries in six years, travelling 150,000 miles. On a trip to Canada, his right hand became so badly bruised and swollen from too many enthusiastic greetings (which he described as pump handling), that he was forced to proffer his left hand for fear of permanent impairment. Adored and feted like a film star, Edward began to behave like one too. His mood swings became all too familiar amongst his equerries and advisors, as he oscillated between buoyed-up exhilaration and lacerating self-pity. He became irritated with official rigmarole and seemed unable to focus on diplomatic matters. On Christmas Day 1919, before embarking on a five-month trip to the Antipodes, he wrote to his private secretary, Godfrey Thomas: "Christ, how I loathe my job now and all the press 'puffed' empty 'success.' I feel I'm through with it and long to die. For

God's sake don't breathe a word of this to a *soul*. No one else must know how I feel about my life and everything. . . . You probably think from this that I ought to be in the madhouse already. . . . I do feel such a bloody little shit."[84]

Another cause of friction with his parents was Edward's obsession with nightclubs and partying in the burgeoning Jazz Age. King George wrote to Queen Mary of his horror, having heard reports that Edward danced "every night & most of the night too," fearing that "people who don't know him will begin to think that he is either mad or the biggest rake in Europe."[85]

Edward found some solace in his romantic life, yet here too, he was irreverent. Instead of seeking a suitable single, eligible bride with whom to settle down, he quickly established a penchant for married women. The patience of his advisors was wearing thin. Tommy Lascelles wrote: "For the ten years before he met Mrs. Simpson, the Prince of Wales was continuously in the throes of one shattering and absorbing love affair after another (not to mention a number of street-corner affairs)."[86] It was Lascelles's contention that the prince never grew up; that he remained morally arrested. Stanley Baldwin agreed: "He is an abnormal being, half child, half genius. . . . It is almost as though two or three cells in his brain had remained entirely undeveloped while the rest of him is a mature man."[87]

Perhaps this partly explains the prince's preference for married women and his desire that they play a bossy, maternal role. His first serious relationship was with the British-born socialite Mrs. Freda Dudley Ward, who was half American and had two teenage daughters, Penelope (Pempe) and Angela (Angie), on whom Edward doted. Between March 1918, when the prince first met Mrs. Dudley Ward sheltering in the doorway of a house in Belgrave Square during an air raid, and January 1921, the prince wrote her 263 letters. In total, during their relationship, which lasted over a decade (surviving his affair with Thelma Furness but not his infatuation with Wallis), the prince penned over two thousand letters to Freda Dudley Ward, many addressing her as "my very own darling beloved little mummie."[88] "It is quite pathetic to see the prince and Freda,"

Winston Churchill observed after traveling with them on a train. "His love is so obvious and undisguisable."[89]

"Freda, whom I knew, was like Wallis in that physically, she was fairly boyish. As far as their relationship went, the prince was a masochist who liked harsh treatment,"[90] said Nicky Haslam. "Freda was lovely," recalled John Julius Norwich. "She was the prince's mistress . . . and everybody liked her."[91] Chips Channon described her in his diaries as "tiny, squeaky, wise and chic."[92] "Mrs. Dudley Ward was the best friend he ever had, only he didn't realise it," said his brother, Prince Henry.[93] Later in life, Mrs. Dudley Ward was asked if her first husband, William Dudley Ward, minded about her affair with the Prince of Wales. "Oh, no," she replied. "My husband knew all about my relationship with the prince. But he didn't mind. If it's the Prince of Wales—no husbands ever mind."[94]

A hint of Edward's desire to be dominated in his relationships lies in a letter he wrote to Freda on March 26, 1918. "You know you ought to be really foul to me sometimes sweetie & curse & be cruel. It would do me the world of good and bring me to my right senses!! I think I'm the kind of man who needs a certain amount of cruelty without which he gets abominably spoilt & soft!! I feel that's what's the matter with me."[95]

Wallis Warfield was twenty years old when, in November 1916, she married her first husband, Earl Winfield Spencer Jr. She had first met the US Navy pilot the previous April during a trip to Florida, when he was stationed at the Pensacola Air Station. The day after she arrived in Pensacola Wallis wrote to her mother: "I have just met the world's most fascinating aviator."[96] Ever since she left Oldfields, Wallis, like her contemporaries, aspired to marriage as the sine qua non of achievement. When "Win," dark haired with brooding looks, proposed eight weeks after their meeting, Wallis was excited to be one of the first debutantes of her coming-out year to get engaged. As much as Wallis thought that she loved Win, a man she barely knew, she later admitted: "There also lay in the back of my mind a realization that my marriage would relieve my mother of the burden of my support."[97]

Despite her mother's fears that a navy life, with no permanent home, constant postings, little money, as well as long and lonely waits for her husband to return from sea, would be too regulated for someone as spirited as her daughter, Alice eventually gave the union her blessing. If only she had not. Wallis discovered on her short, grim honeymoon with Win at a hotel in West Virginia that he was an alcoholic. Wallis—who had only ever had a small glass of champagne at Christmas, as her puritanical family extolled the evils of alcohol—had never tasted hard liquor. West Virginia was a dry state, which further incensed Win, who pulled a bottle of gin from his suitcase. Once inebriated, he would become aggressive, cruel and violent.

Her new life as a navy wife, first in San Diego and then, when Win took a desk job in Washington, DC, became unbearable. Win's insecurity, frustration at his dwindling career and jealous rages were sadistically vented on his young bride. But when Wallis decided to leave and seek a divorce, her mother was aghast. No Montague had ever been divorced. It was unthinkable. Even her stalwart Aunt Bessie said that it was out of the question. Her Uncle Sol was apoplectic. "I won't let you bring disgrace upon us," he shouted.[98]

Wallis persevered with the marriage. Her mother cautioned her that "being a successful wife is an exercise in understanding." Wallis retorted bitterly: "A point comes when one is at the end of one's endurance. I'm at that point now."[99] She moved in with her mother, who was also living in Washington. As Uncle Sol refused her any financial help towards a divorce, her prospects looked bleak. Wallis was suitably thrilled when, in 1924, her cousin Corinne Mustin invited her to go on her first trip to Europe, to Paris. Win continued to write to Wallis and told her that he had been stationed in the Far East. He begged her to join him in China. Perhaps because Wallis could not afford a divorce and was uncertain of her financial and domestic future, she decided to give the marriage yet another go. Win met her in Hong Kong, and soon enough, the familiar patterns recommenced. He became jealous, moody, quarrelsome and offensive. When he began drinking before breakfast, Wallis finally had had enough. She drew their eight-year marriage to a close, seeking a divorce at the United States Court for China in Shanghai.

"Wallis was now twenty-eight and her character was formed," according to Diana Mosley. "She was independent but not tough, rather easily hurt with a rare capacity for making friends wherever she went. She was intelligent and quick, amusing, good company; an addition to any party with her high-spirited gaiety."[100]

Wallis embarked on a year's sojourn in Peking, staying with her good friends Katherine and Herman Rogers. She later described her Eastern sojourn as her "Lotus Year." As a divorced woman travelling in the Far East on her own, she displayed a spirited independence ahead of her time. According to a friend of Duff Cooper's in Paris, a French woman who knew Wallis as Mrs. Spencer in Peking, Wallis was "always good-natured."[101] Unfortunately, when news of Wallis's relationship with the Prince of Wales broke in 1936, her year in China was used against her. It was said that she had visited the "singing houses" of Shanghai and Peking. Unsavory gossip tut-tutted, suggesting that she had acquired "sophisticated sexual techniques" which she then used to entrap and manipulate the Prince of Wales and she became the butt of cheap jokes: "Other girls picked up pennies but Wallis was so proficient that she picked up a sovereign."

Wallis nursed a secret that hit at the very heart of her femininity. She was infertile and had never menstruated. As a young girl, it is unlikely that Wallis would have known that anything was wrong. Perhaps the absence of periods would have been her first sign at puberty that all was not as expected. It has been speculated that Wallis may have had a "disorder of sexual development," or DSD, a modern term encompassing a wide range of rare genetic conditions. Others have claimed Wallis may have had androgen insensitivity syndrome—that is, she was born genetically male, with the XY chromosome. If this had been the case, the male sexual organs would have been internal and barely noticeable and she would have had an extremely shallow vagina. Yet this is unlikely, as Wallis lacked other physical traits associated with the syndrome. We also know that she would go on to have a hysterectomy in middle age.

Whatever the cause of Wallis's infertility, it was a source of profound sadness for her. Over three marriages she bore no children, but not out of choice. Though she and Edward seemed to adore children, their lack of parenthood united them as outsiders to a familial club. Instead, they lavished love on their dogs, which became their child replacements. Wallis later wrote that she mourned never being part of the "miracle of creation" and that her "one continuing regret" was never having "known the joy of having children." The secret inner pain of childlessness must have made the gossip and slurs against her so much harder to bear.[102]

One of the reasons that Wallis kept herself skeletally thin was that she worried that if she put on any weight she would "bulk up in a masculine way."[103] Diana Mosley said that Wallis "loved and appreciated good food, but ate so little that she remained triumphantly thin at a time when slenderness was all important in fashion."[104] Elsa Maxwell agreed that Wallis ate very little at the dinner table. When she challenged Wallis about this, she always replied defensively: "I'm an ice-box raider."[105] Clearly any snacking was confined to minuscule amounts. Wallis and Edward were similar in this respect; they both favored starvation diets and punishing regimes, each obsessed with retaining an almost prepubescent slenderness.

Wallis expressed a traditional femininity through her clothes: her sartorial perfectionism—a love of Cartier and couture—served to create an exaggeratedly feminine outline that was more elegant than sexual. Always immaculately groomed, there was a delicacy about her appearance—from her skirts and dresses cinched in at the waist with tiny belts to neat little pairs of heels. Adorned as she was with exquisite statement jewels, there was nothing androgynous about Wallis's style. She certainly was no "sex siren" or "harlot," as many made her out to be. Although Wallis often liked to be the center of attention socially, in other ways she came across as old-fashioned and reserved; indeed, her upbringing in Baltimore had been ladylike to the point of prudish. Astonishingly, she told Herman Rogers, who eventually gave her away at her wedding to Edward in 1937, that she "had never had sexual intercourse with either of her two husbands."[106] Nor had she "ever allowed anyone else to touch her below" what she described as "her personal Mason-Dixon Line."[107]

Both Wallis and Edward shared insecurities about their sexual identities. Confiding this in each other may have helped forge a strong secret bond between them. Cynthia Jebb, Lady Gladwyn, whose husband was ambassador to France from 1954 to 1960, knew the Windsors in Paris and confided to Hugo Vickers that "the prince had sexual problems. He was unable to perform"—she "called it a hairpin reaction. She said that the duchess coped with it. I commented: 'She was meant to have learned special ways in China.' 'There was nothing Chinese about it,' said Lady Gladwyn. 'It was what they call oral sex.' "[108] Although she could be openly flirtatious in a social setting, Wallis was, as Nicky Haslam observed of her, sassy rather than sexy: her gaiety was more playful teasing than predatory or seriously seductive. "Wallis wasn't obsessed by sex," says Haslam. "If anything, she was rigidly undressable in that she was prudish. Everybody made such a thing of her going to brothels in China, but everyone did that in those days. It was the fashionable thing to do. To have a good look."[109]

"It was just the sort of thing that the press would say, that she was a twice-divorced American adventuress out for what she could get," said John Julius Norwich. "Everything was a bid to discredit her but she was the furthest thing from kinky. You never got the feeling that she was particularly sexually motivated. She was a perfectly normal American woman but not in the least bit depraved. And there was nothing more normal than Ernest Simpson and he fell in love with her."[110]

Winston Churchill summed up the controversial couple's mutual attraction: "the association was psychical rather than sexual, and certainly not sensual except incidentally."[111] Churchill always believed that Wallis was good for Edward; he defended the couple to the last. "Although branded with the stigma of a guilty love, no companionship could have appeared more natural, more free from impropriety or grossness," he said.[112]

Wallis met Ernest Simpson through Mary Kirk, who had now become Madame Raffray, on her marriage to the Frenchman Jacques Raffray.

Raffray, a veteran of the Great War, had originally come to America to train US troops to fight in France. Wallis, then living in Washington, enjoyed staying with the Raffrays at their New York apartment. She spent Christmas of 1926 with them awaiting her divorce from Win. Ernest, who was also in the process of getting divorced, from his American wife, Dorothea, with whom he had a daughter, Audrey, was frequently asked for dinner or to make up a fourth for bridge. A friendship developed, and when both were granted divorces, Ernest asked Wallis to marry him.

A graduate of Harvard, Ernest had been born in New York of an American mother and a British father. After brief service as a captain in the British army, he began work in the family shipping business, Simpson, Spence & Young. Tall, with blue eyes and a neat moustache, he was a fastidious dresser. In the early 1920s, he was much in demand on the London scene and a regular dance partner of Barbara Cartland. (She later described him as a "handsome young bachelor, who was to figure dramatically in the history of England seventeen years later."[113]) The letter Wallis wrote to her mother on July 15, 1928, regarding Ernest's marriage proposal is revealing: "I've decided that the best and wisest thing for me to do is to marry Ernest. I am very fond of him and he is kind which will be a contrast. . . . I can't go wandering the rest of my life and I really feel so tired of fighting the world alone and with no money. Also 32 doesn't seem so young when you see all the youthful faces one has to compete against. So I shall settle down to a fairly comfortable old age."[114] After her peripatetic childhood and abusive marriage to Win, Ernest represented financial and emotional stability, comfort and respectability. Wallis worried briefly that his wholesome ponderousness was the polar opposite to her southern emotionalism. She was fun, spontaneous and extravagant. He was methodical and cautious. Later, he was dismissed amid the upper-class circles into which the Simpsons were propelled as "crashingly middle class" and a bore.

Ernest was transferred to run the British offices of his shipping firm, and in May 1928, Wallis followed him to London. They married on July 21 at Chelsea Register Office. Wallis wore a yellow dress and blue coat that she had bought in Paris the previous summer. Although they considered the clinical nature of the register office ceremony "a cold little job,"[115] she found their honeymoon "a blissful experience."[116] Driving through France, Wallis discovered that her husband was cultured, considerate and spoke French fluently. Ernest may not have been the most exciting or diverting company, but he was a thoroughly decent gentleman. His great-nephew Alex Kerr-Smiley remembers: "Ernest was just a nice person. He was an extremely nice uncle. He was almost like our fairy godfather."[117]

After the harrowing uncertainties of the previous decade, Wallis, aged thirty-two, could finally relax. Looking forward to a new life in London, she "felt a security that I had never really experienced since early childhood."[118] Her domestic equilibrium was to prove short-lived. Three years later, the dull conformity of her marriage was shattered by the arrival in their steady realm of the dazzling Prince of Wales.

2

Ich Dien

After their honeymoon, Wallis and Ernest moved into a small hotel in London while they searched for a suitable home. Ernest's sister, Maud, helped them to find a furnished house in Upper Berkeley Street, which they rented for a year. Wallis, a natural and dedicated homemaker, was keen to secure an unfurnished property on which she could put her decorative stamp.

Initially, Mrs. Simpson was lonely in London, knowing no other Americans. Unaccustomed and resistant to the formality of English mores, she felt like "a stranger in a strange land."[1] Her sense of isolation heightened in October 1929 when she learned that her mother was seriously ill. Alice had been diagnosed with a blood clot in her brain. As Ernest could not leave his business, Wallis crossed the Atlantic alone. She spent three weeks with her ailing mother, who died shortly after Wallis returned to London. The "sadness" that Wallis carried inside was "a long time lifting." She grieved bitterly for her adored mother, who she felt was the only person who truly understood her.[2]

Soon a welcome distraction presented itself. That winter, Wallis found a first-floor flat that both she and Ernest liked in a mansion block on George Street, near Marble Arch. She set about decorating the flat at Bryanston Court with her inimitable flair. She was influenced by two design legends: Syrie Maugham, ex-wife of novelist W. Somerset Maugham, and her good friend Elsie de Wolfe. Professional rivalry simmered between these two eccentrics as to who was the greater visionary. Both were ultrachic, creating light, avant-garde rooms—the antithesis of heavy, dark Victoriana. Wallis enlisted Syrie Maugham's talents at Bryanston Court, while de Wolfe helped shape her later homes in France. Maugham, who pioneered white furniture and white walls against which were showcased Provençal antiques, stripped and painted everything with her secret craquelure technique. From Maugham's workshops, Wallis commissioned a dozen dining room chairs with tall backs, upholstered in white leather and studded with nails. This was considered daringly modern. An Italian dining table, Adam sideboard and console received the Maugham treatment: they were painted blue-green and white. According to Wallis, "when the table was laid for the first time and the candles lighted, the effect was soft and charming."[3] Wallis always chose a mirror-topped table, the center decorated with glass fruits and a silver candelabra at each end. The table service was pink china; one of her most prized possessions was the dinner service inherited from her grandmother. Unconventionally, she served her consommé piping hot in small cups of black Chinese lacquer, with tiny lids.[4] To Wallis, design and presentation were nothing less than moral issues. She adopted both Elsie de Wolfe's streamlined aesthetic and her credo: "What surer guarantee can there be of a person's character, natural and cultivated, inherent and inherited, than taste?"[5]

Ernest, proud of his wife's exceptional talents as a hostess, was pleased with both the style of their home and Wallis's eye for detail. She was always moving furniture into new positions, changing things around in her efforts to perfect a room's look. This continued throughout her life, to her last home, the regal villa she shared with the Duke of Windsor in the Bois de Boulogne in Paris.

In her early days in London, Wallis, far from being able to exhibit largesse in her entertaining, had to budget cautiously. Most of her correspondence to her Aunt Bessie at this time focuses on the trials of trying to find the right cook and of financial concerns. Ernest was meticulous in his housekeeping. One evening a week, he demanded that Wallis show him her weekly expenditures. He would run his finger down the list, scrutinizing each purchase. Wallis ran the house and bought her clothes on a weekly stipend from Ernest. Accustomed to working to a fiscal limit, she discovered that life in Britain was cheap by American standards. If she found herself under budget, she would splurge at Fortnum & Mason on a jar of caviar, brandied peaches or, as a special treat, an avocado.

Wallis shared Elsie de Wolfe's obsession with serving guests food that was the same size, driving her butcher and fishmonger to distraction sourcing six or eight identical trout or grouse; even vegetables were laid out on the plate with military precision. Like her mother, Wallis prided herself on serving only the most delicious food. The Prince of Wales said of his first visit to her "small but charming flat in Bryanston Court" that "everything in it was in exquisite taste and the food, in my judgement, unrivalled in London."[6] Wallis "is the best housekeeper I know," declared Elsa Maxwell. "She is as skilful as a Japanese professional in arranging flowers. She has perfect taste in food as well as furniture and in those little details of forethought and care that mark an imaginative hostess. For instance, last time I lunched with her I noticed that she had found the most enchanting little round porcelain pots with covers to contain the butter and at the bottom, there was ice to keep it firm."[7] According to Lady Pamela Hicks: "She was the most marvellous hostess. Her houses were perfection. At giving parties and serving food, she was the best."[8] When she was the Duchess of Windsor and could afford it, Wallis would spray floral centerpieces with Diorissimo perfume.

Wallis's reputation as a skilled hostess spread around the Simpsons' London set. Naturally, she and Ernest were suitably excited when, having bumped into the Prince of Wales a few times at Thelma Furness's, he accepted their invitation to Bryanston Court in January 1932. Wallis decided to serve a typical American dinner: black bean soup, grilled lobster, fried chicken Maryland and a cold raspberry soufflé. As a concession to her English guests, she followed it with a savory of marrowbones.

Typical of Wallis's dignity, she was "bursting to tell the fishmonger and green grocer" whom she was hosting but "had acquired too much British restraint."[9]

Ten sat down to dinner that January evening, with the prince at the head of the table and Ernest at the foot. Wallis wrote to her Aunt Bessie afterwards, on Sunday, January 24, thanking her for sending butter pat molds with the Prince of Wales's feathers on them. "Darling—the candles arrived and are grand. I enclose cheque. I can't accept everything from you. We [meaning Cain* and self] loved the butter pats, especially the one with HRH's feathers on it. It was a shame it didn't arrive for use the night he dined here which by the way passed off pleasantly the party breaking up at 4 a.m., so I think he enjoyed himself."[10]

The prince paid Wallis the compliment of asking her for the recipe of her raspberry soufflé. The following week, he repaid her hospitality with a prized invitation for the Simpsons to stay as his guests for the weekend at Fort Belvedere, his country residence in Surrey. In 1930 the king had given Edward a grace-and-favor property on Crown lands, bordering Windsor Great Park. This "castellated conglomeration" had been built in the eighteenth century by William, Duke of Cumberland, third son of George II. Eighty years later, the architect Sir Jeffry Wyatville added a high tower which gave the impression of an ancient castle in a forest. From the moment he saw it, Edward adored this "pseudo-Gothic hodgepodge,"[11] despite its wild, untended garden and excess of gloomy yew trees. Fort Belvedere became his first proper home; his only other residence, York House, was more like an office. Edward poured all his energies into doing up "the Fort," as it became known.

"It was a child's idea of a fort," said Lady Diana Cooper. "The house is an enchanting folly and only needs fifty red soldiers stood between the battlements to make it into a Walt Disney coloured symphony toy." Of her host, she said: "The comfort could not be greater, nor the desire on his part for guests to be happy, free and unembarrassed. Surely a new atmosphere for Courts?"[12]

---

* Mary Cain was Wallis's maid.

Edward renovated the inside, modernizing with gusto—creating spaces entirely different from the musty royal houses of his childhood which had made him feel so unwell he could not eat. Each bedroom had its own bathroom—unheard of then in British country houses—and he added showers, a steam bath in the basement, built-in cupboards and central heating. Outside, he felled the yew trees to let in light and air. A muddy lily pond below the battlements was transformed into a swimming pool and acres of dank laurel were cleared for rare rhododendrons. Winding paths cut through fir and birch trees added to the attractive woodland setting. He also improved and developed the Cedar Walk, a sweeping avenue lined by ancient cedar trees stretching from below the terrace to the edge of his property, which became one of his favorite places to walk. Later he added a private aerodrome in the grounds (he was patron of the London Flying Club in 1935) and would ferry friends into and out of Belvedere in his de Havilland Dragon Rapide biplane, which he had painted in the colors of the Brigade of Guards.

"The prince was himself" at the Fort, Thelma, Lady Furness, wrote in her memoirs. "He was free from any obligation to maintain the formalities of his official position. He pottered in the garden, pruned his trees, blew on his bagpipes. We entertained a great deal, but our guests were always the people we liked to have around—there were no dignitaries, no representatives of State and Empire."[13] Of the Fort, Edward said: "I came to love it as I loved no other material thing—perhaps because it was so much my own creation."[14] Guests were pressed into arduous physical labor, hacking out undergrowth and pruning trees. Edward also discovered a love of Windsor Castle, six miles away, of which he had said as a boy "the ancient walls seemed to exude disapproval."[15] Now his reverence grew for the immense grey pile which Samuel Pepys once described as "the most romantic castle that is in the world." Edward would take weekend guests to browse the library and show off the Rubenses and van Dycks in the state apartments on Sunday afternoons.

The Fort became the prince's sanctuary, a place where he could dispense with private secretaries and equerries. He considerately refused to keep staff up late at night, despite the early hours that he often enjoyed and, if he returned home at dawn, let himself into the property with his own latchkey. Unthinkably modern for a future monarch.

Wallis and Ernest set out for the Fort late on the Saturday afternoon, timing their pace to arrive, as invited, at six. It was dark when the car crunched up the gravel driveway. Before they could come to a stop, the prince had opened the door and was supervising the unloading of the luggage, a habit he enjoyed. Unlike the grandeur of Knole, the Kent home of the Sackvilles to which the Simpsons had previously been invited as weekend guests, the Fort struck them as remarkably relaxed. The prince led them into the octagonal hall, which had a black-and-white marble floor and eight bright-yellow leather chairs in the eight corners. The drawing room, also octagonal, was more traditional: pine paneling, yellow velvet curtains, Canalettos and Chippendale furniture. The prince insisted on showing his guests to their room on the second floor. Diana Cooper wrote of her bedroom when staying there: "The stationery is disappointingly humble—not so the conditions. I am in a pink bedroom, pink-sheeted, pink Venetian-blinded, pink soaped, white-telephoned and pink-and-white maided."[16] She did not comment on the gaudy Prince of Wales's feathers engraved into every bed's headboard.

When Wallis and Ernest arrived downstairs for cocktails, they were surprised to see the prince sitting on a sofa, his head bent over a large flat screen. His right hand plied a needle from which trailed a long colored thread. At his feet were his two cairn terriers, Cora and Jaggs. Catching Wallis's look of incredulity at the sight of the Prince of Wales doing needlepoint, he laughed, rising to greet her. "This is my secret vice," he explained, "the only one, in any case, I am at any pains to conceal."[17]

He explained to Wallis that he had learned to crochet from his mother as a young boy. At half past six each evening at Sandringham, Edward and his siblings were called in from the school room and sent to their mother's boudoir, where they would sit at her knee while she crocheted or embroidered. Queen Mary taught them gros point, which Edward kept up and perfected while recovering from a riding accident. He returned to this hobby during his time on the western front in France. On long car journeys he crocheted to kill time. He later said that he was "understandably discreet about my hobby at first. It would hardly have done for the story to get around that a major general in the British army had been seen bowling along the roads behind the Maginot Line crocheting."[18]

While the women all wore simple evening dresses, Edward sported a kilt in Balmoral tartan and produced a small cigarette case from his silver sporran. After cocktails, the small party went through to the dining room—the wood-paneled room seating only ten—where they ate oysters from the Duchy of Cornwall oyster beds, followed by roast beef and salad, pudding and a savory. After coffee in the drawing room, Edward taught Wallis to play a card game called red dog, while others attempted a complicated jigsaw puzzle that was laid out on a long table in front of the main window. Dancing followed in the hallway. Suddenly, the prince tired. Before going to bed, he announced the rules of the Fort: "There are none. Stay up as late as you want. Get up when you want. For me this is a place of rest and change, I go to bed early and get up early so that I can work in the garden."[19]

The following morning, when the maid brought Wallis breakfast in her room, she was informed that His Royal Highness had finished his an hour before and was in the garden. When the Simpsons entered the drawing room, they saw the prince on the terrace outside in baggy plus fours, a thick sweater, hair tousled, hacking at the wild undergrowth with a machete-like billhook, dogs at his heels. Ernest Simpson, not a natural athlete, was ill equipped to respond to the prince's insistence that all guests help him wage war against the dreaded laurel bushes. "It's not exactly a command," a fellow guest informed Ernest, "but I've never known anybody to refuse."[20] Crossing the lawn, brandishing murderous-looking weapons, the house party resembled more a band of revolutionaries ready to do battle than an elite group of guests staying with the Prince of Wales at his country retreat. After two wearying hours in the winter chill the guests returned for a fortifying hot-and-cold buffet lunch laid out in the dining room. That afternoon, the prince took Wallis and Ernest around his home, even showing them his bedroom, on the ground floor off the hall. It was spacious and charming, with red chintz curtains framing spectacular views of his beloved garden.

Later that afternoon, the prince went for a tour outside with his gardener. When he returned, he disappeared to the basement. Thelma explained to the perplexed Wallis that at the same time every day he liked to take a steam bath and was as proud of having installed this as he was of his central heating. He later appeared wearing a bright-yellow polo neck, his face flushed red yet "radiating utter contentment."[21]

As an original thank-you note, Wallis and Ernest composed the prince a jaunty poem on their return to Bryanston Court. As etiquette demanded, it was signed by Wallis only.

Sir—
Bear with me and do not curse
This poor attempt at thanks in verse.
Our weekend at "Fort Belvedere"
Has left us both with memories dear
Of what in every sense must be
Princely hospitality.
Too soon the hours stole away,
And we, who would have had them stay,
Regretful o'er that fleeting slyness,
Do warmly thank Your Royal Highness.
But with your time I make too free—
I have the honor, Sir, to be
(Ere too long my poetic pencil limps on)
Your obedient Servant,
Wallis Simpson[22]

After their fairy-tale weekend, Wallis and Ernest returned to the real world. They did not see the prince for much of the rest of that year, 1932—a year Wallis pronounced "dismal." Ever preoccupied with worsening money worries, she wrote to her Aunt Bessie that Ernest's shipping business was struggling as the world lay in the trough of the Depression.

Britain had also been suffering from the severe economic downturn. Hardest hit were the industrial and mining areas of the north of England, Scotland, Northern Ireland and Wales, where unemployment reached 70 percent. Over the previous few years the Prince of Wales had made extensive tours of Tyneside, the Midlands, Lancashire, Yorkshire, Scotland and Wales. He visited hundreds of working men's clubs and schemes for the unemployed, seeking out the areas of rawest poverty. Although he was sometimes met with sullen apathy, which perturbed him, the prince persevered, inviting himself into slums, eager that the people would not think the monarchy had forsaken them in their misfortune. In 1929 in Winlaton, Durham, he visited the house of Mr. Frank McKay, a seventy-four-year-old miner whose wife had just died. The prince offered his sympathies to the family and "expressed a wish to go upstairs to the room where Mrs. McKay lay dead." As he left, the miners cheered him on the way back to his car. George Haynes, general secretary of the National Council, remembered the Prince of Wales's "way of approach; his transparent interest and concern, and the immense regard people had for him. He had a charisma in those days which was unique."[23] However, the prince was quickly marked down by the establishment as a "dangerous subversive."[24]

The prince would return from his public duties painfully aware that "there was always something lacking."[25] In spring 1932 King George V had what was, for him, an uncharacteristically intimate conversation with his son. He told Edward that while he was still worshipped by the public, he could not expect to survive the erosion of his reputation caused by the increasingly damaging revelations surrounding his private life. The king cited Edward's liaison with Lady Furness and asked his son if he had ever thought of marrying "a suitable well-born English girl?" Strangely, the prince replied that he had never supposed it would be possible.

"What he meant by this was that he liked these married women and he loved Americans," explained Hugo Vickers. "The prince loved golfing pros and tycoons. According to his private secretary he became like a little boy in their presence. He thought that English girls were boring and thought that zinging cocktail girls were what he liked. There was never any question in his mind that he would marry an eligible British girl."[26]

There were suggestions that Princess Ingrid of Sweden might make a suitable bride, but it was never seriously contemplated at York House or Buckingham Palace. Earl Mountbatten of Burma prepared a list of seventeen European princesses who were "theoretically possible," ranging from the fifteen-year-old Thyra of Mecklenburg-Schwerin to twenty-two-year-old Princess Ingrid of Sweden, but these were made with little conviction. No one who knew the Prince of Wales now believed that he would ever marry. The despairing king said to Stanley Baldwin: "After I am dead the boy will ruin himself within twelve months." He apparently later confided to the courtier Ulick Alexander: "My eldest son will never succeed me. He will abdicate."[27]

This was a view shared by the king's youngest surviving son, Prince Henry, who became the Duke of Gloucester. "My brother and I never got on, I'm afraid," Gloucester later said of his relationship with Edward. "We had a hell of a row in 1927. I'd said to someone I didn't think he'd ever be king and it was repeated. He said to me: 'Did you say that or didn't you?' So I said: 'Well I've either got to tell you a lie or tell you the truth and I'm going to tell you the truth. I did say it and I still think it."[28]

The prince's equerry, John Aird, who succeeded Tommy Lascelles in this position, believed that the king and his family were misinformed about his son's activities. He wrote in his diary: "I have been told that HRH's behaviour is killing the king. If so I am very sorry, but feel that it is not probable and quite unnecessary."[29] Lascelles had described the prince as "'an archangel ruined'—though ruined by what, God only knows."[30] John Aird, however, did not share this view. At fault, he felt, were the courtiers at York House eagerly relaying to the king "all the nasty gossip, which is very wrong of them and does no good."[31] Queen Mary's official biographer, James Pope-Hennessy, who was given access to the entire royal family for the writing of his 1959 book, concluded sagely: "It is *courtiers* who make royalty frightened and frightening."[32]

However, those close to the Prince of Wales, the unholy trinity of the monarchy, Church and political establishment, had serious misgivings about Edward's suitability as king. His views were regarded as not conservative enough and he did not seem to take to his official duties with the appropriate solemnity. His high-profile visits to areas of mass unemployment, highlighting the suffering of the laboring classes, raised political hackles during the Depression, while his chief activities—socializing, needlepoint, sewing and gardening—did not match well with contemporary ideas of kingship. There were also concerns about his ability to have children and provide an heir. Several who worked closely with him began to bandy about the word *mad.* His nervous tics, odd speech and constant fiddling with his cuffs did not help solidify his reputation, yet while he could be extremely self-centered, often appearing detached from reality, he was certainly not insane. George V remained infuriated by his eldest son's ways, especially his style of dress. The prince insisted on wearing a bowler hat on official visits to industrial plants, eschewing his father's preference for a top hat. Yet this was a considered move not to further alienate himself from the workers, rather than as a snub to court etiquette. The king and his court dismissed any such attempt of Edward's to modernize the style and approachability of the monarchy as anarchic.[33]

The prince's lack of conformity extended widely to his social circle. Edward's friendship with Lady Diana Guinness (née Mitford) and her lover, the MP and, from 1932, leader of the British Union of Fascists, Sir Oswald, raised questions of political impartiality and judgment. George V knew that the monarchy's survival depended on maintaining its constitutional neutrality, whereas Edward appeared to be enthusiastically pro-German at a time when his parents were going to great lengths to rebrand the royal family as British. Like many members of the British aristocracy in the early 1930s, the prince seemed to view fascism as the latest in political chic. However, Edward was considered too ideologically vacuous to have any genuine interest in a political creed, and his two political mentors, Winston Churchill and David Lloyd George, were both Liberals.[34]

That Edward did not conform to court life, preferring a vigorous and flamboyant social life over the grey strictures of monarchial duty, was tantamount to treachery in the eyes of his advisors. In 1927 Tommy

Lascelles said to Stanley Baldwin of the prince: "You know, sometimes when I am waiting to get the result of some point-to-point in which he is riding, I can't help thinking that the best thing that could happen to him and the country, would be for him to break his neck." "God forgive me," Baldwin said. "I have often thought the same thing."[35]

Edward carried on with his private life, ignoring opprobrium, preferring to spend his time with the wealthy and self-made as opposed to old-school aristocrats. He enjoyed the company of rich Americans, such as Sir Henry "Chips" Channon and Lady Emerald Cunard. Emerald, widow of shipping heir Sir Bache Cunard, was an influential hostess and patron of the arts. Stanley Walker, editor of the *New York Herald Tribune*, wrote: "International society is not always difficult to crash. To be the guest of the Prince of Wales at his country house, Fort Belvedere, is regarded as a high honour. Many of the members of what is known in New York as the 'international set' are accepted in London, and shuttle back and forth between England and America."[36]

During the summer of 1932, Wallis, who suffered from a physically nervous disposition—she felt her stresses in her stomach—had to return from a much-anticipated trip to France and Austria with Ernest, due to a stomach ulcer. She later wrote: "I suppose that the ulcer came from nerves, as I always kept the day-to-day tensions of living bottled up inside me."[37] Beneath her confident, sharp-shooting facade, Wallis nursed a frailty she was at literal pains to conceal. That autumn, Wallis and Ernest were twice invited to the Fort: once for tea and once for the weekend. By December, Wallis was in bed again as her stomach problems had flared up in spite of careful attention to her diet. Her doctor advised her to drink only whisky or water for six months.

From early 1933, the Simpsons received more frequent invitations to the Fort. Wallis wrote to Aunt Bessie from Belvedere on Sunday, January 29: "It is cold for England now and since arriving here we have been skating out on the water with the Duke and Duchess of York.* Isn't it a scream! Also you can imagine me out on the ice but due to having

* The Prince of Wales's brother Albert (Bertie) and his wife, Elizabeth.

roller skated I have not been too bad. The Prince presented T[helma] and self with skates etc."[38]

Wallis's bond with Thelma was strengthening. She wrote to Mary Kirk: "A friend of mine, Thelma Furness, is the Prince of Wales's girl and I chaperone her when she goes out to Fort Belvedere to stay with him."[39] Wallis described her surprise when Thelma arrived to drive her to the Fort, with long struts strapped to the side of the car. Thelma "just laughed and said that I would find out later." It was after dinner that she found out. "The three of us came into the sitting room for coffee. On either side of the fireplace, where a grand fire was blazing, stood a comfortable chair and beside each chair stood something that looked like an artist's easel. When I went closer and looked I found that each of these held a canvas on which was an unfinished piece of embroidery. When we had finished our coffee Thelma and the prince settled themselves down to work and I, sitting between them, was asked to read from a book Thelma handed me."[40]

Thelma encouraged the prince's love of petit point. His first solo effort was a paperweight which he made for Queen Mary. It depicted the royal crown above her initials, M. R., in gold. The prince had it mounted on a silver base and when finished, it was beautiful. He then progressed to sewing a backgammon table cover for Thelma.

The prince had a thoughtful, generous side. Every Christmas he bought all the staff at York House and the Fort a present. This meant buying and wrapping many hundreds of gifts. An eccentricity of his was to involve all his weekend guests during the run-up to Christmas in sessions of after-dinner wrapping. "All the guests became an informal task force," recalled Thelma. "Scissors, paper, ribbon, string were issued to each and the production line started rolling. The prince got down on the floor with his paper and ribbon and manfully struggled through three or four parcels. The results were hardly reassuring; the corners sagged ominously and the ribbons were apparently tied with some sort of knot he had learned to use in securing hawsers during his naval days." Thelma tactfully suggested that he would be of the greatest help if he cut the paper for them, and this became the prince's special task. "I can still see the group sprawled on the floor: Prince George flourishing rolls of ribbon, Wallis Simpson keeping up an animated chatter from one corner, while Ernest stolidly ground out package after package with astonishing skill and artistry."[41]

Wallis sailed for New York that March, thanks to a generous cheque for $500 from Aunt Bessie. When Wallis received it the previous December, she had written immediately to her aunt from Knole, where she and Ernest were weekending. "Dearest Aunt Bessie, I am staggered by the size of the cheque and have a sensation of being a millionairess. You know you should not have sent it and I shall be killed by generosity! I have sworn I shall not pay a bill with it or buy anything for the flat as I have done with your other presents. This I shall invest in myself."[42]

On this visit to America, Wallis was keen to tour, visiting old friends and family. Ernest was due to join her, as his business interests took him to New York, while Wallis would also see friends in Baltimore. The *Mauretania* had barely left the Isle of Wight in its wake when a messenger came dashing up with a radiogram. It was a bon voyage message from the prince, signed "Edward P.," wishing Wallis a safe crossing and speedy return. Word spread on the ship that Mrs. Simpson had received a personal message from the Prince of Wales. "The attention was flattering," Wallis recalled. "I enjoyed every minute of it."[43]

Wallis's time in Washington coincided with the famous first "hundred days" of Franklin D. Roosevelt's presidency, when he presented a series of initiatives to Congress to counter the effects of the Great Depression, including the abandonment of the gold standard. Wallis's mind was on other matters, however, and she made no reference in her letters to American politics. She returned to Europe in May aboard the RMS *Olympic* (Ernest met her at Cherbourg), and, on the seventeenth, wrote to Bessie, thanking her for her generosity. "Darling—What can I ever say to make you know how much I appreciate your giving me this marvelous trip and then a dress and coat besides? Maybe you realize that I am enough like my mother to be completely inadequate at expressing my feelings when I feel the most. I'm afraid I then generally joke the most. I love you better than anyone in the world and will always be on hand when you need me."[44]

On her return from America, Wallis's relationship with the Prince of

Wales entered a new phase, despite Wallis's writing to her aunt that "Thelma is still the Princess of Wales."[45] She and Ernest were accepted into the inner circle of the prince's friends, mixing with his brothers, Prince George and the Duke of York. The Simpsons were regulars at the Fort; they accompanied Edward to nightclubs in London—he was a habitué of the Embassy Club on Bond Street—and the prince dined often at Bryanston Court. Ernest, a staunch monarchist and social climber, was proud of Wallis and the way she had been accepted into this rarefied crowd. He believed in deferential reverence to the Prince of Wales, initially basking in reflected glory at his wife's burgeoning closeness to the future monarch, as William Dudley Ward had once done. "Ernest was initially delighted with Wallis's royal foray," recalled Ernest's nephew Alex Kerr-Smiley. "He benefited from the royal connection. The Prince of Wales had some tweed especially woven. It was made into an overcoat for him. My great-uncle admired it and the Prince of Wales said: 'My dear chap, there is some tweed left over. You may have it.' Ernest had an identical overcoat made up and there is a rude family story saying that he actually swapped his wife for an overcoat."[46]

Initially, though, Ernest refuted rumors that he was a cuckold. Ernest had applied for admission to a Masonic lodge, presided over by Sir Maurice Jenks, a former lord mayor of London. His candidature was supported by the Prince of Wales. When Ernest was refused entry, Edward naturally demanded an explanation. The heir apparent was boldly told that it was against the Masonic law for the husband of his mistress to be admitted. The prince gave his word that this was not the situation and Ernest's candidature was accepted. With Ernest's entrée to the Masonic lodge came introductions to a rich and influential coterie of friends.[47]

"The game of royal mistress, or the royal favorite, had its own set of rules and Ernest played his part," said John Julius Norwich. "Both Wallis and Ernest benefited from the arrangement."[48] Of her association with the Prince of Wales—"a figure of popular legend and the quintessence of youthful charm"—Wallis was "glad to be even a minor satellite in the company revolving around him."[49] Yet she, like her husband, misunderstood the prince's growing admiration for her. "If the prince was in any way drawn to me I was unaware of his interest," she said. "Thelma was always there, and often Prince George, whom I found on closer acquaintance to be altogether as attractive as his brother. He played the piano very well, knew all the latest jazz, and loved to bang away at the keys while the rest of us danced after dinner in the octagonal hall."[50]

Prince George was closest to Edward of all his siblings and had worried the heir to the throne considerably. After he left the navy, George took up residence in York House. Artistic and impressionable, he succumbed easily to temptation. In 1928 he fell into the embrace of an attractive married American socialite called Kiki Preston, who introduced him to drugs. Known as "the girl with the silver syringe," she was addicted to heroin, cocaine and morphine. In the summer of 1929, Edward tried to intervene and even drew closer to his parents, the three of them united in their concern for George. Eventually Edward persuaded Mrs. Preston to move abroad and more or less incarcerated George in the country. He took full responsibility for helping his brother beat his addictions, telling Freda Dudley Ward how exhausting it was to be "doctor, gaoler and detective combined."[51] Aiding Prince George to come off drugs illustrated Edward's capacity for kindness and commendable behavior. Even King George was impressed. He wrote to his son: "Looking after him all those months must have been a great strain on you, and I think it was wonderful all you did for him."[52]

Sadly, Edward could not hold his father's praise for long. Eschewing stuffy court life, he began to drop in on the Simpsons at Bryanston Court for tea or cocktails, enamored with the "gay, lively and informed company" Wallis liked to keep. Young British and American businessmen, foreign diplomats and Wallis's girlfriends would gather. The prince found the conversation "witty and crackling with new ideas."[53] Edward later wrote: "Wallis had an intuitive understanding of the forces and ideas working in society. She was extraordinarily well informed about politics and current affairs. Her conversation was deft and amusing. But most of all I admired her forthrightness. If she disagreed with some point under discussion, she never failed to advance her own views with vigour and spirit. That side of her enchanted me."[54]

Where Wallis was not honest with the prince was concerning the financial strain that she and Ernest were under, constantly trying to keep up with the prince's set. Entertaining lavishly was beyond their means. Although Ernest's father, "Pa Simpson," helped financially, from time to time he would withdraw his allowance, creating huge pressure on the couple. Wallis wrote to Aunt Bessie that "Pa S—the most selfish old pig"—had stopped their allowance. They could only afford to host one dinner party a month.

On June 19, the Prince of Wales threw a surprise dinner party for Wallis's thirty-seventh birthday at Quaglino's, a restaurant off Jermyn Street. Edward gave Wallis an orchid plant as a gift. As it was the prince's thirty-ninth birthday four days later, she gave him a present that she had put much thought and effort into. She had borrowed a royal spoon from Osborne, the butler at the Fort, and had the prince's cipher copied and engraved onto a silver matchbox holder. The first letter the prince preserved from Wallis was the note she wrote accompanying the birthday present:

> Sir—Many happy returns of the day.
> This small "presy" is to conceal Bryant and May's (match) books on your dining table at the Fort. I am also enclosing your own spoon which I borrowed from Osborne for the marking.
> Your obedient servant, Wallis[55]

That summer, news of the Prince of Wales's interest in Wallis reached his mother, Queen Mary. Elizabeth, Duchess of York, wrote to her mother-in-law about the matter on August 1, 1933:

> My darling Mama, when I was at Cowes with you, Papa* one day mentioned to me that he had heard that a certain person† had

---

* King George VI, her father-in-law.

† Wallis Simpson.

been at the Fort when Bertie & I had been there, & he said that he had a good mind to speak to David* about it. I never had the chance to reopen the subject, but I do hope that he won't do this, as I am sure that David would never forgive us into being drawn into something like that. I do hope that you do not mind my mentioning this Mama, but relations are already a little difficult when naughty ladies are brought in, and up to now we have not met the "lady" at all, & I would like to remain outside the whole affair.

With again all my grateful and loving thanks darling Mama for all your kindness and sympathy which I appreciate more than I can ever say,

Ever your loving daughter in law
Elizabeth[56]

Although the Duchess of York had not met Wallis at Fort Belvedere, she had, in fact, been skating with the duke and the prince's party, which included Wallis and Thelma, five months earlier. Queen Mary replied on August 20, reassuring her daughter-in-law:

Darling Elizabeth,
I am so sorry, I quite forgot to answer yr letter to me at Cowes. Of course Papa never said a word to D about Belvedere so all is well for I agree with you that it wld never do to start a quarrel, but I confess I hope it will not occur again for you ought not to meet D's lady in his own house, that is too much of a bad thing!!!"[57]

The Yorks had never been frequent visitors to the Fort. The duchess, ever conscious of her position, was not comfortable with its air of informality. A photograph taken by Thelma Furness during her reign as chatelaine shows a group of eight guests; seven are sitting around the pool

---

* Only Edward's family ever referred to him as David.

relaxing in swimming costumes, while the Duchess of York sits alone, resplendent in a dress, hat and pearls.[58]

Wallis and Edward went on separate summer sojourns in August. The prince holidayed in Biarritz, while Wallis and Ernest extended a business trip of Ernest's in Norway, staying with their friends the Thaws, who were stationed in Oslo. That autumn, they were again regulars at the Fort while Wallis stoically nursed her private strain: more frantic concerns about money. She and Ernest faced the prospect of having to sell Bryanston Court. Dinner parties were reduced to eight guests every six weeks, and she was restricted to having one girls' lunch a month of no more than four women. She continued to lunch at the Ritz or Claridge's with Thelma, à deux, and in November was excited to be invited to a dinner that Thelma gave where she met Noël Coward. (Coward later said of the Prince of Wales that he "had all the charm in the world with nothing to back it up.")

The prince had started giving Wallis gifts: a photograph of himself in a leather frame, a table for her drawing room—that she chose—for Christmas. Wallis declared Christmas "lovely and gay," and that New Year's Eve, she and Ernest partied with the playboy prince until five in the morning.

On January 25, Thelma left for a three-month trip to America to visit her family. In November, Wallis had written to Aunt Bessie: "I am going to miss Thelma terribly when she goes to NY after Christmas."[59] The day before she sailed, Thelma and Wallis met for cocktails. "We rattled along in our fashion," Wallis remembered, "as we said goodbye, she said, laughingly: 'I'm afraid the prince is going to be lonely. Wallis, won't you look after him?' I promised that I would."[60]

Thelma's recollection of events is subtly different. In her memoirs, she wrote: "Three or four days before I was set to sail, I had lunch with Wallis at the Ritz. I told her of my plans, and in my exuberance I offered myself for all the usual yeoman's services. Was there anything I could do for her in America? Were there any messages I could deliver? Did she want me to bring anything back for her? She thanked me and said suddenly: 'Oh,

Thelma, the little man is going to be so lonely.' 'Well, dear,' I answered, 'you look after him for me while I'm away.'[61]

On Monday, February 12, Wallis's letter to Bessie illustrated the extent to which she heeded her friend and in the process became indispensable to the demands of the prince. "Darling—I have been very slow with letters these past 2 weeks. We have inherited the 'young man' from Thelma. He misses her so that he is always calling us up and the result is one late night after the other—and by late I mean 4 a.m. Ernest has cried off a few but I have had to go on. I am sure the gossip will now be that I am the latest."[62] Six days later, she wrote: "Am also behind on my letters to you on account of the prince who is here most of the time or telephoning 2 and 3 times a day being completely at a loose end. However Thelma will be back very shortly."[63]

The prince's interest in Wallis intensified during a dinner that he hosted at the Dorchester Hotel for some American friends on January 30. Earlier that day, he had been in Yorkshire, visiting social welfare projects, villages and working men's clubs. He was astonished that evening, while the other guests were away from the table dancing, when Wallis sat with him, inquired about his day and actually appeared interested in what his role entailed. Instead of the usual "Oh, Sir, how boring for you! Aren't you terribly tired?" response that he was accustomed to, Wallis, who had read about the Council of Social Service in the newspapers, was genuinely keen to know more about it.

Wallis recalled this to be a turning point in their relationship: "He began to talk about his work, the things he hoped to do, and the creative role he thought the Monarchy could play in this new age, and also dropped a hint of the frustration he was experiencing," she wrote in her memoirs. "I was fascinated. It was as if a door had opened on the inner fastness of his character. What I now saw in his keenness for his job, in his ambition to make a success of it, was not dissimilar to the attitude of many American businessmen I had known. I can not claim that I instantly understood him but I sensed in him something that few around him could have been aware of—a deep loneliness, an overtone of spiritual isolation."[64]

Edward was captivated. As the dancing guests returned to the table, he said to Wallis: "You're the only woman who's ever been interested in my job." He later wrote: "She began to mean more to me in a way that she did not perhaps understand. For a long time she remained unaffected by my interest."[65]

Yet the point had come when Wallis could no longer remain oblivious to the prince's attentions. He took to turning up at Bryanston Court for potluck suppers which he, Wallis and Ernest would enjoy *à trois*. According to Wallis, Ernest then "developed the art of tactfully excusing himself and retiring to his room with his papers."[66] The work demands were genuine; thankfully Ernest's shipping business was picking up.

The Prince of Wales would sometimes pop in and stay for a quick drink; at other times he would appear twice a week and stay all evening. On February 18, Wallis reassured her aunt in her regular correspondence: "P.S. It's all gossip about the prince. I'm not in the habit of taking my friends' beaux. We are around together a lot and of course people are going to say it. I think I do amuse him. I'm the comedy relief and we like to dance together—but I always have Ernest hanging around my neck so all is safe."[67]

A few days later, Wallis wrote once more to her aunt: "I am feeling very well but am quite thin not in the face but in the figure. Naturally worry over finances is not fat-making. I weigh 8 stone undressed but eat and drink as usual."[68] Juggling the attentions of Ernest, as well as the prince, who was proving to be a most determined suitor, similarly took its toll on Wallis's nervous disposition. Admirably, she did not "junk old friends" when the prince came into her life, making efforts to keep up her acquaintances in her spare evenings. She told Bessie: "I'm a bit worn—never a restful moment as it requires great tact to manage both."[69] She and Ernest had even been asked by the prince to invite their own friends to the Fort for weekends—a tremendous honor. She asked Bessie to send her a pale-blue summer dress for $20, explaining: "The royalty stuff very demanding on clothes."[70]

Wallis was now playing the coveted hostess role. Unwittingly, Thelma provided the prince the perfect excuse to transfer his affection when she returned from America on March 22. In New York and on the crossing home, she had enjoyed the attentions of Prince Aly Khan, the son of the Aga Khan. Only twenty-three, he had a reputation as a polished seducer. According to Elsa Maxwell, Aly Khan was "*un homme fatal*."[71] Word of their association reached Edward.

"The prince arrived at my house in Regent's Park that night," Thelma recalled. "He seemed a little distrait, as if something were bothering him. Suddenly he said: 'I hear Aly Khan has been very attentive to you.' I thought he was joking. 'Are you jealous, darling?' I asked. But the prince did not answer me."[72] When Thelma asked Wallis why the prince was distant to her at the Fort the following weekend, Wallis replied somewhat disingenuously: "Darling, you know the little man loves you very much. The little man was just lost without you."[73]

"Empty as these sentences were, they were a kind of emotional bulwark," recalled Thelma. Reassured, she invited Wallis and Ernest to the Fort for Easter weekend. However, "that weekend was negatively memorable," said Thelma. "I do not remember who was there, other than the Simpsons, there were about eight of us in all. I had a bad cold when we arrived. . . . Most of Saturday passed without incident. At dinner, however, I noticed that the prince and Wallis seemed to have little private jokes. Once he picked up a piece of salad with his fingers; Wallis playfully slapped his hand."[74] Thelma caught Wallis's eye and shook her head at her. "She knew as well as everybody else that the prince could be very friendly, but no matter how friendly, he never permitted familiarity. His image of himself, shy, genial and democratic, was always framed by the royal three feathers. . . . Wallis looked straight at me. And then and there I knew. That one cold, defiant glance had told the entire story."[75]

Thelma left the Fort, and the prince's life, the following morning. Wallis confirmed that her reign was over in a letter to her aunt on April 15, 1934. Sent tellingly from the Fort, she wrote: "Thelma is still in Paris. I'm afraid her rule is over and I'm trying to keep an even keel with my relations with him by avoiding seeing him alone as he is very attentive at the moment. And of course I'm flattered."[76]

Wallis took to her new role as chatelaine of Fort Belvedere with verve. A footman brought in by Thelma Furness was quickly dismissed; the cook soon followed. Osborne, the butler, was more threatened by Wallis's presence than those of her predecessors, Lady Furness and Mrs. Dudley Ward. When Wallis presented the prince with a small tray on a folding stand, which she thought would simplify the serving of tea, Osborne was reluctant to use it. When the prince insisted that he bring it in for the afternoon tea, the butler snapped the tray into position with a vicious jerk and announced contemptuously: "Your Royal Highness, this thing won't last twenty-four hours."[77]

Wallis's status was further sealed when the prince arrived at Bryanston Court with a cairn terrier pup under his arm. He presented the dog to Wallis, announcing that it was called Slipper and was now hers. In her letters, Wallis tried to reassure Aunt Bessie that Ernest was fully aware of what was happening and, in fact, colluded with the new order. "Ernest is flattered with it all and lets me dine once or twice a week with him *alone*," she wrote, adding: "If Ernest raises any objections to the situation I shall give the prince up at once."[78]

Even at the height of the prince's affair with Thelma Furness, Freda Dudley Ward was in the background as the maternal figure the prince could always rely on. On April 25, when Wallis wrote to Bessie that the royal affair with Thelma was "very much on the wane," she continued: "I shall doubtless be blamed as for the moment he is rather attentive though sees equally as much of Mrs Dudley Ward his old flame."[79]

This is the only mention Wallis ever made of Freda in her correspondence, yet ever since the prince's affair with Freda cooled in 1924 and Thelma came on the scene, he had continued to visit the Dudley Ward family. That month, Freda's daughter, Penelope, suffered complications after an operation for appendicitis. Freda, who spent anxious days beside her daughter's bedside, was too distraught to realize that all was suspiciously quiet from royal quarters. As soon as her daughter recovered, she rang York House to speak to the prince. The telephone operator, whom she had known for years, made a strange choking sound when he discovered Mrs. Dudley Ward was on the line. "He didn't seem able to speak. I suddenly realised to my horror that he was crying," said Freda. " 'Everybody seems to have gone mad around here,' he said. The prince had given orders that none of my phone calls be put through. I never heard from him again."[80]

In that one act of cowardice, the prince coldly dispensed with Mrs. Freda Dudley Ward. From that moment on, Wallis was to be his "one and only."

3

One and Only

By the spring of 1934, Wallis and Ernest's life was almost "completely caught up and submerged in the prince's private world."[1] The Simpsons received the ultimate invitation of society's summer season: to join the prince's party for Ascot week. The royal procession from Windsor Castle to the racecourse was a brilliant piece of pageantry—the king, queen and their family in open landaus, with bewigged postilions astride the grey horses. "That year, as I watched from the Royal Enclosure," Wallis recalled, "I felt an odd surge of pride and admiration when I saw that fleeting, boyish smile directed at us from under his grey topper."[2]

When the prince invited Wallis and Ernest as his guests on his summer holiday to Biarritz, Wallis initially declined. Ernest was due to go to America on business and she had invited Aunt Bessie to stay with her in his absence. Not to be deterred, the prince reassured Wallis that he would welcome Bessie. Her seventy-year-old aunt, would, of course, make the perfect chaperone.

It was a small party that set off for France on August 1: the prince, his assistant private secretary, Hugh Lloyd Thomas, his equerries, "G" Trotter and John Aird, and his old friends, Lieutenant Commander Buist and his wife, Gladys, and Wallis and Aunt Bessie. Edward had rented a sprawling villa called Meretmont, overlooking the ocean. The holiday did not get off to a promising start. There were two days of continuous rain; then their regal host suffered from a surfeit of langoustines and was sick at his table in the Café de Paris. Fortunately, they soon settled into a happier routine. "As at the Fort, life was simple—swimming and sunbathing, golf, sometimes a little bridge," said Wallis. Once a week, Edward and Wallis would leave the rest of the party and dine alone at local bistros. This was their first opportunity to be together as a couple. John Aird wrote in his diary of the prince at this time: "Behaviour in public excellent, in private awful and most embarrassing for others. The prince has lost all confidence in himself and follows W around like a dog."[3]

The prince soon tired of Biarritz. When Mrs. Kenelm Guinness, known as "Posy," joined the party, she invited them to extend their holiday. Her cousin, Lord Moyne, an heir of the Guinness brewing family and Conservative politician, was sailing his yacht, *Rosaura*, nearby. Edward jumped at the chance to spend more time with Wallis. Bessie, who had planned a motoring trip in Italy, refused to be diverted and left Wallis with the royal party. John Aird, who was responsible for organizing the logistics of joining the cruise, later wrote of Wallis: "I feel that she is not basically a bad sort of tough girl out to get what she can, but unless she is much cleverer than I think, she does not know how to work it so as to cash in best."[4]

The yacht was a converted channel steamer. Lord Moyne, a distinguished-looking Irishman, made a point of boasting to his guests that he was an accomplished seaman and the *Rosaura* could override any Atlantic gale. In spite of a furious storm in the Bay of Biscay as the royal party went aboard, Lord Moyne ordered the vessel to get under way, announcing: "I have yet to see the storm that could keep me in port."[5] Wallis, a seasoned seafarer who rarely got seasick, took to her cabin, clinging to the bed as her trunk was flung back and forth across her berth. As the storm mounted in violence, each of the rest of the party retreated to their cabins, with the exception of John Aird. Wallis, convinced that their host would have to accept defeat, asked a steward who checked in on her later that night, how soon they would be in port. He replied: "I've never seen his Lordship in finer fettle. He has just ordered caviar and grouse and a bottle of champagne for Mr. Aird and himself."[6]

The last straw was when Lord Moyne's pet, a terrifying monkey who had the run of the vessel, suddenly leapt on Wallis's bed, having jumped through a skylight. Wallis let out such a scream that Lord Moyne himself was startled from the bridge. A steward was sent to coax the spirited animal from Wallis's berth. Fortunately, the prince, reeling with seasickness himself, struggled to the bridge and, summoning his finest diplomacy, ordered the yacht to the nearby Spanish port of Coruña.

John Aird felt that Wallis's fear of physical danger had an enfeebling effect on the prince. Always before, he had been physically intrepid, even recklessly so. He enjoyed flying in aircraft and was always the one who wanted to push ahead in bad conditions. Of the storm they faced on the *Rosaura*, Aird later wrote bitterly: "He was really frightened, and in my opinion is a coward at heart."[7]

Once the storm had blown over, the party enjoyed a relaxed, delightful cruise down the Spanish and Portuguese coasts. Often finding themselves alone on deck in the evenings, Wallis recognized that here she and Edward "crossed the line that marks the indefinable boundary between friendship and love."[8] Eleven days after leaving Biarritz, they reached Cannes. After dinner with Wallis's friends Herman and Katherine Rogers at their hillside villa, Edward placed a tiny velvet pouch from Cartier in Wallis's hand. It contained a diamond and emerald charm for a bracelet—the first of what would become his legendary acquisition of exquisite jewelry for his beloved.

The prince's advisors were aware of the beneficial influence Wallis could have on him. On holiday, Edward liked to sport the simplest of clothes, an antidote to the constant, starchy dressing up that his position required. But Wallis could see that it was inappropriate for the Prince of Wales to go ashore practically deshabille in shorts, shirt and sandals. It took all her powers of persuasion to entice him into linen trousers and a jacket.

It was their visibility on the Côte d'Azur that inspired the first mention in the press of the new romance. That September, *Time* magazine referred to the fun that "Edward of Wales [was] having at Cannes last week with beautiful Mrs. Wallace Simpson."[9] Still, the courtiers were not alert to any real danger. At the end of the holiday, John Aird concluded of Wallis: "She does not seem to have any illusions about the situation and definitely does not want to do anything that will lose her husband."[10]

The wiser, more perceptive Aunt Bessie queried her niece's motives that September. Over dinner, she asked Wallis: "Isn't the prince rather taken with you?" adding: "These old eyes aren't so old that they can't see what's in his every glance." Bessie cautioned Wallis that if she continued enjoying this kind of life—which Wallis herself described as "Wallis in Wonderland"—it would leave her unsettled and dissatisfied with the life she had known before. Wallis batted away her concerns. "It's all great fun," she told her. "You don't have to worry about me—I know what I am doing." Aunt Bessie's conclusion was wisely prescient: "I can see no happy outcome to such a situation."[11]

Similarly concerned were the king and queen. Up until then, they had publicly ignored Wallis's existence. That September, after his prolonged summer holiday, Edward joined his parents at Balmoral. He had composed a tune for the bagpipes, dedicated to Wallis, called "Majorca." He practiced it relentlessly, marching up and down the castle terrace in the rain until the exasperated king threw open the window and yelled at him to stop.[12]

In November tensions escalated over Wallis in the royal household. The prince had included Mrs. Simpson's name on a list of guests that he wanted to invite to an evening celebration at Buckingham Palace for the wedding of his brother George, the Duke of Kent, to Princess Marina of Greece. When the king saw it he scratched it out. The Duke of Kent later reinstated her on the list.

Wallis resumed her letters to Aunt Bessie, writing from the Fort on November 5 about circulating rumors: "Don't listen to such ridiculous gossip. E[rnest] and myself are far from being divorced and have had a long talk about [the] P[rince of] W[ales] and myself and also one with the latter and everything will go on just the same as before, namely the three of us being the best of friends. I shall try and be clever enough to keep them both."[13]

In the run-up to the royal wedding at Westminster Abbey on November 29, the Simpsons spent many happy times at the Fort with the two princes. George was living there in preparation for his marriage, while Princess Marina was in Paris with her parents, selecting her trousseau. Wallis, Ernest and the princes "had great fun together." Wallis declared Princess Marina "a most beautiful woman" whom Prince George was "genuinely in love with."[14] It amused Wallis to see Prince George jokingly checking the tally at the end of the day of how much the wedding gifts that arrived from all over the world were worth. "Royalty can be just as interested in the cost of things as the rest of us," she sagely observed.[15] She and Ernest gave the royal couple two lamps from Fortnum & Mason, costing ten guineas each. These, she told Prince George, unabashed, were reduced in the sale and were not exchangeable.

For the state reception hosted by the king and queen at Buckingham Palace, Wallis wore a dress designed by Eva Lutyens, daughter-in-law of the famous architect. In a simple column of violet lamé with a vivid green sash, Wallis made a bold impression. Princess Marina, the bride-to-be, was in an unpretentious white evening dress, while Queen Mary was her usual regal staid self in silver brocade with ice-blue paillettes. Wallis, who had borrowed a tiara from Cartier, was understandably thrilled when Prince Paul, Regent of Yugoslavia, the brother-in-law of the bride, told her: "Mrs. Simpson, there is no question about it—you are wearing the most striking gown in the room."[16]

However, the evening would hold far more import than being memorable for Wallis's stylish gown. It would turn out to be the only occasion when she would (briefly) meet Edward's parents. The prince approached Queen Mary with the words "I want to introduce a great friend of mine."[17] Wallis later wrote in her memoirs: "After Prince Paul had left us, David led me over to where they [the king and queen] were standing and introduced me. It was the briefest of encounters—a few words of perfunctory greeting, an exchange of meaningless pleasantries, and we moved away."[18] Afterwards, Wallis described to her Aunt Bessie the "excitement of the prince bringing the Queen up to Ernest and self in front of all the cold jealous English eyes."[19] Many times that evening, Ernest was left standing alone while the heir to the throne took Wallis off to meet his friends and relations. Prince Christopher of Greece wrote of Edward: "He laid a hand on my arm in an impulsive way: 'Christo, come with me. I want you to meet Mrs. Simpson . . .' 'Mrs. Simpson, who is she?' I asked. 'An American,' then he smiled. 'She's wonderful,' he added. The two words told me everything. It was as though he had said: 'She is the only woman in the world.'"[20]

John Aird recorded in his memoirs that the prince introduced Wallis to his mother "and would have done to HM [His Majesty] if he had not been cut off."[21] After the party, the king was outraged that Wallis had slipped back onto the guest list, shouting: "That woman in my house!" He continued to rant that at least Mrs. Dudley Ward had come from a better class, while his son had "not a single friend who is a gentleman."[22] He was referring to Edward's involvement with the international set. King George gave orders to the lord chamberlain that Mrs. Simpson was not to be invited to any of the Silver Jubilee functions the following year, nor ever again to the royal enclosure at Ascot.

During the glamorous reception, the prince also took Wallis over to be greeted by the Duke and Duchess of York. Against Wallis's flat, angular frame and violet column dress, Elizabeth was softer, filling out her pale pink gown. Yet her femininity belied a steely reserve. Wallis curtsied to Edward's sister-in-law, later describing "the almost startling blueness" of the Duchess of York's eyes as she felt her cold, appraising stare. Their blue eyes and affection for the Prince of Wales was all the two women would ever have in common. The Yorks, while studiously polite in public, failed to show any warmth towards Wallis. Elizabeth's close friend the Dowager Lady Hardinge of Penshurst, who was present at the interaction between the two brothers and their amours, later wrote: "I am afraid Mrs. Simpson went down rather badly with the duchess from the word go. It may have been the rather ostentatious dress, or the fact that she allowed the Prince of Wales to push her forward in what seemed an inappropriate manner. The Duchess of York was never discourteous in my experience, but those of us who knew her very well could always tell when she did not care for something or someone, and it was very apparent to me that she did not care for Mrs. Simpson at all."[23]

If Elizabeth, born Elizabeth Bowes-Lyon, once harbored romantic feelings for Edward, as was rumored, it would partly explain her enmity towards Wallis. Elizabeth had initially been reluctant to accept his brother Bertie's wedding proposal. "Prince Albert pursued Elizabeth for three years and she twice turned down marriage proposals, which protocol demanded were made to her through intermediaries," said her equerry, Major Colin Burgess. "On the third time, in 1923, when Prince Albert ignored protocol and asked her directly, she accepted."[24] The twenty-three-year-old daughter of the Earl of Strathmore was considered a suitable royal match. "I believe that it is not impossible that Elizabeth would have liked to marry the Prince of Wales,"[25] said Hugo Vickers, who knew her. "Once the Duke of York took an interest in her, her mother, Lady Strathmore, saw the possibility of a royal union. She thought: 'Why not the older brother?' Edward wasn't interested in any eligible English girl."[26]

Wallis, ever resourceful, did not dwell on the chill of Elizabeth's disapproval at Prince George's wedding celebrations. Instead, she was aware, after the nuptials—where "the prince had provided Ernest and me with very good places on a side aisle, from which we had an uninterrupted view of the altar"[27]—that Edward nursed a sense of sadness and keen loss now that his favorite brother was married. His friendship with his younger brother was, apart from his relationship with Wallis, the most important of his adult life. Wallis, sensitive to the strain of Edward's loneliness, worked hard to divert him with some humorous irrelevancy or by engaging in a more serious topic that interested him. "It was curious to see a man of such dynamic qualities, a man so active and so often filled with the true joy of life, suddenly disappear before my very eyes into uncertainty," she wrote. She felt that he was "reaching out for something that was as yet unknown to him, something which could anchor his personal life."[28]

* * *

Edward described his life before his marriage to Wallis as "a disconnected pattern—duty without decision, service without responsibility, pomp without power."[29] After George's betrothal, this disconnect seemed to weigh on him more heavily. The heir to the throne continued to struggle with the responsibility of his official duties, while railing against the palace old guard. He was at heart a modernizer who felt that many of the institutional practices were out of date. He wanted to be seen as "Edward the innovator," a monarch who would let "fresh air" into the "venerable institution of kingship." In 1969 Edward told an interviewer: "Before I became King, I was in conflict with the government of the day."[30] The prince's visits in 1935 to depressed areas of the country angered the prime minister. Edward later recalled: "When Stanley Baldwin got to hear of these trips he called me to the House of Commons. He said: 'Why are you going up there? Have you not got other important things to do?' So I said, 'No, Mr. Baldwin, I think it's very important to see how these people live. Some of them have been out of work for ten years.'"[31] Edward felt it was his duty to alert the government that little had been done to alleviate the plight of the unemployed. "To some extent I collided with the establishment," he concluded, "but not violently. I'm not being conceited but it might have helped revive their thinking."[32]

As the prince shared the frustrations of his position with Wallis, she realized that she had become a part of his quest, perhaps inextricably so. Each day he drew her ever more intimately into his life. Their dinners alone became more regular and he began telephoning Wallis frequently throughout the day. Flattering, but with his ardor and intense neediness, it was also pressurizing and exhausting. On December 3, 1934, Wallis wrote to Aunt Bessie from the Fort that she had been buying all the prince's Christmas presents for his staff and had to wrap 250 gifts. After her usual domestic update—she had no housemaid—Wallis added, almost casually: "I have 2 more bracelets and a small diamond that sticks into my hair. Smart. Ernest says that the insurance is getting steep! A big kiss and all love—."[33]

Ernest was right to be worried about their insurance premium. That Christmas, Edward gave Wallis £50,000 worth of jewels (including two large square emeralds) followed by £60,000 worth a week later at New Year.[34] The prince should have been more judicious. When the king was alerted by his courtiers that his son and heir had spent £110,000 (£7 million today) on jewels, he feared blackmail. Unbeknownst to Edward, the king asked Stanley Baldwin for police help to ascertain the woman's identity and motives. George V set in motion a controversial surveillance operation that would continue throughout the following year. Sir Vernon Kell, the founder and first director of MI5, initially refused Baldwin's request to spy on the Prince of Wales because he felt that it would be crossing a constitutional line and could not be justified in terms of national security. Eventually, Sir Vernon grudgingly agreed to put Baldwin's request to the board at MI5, which overruled the director and gave its assent.

The covert surveillance operation was authorized by the Home Secretary, Sir John Simon, and undertaken by Superintendent Albert Canning of Scotland Yard. Canning began by confirming Mrs. Simpson as the recipient of the jewels. "She is reputed to be very attractive," wrote Canning in one report, "and spends lavishly on clothes and entertainment."[35] Visitors to Bryanston Court were monitored by the inspector and his team. Detectives also recorded that Mrs. Simpson and the prince called each other "darling" while visiting an antiques shop in South Kensington. In the report, the shopkeeper remarked that the lady seemed to have the gentleman "completely under her thumb." The information collected by Special Branch was often lurid, almost laughably inaccurate and very boys' own. It was asserted that Ernest Simpson was "Jewish" and a "bounder type" who was waiting for "high honours" to be conferred on him.[36] Wallis, who two years later referred to becoming the "convenient tool" in the hands of the politicians who created "an organized campaign" to remove Edward from the throne, had no idea at this stage that she was being spied on.

One trumped-up charge against Wallis that later came to light was that, whilst seeing the prince, she was having "intimate relations" with a Ford car salesman by the name of Guy Marcus Trundle. Trundle, known to his family as a fantasist who liked to boast of his "conquests," made these claims about Wallis to anyone who would listen. However, her close friends categorically deny that she would have even contemplated an affair with such a figure. "There is absolutely no way that she had an affair with Guy Trundle," said Nicky Haslam.[37] "I know this to be true." John Julius Norwich agreed: "She was much too intelligent to have had an affair with a secondhand car dealer when the eyes of the world were upon her. This was merely another bid by the powers that be to discredit her."[38]

Wallis's correspondence to her aunt brims with the strain of juggling two men, her husband and the Prince of Wales; it seems completely out of character that she would jeopardize her situation with a third, let alone a man from such an unlikely background. Far from craving further entanglements, she cherished space for herself. When the prince went to Sandringham with his family for Christmas, she considered it "a lovely rest for us and especially me."[39]

The following year, 1935, was thrilling for Wallis. Her friend Lady Diana Mosley summarized her situation: "Although the great public knew nothing of the Prince of Wales's friendship with Mrs. Simpson, a fairly wide circle in London knew of it, and those who did thought at first it was just Lady Furness all over again and Wallis the prince's latest American friend. Society being what it is, Wallis began not just to have a good time but the time of her life. She was courted and flattered."[40]

Wallis was feted by the Londonderrys (the seventh Marquess was a Cabinet minister and his wife, Edith, Lady Londonderry, held sought-after political receptions); Mrs. Evelyn Fitzgerald, sister-in-law of the press baron Lord Beaverbrook; the Guinnesses; the Cholmondeleys (the fifth Marquess of Cholmondeley would become lord chamberlain at the court of Edward VIII); Mrs. Laura Corrigan (a society hostess from Colorado); Daphne, Countess of Weymouth; Lady Sibyl Colefax; and Lady Emerald Cunard.

"Though nothing about Mrs. Simpson appears in the English papers," the society photographer Cecil Beaton noted in his diary that autumn, "her name seems never to be off people's lips. For those who enjoy gossip she is a particular treat. The sound of her name implies secrecy, royalty, and being in the know. As a topic she has become a mania, so much so that her name is banned in many houses to allow breathing space for other topics. . . ."[41]

There was something touchingly childlike about Wallis's excitement at her recognized status in society as Edward's "one and only." Instead of always feeling an outsider, as she had done since childhood, she began to embrace the (faux) warmth of acceptance. Lady Cunard, the society figurehead always adorned with ropes of pearls who championed Wallis, memorably said: "Little Mrs. Simpson knows her Balzac,"[42] suggesting that Wallis was better read and better bred than people imagined. Emerald Cunard's lunch parties were legendary due to her "throwaway shockers"; invitations to her Grosvenor Square home were coveted. Wallis, who became a regular around her lapis lazuli–topped circular table, was sufficiently savvy to recognize that the fawning society figures were there solely because of the prince. Her glittering position would extinguish the minute Edward lost interest in her. This she accepted and awaited.

Ernest, too, knew that all the attention had nothing to do with him. According to Diana Mosley: "He absented himself more and more, and in fact behaved with dignity. Mrs. Simpson saw only the prince. If she had seen others, everyone would have known, even if there was nothing in the newspapers."[43]

In late January 1935, Chips Channon recorded his first meeting with Wallis. "Lunched with Emerald to meet Mrs. Simpson. . . . She is a nice, quiet, well-bred mouse of a woman with large startled eyes and a huge mole. I think that she is surprised and rather conscience-stricken by her present position and the limelight which consequently falls upon her."[44] Those in the know were abuzz with chatter as to what *exactly* the prince saw in Wallis Simpson. As she herself said later: "I could find no good reason why this most glamorous of men should be so seriously attracted to me. I was certainly no beauty, and he had the pick of the beautiful women of the world."[45] It was her American independence of spirit, she concluded, along with her breezy sense of fun, that he was drawn to.

Although Wallis valiantly told herself and her aunt that Ernest was completely compliant with her situation, the truth was that Ernest, for all his reverence of royalty, was finding his wife's ever-growing attachment to another man increasingly hard to tolerate. For all her protestations to Aunt Bessie that her relationship with Ernest was solid, the marriage was starting to disintegrate. "Until now, I had taken for granted that Ernest's interest in the prince was keeping pace with mine," she later wrote, "but about this time I began to sense a change in his attitude. His work seemed to make more and more demands on his time in the evening. Often he would not return in time for dinner, or when the prince suggested dropping in at Sartori's or the Dorchester for an hour or so of amusement, Ernest would ask to be excused on the plea that he had an early appointment or that papers from the office needed his attention. He also seemed less and less interested in what I had to say about the prince's latest news and interest."[46]

It was the prince's invitation to a two-week skiing holiday in Austria in February 1935 which highlighted the growing frictions between the Simpsons. Wallis relished the chance to get away; when the prince invited them to join him in Kitzbühel, Wallis "naturally accepted for both of us."[47] When she told Ernest, it precipitated their first-ever door-slamming row. Ernest, who had business in New York and was no fan of winter sports, wanted Wallis to accompany him on his business trip. Wallis made her choice—the prince over Ernest—and this, unsurprisingly, created the first irreparable fissure in their marriage.

The prince's staff began to feel alarmed when Edward set off for another holiday with Wallis in the party, yet again without her husband. Accompanying them were Bruce Ogilvy, the prince's equerry; his wife, Primrose; and his sister-in-law Olive. Wallis, who did not take to skiing, discovered a fear of the sport, preferring the less demanding après-ski. She looked forward to the afternoon rendezvous of the whole party in the village inn, sipping hot chocolate before the fire. The prince's entourage stayed in the Grand Hotel and every evening ate at a mountain restaurant where a band played folk music, the prince heartily singing along to the local songs. Edward, loath to return to London, announced after two weeks that he felt like waltzing, "and Vienna's the place for that."[48] So off the royal party swept to the Bristol Hotel in Vienna, crossing the Alps by train. His aides were understandably frantic when, after delightful evenings devoted to Strauss, the prince asserted that "while these Viennese waltzes are wonderfully tender, there is nothing to match the fire of *gypsy* violins."[49] The next morning, on yet another royal whim, they were on their way to Budapest. Edward's insatiable need to indulge every fleeting impulse was more akin to that of a jaded jet-setter, rather than the heir to the throne, with duties and responsibilities to consider.

It was in a dingy local tavern in Budapest, on the Pest side of the river, where they had been guaranteed to hear the best gypsy music in Hungary, that Wallis had a piercing moment of realization about the impossibility of her situation. As the violins swelled with melancholy tunes, amid the flickering candles and rough-hewn wooden tables, she "had the feeling of being torn apart, of being caught up in the inescapable sadness and sorrow of human suffering; and the look in David's eyes told me that he was in the grip of the same flow of feeling."[50] She later wrote that she was "scarcely in a condition to differentiate these two worlds between which I giddily swung, hoping to have the best of both, but not quite sure whether I could maintain my footing in either."[51]

On Wallis's return to London, it became clear that her sense of foreboding was justified. Her marital footing could no longer be guaranteed. Ernest, now cold and distant, had "undergone a change." He showed no interest in her trip and was uncommunicative about his own visit to New York. For the first time, their evenings together were strained, punctuated by arctic silences. Still, Wallis did not act on the warning bells, so enraptured was she to be swept up in the prince's orbit. "My concern was no more than a tiny cloud in the growing radiance that the prince's favor cast over my life," she wrote with insouciance. "I became aware of a rising curiosity concerning me, of new doors opening, and a heightened interest even in my casual remarks. I was stimulated; I was excited; I felt as if I were borne upon a rising wave that seemed to be carrying me ever more rapidly and even higher."[52]

It was the Kitzbühel skiing holiday that convinced royal aides that the prince had gone too far. Sir Clive Wigram, George V's private secretary, visited Edward at Fort Belvedere and told him how concerned the king was about his personal life. In a memo afterwards, he wrote: "The prince said that he was astonished that anyone could take offence about his personal friends. Mrs. Simpson was a charming, cultivated woman."[53] John Aird, meanwhile, could see that putting any pressure on the prince had negligible effect. If anything, he felt that after Sir Clive's visit "the devotion of HRH is if possible greater."[54] Godfrey Thomas, the prince's equerry, said that he believed the prince knew "in his inmost heart" he was behaving badly. Thomas reassured the courtiers that patience was key. "I am sure his eyes will be opened to the folly he is making of himself, and when he does come for help and sympathy, I am sure you will respond as I know I shall."[55]

The rumor mill amongst the staff at the two royal households, York House and Buckingham Palace, was rife with tales of the prince's nocturnal habits. It was said that two bedrooms at the Fort had been turned into one for the couple's benefit, presumably to avoid the risk that, when the house was full, the dressing room adjoining Wallis's bedroom might be occupied and thus access to her impeded. It is a curious detail that Edward always maintained that he never slept with Wallis before his marriage, and sued for libel an author who referred to her as his mistress. Astonishingly, the subject arose between Edward and his father, when Edward challenged the king over his ban on Wallis's appearance at court. He wanted Wallis to be invited to the court ball to celebrate the Silver Jubilee in May 1935. The king said that he could not invite his son's mistress to such an occasion. When the prince swore that she was not his "mistress," the king accepted his son's word and said that Mrs. Simpson could come. "I think that this is all for the best," wrote John Aird in his diary, "but it is rather a shock to think of the Prince of Wales lying on his oath, which a lot of people who know think he has."[56]

Sir Clive Wigram wrote that "the staff were horrified at the audacity of the statements of HRH. Apart from actually seeing HRH and Mrs. S in bed together, they had positive proof that HRH lived with her."[57] Tommy Lascelles said that he would find it as easy to believe in the innocence of their relationship as "a herd of unicorns grazing in Hyde Park and a shoal of mermaids swimming in the Serpentine."[58]

Despite the unraveling of their marriage, the Simpsons put on a brave front. That April, Ernest wrote warmly to his mother, keen to impress her with his royal connections and wanting to reassure her that all was well in his marriage:

> My dearest one and only Mother,
> The Prince took two other married couples and ourselves to the Grand National Steeple chase near Liverpool. We had a special car on the train and we were met by a fleet of motors. We lunched in state with Lord Sefton, the owner of the course and had a splendid view from his private stand. It was great fun.
> Much, much love, in which Wallis joins, and a big hug,
> Affectionately, Ernest.[59]

At Easter, Ernest joined Wallis motoring around Cornwall with the prince, and their friends the Hunters, to see the camellias and rhododendrons in bloom. According to Wallis, whatever Ernest was "thinking or feeling, he loyally played his part."[60] Whilst staying on the Duchy estate, Edward began penning Wallis intimate billets-doux, which he had delivered to her room. But a shadow was now cast over the trio. Where the arrangement had previously been chummily inclusive, Ernest was now excluded. Wallis and Edward were sufficiently emotionally entwined to have developed their own private language, which spelt out the intensity of their relationship. They referred to themselves as "WE," representing their joint first names and symbolizing their union. They also devised the adjective *eanum*, which to them meant tiny, "poor," "affecting" and "pathetic." Edward wrote to Wallis from St. Austell Bay Hotel, his note accompanying an Easter gift of a bracelet:

> My [*twice underlined*] Eanum—My [*thrice underlined*] Wallis
> This is not the kind of Easter WE want but it will be alright next year. The Easter Bunny has brought this from Us All [twice underlined] & Slipper says he likes it too but it has to be fitted and christened later. I love you more & more & more each & every

minute & miss you so [thrice underlined] terribly here. You do too dont you my sweetheart.

God bless WE. Always your[s] [*twice underlined*].[61]

Edward's obsession with Wallis was causing him to act with increasingly rash indiscretion. Wallis would have received the letter, and the accompanying piece of jewelry, while sharing a room with Ernest. She, meanwhile, was no longer under any illusions that this was a romantic relationship that the prince seemed wholly committed to. The mounting tension between the trio finally erupted in a terrible row between Wallis and Ernest on their return from Cornwall. This provoked Wallis to write her first stern letter to the prince. It reveals how she by now fully assumed the role of disapproving mother, reprimanding a thoughtless naughty boy.

Tuesday a.m.
David dear—
I was and still am most terribly upset. You see my dear one can't go through life stepping on other people. . . . You think only of what you want and take it without the slightest thought of others. One can arrive at the same result in a kinder way. I had a long quiet talk with E last night and I felt very eanum at the end. Everything he said was so true. The evening was difficult as you did stay too late. Doesn't your love for me reach the heights of wanting to make things a little easier for me. The lovely things you say to me aren't of much value unless they are backed up by equal actions.

I was upset and also very disappointed in a boy—because David what are all those words if what they say isn't enough for a little sacrifice on our part to do what is the right thing for all concerned. So far you have always come first in my actions if there had to be a choice (like Sat). It isn't fair and cannot always be that way.

Sometimes I think you haven't grown up where love is concerned and perhaps it's only a boyish passion for surely it lacks

> the thought of me that a man's love is capable of. . . . Your behaviour last night made me realise how very alone I shall be some day—and because I love you I don't seem to have the strength to protect myself from your youthfulness.
>
> God bless WE and be kind to me in the years to come for I have lost something noble for a boy who may always remain a Peter Pan.[62]

Those close to the couple could see the inherent insecurity in Wallis's position. As Chips Channon wrote on May 14, the day of the Silver Jubilee Ball: "She is madly anxious to storm society while she is still his favourite so that when he leaves her, as he leaves everybody in time, she will be secure."[63] Chips continued to comment on the gossip fizzing about Wallis's appearance later at the ball. "There is tremendous excitement about Mrs. Simpson. It is a war of the knife between past and present. Officially I am on-side—but secretly delighted for she always was an appalling, selfish, silly influence. Mrs. S has enormously improved the prince. In fact, I find her duel over the Prince of Wales between Mrs. Simpson, supported by Diana Cooper, and strangely, enough, Emerald, and the ——* camp, is most diverting. In fact, the romance surpasses all else in interest."[64]

Of the state ball, Wallis recalled that after the king and queen had made their entrance, the dancing began. "As David and I danced past, I thought I felt the king's eyes rest searchingly on me. Something in his look made me feel all this graciousness and pageantry were but the glittering tip of an iceberg that extended down into unseen depths I could never plumb, depths filled with an icy menace for such as me." A chill ran through Wallis, and in spite of being seen dancing the fox-trot with the Prince of Wales, "in that moment I knew that between David's world and

* When Chips Channon's diaries were published in 1967, his views on the royal family were seen as so controversial that certain names were redacted. In this instance it is likely that he is referring to the Duchess of York and then the battle between the king's camp and the York camp, which would include the attitude of the king and queen.

mine lay an abyss that I could never cross, one he could never bridge for me."[65]

Wallis kept up her jovial, reassuring front in her correspondence with Aunt Bessie. After the ball, she wrote of her evening, describing the diamond clips she received as a jubilee present. "The Prince danced with me after the opening one with the Queen so you see I am not neglected on the right things."[66] She continued to regale her aunt with examples of her popularity, explaining that she was besieged by invitations. Wise to the situation she explained: "They think that in asking me they'll get him." Before adding, tellingly: "It will be lovely when something happens to break it up."[67]

However, Edward had no intention of letting Wallis go. He later wrote: "A prince's heart, like his politics, must remain within the constitutional pale. But my heart refused to be so confined; and presently and imperceptibly the hope formed that one day I might be able to share my life with her, just how I did not know."[68] The prince and Mrs. Simpson continued to storm society, while Special Branch continued to spy on Wallis and the royal family made every effort to avoid her. The battle lines that Chips Channon referred to were drawn between the old-guard traditionalists (chiefly King George V, Queen Mary, the Duke and Duchess of York and Princess Marina) and the pro-Wallis camp (which included the Prince of Wales, the Duke of Kent, Lady Cunard, Lady Colefax, Chips Channon, the Duff Coopers, Cecil Beaton and Winston Churchill).

Later that May, on Empire Day, Chips Channon wrote in his diary: "We had cocktails at Mrs. Simpson's little flat in Bryanston Court. The Prince was charm itself. He is boisterous, wrinkled and gay. His voice is more American than ever. (It doesn't matter, since all the Royal Family except the Duke of Kent have German voices.) He wore a short black coat and soft collar, checked socks and a tie. . . . He shook and passed the cocktails very much the *jeune homme de la maison*."[69]

A few nights later, Chips joined the prince and "the ménage Simpson" in Emerald Cunard's box at the opera. He noted the positive influence and mesmeric hold Wallis had over the heir to the throne. It was she who chided Edward to leave, reminding him not to be late in joining the queen for a ball. As he left, she removed a cigar from his breast pocket, admonishing: "It doesn't look very pretty." The party noted that the prince left but was back within half an hour.

Wallis's reign at the Fort was similarly in its zenith. That summer Lady Diana Cooper and her husband, Duff, were weekend guests. "We arrived after midnight (perhaps as chaperones)," recalled Lady Diana:

> Jabber and beer and bed was the order. I did not leave the "cabin's seclusion" until 1 o'clock, having been told that no one else did. HRH was dressed in plus-twenties with vivid azure socks. Wallis, admirably correct and chic. Me bang wrong! Everything is a few hours later than other places (perhaps it is American time). A splendid tea arrived at 6.30 with Anthony Eden and Esmond Harmsworth [son and heir of Lord Rothermere]. Dinner was at 10. Emerald arrived at 8.30 for cocktails, which she doesn't drink although the prince prepares the portions with his own poor hands and does all the glass-filling. The Prince changed into a Donald tartan dress-kilt with an immense white leather purse in front, and played the pipes round the table after dinner, having first fetched his bonnet. We "reeled" to bed at 2 a.m.[70]

While the British press had yet to write anything about the royal romance, keeping the public completely in the dark about the affair, American publications were less reverential and inhibited. That June, Wallis wrote to Aunt Bessie, who was "upset by Hearst [Newspapers'] reporters lies." She tried to put her aunt's mind at rest. "You know I am not going to get a divorce. Ernest and I are perfectly happy and understand each other so please put it all out of your head and tell people they can't believe the press."[71]

It was not just the whispers in the press that were mounting. Superintendent Canning's report, delivered to the Metropolitan Police Commissioner Sir Philip Game on July 3, not only alleged that Wallis was having an affair with Guy Trundle; it also speculated about a controversial liaison between Wallis and Joachim von Ribbentrop, Hitler's ambassador to Britain. The relentlessly charming Ribbentrop, a former wine salesman, had for the last two years been peddling the Third Reich to the British aristocracy. He cultivated Lady Cunard as a route to the Prince of Wales. In June, Wallis and the prince had met Ribbentrop at a large gathering at Emerald's. Winston Churchill, also in attendance, listened as the German droned on about the achievements of the führer. When he left, Churchill turned to his hostess and said: "Emerald, I hope we never have to hear that broken gramophone record again."[72]

Chips Channon noted in his diary: "much gossip about the Prince of Wales' alleged Nazi leanings; he is alleged to have been influenced by Emerald (who is rather éprise with Herr Ribbentrop) through Mrs. Simpson. . . . He has just made an extraordinary speech to the British Legion advocating friendship with Germany; it is only a gesture, but a gesture that may be taken seriously in Germany and elsewhere. If only the Chancelleries of Europe knew that his speech was the result of Emerald Cunard's intrigues, themselves inspired by Herr Ribbentrop's dimple!"[73]

In July, Edward took part in a naval review in the Channel. His separation from Wallis inspired him to write to her at one o'clock in the morning on board his ship:

> A boy is holding a girl so very tight in his arms tonight. . . . A girl knows that not anybody or anything can separate WE—not even the stars—and that WE belong to each other for ever. WE love [twice underlined] each other more than life so God bless WE.
> Your [*twice underlined*] David[74]

For his August holiday that year, the prince rented the Marquess of Cholmondeley's summer residence, Villa Le Roc, in Cannes. As Edward was not allowed to receive gifts from his subjects, he paid George Rocksavage a token £5 for the fortnight's stay. Wallis wrote to Aunt Bessie of the villa, with its pretty terraced gardens bursting with zinnias and plumbago: "We got here on Monday to find a lovely villa on the water—our own rocks and all the privacy in the world but very hot."[75] The Duke of Westminster's yacht, *Cutty Sark*, was at their disposal. Again, Wallis accompanied the prince without Ernest. Ernest absented himself because his mother was visiting him in London, then he was due on business in America. Wallis gushed to her aunt: "My party consists of Lord and Lady Brownlow, Buists, Mrs Fitzgerald and Lord Sefton. Très chic. E. is quite content for me to go as he can do nothing for me in the way of a holiday." She ended her missive by asking her aunt to go and see her husband when he is in the States. Ernest, she revealed, "is still the man of my dreams."[76]

John Aird, who was in attendance on the trip, was alarmed when, on arrival at the villa, the prince rushed in and gave the best bedroom to his equerry, apportioning himself "a rotten little room next to W." An hour later the decision was reversed. "At whose suggestion I do not know," recorded Aird.[77] Most likely Wallis's, given that only she could steer the prince towards more dignified behavior. Indeed, the couple's correspondence during the trip bears witness to Wallis's eye for detail. She writes to him from her room in the morning, suggesting that as they have a lunch for ten later that day, including with Sir Robert Vansittart, the permanent undersecretary at the Foreign Office, it would be more comfortable if the butler could organize "chairs without arms." As well as seating plans, menu plans—"I didn't see a green vegetable on the menu"—she explains: "I like everyone to think you do things well."[78]

Wallis always needed to be in control. "She liked to know exactly what was going on," said Hugo Vickers. "Later in their life together, if someone dropped a plate in their house in the French countryside and the duchess was in Paris, she would know as if by radar. She said to her butler: 'If something breaks, please tell me. I won't mind but please always let me know.' She was incredibly straightforward like that and her staff adored her for it."[79] Indeed, a kitchen maid who later worked for Wallis attests to this: "All the maids spoke well of Mrs. Simpson."[80]

Oblivious to the dramatic extent of it, Wallis, with her maternal chiding, vigilant housekeeping, lack of sycophancy, genuine intelligent interest in Edward's official duties and air of assured competency, had become indispensable to the prince. She was his oxygen. Without her, Winston

Churchill observed, he was haggard and dejected.[81] By the end of the long summer holiday, having stretched their European sojourn through to October, Edward knew that he wanted to marry her. How he would realize this became his principal obsession. "It was all quite vague but nonetheless vivid," he later wrote. "This dream of being able to bring into my life what for so long had been lacking."[82] He intended to discuss the matter with his father that autumn. Meanwhile, he wrote to Wallis, pleading with her not to forsake him: "Please, please Wallis don't get scared or loose [*sic*] faith when you are away from me. I love you more every minute and no difficulties or complications can possibly prevent our ultimate happiness."[83]

His obsessive desire for Wallis now left no room for Ernest. "I do hate and loathe the present situation . . . and am just going mad at the mere thought (let alone knowing) that you are alone there with Ernest. God bless WE forever my Wallis. You know your David will love you and look after you so long as he has breath in his eanum body."[84]

4

God Bless WE

The prince's attempts to speak to his father at any length about his personal life were thwarted by events. On November 6, 1935, Edward's brother Prince Harry was married in the private chapel at Buckingham Palace to Lady Alice Scott. Eminently suitable, she was the third daughter of the king's friend the Duke of Buccleuch. Sadly, the duke died just before the wedding, rendering it a quiet affair. Queen Mary recorded in her diary how charming the bridesmaids looked: "Lilibet and Margaret* looked too sweet."[1] In his diary, King George wrote: "Now all the children are married but David." In a state of resigned despair, weakened by concerns over Edward's private life, he memorably said: "I pray to God my eldest son will never marry and have children, and that nothing will come between Bertie and Lilibet and the throne."[2]

Later that month, the general election saw the National Government return to power with a reduced majority and Stanley Baldwin enjoying his third term as prime minister. The prince sensed that his father was too engrossed with the political aspect of his duties to be disturbed. Then, a bitter blow befell the royal family. On the day that the seventy-year-old king was due to open Parliament, his favorite sister, Princess Victoria,

* The princesses Elizabeth and Margaret.

died. The siblings were exceptionally close; King George would begin each day with a telephone call to her at her Buckinghamshire house, Coppins, in Iver, at 9:30 a.m. Weighed down by grief, it was the first time in his life that the king had canceled a state ceremony. His health rapidly deteriorated and he never appeared in public again.[3] His family believed that the loss of his beloved sister sounded his own death knell.

Aware that King George's life was ebbing away, all efforts were made by the family to try and ensure that Christmas at Sandringham was especially memorable. In the White Ballroom, nine-year-old Princess Elizabeth romped around the Christmas tree with her younger sister, Margaret, their childish effervescence lightening the somber mood. Edward, the only family member not to have a spouse by his side, felt "detached and lonely." He later wrote: "my brothers were secure in their private lives; whereas I was caught up in an inner conflict and would have no peace of mind until I had resolved it."[4] On Boxing Day he wrote to Wallis from Sandringham: "I couldn't believe it was possible to miss this way but it's so lovely although hell while it lasts. It really is terrible here and so much the worst Xmas I've ever had to spend with the family. . . . Oh! to be alone for ages and ages and then—ages and ages. God bless WE sweetheart but I'm sure he does—he must. Your David."[5]

Wallis and the prince saw in the new year together at a house party at Melton Mowbray, hosted by their friends the Buists. Both dressed as pirates for the evening fancy dress gala. Ernest was again absent—he had traveled to Canada for business. The prince's need for Wallis to be permanently at his side was now insatiable. On New Year's morning he sent a note to her room: "Your lovely New Year message helped a boy a lot in his lonely drowsy and he was feeling sad. . . . Oh! my Wallis I know we'll have *Viel Glück* to make us *one* this year."

The deteriorating health of the king dominated the thoughts of the nation over New Year. Suffering from a chronic bronchial complaint, King George continued his daily habit of riding out on his white pony, Jock. With Queen Mary walking beside him, he looked his last upon the gardens and grounds of Sandringham, the home he had enjoyed most in the world.

On January 16, Edward hosted a day's shoot in Windsor Great Park. Duff Cooper noted that the Prince of Wales was "in the highest spirits." It was snowing and bitterly cold when the party broke for lunch at the Fort.[6] That afternoon, the prince received an urgent note, while still in the field, from his mother. "I think you ought to know that Papa is not very well," she had written. Lord Dawson, the king's physician, was "not too pleased with Papa's state at the present moment." The note was carefully worded so as not to arouse undue concern in the heir to the throne, while she was similarly anxious that his sudden arrival must not alert the suspicions of the king to his own perilous condition. Edward hastened back to the Fort, where Wallis was waiting for him, and silently handed her the note. As she was reading it, he telephoned his pilot to tell him to have his airplane ready to fly him the following morning to Norfolk.

At Sandringham, he found his father sitting in front of the fire in his old Tibetan dressing gown, gazing through the window at the church tower jutting above the leafless winter trees.

On Saturday night, as all the members of his family were gathering, Edward wrote to Wallis, his longing and loneliness palpable:

> My own sweetheart,
> Just a line to say I love you more and more and more and need you so to be with me at this difficult time. There is no hope whatsoever for the king it's only a matter of how long. . . . But I do long long [*sic*] to see you even for a few minutes my Wallis it would help so much. . . . You are all and everything I have in life and WE must hold each other so tight. It will all work out right for us. God Bless WE.[7]

That evening, Chips Channon wrote: "My heart goes out to the Prince of Wales tonight, as he will mind so terribly being King. His loneliness, his seclusion, his isolation will be almost more than this highly strung and unimaginative nature can bear. Never has a man been so in love. . . . How will they arrange their lives, these people?"[8]

On Sunday, January 19, Edward drove up to London to inform

Mr. Baldwin that the king was dying—expiring painfully from bronchitis. The prince joined Mr. and Mrs. Baldwin for tea at No. 10 Downing Street. The heir apparent appeared unmoved when Stanley Baldwin announced: "I wonder if you know, Sir, that another great Englishman died yesterday?"[9] The prince, no great fan of literature, was unaware that it was Rudyard Kipling, Baldwin's first cousin.

The following day, Queen Mary recorded in her diary: "G. about the same, sat with him from time to time—did not go to church as the place was surrounded by reporters & photographers, too heartless."[10] Meanwhile, privy councillors gathered in the king's study as the red dispatch boxes piled up; matters of state would wait for no one, not even death. The dying king was propped up in a chair and, with a shaky hand, pen held in place by Lord Dawson, managed two marks to appoint a Council of State, composed of the queen and their four sons. Edward recalled: "Signing documents provided a distraction from the strain of waiting. It is a harrowing experience to watch anyone die, let alone one's father, and especially when one's father is king. When a king starts to die, the whole world crowds in for the death watch. Inside the Big House, a sad quiet came over our family circle."[11]

Cosmo Lang, the archbishop of Canterbury, later recorded that at tea time on Monday, January 20, the Prince of Wales was "touchingly attentive to the Queen."[12]

Soon afterwards, a news bulletin was issued to announce that "the king's life is moving peacefully towards its close." Dawson had already taken the precaution of telephoning his wife in London to ask Lady Dawson that she "advise *The Times* to hold back publication." This was to ensure that the death was reported in respectable morning papers rather than in "the less appropriate evening journals."[13] At eleven o'clock in the evening, Lord Dawson gave the king two injections: a mixture of morphine and cocaine to hasten his passing.[14]*

---

* Lord Dawson subsequently campaigned against euthanasia in the House of Lords. A popular ditty emerged after King George's death: "Lord Dawson of Penn / Killed many men / That's why we sing / God Save the King."

At five to midnight, the king died. No sooner had King George V died than Queen Mary, with characteristic sangfroid, took the hand of her eldest son and kissed it. Edward's brother George, Duke of Kent, who was standing beside her, stepped forward and followed her example. Although he recognized that this form of homage was by custom his due, Edward was momentarily embarrassed by it. "Nevertheless, these two spontaneous gestures served to remind me, however needlessly, that I was now King."[15] He was His Most Excellent Majesty Edward the Eighth, by the Grace of God, of Great Britain, Ireland, and the British Dominions Beyond the Seas, King, Defender of the Faith, Emperor of India.

The new king began crying hysterically. His sudden undignified outburst of grief stunned his family. He kept embracing his mother, weeping against her. Was he lamenting his father or mourning the biting reality of his new position? His emotion was "frantic and unreasonable," wrote an appalled Helen Hardinge, wife of King George's assistant private secretary. "In its outward manifestation, it far exceeded that of his mother and three brothers, although they had loved King George at least as much as he had. . . . While he demanded attention for his own feelings, he seemed completely unaware of those of others."[16]

Shortly afterwards, Edward left his family and went to telephone Wallis, who was dining with friends, the Lawson-Johnstons, after a charity film premiere. "It's all over," he told her. "I could think of nothing better to say than 'I'm so very sorry,' " Wallis later recalled.[17] Grief and its close ally, shock, create the most uncharacteristic individual reactions. The future monarch had barely left his father's deathbed when he ordered that the clocks at Sandringham, which had always been kept half an hour fast to give extra daylight for shooting, be put back to normal time. "I wonder what other customs will be put back also," ruminated a concerned Cosmo Lang.[18]

King Edward VIII immediately broke with tradition by flying to London—the first time a British monarch had traveled in an airplane—and further surprised courtiers by watching his own proclamation ceremony, in which he was declared king-emperor, from a window in St. James's Palace, Wallis and Ernest standing close behind him. As he surveyed the historic scene, with mace bearers and trumpeters in state dress and the "tremendous words rolled out," Edward was "swept by conflicting emotions. There was a flash of pride in becoming King-Emperor of the vast and liberal Commonwealth I knew so well. At the same time, these words seemed to tell me that my relations with Wallis had suddenly entered a more significant stage."[19] As they walked away, Wallis turned to Edward. "It was all very moving," she said. "But it has also made me realize how different your life is going to be."[20]

Chips Channon wrote of the proclamation: "It was a fleeting brilliant ceremony. . . . Afterwards, I saw a large black car (the king's) drive away, with the blinds pulled half down. The crowd bowed, thinking that it contained the Duchess of Kent but I saw Mrs. Simpson."[21] Like the rest of society, Chips was "riveted by the position of Mrs. S. No man has ever been so in love as the present King but can she be another Mrs. Fitzherbert?* If he drops her she will fall—fall—into the nothingness from whence she came but I hope he will not, for she is a good kindly woman, who has had an excellent influence on the young monarch."[22]

On January 20, Stanley Baldwin called Duff Cooper into the Cabinet Room at 10 Downing Street. To Duff's surprise, Baldwin wanted to talk to him about the prince's relationship with Mrs. Simpson. "If she were what I call a respectable whore, I wouldn't mind," Baldwin told Cooper.[23] Cooper assumed that he meant somebody whom the prince occasionally saw in secret but did not spend his whole time with.

"It was perfectly all right for a gentleman to have affairs with married ladies, not girls, always married women," explained Duff Cooper's son, John Julius Norwich. "People knew that affairs were going on and they put people next door to each other in country house weekends. That was fine. What mattered was the way that things looked. It was the outside show that counted and appearances had to be maintained."[24]

---

* Twice-widowed Maria Fitzherbert was the secret wife of King George IV. As her Roman Catholic beliefs would not allow her to be the prince's mistress and King George III would not allow his son to marry a Roman Catholic nor a commoner, George married her in secret in 1785 in a union that was not deemed legal.

In his meeting with the prime minister, Stanley Baldwin suggested to Duff that he tell Mrs. Simpson "to clear out—for a bit at any rate" as he felt that that "would be the best thing that could happen." Cooper decided that he would "certainly do nothing of the kind. She would tell the prince who would never forgive me."[25]

Later that day, the prince received an idolatrous letter from Ernest Simpson. Characteristic of Ernest's decency, despite the fact that the new king was responsible for the collapse of his marriage, he wrote to his monarch as his "devoted, loyal subject." The dignified Ernest offered him the "warmest sentiments that friendship can engender."[26] Ernest "has of course been marvelous about it all," Wallis wrote to Aunt Bessie. "He has the makeup of a saint and is much too good for 'the likes of me.'"[27]

On January 23, Edward marched with his brothers behind the gun carriage taking the body of their father to lie in state at Westminster Hall. The new king, who at forty-one still appeared boyishly young, looked lost and bewildered, dwarfed in a heavy, long overcoat. As the cortège made its way into New Palace Yard, the jeweled Maltese cross on top of the imperial crown—set with a square sapphire, eight medium-sized diamonds and 192 smaller diamonds—came loose. The jolting of the heavy gun carriage caused it to fall to the ground. Out of the corner of his eye, Edward caught sight of a flash of light dancing upon the pavement. He resisted the urge to retrieve the cross, resolutely marching on, barely breaking step, as a Grenadier Guardsman scooped up the cross with one hand and dropped it into his pocket. This strange occurrence was considered a bad omen. "Christ! What will happen next?"[28] King Edward was heard to say. "A fitting motto," MP Walter Elliot remarked to his companion, "for the coming reign."[29]

Over the four days in which the king lay in state, over a million people paid their respects before the purple-draped catafalque containing his coffin. On the day of the funeral procession at Westminster Abbey, which was to be followed by a service at St. George's Chapel, Windsor, Edward had arranged for Wallis to watch from St. James's Palace. According to Chips Channon: "half the house had been commandeered for Mrs. Simpson and her party. I didn't see her. Apparently she did not go to

Windsor [for the burial] having refused, with dignity, I consider, the offered invitation."[30]

Edward and Wallis saw less of each other during this period due to the immense commitments placed upon the new king. If Wallis assumed that his duties as monarch would eclipse his need for her, she could not have been more mistaken. The king found his exalted new position an intolerable burden, exacerbating his loneliness. Seeking relief and emotional succor, the only person he could turn to was Wallis. With her he could relax and confide, while she provided a warm antidote to sterile and strategic court life. Although they could not physically spend as much time together as before, his desperation to be permanently with her intensified. Tommy Lascelles's view of it was: "the Prince of Wales was caught napping by his father's death . . . he had expected the old man to last several years more, and he had, in all probability, already made up his mind to renounce his claim to the throne, and to marry Mrs. S. I know that, long before this, he had confided to several American friends of his that he could never face being king."[31]

On January 22, King George V's will was read at Sandringham. Each of his brothers received about £750,000 in cash—worth around £28 million today. Edward was left no money, and was prevented from selling any of the inherited assets such as a rare stamp collection and a stud of valuable racehorses. Furious, he kept repeating: "My brothers and sister have got large sums, but I have been left out."[32] Advisors tried to reassure him that his father, who had received no cash either when he became king, would have assumed that, as Prince of Wales, he had built up a substantial fortune from the revenues of the Duchy of Cornwall.

Lascelles, who passed the king in the corridor after the reading of the will, recalled he had a "face blacker than any thunderstorm."[33] Edward went immediately to telephone Wallis. He told her that while he had a crown, which he didn't want, he had no fortune, which they had both keenly anticipated. Although as Prince of Wales he had already accumulated great wealth and could expect to do so again out of savings from the civil list and the privy purse, he had believed that another vast fortune would soon be his. His disappointment was compounded because he feared letting down the woman he loved and desperately wanted to impress.

Of the thousands of people who wrote to the new king offering condolences for his father's death, only Lady Diana Cooper, it seemed, mentioned Wallis. Edward replied: "Dear Diana—Your letter was most kind and human. Wallis . . . is and always will be the most wonderful friend and help to me. She gives me the courage to carry on. Yours Sincerely Edward RI."[34]

The prince's advisors were aware of the beneficial influence Wallis had on Edward in the early days of his "Kinging," as he called it. Duff Cooper recalled sitting next to Wallis after a formal day in which the Privy Council addressed the new monarch. "She talked to me a great deal about the king," he said. "I told her how well his informal little speech had gone with the Privy Council whereupon she repeated it word for word. . . . She talked very sensibly—said she has not allowed him to come to her flat since his father's death, and had insisted on his using the large Daimler type of motor car in which people could see him—and even suggested that it would be better if she were to go away altogether."[35]

It was no good. Edward's need for Wallis escalated to a suffocating degree. He telephoned her frequently throughout the day, sent her billets-doux and arranged for regular deliveries of grand bouquets of flowers. It was clear he felt that she, like no one else, understood him and only she could meet his emotional needs. The Conservative MP Victor Cazalet considered her "the one real friend he has ever had." He added: "She does have a wonderful influence over him, but she knows how stubborn he is, and how difficult to influence."[36] Wallis bolstered Edward, she boosted his confidence, listened so attentively as he recited his speeches that she could later repeat them herself, supported his fragile ego, mothered and soothed. As she wrote to Aunt Bessie in late January: "I am implored on all sides not to leave him as he is so dependent on me and I am considered to be a *good* influence believe it or not and right in the things I try to influence him to do. Of course I am very fond of him and proud and want him to do his job well and he is so lonely and needs companionship and affection, otherwise he goes wrong."[37] Chips Channon observed:

"It appears that the king is Mrs. Simpson's absolute slave, and will go nowhere where she is not invited, and she, clever woman, is behaving well. She encourages the king to meet people of importance and to be polite; above all she makes him happy. The Empire ought to be grateful."[38]

Edward VIII's accession was greeted by his subjects with enthusiasm and hope. The new monarch, who in some moods liked his job, began his reign with impressive zeal. He carried out most of his ceremonial functions with affability and aplomb. At this time, the king was considered the "most popular man in the world,"[39] according to the writer Philip Gibbs. Protected by the deference of the media, his adoring subjects had no idea about his unhealthy dependence on Wallis Simpson. They believed that the king's charisma, modernity and interest in reform hailed a new, exciting era. However, this "faith and confidence in the new reign, which I shared with the majority of the British people, were not held by the Prime Minister or the Archbishop of Canterbury," according to Lord Beaverbrook.[40] A seismic clash seemed inevitable. "Even if I had remained a bachelor, I would definitely have collided with the establishment," Edward said later.[41]

Max Beaverbrook, the Canadian-born press baron and business tycoon, who was a self-made millionaire by the age of thirty, was to become a staunch ally of Edward's. He astutely observed: "Members of the aristocracy wished to destroy the king. They deplored his liking for the company of married women and in particular Mrs. Simpson. They disliked his neglect of their circles with abhorrence for his addiction to what they called 'Café Society'—they declared that Buckingham Palace was drifting into the status of an American nightclub."[42]

Encouraged by Wallis, Edward at first worked diligently on his official red boxes. According to Wallis, weekends at Fort Belvedere continued, but with a difference. "There was a perceptible stiffening in protocol, a heightening of formality." As more time was devoted to the documents of state, there was less time for the garden and "the forays against the last remaining stands of laurel all but came to an end."[43] The king kicked off reforms: he ended the prime ministerial custom of sending regular political reports to Buckingham Palace; he championed the King George's

Field Foundation, creating the provision of playing fields throughout the country as a memorial to his father; and he laid down new laws about formal decorations and dress. He dispensed with the frock coat as an item of court apparel, as well as with mourning caps, veils and crepe.

He also concerned himself with relative trivia, however. In an act of supreme hauteur, Edward dismissed the new design for stamps and coins of his profile because they had been sketched from his right side; believing that his left profile was more flattering, he insisted the illustrations be redone. Full of ideas, he liked change for change's sake. Yet in few areas was his interest sustained, apart from those relating to finance. He showed a continuing and almost pathological preoccupation with money. While there was plenty of room for fiscal reform in certain domains of the royal palaces, the king betrayed a compulsive stinginess and lack of sensitivity to the devoted service of retainers. There was understandable resentment at Buckingham Palace from staff who had had their beer money cut down, when they were often loading cases of champagne or furniture destined for Mrs. Simpson's flat.

One of the king's many eccentricities was his obsessive concern with trifling matters of housekeeping. On one occasion he summoned the head housemaid at the Fort and asked her what happened to the guests' soap after they had left the house. She informed him that it was taken to the servants' quarters and used there. Edward instructed that all the used guest soap was to be brought to him for his own use. "The king used to complain about the most ridiculous things, like the fact that he never got a new bar of soap," remembered John Julius Norwich. "That was literally the level of his concerns and standard of his conversation."[44]

It was not long before Edward came into opposition with the Church, in the form of the archbishop of Canterbury. Cosmo Lang's conservatism symbolized everything the king disliked and mistrusted about the old establishment. The day after George V's funeral at Windsor, Lang had called at Buckingham Palace to pay his respects to Queen Mary. He then asked to see the new king. Edward was taken aback when the archbishop said to him: "I want you to know that whenever the king questioned your conduct I tried in your interest to present it in the most favourable light."[45] Edward later recalled that during their awkward audience, "Wallis's name had of course not been mentioned, but I knew that the archbishop intended that I should know that she was the hidden burden of his discourse. He was clearly against our continued friendship. He would undoubtedly muster powerful forces in opposition to my project when I came to press it."[46] Of the king, Lang said: "It is clear that he knows little and I fear, cares little about the Church and its affairs."[47] Stanley Baldwin told his daughter Monica that once when he was waiting to see the king, the Duke of Kent came into the room and announced that his brother was "damning the whole root and stock of the Episcopacy. He has just shooed the Archbishop of Canterbury out of the house."[48]

The king lacked the intellectual stamina to concentrate on serious state matters for long, particularly since, according to Baldwin, his infatuation with Mrs. Simpson "obliterated part of his mind."[49] Although the king had lost none of his power to bewitch when he responded to public crowds, he generally reacted to the outside world with impatience and anger because it kept him away from Wallis. Major Alexander Hardinge, his private secretary, wrote: "It was scarcely realised at this early stage how overwhelming and inexorable was the influence exerted on the king by the lady of the moment. As time went on it became clearer that every decision, big or small, was subordinate to her will. . . . It was she who filled his thoughts at all times, she alone who mattered, before her the affairs of state sank into insignificance."[50]

Wallis, meanwhile, oscillated between a state of heady delight at her exalted court position and a burgeoning sense of isolation. In the early days of the king's reign, she had been inundated by flattering and admiring letters from her society friends. The hostess and interior designer Sibyl Colefax wrote to Wallis that she had "grown every month more full of delighted admiration for not only your immense wisdom & lovely common (so miscalled!) sense, but also for your unfailing touch of being exactly right in all judgements & all kinds of moments in life at every angle."[51] Margot Oxford considered that she had "every quality to be liked—you are very natural, very kind, never pretend to know what you don't know (a rare quality believe me) & a genuine desire to help the man you love in his every difficult task."[52] While Diana Cooper found her "good and kind and loveable—what more can one be?"[53]

"Though the king is in mourning," Wallis wrote to Aunt Bessie, "everyone is over anxious to see that I am asked to all small dinners in the official world, all sending messages via me. Isn't it all funny and strange too? I'm just the same however and enjoying it all as a huge game—laughing a lot inside and controlling my tongue and sense of humour on the outside."[54] On February 2, Chips Channon confided: "We are concerned that some of our friends should be trying to poison the Kents against Mrs. S. and hence the king, and are attempting to drive a wedge between the royal brothers."[55]

Wallis was trying to prepare herself for what she considered the inevitable: permanent separation from the king. In early February she wrote to him: "I am sad because I miss you and being near and yet so far seems most unfair. Some day of course I must learn to be always alone for I will be in my heart also I must develop strength to look at papers containing your photographs and accounts of your activities—but also perhaps both of us will cease to want what is hardest to have and be content with the simple way."[56] To Aunt Bessie, she observed of being king: "It's a very lonely job—and it's a tragedy that he can't bring himself to marry without loving. The English would prefer that he marry a duke's daughter to one of the mangy foreign princesses left."[57]

Wallis recalled in her memoirs: "In the back of my mind I had always known that the dream one day would have to end—somewhere, sometime, somehow. But I had characteristically refused to be dismayed by this prospect. I was prepared to take whatever hurt was in store for me, when the day of reckoning came."[58]

What she was not prepared for was the heartache she felt when the day of reckoning came for her marriage to Ernest. In spite of his noblesse oblige, Ernest had tired of being a cuckold. He had developed a relationship with Wallis's school friend Mary Raffray, spending time with her on his business trips to America. Although Wallis had encouraged the friendship, regularly hosting Mary as a houseguest, it stung when Mary fell in love with Ernest. She even expressed her shock to Aunt Bessie when she found an incriminating letter which told of their affair. Like her relationship with the Prince of Wales, it was another situation of which Wallis believed she could control the outcome but came to regret. Mary turned against Wallis, later writing about the level of her friend's manipulation. "She tricked me into going to the opera," she later wrote, "and then at the last minute failed to appear because she told everyone Ernest's mistress was there. . . . She thought that she could use me as a scapegoat and did."[59]

Mary, understandably, took Ernest's side; yet beneath her hostility to Wallis lurked envy. Mary Raffray's letters to her sister Buckie brim with her pride at being invited to weekends at the Fort and dinners at York House. She describes the delight she felt at being able to wander around Windsor Castle after houseguests from the Fort had driven over to see movies of the Grand National. "Wallis," she told her sister, "is in the very thick of things, received and toadied to by everyone."[60] Mary later wrote to her sister, from a London hotel, of an unfortunate scene at Bryanston Court. When Wallis accused Mary of having seduced Ernest, Mary simply walked out of the room, packed up her things, phoned for a taxi and left Bryanston Court "and Wallis's life forever."[61]

Ernest, despite his new relationship, remained loyal to Wallis. His concern for her was revealed when he decided to challenge the king over his intentions. Like a Victorian father, he wanted to confront the errant suitor. In February, Ernest dined with the king at York House, taking his friend Bernard Rickatson-Hatt, editor in chief of Reuters, to witness what he felt he must say to the king. When the king rose after dinner, Ernest asked him to remain. Turning to Edward, he made a dramatic statement: Wallis, he said, would have to choose between them. He asked the king what he intended to do about it—did he intend to marry her? Edward VIII rose imperiously from his seat and said: "Do you really think that I would be crowned without Wallis by my side?"[62] Rickatson-Hatt firmly believed that if it had not been for the king's "obstinacy and jealousy," and his obsessive need to have Wallis to himself regardless of whose life he trampled over, Wallis and Ernest "would have remained man and wife."[63]

Wallis knew nothing of the dinner and was oblivious to the machinations that her husband's meeting with the king set afoot. She later spoke of the bid to discredit her by powerful establishment men, writing two weeks after the abdication: "the pitiful tragedy of it all is that England still remains in the hands of the men that caused the tragedy—using a woman as their means."[64] Little did she know then, ten months beforehand, of the documents and memorandums drawn up after this encounter, with their malice towards her and undertone of hysteria.

Ernest's meeting with the king triggered terror in court circles. Immediately after the York House dinner, Lord Davidson, a close ally of Baldwin, wrote a detailed account of Ernest's meeting with Sir Maurice Jenks, who presided over the Masonic Lodge that Ernest had been admitted to through the king's influence:

> Simpson Mason asks to see Jenks Mason—the *Mari Complaisant* is now the sorrowing and devastated spouse. He tells Jenks that the king wants to marry Mrs. S, (unbelievable) & that he—S [Ernest]—would like to leave England only that would make divorce easier—what he wants is his wife back. S suggests he should see the P.M. SB [Stanley Baldwin] replies to this suggest [*sic*] with a flat negative. He is the king's chief advisor not Mr. S's. . . . Clive Wigram, SB and I have a frank talk. I am quite convinced Blackmail sticks out at every stage. HM has already paid large sums of money to Mrs. S and given valuable presents. I advocate most drastic steps (deportation) if it is true that S is an American but if he isn't the situation is very delicate. The Masonic move is very clever. The POW [Prince of Wales] got S in on a lie—is now living in breach of the Masonic Law of chastity because of the lie he first told. S and Mrs. S, who is obviously a gold digger, have obviously got him on toast . . . Mrs. S is very close to [the German Ambassador Leopold von] Hoesch and has, if she likes to read them access to all Secret and Cabinet papers!!!!![65]

Sir Maurice Jenks managed to reassure a jumpy Clive Wigram, the king's private secretary, that, as a British subject, Ernest could not be deported. And that he was, in fact, an honorable man who, far from planning to blackmail the king, as courtiers fantasized, was keen to avoid a scandal. The Davidson memorandum illustrates the establishment's panic at the mere hint of Wallis becoming queen. It also highlights the bubbling levels of paranoia engendered by the escalating international situation, that Wallis Simpson should be seriously suspected of passing on official state secrets to the Germans. Reports coming from the Fort that the king now left his red boxes open with state papers spilling out, barely bothering to read them, as he found them "complete drudgery," were translated to mean that Wallis was avidly reading them and passing on the contents to the Nazis. Ministers began to starve the king of confidential information, screening Foreign Office papers before they were sent to him.

As rumors circulated amongst the government that Wallis "was in the pocket of the German ambassador" and had access to state papers, Clive Wigram approached the king. He told him that there was much concern over the safety of secret documents in his possession. "HM assured me that he was very careful, and read them going down to the Fort in his car," Sir Clive reported. "As HM leaves about 3 am in his car, I did not feel there was much light to read!"[66]

Weekend guests at the Fort observed the king's reluctance to tend to his dispatch boxes. Diana Cooper witnessed Wallis, far from exploiting Edward's lax attitudes, repeatedly trying to persuade him to pay more attention to his kingly duties. "Wallis must not get too bossy," she wrote. "I had rather she had not said to him at dinner that she wanted to encourage his *reading* his papers and documents, that he was inclined to have them read to him—but that it was essential he should learn to master the points in them. She is right of course, as he made haste to say. 'Wallis is quite right. She always is. I shall learn it quite soon.'"[67]

Unsurprisingly, there are no mentions in the official records of Wallis's attempts to positively influence the king. Instead, she is conveniently denounced as pro-Nazi, a character assassination which haunts her reputation to this day. Despite the fact that Wallis only met Ribbentrop twice at Lady Cunard's, and was the beneficiary of bouquets of flowers from him as he tried to inveigle his way into London society, wild rumors of her affair with him persist.

There is no evidence that any ardent German Nazi sympathizers ever visited Fort Belvedere, and nothing was ever found in the German state archives after the war to indicate that Wallis, or anybody else, passed on to the German government information gleaned from papers in the king's keeping.[68] Far from planning covert operations with German envoys, all of Wallis's considerable energies and resources were deployed in the continuing struggle to "please, amuse, placate two men."

On May 4, she wrote a startling confessional letter, running to over twenty pages, to her beloved Aunt Bessie. Detailing the new direction her life had been forced to take, the letter is infused with an unnerving sense of uncertainty and fresh sorrow. She tells her aunt that for the past year she has been living under the "most awful strain," trying to juggle the two separate lives with Ernest and the king. Her nerves are shredded; she feels tired and irritable and her stomach is playing up again from stress. Trying to break it as gently to her aged aunt as possible, she confirms that she and Ernest are to split up. "Ernest and HM have talked the situation out so everything has been on a most friendly and arranged basis," she explains. She hints that Ernest is in a new relationship, "having his own reason for allowing the world to call him the 'complacent husband.'"[69] She and Ernest are to separate, but she is not planning on divorce "at the moment." Wallis then makes reference to the king's wish to marry her: "The K on the other hand has another thing only on his mind. Whether I would allow such a drastic action depends on many things and events and I should never allow him if possible to prevent a rather stubborn character to do anything that would hurt the country and help the socialists." She reassures Bessie that the king has settled a large sum of money on her, enough "for my lifetime."[70]

She concludes wearily: "I am 40 and I feel I must follow my own instincts as regards my life and am quite prepared to pay for a mistake. I know I can only control the financial side of the future and that I can't insure against heartache, loneliness etc. but if the worst happens I shall have to be like the Arabs and fold my tent and steal silently away."[71]

Wallis knew that the king's formerly "pleasant daydream" to marry her, which had previously been "tantalizingly remote and evanescent,"[72] was now hardening into a resolution. While this was undeniably flattering, Wallis could not entertain how it could ever become feasible—or was even desirable for her.

One spring day, she and Edward were sitting in the garden at the Fort, when the king mentioned that he had invited the prime minister to dinner in London and wished for Wallis to be present. "Then he paused, and after a moment, with his most Prince Charming smile said: 'It's got to be done. Sooner or later my Prime Minister must meet my wife.'"[73] Far from being elated, Wallis was "filled with apprehension." "David," she exclaimed, "you mustn't talk this way. The idea is impossible. They'd never let you."[74] Edward's lighthearted insouciance continued, despite Wallis's protests—until she mentioned his mother.

"Yes, that may be difficult," he conceded. Wallis relaxed inside. "Being convinced that even his strongest hopes would be unavailing against his mother's unwavering principles," she later wrote, "I could not take his aspirations seriously."[75]

On May 27, the king held a dinner party at St. James's Palace. Wallis took care of the menu and table decorations. Mr. and Mrs. Baldwin, Lord and Lady Mountbatten, Lord and Lady Wigram, Mr. Duff and Lady Diana Cooper, Lord and Lady Chatfield, Colonel and Mrs. Lindbergh, Lady Cunard, and Mr. and Mrs. Simpson were invited. The following morning, Edward published this exact list of his guests in the Court Circular (published daily in the major national newspapers). Using this official listing to publicly announce his friendship with the Simpsons was considered wholly unusual. But the king had a point to make, and he had already set his campaign to marry Wallis in motion. This was the last time that Ernest would ever be the king's guest, a fact noted by avid followers of the Court Circular; once considered dreary and dull, the listing became, according to Lady Diana Mosley, "a source of endless gossip and conjecture in London society."[76]

It was considered equally singular when, that spring, the king bought an American station wagon, a car almost unheard of in England. One afternoon, when he and Wallis were at the Fort, Edward declared: "Let's drive over to Royal Lodge. I want to show Bertie the car."[77] He took Wallis and his house party to see the Duke and Duchess of York at their home, Royal Lodge, in Windsor Great Park. Edward showed his brother the car, briefly driving off with him, leaving Wallis and the guests with the Duchess of York. This cannot have been easy for Wallis, as she had already experienced the duchess's froideur at Prince George's wedding. After touring the gardens, the party went inside for tea. In the drawing room, they were joined by Princess Elizabeth, aged ten, and Princess Margaret Rose, then nearly six. "They were both so blonde, so beautifully mannered, so brightly scrubbed, that they might have stepped straight from the pages of a picture book," Wallis observed.[78]

The young princesses' Scottish governess, Marion Crawford, who accompanied the girls into tea, later said of Wallis: "She was a smart, attractive woman, already middle aged, but with that immediate friendliness American women have. She appeared to be entirely at her ease; if anything, rather too much so."[79] Crawford was taken aback by Wallis's "distinctly proprietary way of speaking to the new king. I remember she drew him to the window and suggested how certain trees might be moved, and a part of a hill taken away to improve the view."[80]

The king and his sister-in-law held most of the conversation, with the nervous duke throwing in the occasional word. After an hour, the party took their leave. "I left with the distinct impression that while the Duke of York was sold on the American station wagon, the duchess was not sold on David's other American interest," Wallis said, with polished understatement.[81] While Marion Crawford wrote: "I have never admired the duke and duchess more than on that afternoon. With quiet and charming dignity they made the best of this awkward occasion and gave no sign whatever of their feelings. But the atmosphere was not a comfortable one."[82]

That summer, weekends continued at the Fort whenever possible. Barbie Wallace, a daughter of Sir Edwin Lutyens, stayed several times with her husband, the Conservative MP Euan Wallace. "It was," she wrote:

> an Alice-in-Wonderland atmosphere and the only royal occasions I have ever enjoyed. I have always felt it's torture to be with royalty as one can't do right. . . . If one talks to them one's a snob, if one doesn't one's not pulling one's weight. With life at the Fort it was quite different. Wallis was very formal with the king, plenty of curtsies and Your Majesty, but managed to make everyone happy and at ease and of course, delicious food. Wallis was a wonderful hostess and had the best manners I've ever seen. She always talked to everyone and even engaged Sir Arthur Colefax in animated conversation. No one had ever spoken to him before.[83]

This was a tribute not just to Wallis's etiquette but also to her kindness. Sir Arthur Colefax, a Conservative politician and husband of Wallis's friend Sibyl, was a legendary bore. (Society figure Lord Berners, a composer and novelist, once quipped that the government had offered Sir Arthur "£30,000 to bore the Channel Tunnel."[84]) After dinner, the guests were driven to Windsor Castle to watch a film. "Endless footmen in royal livery crawled about on all fours (in order not to spoil the view of the screen) offering champagne," recalled Barbie Wallace. "When the lights went on most of the guests were asleep."[85]

While rising splendidly to the demands of acting as an unofficial shadow queen, Wallis confided to Aunt Bessie the toll her prestigious position was taking. Her health was poor again, with physical ailments caused by the continuing emotional turmoil and pressure. She complained of the "luncheons and dinners without a breathing space, with so many problems revolving in my mind."[86] Existing in limbo, uncertain of her future, was understandably taxing. "Life is very full at the moment and should grow more and more so and I can only hope that HM will remain fond of me for some more time—but I don't plan my future relying on that in any way."[87]

Ernest had moved out of Bryanston Court and taken rooms at his club, the Guards'. He wrote Wallis a heartrending farewell letter: "I think something in me quietly died when I closed the door of the flat for the last time this evening. I have no tears left to shed. I know that somewhere in your heart there is a small flame burning for me. Guard it carefully my darling and don't let it go out—if only in memory of the sacred lovely things that have been. Someday I pray God will fan it into a blaze again and bring you back to me."[88]

Wallis nursed deep unhappiness and self-reproach at her treatment of the blameless, decent Ernest. This served to increase her feelings of self-criticism and unworthiness. "I'm sorry to be a source of worry to you and not of pleasure,"[89] she apologized to Bessie. The American press was abuzz with her relationship, while at home, the name Mrs. Simpson still meant nothing to the British public at large. It was well known to the members of the Cabinet, however, the court and a tiny circle of informed Londoners. Ramsay MacDonald spoke out about the king's "appalling obstinacy" in sending Wallis to Ascot in a royal carriage and including her in court circulars. He famously told Harold Nicolson that it would not have mattered so much if she had been a widow: "The people of this country do not mind fornication but they loathe adultery."[90]

Chips Channon detected Wallis's distress. "The Simpson scandal is growing, and she, poor Wallis, looks unhappy. The world is closing in around her, the flatterers, the sycophants and the malice. It is a curious social juxtaposition that casts me in the role of Defender of the King. But I do, and very strongly in society, not for loyalty so much as in admiration and affection for Wallis, and in indignation against those who attack her."[91]

5

Down with the American Harlot

In July 1936 the king presented new colors to various battalions of the Brigade of Guards. He addressed the troops in Hyde Park in a speech that he had drafted himself, before sending it to Winston Churchill for tightening and emboldening. Edward chose to stress the horrors of war: "Humanity cries out for peace and the assurance of peace, and you will find in peace opportunities of duty and service as noble as any."[1]

"David did it beautifully," noted Queen Mary.[2] As the king rode back towards Constitution Hill, he coolly dodged an assassination attempt. From the crowd, a mentally unstable man wearing a brown suit pulled out a loaded revolver. He was grappled to the ground by a policeman and the gun was thrown onto the road at the feet of the king's horse. John Aird, who had accused Edward of being lily-livered on the Guinness yacht the previous summer, now wrote: "I have held the opinion that HM is a coward but after today I must reconsider my opinion and give HM fullest marks for not looking round, even when it happened. The King rode on in complete calm, not even quickening the horse's pace."[3]

The sovereign's unruffled response won him further praise from his adoring public, who were looking ahead with excitement to his coronation, due the following May. Preparations were well under way; thousands of new prayer books had been produced for the occasion, as well as flags, souvenirs, bunting, colored lights and over seven million coronation mugs.[4] The king's intention to be crowned must have held fast in his early months as monarch. He sat for a coronation portrait wearing the imperial robe of purple velvet, and a cape of ermine and silk. Painted by Albert Collings, the eminent royal artist of the day, it depicted a handsome, thoughtful, incredibly youthful-looking monarch standing next to a velvet cushion on which rested the crown and a bejeweled golden orb.[5]

Queen Mary was meanwhile preparing to move from Buckingham Palace to Marlborough House, anticipating that Edward would take over Buckingham Palace that autumn. She spent the early part of the summer sorting out her own possessions from those he was to inherit. On July 13, she divested herself of the crown jewels, which, she wrote, "have been in my care since 1910—Felt very sad at parting."[6]

Edward, who saw his mother regularly during this time, was sensitive both to her grief and the strain created by this transition. On July 30, she left Buckingham Palace and drove to Sandringham. Edward came to bid her farewell. On arrival in Norfolk, she wrote to her son: "I fear I was very quiet today when you came to see me but I feel sure you realised that I felt very sad at leaving those lovely comfortable rooms which have been my happy Home for 25 years, & that I was terribly afraid of breaking down—It was dear of you to come & see me off & I thank you with all my heart."[7]

Whenever he seemed to hold his parents' good favor, Edward was incapable of sustaining it. Instead of following his father's tradition of spending August quietly at Balmoral on the grouse moors, the new king raised eyebrows by preferring to take a Mediterranean summer sojourn. As he planned his holiday, Edward was "conscious of the clouds that were rolling up on the horizon—not only clouds of war but clouds of private trouble for me." While the British press maintained a deferential silence, "the American press had become fascinated with my friendship for Wallis, and now pursued us everywhere."[8]

The king had originally wanted to take a villa near Cannes, so John Aird was dispatched to find somewhere suitable. The actress Maxine

Elliot was asked to lend the king her villa, Le Château de l'Horizon, which boasted a twenty-five-foot slide down which her houseguests, who included Winston Churchill, shot from the edge of the saltwater swimming pool into the Mediterranean. Edward had visited L'Horizon before and liked it, describing "the long marble chute from the lower terrace down to the sea. Zzzzip! Splash! Wonderful!"[9] However, the British ambassador in Paris warned against a visit to the South of France, due to the political instability in the area caused by the Spanish Civil War. "I really am very annoyed with the FO for having messed up my holiday in this stupid manner," Edward wrote to his mother. Instead he decided to charter a yacht and cruise from the Adriatic to the Bosphorus. Lady Yule's vessel, the *Nahlin*, was declared suitable, even if it was, according to Diana Cooper, "furnished rather like a Calais whore-shop."[10] In spite of its gaudy interior, Wallis declared it "a lovely comfortable boat."[11] At the king's request, all the books were removed from the yacht's library, as an extra bedroom was deemed more useful. A plentiful supply of golf balls was stowed aboard for one of Edward's favorite pastimes: driving them into the sea.

Although he wanted to start the cruise in Venice, the Foreign Office advised against it due to Mussolini's intervention in the civil war in Spain. Edward was irritated that his party would now embark at the less romantic port of Šibenik on August 10. Crates and cases addressed to the "Duke of Lancaster"—the king's ducal alias—were carried on board. On August 8, Wallis and the king left England on an aircraft of the King's Flight. In Paris that evening, they met some of their guests and boarded a private coach attached to the Orient Express, whereby they continued to Yugoslavia. There, they were met by the yacht and two destroyers, HMS *Grafton* and *Glowworm*, known on board as the "Nanny-boats," which were to accompany the ship.

The guests, who were staggered throughout the trip, included Duff and Diana Cooper, Lord Sefton, Helen Fitzgerald and old friends of Edward's and Wallis's, the Butlers and the Rogerses. From the royal household, John Aird, Godfrey Thomas and Tommy Lascelles were present. "Outwardly as respectable as a boatload of archdeacons," commented

Lascelles. "But the fact remains that the two chief passengers (the king and the earl) were cohabiting with other men's wives."[12]

"To my parents' great surprise, they were invited to spend a week in Greece on the *Nahlin* cruise," said John Julius Norwich. "A good deal of reasoning behind this invitation was that the king had determined to marry Mrs. Simpson and at this stage, he thought he could get away with it without abdication. Because my Papa had an extremely good reputation for womanizing, the king thought that he would have far greater sympathy with him and his situation than the rest of the cabinet. The king would not have got far with Neville Chamberlain, for example."[13]

The voyage attracted a blaze of publicity. Thanks to the efforts of the American press, twenty thousand locals assembled in Yugoslavia to welcome the royal party. Due to the newspaper coverage, this laughing, shouting mob seemed as interested in Mrs. Simpson as the king; no English crowd would have recognized her at this time. The *Daily Telegraph* even omitted Mrs. Simpson's name from the *Nahlin* guest list. This exuberant welcome was repeated at every port of call, the American press avidly in tow. In Dubrovnik, they were greeted with cries of "*Živela ljubav!*"—the equivalent of "*Vive l'amour*!"

Swept up in euphoria, Wallis and Edward were buoyed by these displays of approval for their fairy-tale romance. Far from being a warning of the savage attention their union would attract now that their relationship was "becoming the property of the whole world," they could not have taken the ramifications less seriously. "I was oblivious to the dangerous undercurrents of this charming and seemingly irrelevant incident," Wallis later recalled. "It delighted both of us that strangers of uncomplicated hearts should spontaneously wish us well."[14]

Lady Diana Cooper, who spent the cruise suffering from a septic throat, boarded the ship with Duff in Split. She was taken aback by the king's informality: he sported little shorts, straw sandals and two crucifixes on a chain round his neck. Wallis wore duplicates of the crosses on a charm bracelet on her wrist. When they went ashore to visit a local village, they were greeted by "a million children and gay folk smiling and cheering." Diana waspishly added that half of them didn't know which one was the king and must have been surprised when they were told. "He had no hat (the child's hair gleaming), espadrilles, the same little shorts and a tiny blue-and-white singlet bought in one of their own villages."[15]

The trip created the unfavorable impression in the press that the king, his mistress and a group of hangers-on were carousing the eastern Mediterranean, shocking locals with their underdressed attire and over-casual attitudes. While the king made undignified appearances everywhere—he sailed through the Corinth Canal, dined in a disreputable Athens bistro and wandered naked around a Turkish bath in Vienna—he also gained a measure of diplomatic goodwill. He met with dignitaries such as Turkey's great secular head of state, Kemal Atatürk, with whom he conversed in German. This was the first visit in history by a British king to the country. "Psychologically, it transformed the attitude of the Turkish people towards Britain, to whom they had grown used, from the outbreak of First World War, as an enemy," wrote Lord Kinross.[16]

While cruising the Aegean, Edward took advantage of Duff Cooper's counsel regarding his relationship with Wallis. "The king and Papa had a great many conversations on board about the issue," said John Julius Norwich. "Papa said that he should delay his coronation, go and do a big durbar in India and give the issue time to resolve. Papa could see that this thing had got too big for Wallis and that she was longing to get the hell out. My father saw that and wanted to give her a chance to get away. But the king was absolutely determined to marry her. It was a schoolboy love, as though he had never been in love before, and poor Wallis was in a completely impossible position. My father felt deeply for them both."[17]

Everywhere that they went, Edward and Wallis were photographed. Like modern celebrities, they were chased by the press, an early foretaste of paparazzi hounding. They were photographed passing through Salzburg, driving in Athens, bathing in the sea (the king did an hour's rowing in the ship's dinghy every day for exercise); but probably the most memorable photograph, of which the world took note, was of the royal couple getting into a small boat. Wallis's hand is proprietorially placed on the king's forearm—a breathtaking breach of protocol—while he is bending attentively towards her, every sinew of his body strained in devotion.

The photographs, which circled the globe, were startling because they captured the couple's unguarded intimacy and tenderness.

Of the king, Diana Cooper wrote: "He is utterly himself and unselfconscious. That I think is the reason why he does some things (that he likes) superlatively well. He does not *act*. In the middle of the procession he stopped for a good two minutes to do up his shoe. . . . We were all left staring at his behind. But it did not occur to him to wait, and so the people said: 'Isn't he human! Isn't he natural! He stopped to do up his shoe like any of us!'"[18]

Edward could be both a thoughtful, courteous host and an insufferable egotist. Endearingly, he adored childish pursuits such as fishing jellyfish out of the sea. He would lean out of his dinghy, scooping them up in an old shrimping net, while his guests stood at the ship's prow, shouting: "There's a big one, Sir." He did not create a fuss when at every mealtime on the *Nahlin* he was served last—an example of his impeccable manners and out of deference to his guests—with the result that there was never enough food for him. Even though he was fastidious about what he ate—he, like Wallis, was forever terrified of gaining weight—every day he had to say at least once: "Yes, but I do want *something* to eat."[19] This he took in good humor. But it was after a dinner with his cousin, King George II of the Hellenes, recently returned to the throne following his exile, that the tenor of the cruise soured. Edward went into a troubled and prolonged mood, which naturally his guests found dispiriting.

The dinner at King George's magnificent rented villa in Corfu, up a winding hill lined with cypress trees, was, according to Diana Cooper, "A1." On the large formal terrace, she sat next to the Greek monarch, with Wallis on George II's other side. Diana observed Edward turn the full force of his charm onto "an exceedingly good-looking Englishwoman" called Joyce Brittain-Jones. Lady Diana disparagingly referred to her as "Mrs. Jones." Diana noted Wallis "doing splendidly, the wisecracks following in quick succession, the king clearly very admiring and amused."[20] The dinner went on until 1.30 a.m., by which time Diana was "nearly crying" with fatigue.[21]

Back on board the *Nahlin*, the group was discussing the evening and George II's attachment to divorcée Mrs. Brittain-Jones. She was his constant companion, with whom the king had found great love and solace since his loveless marriage to Princess Elisabeth of Romania had ended in divorce the year before. "Why doesn't he just marry her?" asked Wallis. Without thinking, one of the guests replied in astonished tones that it was impossible for the king to marry a woman who was both a commoner and a divorcée. Hearing this statement of fact voiced out loud, mirroring his own plight, clearly rankled with Edward. His own dilemma was brought into focus, triggering days of melancholy. Whichever way he now turned, a dereliction of duty was inevitable. To the woman he loved or to the Crown. Wallis, finely attuned to the king's mood swings, became tetchy that night too. Later that evening, when her dress—an exquisite filigree material embroidered with dragonflies—caught under the legs of a chair, the king got down on his hands and knees to try to free it. Diana Cooper said that Wallis stared at him coldly and cut him down, saying: "Well, that's the *maust* extraordinary performance I've ever seen."[22]

Wallis, increasingly aware that she was trapped in a dependent position, found ways to diminish and punish Edward in public. Just as she knew how to soothe him, she knew exactly how to torment him. It showed an unappealing side to her character—a rebellion and release against feelings of suffocation and loss of control over her own life. While the masochistic side of the king believed he deserved and benefited from Wallis's censure, no doubt he received her forgiveness as a form of benediction. This was part of the power that Wallis had over him.

Everyone saw the end of the cruise as a blessing. "I feel the sooner the trip ends for us, the better," wrote Diana Cooper to a friend. "It's impossible to enjoy antiquities with people who won't land for them and who call Delphi Delhi."[23]

Wallis and Edward took a private train from Turkey, through Bulgaria to Yugoslavia, before ending up in Vienna. The king was delighted that Tsar Boris III of Bulgaria joined the train before Sofia and, as a keen driver of locomotives on his state railways, allowed Edward to join him up front. "We had two kings in the cab of the engine," Wallis recalled. "The King of Bulgaria was at the throttle and the King of England was allowed to blow the whistle at the crossings."[24]

The royal party stayed once more for a few days at the Bristol Hotel in Vienna. Elsa Maxwell (who had not yet met Wallis but would later be a close friend) happened to be in the lobby when the party arrived. "The clicking of heels by the manager and his staff sounded like castanets and a crew of porters scurried through the door with mountains of luggage," she wrote.

> Then the king's entourage entered, led by a small, distinguished-looking woman. Her expression and the purposeful way she walked gave me the impression that she would brush aside anyone who had the temerity to get in her path. I took a second, startled look when I saw the king following a few paces behind. I had never seen Mrs. Simpson. It was difficult to believe that this was the woman who was going to create such a turmoil throughout the British Empire. Yet a few nights later, when I saw the king's look of adoration when he danced with the woman he was to marry, I knew he was utterly in love with her.[25]

On September 14, the king flew back to England from Zurich and Wallis went with the rest of the party to Paris to stay at the Hôtel Meurice. Of the trip, Tommy Lascelles said to John Aird that he "could not be better pleased with HM's behaviour as compared to past trips."[26] He was alluding to the prince's previous womanizing, so could at least see that Wallis had a stabilizing influence in this respect.

While most of the Western world outside Britain was agog with the relationship of King Edward and Mrs. Simpson, still not a word was whispered in the British press. Upholding a dignified reserve, even Queen Mary did not refer to Mrs. Simpson when Edward went to dine with her at Buckingham Palace on his return. "Greeting her, I wondered how much she knew about the stories appearing in the American press," Edward wrote later. Queen Mary's conversation revealed nothing. She asked her son if he had enjoyed the cruise and about the heat in the Adriatic. They discussed King George II of Greece. "David got back from abroad looking very well," was all Queen Mary noted in her diary, "—and came to dine with me and we had a nice talk."[27]

The queen was delighted that her son planned to spend the last two weeks of September at Balmoral. If she hoped that the *Nahlin* trip was his last hurrah before he settled dutifully into his role as monarch, returning to the more traditional ways of her husband, King George V, she would soon be disappointed. Yet Edward, who loved the life in the Highlands—if not the formality of court life at Balmoral—looked forward to his Scottish trip after the enervating heat of the Balkans. True to form, he would do Balmoral *his* way. "The deerstalking would be at its best; there would still be plenty of grouse on the moors and the exhilarating air and hard exercise to put me in condition for the heavy schedule awaiting me," he said.[28]

Meanwhile in Paris, Wallis, recuperating from a nasty cold, was "amazed and then shocked" to read American press clippings sent to her by friends and family. Her relationship with the king, which "heretofore had been purely personal between David and me was now a topic of dinner-table conversation for every newspaper reader in the United States, Europe and the Dominions."[29] When the king telephoned her, she confided her "deepening misgivings" and told him some of the scurrilous rumors being bandied about. Edward batted away her anxieties, reassuring her that there would be no public comment in England and that the furore would soon quieten down.

On September 16, Wallis wrote Edward a revelatory letter. Seized with panic, it was as if she had suddenly shaken herself awake from a skittish dream that had lasted two and a half years, to be confronted with the stark reality of her situation.

That July, through the king's solicitor, Theodore Goddard, Wallis had begun divorce proceedings against Ernest. A date had been set for the trial of October 27. Goddard had retained the services of Norman Birkett, the most celebrated and publicized advocate of his day. The king knew that if Wallis received her decree nisi, she would be eligible to apply for her divorce to be made absolute six months later, at the end of April 1937.

It would therefore be technically possible for her to remarry before the May coronation. Goddard had decided that the case should be tried outside London, as he naively thought that it would attract less attention. He chose Ipswich Assizes in Suffolk, where Wallis would have to live prior to the trial in order to gain the necessary residential qualification for the hearing. A suitable cottage, Beech House, near Felixstowe, was found. The arrangements had been set in motion. At this late hour, the fearful Wallis suddenly did a volte-face and begged to return to Ernest.

> Dear David,
> This is a difficult letter to write—but I feel it's easier than talking and less painful. I must really return to Ernest for a great many reasons which please be patient and read. The first being because we are so awfully congenial and understand getting on together *very* well—which is really an art in marriage. We have no small irritations one for the other.

Wallis detailed the benefits of the less exhilarating but more stable union with Ernest, even accommodating being poor and "unable to do the attractive amusing things in life which I must confess I do love and enjoy—also the possession of beautiful things is thrilling to me and much appreciated but weighed against a calm congenial life I choose the latter for I know that though I shall suffer greatly now I shall be a happier calmer old lady." In no uncertain terms, she tried to break from the king.

> I know Ernest and have the deepest affection and respect for him. I feel I am better with him than with you—and so you must understand. I am sure dear David that in a few months your life will run again as it did before and without my nagging. Also you have been independent of affection all your life. We have had lovely beautiful times together and I thank God for them and know that you will go on with your job doing it better and in a more dignified manner each year. That would please me so. I am sure you and I would only create disaster together.

Wallis, who was regularly accused of being avaricious and an adventuress, out for whatever material gain she could get, said that she would contact the king's lawyer to "arrange the return of everything." This included the life-changing sum of money that had been settled on her. "I want you to be happy," she concluded to Edward. "I feel sure I can't make you so and I honestly don't think you can me. . . . I am sure that after this letter you will realise that no human being could assume this responsibility and it would be most unfair to make things harder for me by seeing me. Good-bye WE all say. Wallis."[30]

Hugo Vickers believes that by this time Wallis and Ernest had more of a "brother-sister relationship." "He was the only one she could turn to," he said. "Whether she was still in love with him or not, I'm not sure, but he represented stability and security and one thing is for certain, she absolutely did not want the abdication."[31] A legal advisor and old friend of Edward's, Sir Walter Monckton, wrote: "The easy view is that she should have been made to give him up. But I never knew any man whom it would have been harder to get rid of."[32]

Before putting her feelings in writing, Wallis had tried to explain her misgivings to Edward on the telephone. He responded with the following letter, written from the Fort at half past midnight:

> Good night my Wallis.
> Why do you say such hard things to David on the telephone sometimes? Hard things like you would prefer to have someone else with you tonight when you are sick that I would be bored that I don't understand and lots of others which hurt me so. . . . I feel like bursting tonight with love and such a longing to hold you tighter than I ever have before. You see I do love you so entirely and in every way Wallis. Madly tenderly adoringly and with admiration and such confidence.[33]

Bit by bit, Edward wore Wallis down with his protestations of love and declarations of need. He phoned her frequently, rarely giving her space to gather her thoughts. He simply would not hear of letting her go. In a state of agitated confusion, her nerves shredded, she succumbed to the king's considerable pressure, continuing with plans to join him at Balmoral. She stopped briefly in London, where she met with Theodore Goddard to settle the final arrangements of her divorce.

The king, already in the Highlands, was surrounded by his family. The Duke and Duchess of York resided at Birkall, seven miles away from Balmoral, while his brother Harry and his wife, Alice, stayed at Abergeldie Mains, another estate house. Instead of the usual and anticipated roll call of Cabinet ministers, archbishops, admirals, generals and the aristocracy customarily invited to Balmoral, Edward "wanted others to see it and enjoy with me its famous sport and amenities."[34] He said: "Naturally Wallis was included in the house party, and her arrival with Mr. and Mrs. Herman Rogers a few days later was duly recorded, with my instructions, in the Court Circular."[35]

On September 19, Elizabeth, Duchess of York, wrote to Queen Mary, who had asked her to go to Balmoral to remove certain personal photographs which she wanted to keep. In her letter, Elizabeth talked about going to Aberdeen the following week. The king had been asked to open the Aberdeen Infirmary but had told the Lord Provost of Aberdeen that he would not be able to do so because the court was still in mourning. He asked his brother Bertie to deputize for him, despite the fact that he, too, was in mourning.

"Next week we go to Aberdeen to open the new hospital," wrote Elizabeth. "I do wish that David could have done it, as they have all worked so hard and for so long, & it will be one of the best in Scotland, and it would have given enormous pleasure to the countryside round here. But he won't, so there it is!" She went on to add: "I am secretly rather dreading next week, but I haven't heard if a certain person is coming or not—I do hope not as everything is talked of up here."[36]

On September 23, instead of fulfilling his official engagements for that day, the king drove himself sixty miles to Aberdeen station, to meet Wallis off the train. Wallis, in a party with fellow guests, could have waited at Aberdeen and changed trains for Ballater, the nearest station to Balmoral, eight miles away. But Edward, who could not bear the thought of his beloved changing trains and would not wait a moment longer than necessary to be reunited with her, decided to drive to Aberdeen—the city where he had said he could not open the infirmary. Barely disguised in motoring goggles, he arrived at the station at the same time that his brother was carrying out his official duties on the other side of the city. Later that day, on the front page of the Aberdeen evening newspaper, two photographs were published side by side: one of the Yorks opening the hospital, the other of the cavalier king, with the caption: "His Majesty in Aberdeen. Surprise visit in car to meet guests."

This staggering lack of tact and sensitivity did the king irreparable damage. "This has done him more harm than anything else and has lost him Scotland," wrote Sir Godfrey Thomas in his diary.[37] In Aberdeen, someone daubed a wall with graffiti: "Down With the American Harlot."

The following morning, Wallis took precedence over the Duke and Duchess of York in the Court Circular. In his overzealous desire to secure Wallis in his life, Edward's sanity was again coming under question by horrified courtiers. The king's obsession with Mrs. Simpson was making him lose what limited judgment he had previously possessed. "The king was like the child in the fairy story who was given every gift except a soul," wrote Tommy Lascelles acerbically. "He had no real friends for whom he cared a straw. His private secretaries had a devil of a time."[38]

At Balmoral, Edward put Wallis in the best guest room and refused to sleep in the king's room, installing himself instead in the dressing room of Wallis's suite. The couple still corresponded through notes. The king sent Wallis a list of local dignitaries who were invited that evening for a film screening. "Darling—here are the people who are going to bore us for eanum time tonight."[39] Wallis replied on a slip of Balmoral writing paper: "DDD—have you thought of changing the film as all the nuts have seen it? WE can see it in London."[40]

To his mother, the king wrote breezily that the weather was fine and that Balmoral, where Queen Victoria's wallpaper still hangs, was most comfortable: "only a few more baths will have to be added for another year."[41]

On Saturday evening, Edward threw a dinner and reception to which the Duke and Duchess of York were invited. Most of the guests, including the Duke and Duchess of Kent, were already assembled when the Yorks arrived. As Elizabeth preceded her husband into the drawing room, Wallis walked forward to receive her. The eighteen other people present in the room read Wallis's gesture in different ways. Some saw it as a mistaken act of politeness, others saw it as an insouciant flouting of her power. The Duchess of York, still furious about events in Aberdeen only days earlier, openly showed her resentment at being received by Wallis. Devoid of her usual smile, her face set in a "freezing expression," Elizabeth walked straight past Wallis and said, to no one in particular: "I came to dine with the king."[42]

The Duke of York looked on, nervous and highly embarrassed. The king, noticing this, broke off his conversation with a group of guests and came forward to greet his brother and sister-in-law. The Duchess of York took precedence at dinner, sitting on the king's right, with the Duchess of Sutherland on his left. Wallis sat at the head of the table, but it was Elizabeth who led the ladies from dinner, without even glancing in Mrs. Simpson's direction.

Whatever Wallis did and however she behaved, she was in an impossible situation; the Duchess of York's disdain for her severely influenced her detractors, and this antipathy lasts to this day. Although Mary, Duchess of Buccleuch, a guest at the house party, wrote that she "saw no signs of Mrs. Simpson acting as official hostess" during her stay at Balmoral, amongst Scottish grandees, the die was cast. Word among the estate was that Wallis had offended long-serving staff by introducing the triple-decker sandwich to the menu, and another innovation: after-dinner films. The club sandwiches proved incredibly popular with guests, who made repeat orders, but less so with the already busy staff. It was also suggested that old and loyal retainers had been dismissed by the king on Wallis's advice. The Balmoral trip attracted nothing but bad press for Edward and Wallis.

Yet after he left the castle, George, Duke of Kent, who had enjoyed his brother's hospitality, wrote: "I could never believe that any place could change so much and have such a different atmosphere. It was all so comfortable and everyone seemed so happy—it really was fun."[43] Cecil Beaton recalled being shown a cine film taken by Herman Rogers of the Balmoral house party which captured the lighthearted gaiety Prince George referred to. "Here, against the Highland setting, more candid shots of the turreted castle, which caught the king demonstrating to his guests an Austrian game by shooting some kind of arrow through the air. Lord Louis Mountbatten tried after him, then the Duke of Kent. They fared badly making everyone laugh. As they sat on the terrace waiting for lunch, the ladies looked untidy and relaxed. . . . Every few feet of film, the king appeared with Wallis. She looked very different from the others, neat and towny in smart clothes and a black felt hat."[44]

By October, Wallis and the king were back in London. Both were relocating. Wallis stayed at Claridge's while she waited for the lease to become free on her new London home, a four-storey furnished property at 16 Cumberland Terrace, Regent's Park. Cecil Beaton was commissioned by the king to photograph Wallis in his studio. Beaton, who had dismissed Wallis as "brawny and raw-boned" in 1930, now found her "bright and witty, improved in looks and chic." He "liked her immensely," he said. She came to his studio "rather shyly" and had scarcely arrived when the telephone rang for her. "It seems that incessant callers make demands upon her all the time," he wrote. " 'Will you lunch?" "May I come in for a cocktail?" To accept all this lionizing required careful arranging, which she manages well. She has learned how to keep people at a distance: 'Wait till I get home and look at my book.' 'My secretary will give you a ring in the morning.' Her voice seemed quieter."[45]

Beneath her popularity, valiant facade and rigid impeccability, the mounting emotional strain was taking its toll. "Whatever fantastic changes have taken place in Mrs. Simpson's life," Beaton noted, "she has obviously suffered. There is a sad look to her eyes. The camera was not blind to this."[46]

Now that his mother had completed her move to Marlborough House, Edward, meanwhile, was very unhappily installing himself in Buckingham Palace, a place he had loathed since childhood. As he did not want to occupy his father's rooms on the second floor, he moved into the Belgian Suite on the ground floor. This five-room apartment with tall French windows opening onto the gardens was named after Queen Victoria's uncle Leopold I and was usually kept for visiting monarchs. The king made no changes to the rooms, bar adding a shower to the bathtub and replacing the ornate four-poster with a single bed. With some prescience, he said that he "had a feeling that I might not be there very long."[47] He installed an extra switchboard to handle his private calls, no doubt with Wallis in mind, and a private line to the Fort.

The king planned to throw himself into his work "with energy"; his schedule was packed until Christmas. Yet rifts in the royal household were creating an anxious, unsettled atmosphere. The Duke of York, increasingly shut off from his brother, confided to his wife that he felt neglected and ignored. The duchess put the couple's distress into a letter to Queen Mary on October 11. She wrote from Birkhall, telling her mother-in-law about the lovely late summer weather, before turning to her main theme: "David does not seem to possess the faculty of making others feel wanted. It is very sad, and I feel that the whole difficulty is a certain person. I do not feel that I can make advances to her & ask her to our house, as I imagine would be liked, & this fact is bound to make relations a little difficult. . . . The whole situation is complicated and horrible and I feel so unhappy about it sometimes, so you must forgive me darling Mama for letting myself go so indiscreetly."[48]

A few weeks later, Elizabeth wrote to the king, betraying no trace of her "indiscretions" to her mother-in-law. In luminous terms, she thanked her brother-in-law for lending her and Bertie Birkhall for the summer. "Darling David . . . It was ANGELIC and kind of you to let us have it. I do thank you from all my heart—you are always so sweet and thoughtful for us, and I wish that I could thank you as I would wish." She signed off: "Your loving sister in law Elizabeth."[49]

On October 1, Wallis moved temporarily to Suffolk. Her friends George and Kitty Hunter offered to stay with her while she waited for her divorce case to come to court. They drove to Felixstowe in Wallis's Buick.

Disheartened by the small, uninspiring cottage that awaited them, which would barely fit three people, let alone a cook and a maid too, Wallis felt low and melancholic. Seaside resorts can be bleak out of season; Felixstowe was particularly dreary, stormy and wet. Yet due to the silence of the British press, Mrs. Simpson and the Hunters passed unrecognized as they strolled into the town to collect their post and the newspapers, when the weather held. During blustery beach walks, Wallis agonized over her plight. Generally feeling depressed and anxious about the unflattering depictions in the foreign press, she tried again to make Edward see sense.

On October 14 she wrote to him on Claridge's writing paper, though from Beech House, Felixstowe:

> My dear—
> This is really more than you or I bargained for—this being haunted by the press. Do you feel you still want me to go ahead as I feel it will hurt your popularity in the country. Last night I heard so much from the Hunters that made me shiver—and I am very upset and ill today from talking until 4.

She detailed what she had heard: that the king was hissed at in the cinema; that a man in white tie refused to get up in the theater when they played 'God Save the King.' Wallis continued:

> Really David darling if I hurt you to this extent isn't it best for me to steal quietly away. . . . I'm sorry to bother you my darling—but I feel like an animal in a trap and these two buzzards working me up over the way you are losing your popularity—through me.[50]

Wallis tried to disguise the extent of her despair in letters to Aunt Bessie, asking her to come to visit her in London in November. "Darling—I can never put a foot in the US on account of all the publicity. I am sorry you are in the dark but it is best for you to be that way. I love you and everything will eventually be alright—just now I am having a bad time."[51]

Edward knew that the British press's silence over the private lives of the royal family would not hold indefinitely. "Something was bound to give before long," he later wrote. "And, believing in the direct approach, I decided to enlist the aid and understanding of two powerful newspaper friends, Lord Beaverbrook and the Honorable Esmond Harmsworth."[52] Max Beaverbrook controlled the *Evening Standard* and the *Daily Express*—which had the largest circulation in Britain—while Harmsworth, the son of Lord Rothermere, controlled the rival *Daily Mail* and *Evening News*. At the king's request, Beaverbrook was asked to a meeting at Buckingham Palace. "Name your time," the king had said, an unusual indication of how urgently the press baron's presence was required. Beaverbrook, who was suffering from acute toothache, delayed the king by two days. When they finally met, Edward asked Beaverbrook to protect Wallis from "sensational publicity" in his own country.[53]

"The king asked me to help in suppressing all advance news of the Simpson divorce, and in limiting publicity after the event," Beaverbrook later wrote. "He stated his case calmly and with great cogency and force. The reasons he gave for his wish were that Mrs. Simpson was ill, unhappy and distressed by the thought of notoriety. Notoriety would attach to her only because she had been his guest on the *Nahlin* and at Balmoral. As the publicity would be due to association with himself, he felt it his duty to protect her."[54]

Beaverbrook secured a "gentleman's agreement with other press owners who censored themselves, agreeing to make no mention of Mrs. Simpson's friendship with the king." This conspiracy of silence was even assisted by newsagents who literally cut out revelations from foreign journals. The *New York Times* was stunned by this "voluntary surrender of the freedom of the press."[55] At this stage, Lord Beaverbrook was unaware that the king had marriage in mind. But he said that, if he had known, he "would still have done what I did. But the fact remains that I did not know, although I was having conversations with the king almost every day."[56]

Following his satisfactory meeting, the king went to Sandringham on Friday night to prepare for a partridge-shooting party he was hosting the following week. This was to be the only time he would act as host at Sandringham. On his arrival, as the Royal Standard was hoisted on Sandringham Church, the flagpole snapped. A carpenter was instructed to work through the night to mend it, to prevent the press from labeling it a portent of doom similar to the Maltese cross falling from the imperial crown.

On Saturday, October 17, Edward wrote to Wallis, who had returned to London for the weekend: "This eanum note to welcome a girl back and to say that a boy loves her more and more and that he will be hurrying back to her very soon now. Oh my sweetheart what a nightmare these days—that are thank God ending now—have been. God bless WE my Wallis Your David."[57]

As news of Wallis's impending divorce circulated around the inner circles of the court and Whitehall, there was a renewed sense of alarm. Stanley Baldwin, who initially resisted pressure to confront the king, could delay no longer. A message was sent to Edward at Sandringham saying that the prime minister needed to see him as a matter of urgency. It was decided that Baldwin's sudden appearance at Sandringham would create too much speculation amidst the shooting party, so Edward agreed to meet him at Fort Belvedere. He drove there on Monday evening, in preparation for the meeting set for ten o'clock the next morning.

"Friendly, casual and discursive, he might have been a neighbour who had called to discuss a dispute over a boundary fence," Edward later said of Baldwin. After Baldwin complimented the king on the beauty of the Fort's grounds, they retired to the fireside in the octagonal drawing room. Tired from the drive in an unpleasant little car, which the king noted "didn't seem half big enough for him,"[58] the prime minister, while outwardly composed, was agitated and in pain from his arthritis. The king was taken aback when, at eleven in the morning, Baldwin asked, almost apologetically, if he could have a whisky and soda. The king refused to join him on the grounds that he never drank before 7 p.m. But both produced their pipes and tobacco pouches and began to smoke.

Baldwin started by speaking of his high regard for the king, as a man, and his belief that he had the qualities to make an admirable monarch.

"You have all the advantages a man can have. You are young. You have before you the example of your father. You are fond of your house and you like children. You have only one disadvantage. You are not married and you ought to be."[59] Baldwin then told Edward that the ministerial correspondence on his relationship with Mrs. Simpson was growing larger every day. A tide of public outrage could no longer be stemmed. He produced a file which contained samples of damaging material: "The American papers are full of it and . . . the effect of such comment in the American press would be to sap the position of the throne unless it is stopped."[60] He pointed out that while the British public would tolerate a considerable amount in a private life, when it spilled over into public life, they resented it. Citing Mrs. Simpson's appearance in the Court Circular at Balmoral as inflammatory, he urged the king to conduct his affair more discreetly.

"The lady is my friend and I do not wish to let her in by the back door," responded Edward, at his most dignified.

Then, suggested Baldwin, could he not put off the divorce?

"Mr. Baldwin, I have no right to interfere with the affairs of an individual. It would be wrong were I to attempt to influence Mrs. Simpson just because she happens to be a friend of the king's," came the disingenuous reply.

Could Mrs. Simpson perhaps leave the country for six months? Baldwin continued.

The king remained silent.

Baldwin failed to summon the courage to ask Edward if it was his intention to marry Wallis if she became free. Instead, he left mumbling that he was glad that the "ice had been broken." He reported to colleagues that he found the king "stiff and in the toils."[61] However, he relayed to Mrs. Baldwin that the king had told him that Mrs. Simpson was "the only woman in the world and I cannot live without her."[62]

According to Lord Beaverbrook, despite what he actually said to the king, Stanley Baldwin "did not want King Edward." The prime minister had already clashed with Edward, when, as Prince of Wales, he had visited the unemployed in Wales and Northumberland without the government's approval. "Baldwin did not believe in the capabilities of His Majesty for the art of kingship," said Beaverbrook, "and resented his independence of politicians and his addiction to declaring himself on political issues, without consultation with his constitutional advisors."[63]

Beaverbrook, who, like Churchill, came to deplore Baldwin, believing that he played a sinister and deceiving hand in Edward's abdication, said: "He was a thoroughly lazy man, but was capable of immense energy when his own position was threatened. Whenever he was in danger he became a cool, determined, relentless and far-sighted adversary. He showed all the wisdom of the serpent. In the crisis of the king he was to do more. He was to show the serpent's venom as well."[64] The king, who, according to Beaverbrook, "found Baldwin something of a bore," had similar misgivings about his prime minister's loyalties. He later wrote: "My talk with the prime minister perturbed me." Of his relationship with Wallis, he now fully realized that "a friendship that had so far remained within the sheltered realm of my private solicitude was manifestly about to become an affair of state."[65]

Edward decided to talk to Sir Walter Monckton, a barrister and old friend from his Oxford University days. Appointed attorney general to the Prince of Wales in 1932 and legal advisor to the Duchy of Cornwall, Monckton was the first person Edward had knighted as king. Invited to lunch at the Fort a few days later, Monckton and the king strolled after coffee along the Cedar Walk. Edward stopped and faced him. "Listen, Walter. One doesn't know how things are going to turn out. I am beginning to wonder whether I really am the kind of king they want. Am I not a bit too independent? As you know, my make up is very different from that of my father. I believe they would prefer someone more like him. Well, there is my brother Bertie." According to the king, Monckton did not wholly agree, yet "conceded the logic of my argument."[66]

Although Wallis's imminent divorce seemed certain to increase the risk of public scandal, still few people, even those close to the king, believed that he would actually marry Mrs. Simpson. Wallis herself did not entertain this possibility. When, in one of her meetings with Theodore Goddard, he tentatively raised the question of marriage, she blazed back:

"What do you take me for? Do you think I would allow such a thing? I would never think of it. . . . Some day I shall just fade out."[67]

The American press were in full cry to the opposite. The day before Wallis's divorce petition was heard, the New York *Daily Mirror* ran a blaring headline that took up three-quarters of its front page: "KING TO MARRY 'WALLY.' WEDDING NEXT JUNE."[68]

The night before her court appearance, Wallis could not sleep. She packed her suitcases from her unhappy stay in Felixstowe, ready to leave the following morning for London, then paced the bedroom floor, agitated as to whether she was doing the right thing. The burden upon her was intense. Yet as dawn broke, a measure of calmness settled over her. It was too late to turn back.

6

Oceans of Agony

At 2:17 p.m. on Tuesday, October 27, the case of *Simpson W. v. Simpson E.A.* came before Sir John Hawke at Ipswich Assizes. The court was surrounded by police, preventing the throng of press on the pavement from taking photographs, smashing two cameras in the process. Wallis arrived with Goddard and was given a seat in the witness box (although it was normal custom for a woman to stand while testifying). She was struck by how quiet the courtroom was and that there were only two women present in an otherwise empty gallery. "It's the judge's wife and a friend," whispered Goddard.

The evidence revealed that on July 28, 1936, Ernest Simpson had spent the night in bedroom number four of the Hotel de Paris, at Bray in Buckinghamshire, with a "Mrs. Simpson" who was not his wife. She was the implausibly named Buttercup Kennedy (this was, in fact, the pseudonym under which Mary Raffray had booked into the same hotel with Ernest). The judge said testily: "Well, I suppose that I must come to the conclusion that there was adultery in this case." When Wallis's counsel responded, "I assume what your Lordship has in mind," Sir John Hawke replied: "How do you know what is in my mind, Mr. Birkett?"[1]

"I was much too tense to pay attention to my surroundings or even to follow the details of the proceedings, which lasted only a few minutes," Wallis later wrote. "All I remember of that ordeal was the hostility of the judge as he scrutinized me while I was testifying, and his obvious attempts to discomfit Mr. Birkett. For a terrible moment I felt sure he was determined to deny me my divorce."[2]

Wallis was granted a decree nisi, with costs against Ernest. "A moment later, Mr. Goddard had me by the arm and was guiding me out of the courtroom and into the car. We started at once for London," remembered Wallis. Due to the press throng and the police, George Ladbroke, the king's chauffeur, whom Edward had sent to collect Wallis, had to skillfully maneuver the car to get away. On the long journey back to London, while Goddard exuded an air of quiet triumph, Wallis sank back, exhausted. She was thankful the ordeal was over but, as always, anxious. Few around her realized, let alone were sensitive to, her fragility.

All day, in between carrying out his duties, the king had waited for news. After lunch, he heard that Wallis had been granted a decree nisi. He knew that it would be six months before the absolute. "Wallis therefore could not remarry before the end of April 1937," he deduced. "However, with my Coronation fixed for May 12th, this seems to allow ample time for me to work things out. Inwardly relieved—mistakenly, as it proved—I returned to my engagements."[3]

That evening, Wallis and Edward enjoyed an initially happy reunion dinner at Cumberland Terrace. Their ease was short-lived. Detecting his "suppressed anxiety," Wallis coaxed the truth out of Edward. He told her about Baldwin's visit and the prime minister's wish that he had prevented Wallis's divorce proceedings. "My first reaction was one of utter bewilderment; then as I began to grasp the enormity of what was on Mr. Baldwin's mind, I was appalled," said Wallis. "For there could be only one explanation for his unasked-for and unprecedented intervention: he had clearly made up his mind that David wanted to marry me and he wished to foreclose such a possibility, once and for all." Edward promised that he would "fix things," but, the more perceptive of the two, she was to be correct when she surmised: "David's reassurance notwithstanding, I was still convinced that we had not heard the last of Stanley Baldwin."[4]

Faithful to its word, the British press reported the divorce hearing in brief, discreet paragraphs. Elsewhere in the world, lurid headlines screamed, the most unedifying being one Chicago newspaper's "KING'S MOLL RENO'D IN WOLSEY'S HOME TOWN"—a reference to Ipswich and Thomas Wolsey, Henry VIII's ill-fated divorce broker.

"Already the press here is beginning to register digs and slight disapproval," noted Chips Channon. "And it is quite true that the monarchy has lost caste enormously since last January. All the world knows is that the king is the slave of an American, who has had two husbands and two divorces. It does not know how charming, how wise, and sympathetic she is, nor what an edifying influence. It seems the whole press angle has been clumsily handled. The king is at his worst with Fleet Street, off-hand, angry and ungracious; he never treats them in the right way, or realises that his popularity largely depends on them."[5]

While serious rumors circulated that the king intended to marry Wallis, she was at pains to refute such gossip. Cecil Beaton attested to this when she invited him to her new Regent's Park house to photograph her, and then, a few days later, sketch her. Beaton sat in her pale-white and olive-green drawing room, noting the extravagant Constance Spry flower arrangements, mixed with bark and wild grasses. The king sent Wallis bouquets from Spry almost every day, at a cost of £5 a bouquet (around £100 today). Beaton considered that Wallis looked astonishing: "Immaculate, soignee and fresh as a young girl. Her skin was as bright and smooth as the inside of a shell, her hair so sleek she might have been Chinese." He cheekily suggested a background of scrolls and ermine pinned on a white cloth for the shoot. "Don't do anything connected with the Coronation for me," Wallis immediately responded. "I want none of that now."[6] Beaton reported that when he asked her to lower her chin, "as though bowing," the unfortunate reference caused her to look sharply at him.

Wallis's elusive quality was tricky for even Beaton to capture. None of his sketches quite came off. "Mrs. Simpson proved an exceptionally difficult woman to draw," he said, reflecting the complexity of Wallis's persona. Yet he found her conversationally open, spirited and fun to be around. "She spoke amusingly, in staccato sentences punctuated by explosive bursts of laughter that lit up her face with great gaiety and made her eyebrows look attractively surprised." Towards the early evening the door opened and the butler announced: "His Majesty." Wallis let out a cry of surprise: "Oh, Sir, we were just talking about you."[7] Edward, who struck Beaton with his relaxed ease, examined the photographic proofs of Wallis which were laid out on the sofa. He announced that he wanted to buy them all. With a whisky and soda in hand, he allowed Beaton to sketch him, stressing he must capture the left side of his face as it showed the parting of his hair.

The "cocktail hour" that Beaton described at Cumberland Terrace was so full of life and laughter that is it easy to see why Edward, lonely at Buckingham Palace, sought the comfort of Wallis and her inimitable homemaking. Aunt Bessie, who had recently arrived in England as a support to Wallis, joined them for drinks later that evening before they were all due to go to a dinner at Emerald Cunard's. Hot hors d'oeuvre, served on a silver tray, accompanied by green grapes stuffed with cream cheese, were passed around.

"The king talked very fast," remembered Beaton, "darted around the room, rang bells, busily untied parcels with red, slightly horny hands that looked surprisingly like a mechanic's. He had a bad cold and wore a heavy silk jersey. Wallis's eyes sparkled; her brows lifted in mock-pain; her mouth turned down at the corners as she laughed. The aunt sat back quipping. At last the king (like a child whose before-dinner play hour had come to an end) was told that we must all go. Wallis, who had only a few minutes to dress for Emerald Cunard's dinner, was already beginning to unbutton her dress."[8]

Diana Vreeland said of Wallis at this time, "suddenly she had the most beautiful clothes in London and the most divine house in

Cumberland Terrace, filled with white lilacs and burning perfume and the whole lot."[9]

On the surface, the king's life seemed to proceed normally during the first half of November. He later wrote: "But now that I myself was caught up in a struggle of the heart and the spirit, the old, easy sense of security crumbled away. And as I discharged my kingly duties, the ceremonial parts, especially, took on an air of unreality."[10] The state opening of Parliament on November 3 demonstrated that Edward Windsor, when inspired, could fulfill his role with consummate skill. As it was pouring with rain, and Edward maintained that "pageantry needs sunshine," he canceled the traditional state procession, driving to Westminster in a closed Daimler. This raised disapproving eyebrows in court circles. Yet once at the Houses of Parliament—at what would be King Edward VIII's only opening of Parliament—he determined to excel.

"Well do I recall the hush inside the House of Lords as I mounted the steps to the throne," he wrote. "As I looked out over the brilliant scene, my senses were suddenly assailed by an almost suffocating odour of mothballs given off by the colourful robes removed from storage for this formal airing. The smell was nauseating, and sitting there on the throne I could feel the pumping of my own heart."[11] *The Times* reported that his speech was exemplary: "One more page in the history of Parliament has been written. A young King had made his first speech from the Throne. Not alone the fact that his was a Throne by itself, but his whole Royal demeanour make one feel that 'in himself was all his state.'"[12] But under the surface there was disquiet. "I dined at the House of Commons," wrote Chips Channon, "and what was to have been a quiet snack developed into an acrimonious argument over the eternal problem—will the king marry Mrs. Simpson? MPs are like a lot of old concierges on this matter, and can think and talk of little else. But the situation is extremely serious, and the country is indignant; it does seem foolish that the monarchy, the oldest institution in the world after the papacy, should crash, as it may, over dear Wallis."[13]

Wallis, finding her infamy uncomfortable, was "beginning to be seriously disturbed by the reaction of people much closer to home."[14] She could no longer go out, even to the hairdresser's, without people stopping and staring at her. In spite of the continuing silence of the British press, the London circles in which she moved were well aware of the trumpeting foreign press. Wallis, for whom dignity was a supremely important element of her character, found these public embarrassments excruciating.

Over the next week, Edward took his part in the Armistice ceremonies and celebrations. It is a poignant irony that the king fulfilled what were to be his last ceremonial duties that autumn conscientiously and with flair. Whether deliberately or not, he made a regal last hurrah. His visit to inspect the Royal Navy's Home Fleet at Portland on November 12 and 13 was highly successful, while bearing his own stamp. He won the hearts of everyone present and turned the still-pouring rain to his advantage. Unlike Sir Samuel Hoare, the first lord of the Admiralty, Edward rejected a waterproof while inspecting men similarly drenched. Sir Samuel reported that it was a "small thing, but sailors take note of small things, and in this they saw a real difference between the politician and the Monarch."[15]

That evening the king displayed his finest talents, his charm and sense of camaraderie ensuring his absolute popularity. At a concert on board the aircraft carrier HMS *Courageous*, the vast underdeck was packed with thousands of sailors. Elbowing his way through the crowd, Edward wanted to see what was happening at the other end of the hall, whereupon he started a singsong to the accompaniment of a sailor's mouth organ. "When he came back to the platform, he made an impromptu speech that brought the house down," said Sir Samuel Hoare. "Then, a seaman in the crowd prompted three cheers for him, and there followed an unforgettable scene of the wildest and most spontaneous enthusiasm. Here, indeed, was the Prince Charming, who would win the hearts of all sorts of conditions of men and women and send a thrill through great crowds."[16]

"The king could be incredibly thoughtful and could be brilliant with the armed forces, especially the Navy, which he loved," said the Duke of Fragnito. "Once when, as the Prince of Wales, he went to Dartmouth on an inspection, a family cousin of ours was there and the prince knew of him. He asked to be introduced to him and, in the parade, pulled him out and walked up and down for a minute or two, then dismissed him. But it was to help my cousin; to show that he had the friendship of the royal family. We thought he was so kind to improve the position of the young cadet."[17]

The king's two days of naval inspection in Portland were, he later said, "good days." "Engrossed in inspecting the ships, talking to sailors and reminiscing with old shipmates, I was able to put aside for a few hours the burning issue that was pressing for decision."[18]

While away, Wallis had written to inform him that a British weekly news magazine, *Cavalcade*, had mentioned "the king's matter." The magazine also claimed that an unnamed London hostess had imposed a fine of five shillings on any guest discussing the king's "non-state activities" in front of the servants.[19] "They are selling *Cavalcade* in the streets of the City [of London]," Wallis wrote, alarmed. "Think of the harm among *that* class. Goddard says it is a libel. Something must be done at once. I hope your pain is better and that soon we will be able to be happy although now one's eyes are sad & worried. I long to be gay and open with everybody. Hiding is an awful life."[20]

On the evening that the king returned from Portland, he joined Wallis and Bessie at the Fort. "Now out of the darkening sky came a thunderclap, all the more shattering because of the unexpected quarter from which it came,"[21] Wallis recalled. The king was in a buoyant mood when he met Wallis and her aunt. After giving them a brief account of his trip, he excused himself, explaining that an urgent dispatch from the palace awaited his attention. His butler had informed him that there was a letter from Major Hardinge, who was anxious that the king read it straight away. Placed on top of the pile of red dispatch boxes, it glared: "Urgent and Confidential." The king, still cold to the bone from the naval review, but forgoing a longed-for bath, carefully read the letter from Hardinge instead. "An instant later," he wrote, "I was confronted by the most serious crisis of my life."[22]

> Buckingham Palace
> 13th November 1936
>
> Sir,
> With my humble duty,
> As your Majesty's Private Secretary, I feel it my duty to bring to your notice the following facts which have come to my knowledge, and which I *know* to be accurate …

Alec Hardinge went on to inform the king that the prime minister and senior members of the government were meeting that day to discuss the government's possible action in the light of "the serious situation which is developing" over the king's intentions towards Wallis. Hardinge also warned that the silence of the British press was not going to be maintained and would burst in a matter of days. Even more alarming, he told the king that the resignation of the government was an eventuality that could not be excluded and that, with the dissolution of Parliament and a general election, Hardinge had "reason to know" that the king would find it impossible to form a new government.

He ended by "*begging*" the king to insist that "Mrs. Simpson go abroad *without further delay*," and concluded: "Owing to the changing attitude of the Press the matter has become one of great urgency."[23] (This exigency, however, did not preclude Hardinge from adding in his postscript that he was going to High Wycombe after dinner for a shoot the following day, but that the Post Office would have his telephone number.)

The king's reaction was one of shock and anger. "Angry because of the way it was launched, with the startling suggestion that I send from my land, my realm, the woman I intended to marry."[24] Sensibly he resisted seizing the telephone, had a hot bath and, after dinner, read the letter again. As a conscientious private secretary, it was Hardinge's duty to alert the king to what was happening. Yet the messenger was a man whom

Edward now disliked and distrusted. He suspected that Hardinge was Baldwin's agent, querying: "Who would have told Alec Hardinge all this but the prime minister?"

"I was obviously in love," the king later recalled. "They had struck at the very roots of my pride. Only the most fainthearted would have remained unaroused by such a challenge. There was little sleep for me that night. This was not the crisis of a prince; it was the crisis of a king. And, because it was not my nature to watch and wait, I resolved to come to grips with Mr. Baldwin and the nebulous figures around him."[25]

Admirably, Edward carried his disturbing secret alone for two days, "pressing with deadly weight upon my every thought and action."[26] Of this gallant approach, not wanting to worry Wallis until absolutely necessary, Wallis recalled: "He always had an extraordinary capacity for keeping his inner tensions locked up inside his mind and heart."[27]

That Friday night, Edward played after-dinner cards with Wallis and Aunt Bessie, his gaiety temporarily restored with rounds of three-handed rummy. The next day, friends came for lunch at the Fort, oblivious to the immense strain the king was under. On Sunday afternoon, Wallis and Edward had been invited to the Duke and Duchess of Kent's for tea at Coppins. Excusing himself from lunch on the pretext of business with the librarian at Windsor, Edward left for a secret rendezvous with Sir Walter Monckton, reassuring Wallis that the car would return in an hour, so she could collect him from Windsor for their trip to tea.

Monckton was waiting for the king in his old rooms on the second floor of Windsor Castle. Edward handed him Hardinge's letter, which Monckton read slowly. The lawyer's expression turned to shock. He agreed with the king that it could not have been written without some discussion with Mr. Baldwin.

"The first thing I must do," said Edward, "is to send for the prime minister—tomorrow. I shall tell him that if, as would appear, he and the government are against my marrying Mrs. Simpson I am prepared to go."

"He will not like to hear that," said Walter gravely.

"I shall not find it easy to say."[28]

The king asked Monckton if he would act as his personal advisor and liaise with Downing Street; Sir Walter, who would prove a calm, expert support to the king, agreed.

Wallis and Edward went to tea with the Kents, which the king described as "an agreeable but brief visit."[29] But back at the Fort, it became impossible for him to conceal his burdens a moment longer. He took Wallis into his study and said: "A most serious thing has happened. I have kept it from you since Friday evening. But since it concerns you no less than it does me, you must know what is involved."[30] On his desk stood his red dispatch box, which he opened with a key. He took out the letter and handed it to Wallis. Asking her to read it alone, he left the room.[31]

After she had read the explosive missive, Wallis felt numb. She said: "This was the end I had always known in the back of my mind was bound to come." Realizing that the government's stance would trigger a crisis with the king, Wallis concluded: "Clearly, there was only one thing for me to do: it was to leave the country immediately as Hardinge had implored."[32]

When Edward returned a few moments later, Wallis told him that her departure would be in everyone's best interests. "You'll do no such thing," he told her. "I won't have it. This letter is an impertinence."[33]

"That may well be," replied Wallis. "But just the same, I think he's being sincere. He's trying to warn you that the government will insist that you give me up."

"They can't stop me. On the throne or off, I'm going to marry you."[34]

"Now it was my turn to beg him to let me go," Wallis later recalled. "Summoning all the powers of persuasion in my possession, I tried to convince him of the hopelessness of our position. For him to go on hoping, to go on fighting the inevitable, could only mean tragedy for him and catastrophe for me."[35]

Edward remained deaf to her entreaties. Taking Wallis's hand, he said: "I'm going to send for Mr. Baldwin to see me at the palace tomorrow. I'm going to tell him that if the country won't approve of our marrying, I'm ready to go."[36]

At this, the first mention between them of abdication, Wallis burst into tears. "David was determined that I stay," admitted Wallis. "He insisted that he needed me, and as a woman in love I was prepared to go through rivers of woe, seas of despair, and oceans of agony for him."[37] She had fallen in love with Edward and was now all too aware of the sacrifice this would entail. Yet the thought of the vicissitudes of her suffering never seemed to register with him. Surely, the greater act of love would have been for Edward to let Wallis go? Yet he did not seem to be able to see matters from any other perspective than his own. As far as he was concerned, *he* could not live without *her* and could not see that she might not be able to live with the consequences of his single-mindedness. Being blamed in perpetuity for stealing a beloved, popular king from his throne and almost destroying the British monarchy would prove to be a lifelong annihilating burden that Wallis was forced to bear.

Typically, Wallis later reproached herself—rather than Edward and his narcissistic neediness—for being deflected from her decision to leave England immediately. "I should have realised that this was the fateful moment—the last when any action of mine could have prevented the crisis."[38] She still could not fully comprehend that Edward was not going to let her go anywhere. Wallis also blamed herself for not realizing the true position of the king in the British constitutional system. Because she was accustomed to witnessing the apparent deference to his every wish, the fawning adulation that surrounded him, she was unaware of how vulnerable he really was and how little power he actually had vis-à-vis his ministers and Parliament. As a result, it was still inconceivable to her that his adoring public in Britain and the Empire would "ever allow anybody who had served and loved them so well to leave them."[39]

The king summoned Stanley Baldwin to a meeting at Buckingham Palace on Monday, November 16, at 6:30 p.m. In the meantime, he tried to get hold of Beaverbrook, only to discover that he was halfway across the Atlantic on the ocean liner *Bremen*. A chronic sufferer from asthma, Beaverbrook was heading for the drier, healing climes of Arizona. Edward managed to persuade his powerful ally to head back to Britain when the ship set sail from New York twelve days later.

* * *

In his audience with Baldwin, the king came straight to the point. "I understand that you and several members of the Cabinet have some fear of a constitutional crisis developing over my friendship with Mrs. Simpson?"

"Yes, Sir, that is correct." Baldwin went on to elaborate that he and his colleagues were disturbed and upset over the prospect of the king marrying a divorcée. Edward was taken aback because until that moment, the word marriage had not been mentioned between them. Baldwin, according to the king, then launched into a "dissertation concerning the moral outlook of the British people."[40]

"I believe I know what the people would tolerate and what they would not," the prime minister declared haughtily. "Even my enemies would grant me that."[41]

Edward tried to explain his personal philosophy to the rigidly traditional Baldwin: that he found it less sinful to wish to marry the woman he loved than to take a mistress. Baldwin pointed out that the position of the king's wife was different from the position of any other citizen in the country. It was part of the price the king had to pay. "Your wife becomes Queen; the Queen becomes the Queen of the country; and, therefore, in the choice of a Queen, the voice of the people must be heard,"[42] maintained the prime minister.

As dispassionately as he could, the king responded that marriage had become an indispensable condition of his continued existence, whether as king or as man. "I intend to marry Mrs. Simpson as soon as she is free to marry. If I could marry her as king well and good; I would be happy and in consequence a better king. But if on the other hand the government is opposed to the marriage, as you prime minister have given me reason to believe that it would, then I am prepared to go."[43]

"Sir, that is most grievous news, and it is impossible for me to make any comment on it today,"[44] said Stanley Baldwin, visibly startled.

Although no one could see it at the time, due to the blinding social stigma of Wallis being a divorcée, Edward's desire to have Wallis as his wife, rather than a mistress, was indeed decent and honorable. As he said, it would have been far more acceptable to the establishment for him to have been a known adulterer than to openly acknowledge the woman he loved and publicly commit to her. The subtext of his talk with the prime minister was: "I should have taken a mistress. A discreet house nearby, a key to a garden door, decorous associations—the relationship might be privately deplored, but it had notable precedents."[45]

Although an often befuddled thinker, Edward was ahead of his time in his views on marriage and divorce. He hated much of what he saw of conventional morality. As a young Prince of Wales, he had found the idea of an arranged marriage "altogether repugnant."[46] He determined early "that my choice of wife would be dictated not by considerations of State but by my own heart."[47] Under the Royal Marriages Act of 1772, as sovereign, he was actually free to marry anyone he liked except a Roman Catholic. It was Baldwin who said that marriage to Wallis Simpson would be impossible. Edward found it equally "outmoded and hypocritical" that no divorced person, even if the innocent party, could be received at court. He had set in mind that when he became king, he would end this form of social exclusion and ostracism. Yet the mores of the day were against him; his radical way of thinking was too avant-garde for the establishment, and unthinkable for the Church of England. (Indeed, the fact that the Church of England so abhorred divorce is something of an irony, since it had been founded upon an adulterous monarch's desire to end his own marriage.)

"I never underestimated the weight and authority of the group whose views the Prime Minister represented," he later wrote. "His senior Ministers, the men closest to him were deeply conservative, not alone in their politics but equally in their way of life. Behind them, I suspected, was a shadowy, hovering presence—the Archbishop of Canterbury. Curiously enough, I did not once see him throughout this period. He stood aside until the fateful fabric had been woven and the crisis was over. Yet from beginning to end I had a disquieting feeling that he was invisibly and noiselessly about."[48] Edward later said of Cosmo Lang that "he was a wicked man."[49]

Edward recognized that he had placed Cosmo Lang in a "quandary." Lang was preparing to use King Edward's coronation as a sounding board for an emotional call for Christian revival, where the main theme would be to attack divorce. "Thus the Archbishop and I were both fighting for a principle; I to marry someone who possessed all the womanly qualities that I desired in a consort, and he to prevent the marriage because the lady had been divorced."[50]

The king concluded his fateful meeting with Stanley Baldwin by agreeing that he would tell his mother about his decision and he gave the prime minister permission to tell one or two confidants. They agreed on Sir Samuel Hoare, the first lord of the Admiralty, and Duff Cooper, the war secretary. That evening, Lucy Baldwin wrote: "All the time the king was most charming but S said that king simply could not understand and he couldn't make him. S said that he felt a streak of almost madness. The king was obsessed by a woman & that was the long & short of it. On leaving, the king held Stanley's hand for a long time and there were almost tears in his eyes when he said goodbye."[51] The prime minister told his family: "The king's face wore at times such a look of beauty as might have lighted the face of a young knight who caught a glimpse of the Holy Grail."[52]

Later that evening, Baldwin bumped into Duff Cooper in the House of Commons. He told Duff about his meeting with the king. "As we separated he said that he was not at all sure that the Yorks would not prove the best solution," Duff recalled. "The king had many good qualities but not those which best fitted him for his post, whereas the Duke of York would be just like his father."[53]

After his meeting with Baldwin, Edward had the even more onerous task of telling his mother. Before dinner that evening, which he had prearranged with Queen Mary, he rang Wallis, anxiously waiting at Cumberland Terrace for news. For Wallis, it had been "a tense day," as she worried how the meeting with Baldwin would go. "David was always guarded in his telephone conversations," said Wallis. "Not only because of his innate reserve, but also because he could never be sure that someone was not listening in." Edward was even more noncommittal than usual with Wallis, presumably in a bid not to further alarm her. "The succeeding days were extraordinary," Wallis wrote. "I knew that momentous happenings were going on all around me. But to me, waiting alone Cumberland Terrace, these were only dimly outlined shadows."[54]

At 8:30 p.m. on the dot, the king arrived at Marlborough House in white tie and tails to dine with Queen Mary. "With maternal intuition she must have guessed that I had something serious to tell—indeed, I rather suspected that she knew what it was, for when I entered her boudoir, I found my sister Mary there as well." Grateful for Mary's presence, the king was thoroughly put out to find his sister-in-law Alice also included. Alice, Duchess of Gloucester, newly wedded to his brother Harry, was "almost a stranger."[55]

"He was in a great state of agitation,"[56] remembered Princess Alice. Accounts of what happened next differ. The king believed "my mother put both of us at our ease by announcing, with a reassuring smile, that Alice was tired and would go to bed directly after dinner."[57] However, Princess Alice recorded in her memoirs that after dinner the king "asked his mother if I could leave the room as he had a very serious matter to discuss. Queen Mary was discernibly angered by this request, but with many apologies she asked me to go, which of course I did."[58]

The four of them ate dinner, making polite conversation. Queen Mary expressed her pleasure that Edward had agreed to have the exterior of Buckingham Palace painted before the coronation the following spring. He conversed with his sister, Mary, a keen racehorse owner, about the Newmarket sales, Europe's premier sale for thoroughbred livestock. His sympathies lay with "poor Alice. Shy and retiring by nature, she had unwittingly sat down at my mother's table only to find herself caught up in the opening scene of one of the most poignant episodes in the annals of the British Royal Family." According to Edward, as the party got up to leave the table, Alice "after making her curtsy, almost fled from the room."[59]

The king retired with his sister and mother to Queen Mary's boudoir. Queen Mary reclined on her chaise longue (where she often polished her nails, of which she was proud), while she listened to family discourse.[60] "I told them of my love for Wallis and my determination to marry her and of the opposition of the Prime Minister and the Government to the marriage," Edward later wrote. "As I went on and they comprehended that even the alternative of abdication would not deter me from my course, I became conscious of their growing consternation that I could even contemplate giving up the Throne for my forebears."[61]

For Queen Mary, to whom "the Monarchy was something sacred and the Sovereign a personage apart," the concept that Edward could shirk his duty as king was appalling. Edward tried to explain that, far from shirking his duty, he could not carry out his duties as king without the "help and support" of Wallis. In this sense, it seemed to Edward that his duty was to abandon the throne, while to his mother, it was equally plain that his duty was to stay on it.

"All the while I was waiting for the right moment to make a request that I did not believe would be refused," recalled Edward. He asked his mother if she would formally receive Wallis, saying: "if you were to meet her, you would understand what she means to me and why I cannot give her up. I have waited a long time to find the person whom I wished to marry. For me the question now is not whether she is acceptable but whether I am worthy of her."[62]

Queen Mary refused her son's deeply held desire that she would accede to a proper introduction to Wallis. According to Diana Mosley: "She did not tell her son that she had given word to George V that she would never receive Mrs. Simpson—even though she had confided this to her lady-in-waiting, Countess Airlie, adding 'He's very much in love with her, poor boy.' "[63] Queen Mary also remained silent about the late king's prayer that the Duke of York should succeed him. Instead, she drew the harrowing evening to a close, wishing the king well for his next trip, a tour of the south Wales collieries.

The following day, Queen Mary sent her son a poignant little note: "As your mother, I must send you a line of true sympathy in the difficult position in which you are placed—I have been thinking of you all day, hoping you are making a wise decision for your future—I fear your visit to Wales will be trying in more ways than one, with this momentous action hanging over your head."[64]

The seventeenth of November was a day of flurried activity in

Parliament and at the palace. The king took his brother Bertie into his confidence. "Bertie was so taken aback by my news that in his shy way he could not bring himself to express his innermost feelings at the time," Edward said. "His genuine concern for me was mixed with the dread of having to assume the responsibilities of kingship."[65] He confessed his fears to his wife, Elizabeth, the Duchess of York, who immediately wrote to Queen Mary:

> My darling Mama,
> Bertie has just told me what has happened, and I feel quite overcome with horror & emotion. My first thought was of you, & your note, just arrived as I was starting to write to you, was very helpful. One feels so helpless against such obstinacy.

She asked her mother-in-law if she and Bertie could visit her the following morning, before signing off: "God help us all to be calm & wise. Your devoted daughter in law, Elizabeth."[66]

Meanwhile, the king sought the counsel of the only two men in the Cabinet whose advice he felt he could trust: Duff Cooper and Sir Samuel Hoare. "I was more nervous of the meeting than I had even been of my first encounter with Gandhi," Hoare later admitted. However, he stuck to his guns, saying he would not be drawn into the king's corner, insisting that the country would be fully behind Baldwin in opposing the match. Of the meeting, Hoare noted: "Decision irrevocable. No single middle-aged man willingly stays in a tomb."[67]

Duff Cooper listened patiently to the king's arguments: that he could not be an effective king without Wallis and that if he could not marry her and remain king, he must abdicate. Duff seems to have been the only person among the king's circle of friends and confidants to emphasize "that the whole blame for the catastrophe if it occurred would be placed on Wallis both now and in history."[68] In response, the king "seemed a little shaken by this and said that it would be very unfair. I agreed, but repeated that it would be so."[69]

It seems inconceivable that Edward had not fully considered that the woman he professed to love beyond all else would pay the highest price for his decision. "My father did give him pause, as this certainly had not struck him," said John Julius Norwich. "But it did not give him pause enough. He was incredibly stupid. You don't need to be intelligent to be king—you have many intelligent advisors—but you do have to put up with your life. This Edward refused to do."[70]

Duff then asked the king if he had considered what sort of life his would be. "I had always thought that the life of an ex-monarch was the most miserable that a man could lead," recalled Duff. "Minor royalties could fall into the position of private citizens but those who had once been rulers could never find a normal place in society."[71] He quoted the case of the King of Spain. "Oh, I shan't be like Alfonso," Edward exclaimed. "He was kicked out. I shall go of my own accord."[72]

Duff tried to persuade Edward to calm things down by taking his time. He suggested that he dismiss the idea of getting married before the coronation and wait a year. Why didn't he go through with the coronation and then go to India for the durbar? If he ostentatiously separated himself from Wallis—who should maybe go to America but definitely leave the country—in a year's time, his position would be immensely strengthened. The people would see that he had done his best to get on without her but that he had found that impossible. Sympathy for him would then be higher.

Again, Edward stuck to his own moral code, which had logic and emotional resonance. He felt it would be disingenuous and disloyal to his people to partake in such an official solemn ceremony as the coronation, while keeping the whole truth of the situation "up his sleeve."[73] Though blinkered, in some ways his stance was honorable. Of the religious service, he said: "The king is anointed with holy oil; he takes the Sacrament; and as Defender of the Faith he swears an oath to uphold the doctrines of the Church of England, which does not approve divorce." For him to have gone through the coronation ceremony while harboring a secret intention to marry would have meant being "crowned with a lie on my lips."[74]

"Whatever the cost to me personally," he later said, "I was determined, before I would think of being crowned, to settle once and for all the question of my right to marry."[75]

Aware that the British press would not remain silent much longer, Edward asked Duff Cooper if he could not make some sort of statement to appeal to his subjects. Duff considered this a tricky undertaking. "Although there had been a great deal of gossip the average man in the street still knew nothing," Duff recalled. "And, frankly, it would come to him as a tremendous shock to learn that the King of England intended to marry an American lady who had been twice married already." As he said this, the king "winced at the word twice and said that the first marriage hadn't really counted. What, if anything, he meant by that I didn't enquire."[76]

Meanwhile, Queen Mary, bewildered and still stunned by her son's confession, received the prime minister at Marlborough House. "Well, Mr. Baldwin!" she exclaimed, hastening into the room, her hands held out before her in a gesture of despair and adopting a funny little voice: "*This* is a pretty kettle of fish."[77]

That evening, Wallis dined at Emerald Cunard's. Chips Channon declared it a "pompous, manqué dinner." During the meal, Emerald slipped a crumpled note into Chips's hand. It was an anonymous missive that she had received, which read: "You old bitch, trying to make up to Mrs. Simpson, in order to curry favour with the king." According to Chips, "Emerald was frightened, yet rather flattered. It was an educated hand-writing."[78]

After dinner, Chips sat with Wallis—whom he described in his diary as looking "very well tonight, like a Vermeer, in a Dutch way"—and with Prince Paul and Princess Olga of Yugoslavia. The conversation turned to tiaras, and "Princess Olga said hers gave her a headache. Wallis Simpson laughingly added: 'Well, anyway, a tiara is one of the things I shall never have. . . .' There was an embarrassed pause. Diana [Cooper] is convinced that Wallis and the king will marry in secret, immediately after the Coronation. I half hope so, half believe it is fated."[79]

Meanwhile, Edward left London for what would be the last official engagement of his reign: a tour of the depressed coalfields of south Wales.

This was a bold and seemingly deliberately provocative move; he was not going to be told what to do by Stanley Baldwin. As the king's train rattled through the night, he lay in his berth reflecting on the turmoil that he knew gripped Whitehall. "Yet, I was at peace with myself," he recalled. "My spiritual struggle was over. I had passed the climax. The public struggle remained, and in many ways it would be more pitiless. But I had declared myself."[80]

7

The Last Hour

In 1936 there was still mass long-term unemployment and widespread poverty in Britain. This was the year that George Orwell lived among the poor of Wigan (as he famously chronicled in *The Road to Wigan Pier*). The areas worst affected were those associated with traditional heavy industries, such as south Wales and the north of England. Years of protest and hunger marches now culminated in the epic Jarrow Crusade of October 1936, when two hundred men marched from County Durham to London to deliver a petition to Baldwin's government, pleading for help and asking for the reestablishment of industry following the closure of the area's main shipyard.

On November 18 the king travelled to the impoverished Welsh heartlands of the Rhondda and Monmouth Valleys. Against a background of slag heaps and shuttered, empty shops, thousands of people turned out in their best clothes, hung Union flags and stood for hours in the cold on roadsides or at abandoned works to see their sovereign. Edward was given a euphoric and rapturous welcome. A few years earlier, when, as Prince of Wales, he had visited the same region, a banner had greeted him with the words "Welcome to Our Prince." Now it read: "We Need Your Help." Over the next few days, Pathé newsreels praised the king for "bringing the whole problem [of unemployment] out of the shadows and into the floodlight of world attention."[1] The "People's Prince" had become the "People's King." Unloved by the establishment and a source of growing concern for the government, he was plainly adored by the masses. As with his visit to the Home Fleet, the occasion bought out the consummate qualities of the king. Edward moved amongst the crowds, speaking to dozens of men directly, showing open concern and sympathy for their plight. He deviated from the official schedule, ending his already long day late because he insisted on making a detour. After visiting a labor exchange, he called at the dismantled Bessemer Steel Works in Dowlais. Years earlier, it had employed over nine thousand men; now three-quarters of the workforce was unemployed and the plant derelict. Hundreds of men awaited him, sitting on piles of twisted, rusting metal. When the king arrived, they stood and sang the hymn "Crugybar." Their monarch listened, bareheaded, clearly intensely moved. It was here that he turned to an official and uttered the now infamous words: "Terrible, terrible. Something must be done."

Edward later explained that he had made this bold declaration in order to help "repair the ravages of the dreadful inertia that had gripped the region."[2] The following day, though uncertain of his own future, he promised the unemployed workers: "You may be sure that all I can do for you I will." Afterwards, he explained that "the statement was the minimum humanitarian response that I could have made to what I had seen," and was pleased that the liberal press took approving note. But in certain political circles, the king's comments were seen as causing the government further embarrassment and shining a light on its unwillingness to help. Years later, Edward spoke of his conflict with Baldwin over his visits. "Mr. Baldwin was suddenly conscious of the fact that he and his government had actually done very little to alleviate the plight of the unemployed of which there were thousands at that time."[3]

Alec Hardinge was nonetheless pleased to report to the prime minister that "the Welsh visit went extremely well. The reception was everywhere splendid and there was no discordant note."[4] That the king was genuinely moved by what he saw was never in doubt. Edward told Queen Mary that the trip had been "very strenuous and heart-rending but the spirit of these poor people is marvellous."[5] His authentic reaction, his anger on their behalf, his sympathy and his public charisma enhanced his already widespread popularity. "Nothing that ever happened afterwards ever altered the love that ordinary people bore King Edward VIII," wrote Diana Mosley. "It was a fact, sometimes awkward, that had to be taken into account every time his future and in particular his place of residence was under discussion."[6]

While Edward was away in south Wales, Wallis had been invited to lunch at Claridge's by Esmond Harmsworth. After politely chatting, he asked her if she and Edward had considered a morganatic marriage. "His directness quite took my breath away," said Wallis, who then asked the press baron to explain exactly what a morganatic marriage was. ("It was one whereby a king or a prince could contract a legal marriage with a woman outside the royal circle—with his wife, however, not sharing her husband's position and titles,"[7] she was told.) The idea had been mooted by Winston Churchill in discussions with Harmsworth's father, Lord Rothermere. "I realise, Wallis, that this is not very flattering to you. But I am sure that you are one with us in desiring to keep the king on the throne,"[8] Esmond continued. He urged Wallis to raise the idea with the king, leaving her with the notion that a suitable title for her might be the Duchess of Lancaster, an ancient and subsidiary title and in keeping with the alias used by the duke when traveling abroad.[9] The scheme would become known as the "Cornwall plan" because Churchill's original idea was that Wallis could be styled the Duchess of Cornwall.[10]

Wallis felt "completely at sea" after the lunch. Her position in society was a constant worry to her. Harold Nicolson reported that Lady Colefax had a heart-to-heart with Wallis "and found her really miserable. All sorts of people had come to her reminding her of her duty and begging her to leave the country. 'They do not understand,' she said, 'that if I did so, the king would come after me regardless of anything. They would then get their scandal in a far worse form than they are getting it now.'"[11]

The evening that the king returned from Wales, the Channons held a party at their London mansion. Tout le monde attended, including Prince Paul and Princess Olga of Yugoslavia, the Duke and Duchess of

Kent, Duff and Lady Cooper, and Wallis and Edward. Honor Channon sat next to the king, "who ate a lot, drank claret and laughed a lot."[12] The dining room was "a cascade of beauty," according to Chips; "the table seemed literally to swim with Dresden . . . tiaras nodded, diamonds sparkled, the service was excellent and conversation flowed."[13]

Wallis's good influence was again illustrated when Prince Paul asked the king if he would telephone the Spanish infanta, Beatrice, who was staying at Claridge's, to offer his condolences. Earlier that day her second son, Don Alonso, had died in an air accident while fighting with Franco's nationalists in Spain. "Can't I do it in the morning?" pleaded the king. Prince Paul appealed to Wallis, who turned to Edward: "No, now, to please me, Sir." Edward dutifully followed Chips into his study, where he found the number and put the call through to the infanta.[14]

Duff Cooper recalled of the evening: "The king was in the highest spirits. He talked to me about recruiting, about the Artillery Mess and about the BBC. I explained to him the measure of its independence. 'I'll change that,' he said. 'It will be the last thing I do before I go.' He said this quite loud and with a laugh, as though he were looking forward to going." Duff took Wallis aside at the end of the evening in a bid to persuade her to leave the country. She told Duff that the king wouldn't hear of it and had said that wherever she went, he would follow.[15]

The following day, an anxious and still-shocked Duchess of York wrote to Queen Mary from Wilton House near Salisbury, where she was a guest of the Pembroke family. "Staying here, in a very normal English shooting party, it seems almost incredible that David contemplates such a step," she wrote. "Every day I pray to God that he will see reason and not abandon his people. It is a great strain having to talk & behave as if nothing was wrong during these difficult days—especially as I do not think that anybody here dreams of what is worrying all of us . . . it is truly the sword of Damocles again. Ever your loving daughter-in-law, Elizabeth."[16]

That evening, Wallis and Aunt Bessie joined the king at the Fort. According to Wallis, "he looked exhausted and, more than that, harassed; the tension of the inner struggle was obviously eating into his soul, and I felt that the appalling strain he was under could not be allowed to go on." With "many misgivings," she brought up the idea of a morganatic marriage.[17]

"My first reaction to the morganatic marriage proposal was one of distaste," Edward recalled. "The term itself repelled me as one of the least graceful that might be applied to the relations between men and women."[18] But, as the weekend wore on, and the king's options diminished, he rallied to the idea. On Monday he summoned Esmond Harmsworth to see if he would put the idea to Baldwin. The king had decided that "even without the formal symbolism of the two gilt thrones side by side," Wallis "with her American charm and energy" would skillfully fulfil the role of king's consort.[19] At this stage, he was keen to find a way to marry while on the throne without precipitating a political struggle. Buoyed up by his popularity following his tour of south Wales, the king was also having second thoughts about the need for abdication. The next day, the *Daily Mail* published a leader with praise for the king "so fulsome and exaggerated as to be almost dangerous," according to Chips Channon's diaries.[20] Baldwin told Cosmo Lang that "on his return," the king "seemed to waver."[21]

Harmsworth visited Duff Cooper after dinner, at 11 p.m., to discuss the idea. It was proposed that the king should confer a ducal title on Wallis; that he should marry her but she should not become queen. Duff reiterated his view that the couple ought to wait awhile. He did not think that the public would accept the king marrying in such seeming haste, in the short period between the end of April, when Wallis's divorce came through, and the coronation on 12 May. He stressed the importance of a year's separation. Harmsworth agreed. The next step was to put the idea to the prime minister.

Unlike the bullish king, Wallis was keenly attuned to the complexities of the characters involved. She immediately sensed danger, fearing Edward could be playing into Baldwin's hands. "David was obviously allowing his better judgment to be swept aside by his impatience to break the deadlock," she wrote later. "I began to suspect that the whole idea, however well meant, would turn out in reality to be a trap. He would be putting his head on Mr. Baldwin's chopping block."[22] She understood that the formal presentation of the morganatic proposal would give the prime minister the constitutional right to proffer the king advice, and that Edward would be given little choice but to take it.

Wallis's fears proved to be well founded. When, on November 25, the king met with the prime minister to discuss the marriage proposal, Baldwin appeared determined to derail the scheme. He said he found the idea of a morganatic marriage repugnant. (Indeed, the mere fact that it had been proposed by Harmsworth, via Winston Churchill, was probably enough to make him reject it out of hand. Baldwin regarded Harmsworth as "a disgustingly conceited fellow" and told the king that Harmsworth's paper the *Daily Mail* was "the worst judge in England of what people were thinking."[23]) Besides, said Baldwin, the British public would never tolerate it. "I believe many people would be sorry to see me go," Edward responded wistfully. The prime minister offered to put the idea before the Cabinet—at the same time expressing his private view that Parliament would never pass such a bill—and also the leaders of the Dominions. The king gave his assent. "Many were to argue afterwards that this was a tactical error on my part of the first magnitude," Edward later confessed. "The automatic effect of my action was to deliver the imperial passkeys into Mr. Baldwin's hands; once inside the door, he carefully locked me out."[24]

Over lunch at the Fort, Edward updated his ally Max Beaverbrook on the meeting. Beaverbrook was immediately against the idea, suspicious of giving Parliament the power in the decision. He advocated presenting to the British people what he called the "king's case for the marriage." Yet it was too late: Edward had already handed all bargaining tools to the prime minister.

Beaverbrook was right about Baldwin's influence over Parliament. Before his meeting with the king, the prime minister had sounded out the opposition. There was a strong emotional attachment among many socialists to Edward due to his long-term stand on poverty and unemployment. Francis Williams, editor of the *Daily Herald*, declared: "Good luck to the king, and let him marry whoever he pleases."[25] Yet there was a belief that many Labour voters would not accept Mrs. Simpson. "Our people won't 'ave it," claimed the trade union leader Ernest Bevin.[26] Buoyed by this cross-party support, when Baldwin raised the matter with the Cabinet on November 27, the morganatic marriage proposal was overwhelmingly rejected.

The following morning, the king waited anxiously for the arrival of the red box containing the confidential minutes of the Cabinet meeting. He opened it with the gold key that had been his father's. "But the solitary paper that I found inside, purporting to discuss the momentous decisions of the day, was blank except for a perfunctory paragraph relating to the carriage of arms to Spain."[27]

Beaverbrook, on learning about the Cabinet meeting, hurried to Buckingham Palace, where he told the king: "Sir, you have put your head on the execution block. All that Baldwin has to do now is swing the axe."[28] Beaverbrook advised against sending telegrams to seek the consent of the Dominions. "I am Canadian, I know the Dominions," he said. "Their answer will be a swift and emphatic no."[29] He also conveyed that he understood all too clearly how Baldwin would frame the question of the hour in his communiqués: "Do you recommend the king's marriage to a woman with two husbands living, or do you recommend Abdication?"[30]

Wallis, meanwhile, waited with Aunt Bessie at 16 Cumberland Terrace, desperate for news, the tension and uncertainty becoming unbearable. "These complex, and for David, desperate maneuverings, were scarcely known to me," she said. "What little I knew at the time came to me in bits and snatches from David, by now seemingly withdrawn even from me. But as that terrible week wore on, even I, remote as I was from the center of the storm, could feel the mounting menace in the very atmosphere."[31] Although the British press still remained silent on the king's relationship with Wallis, and not a word had been breathed about the breach between the king and his ministers, Wallis felt that "it was as if some mysterious and silent means of communication was carrying the story of the hidden crisis into ever-widening circles of the British public."[32]

Tensions were justly running high in palace circles too. The Duke and Duchess of York similarly awaited their fate based on the king's decision.

On November 23, the duchess wrote to Edward in a letter marked "Private":

> Darling David,
> Please read this. Please be kind to Bertie when you see him, because he loves you and minds terribly what happens to you. I wish that you could realize how loyal & true he is to you, and you have no idea how hard it has been for him lately. I know that he is fonder of you than anybody else, & as his wife, I must write & tell you this. I am terrified for him—so DO help him. And for God's sake don't tell him that I have written—we both uphold you always, E.[33]

During this time, unable to venture out due to the constant gawping of strangers, Wallis and Bessie became virtual prisoners at Cumberland Terrace. Bessie would stand at the window and peer through the curtains at people staring up at the house. Worse, Wallis began to receive threatening hate mail, some signed, some anonymous. Already feeling like a "hunted animal" she was understandably alarmed when the king informed her—by note—that he had received news of a rumored plot to blow up her house. It was agreed that he would take them to the safety of Fort Belvedere, and that her staff should not disclose her whereabouts.

Early that evening, the king's car came to collect them. Wallis and her canine companion, Slipper, sat in the back with Edward, who squeezed her hand reassuringly. "As the lights of London receded into the distance behind us, little did I know that this was the last time I was to see them for nearly three years,"[34] she recalled.

The moment she entered the Fort, Wallis was hit by the tense change in atmosphere: the servants' faces looked strained; the telephone was constantly ringing. Wallis realized with sadness that this "was no longer the enchanted Fort; it was the Fort beleaguered."[35]

That weekend, Belvedere was abuzz with the constant comings and goings of palace aides, government advisors and couriers. The king was either on the phone or locked in his study. He had five private lines installed, one direct to Lord Beaverbrook.[36] On Sunday afternoon, after a lengthy conference with Sir Walter Monckton and the king's solicitor, George Allen, Edward took Wallis into the library and told her the truth of the situation. The government, he said, would not approve a morganatic marriage, and he did not want to follow Winston Churchill's and Duff Cooper's advice to temporarily forsake her in order to be crowned king, and to reunite with her after a suitable length of time.

"I was crushed," Wallis recalled. "I felt unutterably sorry for him in the dilemma into which his love for me had brought him so early in what had promised to be a glorious reign."[37]

The shock of Edward's stance triggered a huge physical and psychological collapse. Desperate and forlorn, Wallis was ordered to rest, there being genuine fears for her health and her heart. According to Honor Channon, Wallis sent her a "charming note" during this time in which she described having "a sort of break-down."[38] She also wrote two letters to her closest girlfriends, the first to Sibyl Colefax:

> Dear Sibyl,
>
> I have been put to bed for a week's isolation policy. I am very tired with and of it all—and my heart resents the strain—so I am to lie quiet. I am planning quite by myself to go away for a while. I think everyone here would like that—except one person perhaps—but I am planning a clever means of escape. After a while my name will be forgotten by the people and only two people will suffer instead of a mass of people who aren't interested anyway in individual feelings but only the workings of a system. I have decided to risk the result of leaving because it is an uncomfortable feeling to remain stopping in a house where the hostess has tired of you as a guest. I shall see you before I fold my tent.
>
> Much love,
>
> Wallis[39]

To her American friend Foxie Gwynne, she wrote more openly:

> Darling Foxie,
> Everything is wrong and going more wrong—and I am so tired of it all. Even the heart has been acting up and I have been put to bed for a week's rest—no calls, no callers. The US press has practically ruined two people's lives however—they go on pounding away—it does get one's morale down. I think I shall remove myself when I am well enough for a small trip and give it all time to die down—perhaps returning when that d---d crown has been firmly placed. I want to see you so much and hear your news which must be cheery and happy. So when I can I'll ring you.
> Much love, Wallis[40]

Wallis had finally made the decision to remove herself from the scene, regardless of Edward's protestations. She needed a few days' bed rest to recover her health and garner strength. Sadly for her, events were moving too quickly for her to gain control of the situation.

On December 2, Edward motored to London to meet Stanley Baldwin at Buckingham Palace. There he was told, unequivocally, that the government would not sanction the necessary legislation for a morganatic marriage and that the support of the Dominions would not be forthcoming. More blows were to follow. That same day, an inflammatory speech was delivered at the normally sedate Diocesan Conference in Bradford. The bishop of Bradford, the Right Reverend A. W. F. Blunt, gave a sermon lamenting that the king was not a more diligent churchgoer. In his dissertation on the religious nature of the coronation ceremony, he made some highly pointed remarks about Edward: "The king is a man like any other—if he is to do his duty properly. . . . We hope that he is aware of this need. Some of us wish that he gave more positive signs of such awareness."[41] This was taken to mean that the king needed divine guidance in his marriage.

The bishop's open criticism, in such a charged atmosphere, proved to be the catalyst. For weeks, the editor of the *Times*, Geoffrey Dawson—whom Edward regarded as an archenemy and in the pocket of Stanley Baldwin—had had a leading article ready to be printed, demanding that the king reply to the claims made about him in the foreign press. When Edward heard that the *Times* was also about to come out with a fierce attack on Wallis, he asked Baldwin to get it stopped. Baldwin replied that he could not control the press, but offered to pass on the king's request to the editor.

In his meeting with Baldwin, Edward had made it clear that he would not contemplate remaining on the throne without Wallis by his side as his wife. "Whether on the Throne or not, Mr. Baldwin, I shall marry; and however painful the prospect, I shall, if necessary, abdicate in order to do so."[42] Edward later wrote of this decision: "My whole life—the ordered, sheltered existence that I had known since birth—had blown up and was disintegrating. And in the chaos around me I had three distinctive desires: to dampen the uproar if I could; to avoid the responsibility of splitting the nation and jeopardising the Monarchy on the issue of my personal happiness; and to protect Wallis from the full blast of sensationalism about to overwhelm us both."[43]

The king arrived back at the Fort for a late dinner with Wallis and Bessie. "One look at his face told me that the worst had happened," Wallis said. Characteristic of his chivalrous nature, not wishing to alarm Aunt Bessie, Edward made no mention at the dining table of that afternoon's earth-shattering events. After dinner he suggested that he and Wallis take some air. It was a cold, foggy night, and as they walked up and down the flagstone terrace, Edward told Wallis that "it has been a bad day" and that there had been an emphatic rejection of the morganatic marriage.[44] "A damp fog had rolled up across from Virginia Water; peering in the direction of London, I could almost feel the vibration of the Fleet Street presses," he said. "So it comes to this. Either I must give you up or abdicate. And I don't intend to give you up."[45]

Wallis reiterated over and over that abdication was unthinkable. That his place was at the head of his people. "He was scarcely listening. His mind was far away, Now, with everything on the brink of disaster, with the Throne tottering and David beyond my reaching, I realized that the time had come for me to take matters into my own hands to the extent that I could."[46] Standing in the darkness, Wallis calmly and firmly told him that she was going to leave the country. She had already stayed too long; she wished that she had gone after he had showed her Hardinge's letter. To her great relief, in fear of what the next day's press onslaught would bring, Edward did not try to prevent her. "It will be hard for me to have you go," he finally said. "But it would be harder still to have you stay. Your situation here would become harrowing beyond belief. You are right to go. I must handle this in my own way, alone."[47]

Edward later wrote: "I suppose that every actor in the Abdication drama has his own idea of where and when the real turning point occurred. For me, scanning across the years, it came, I am sure, that evening on the flagstones at Fort Belvedere. For in agreeing with Wallis that it would be better for her to leave Great Britain I must have unconsciously made up my mind that the struggle to save my Throne was hopeless, and that in the end, come what may I would follow her."[48] That night, he "felt grievously responsible for the trouble and sorrow that" his love "had brought down upon her head."[49]

In the early hours, unable to sleep, Edward rang Max Beaverbrook. "He told me that he meant to retire into private life," recalled Beaverbrook. "If this statement was final, there was no sense in carrying on the struggle. But I did not believe it was final. For though the king often spoke of abdication he always indicated that he was anxious to stay on the throne."[50]

The following day, Beaverbrook and Churchill busied themselves in a campaign to secure favorable press for the king. "When the lines of battle were clearly drawn, the newspaper support for the king was certainly more powerful in the country than the opposition," said Lord Beaverbrook. "*The Times*, *Morning Post*, *Daily Telegraph* and *Daily Herald* were against him. On the other hand, the *Express* and the *Mail* groups were strongly for him, along with some of the provincial papers."[51]

Although Wallis thought that she "was braced for the blow," she was unprepared for what faced her in the papers on her morning breakfast tray on December 3. "There in black type," in newspaper after newspaper, "were the words 'Grave Constitutional Issue,' 'Grave Crisis' and 'Constitutional Crisis.' The dam was broken; I felt unnerved; self reproach flooded through me. Everything that David and I had created between us—everything that David in his tenderness had seen in me—was about to be rendered public and common."[52]

The king himself felt "really shocked" by the press. "Could this be the king or was I some common felon?" he wondered. "The press creates, the press destroys. All my life I had been the passive clay that it had enthusiastically worked into the hackneyed image of a Prince Charming. Now it had whirled around me and was bent upon demolishing the natural man who had been there all the time."[53]

Wallis dressed hastily and sought Edward, whom she found at his writing desk in the drawing room. Hearing her enter, he quickly pushed aside the heap of newspapers at his elbow. She told him that she had already seen them all. As he took her in his arms, Wallis said: "Dearest David, I am sorry I've done this to you."[54] They decided that she should leave that day and discussed Wallis going to stay with Katherine and Herman Rogers in the South of France. True intimates, the Rogers responded immediately to the request for sanctuary: "of course you must come to us."[55] Bessie would stay behind, then return to America.

Edward insisted that his lord-in-waiting, Lord Brownlow, accompany Wallis to France. Wallis was well acquainted with Perry Brownlow and his wife, Kitty, as they were frequent visitors to the Fort. Anticipating that every road from Belvedere was being watched by the press, the king arranged for Ladbroke, his chauffeur, to drive Wallis's Buick to Newhaven and board the night ferry to Dieppe as a decoy. Inspector Evans of Scotland Yard was to accompany Ladbroke, and together they would then meet up with Perry Brownlow and Wallis in France. Perry would come to the Fort later that evening under the cover of darkness to chaperone Wallis. But on "the one day in history when the king really needed Lord Brownlow, he was nowhere to be found," remembered Diana Vreeland, who was related to Perry. "*Finally*, they found him in a Turkish bath. He'd been a bit of a toot, and was having a good old massage when the message came through: would he please go directly to Fort Belvedere, bringing a change of clothing?"[56]

Unable to return to Cumberland Terrace, which since rumors of the king's abdication had broken had been besieged by a baying, stone-throwing mob,[57] Wallis nervously sent a maid to fetch some clothes on her behalf. She then summoned George Allen to her bedroom, to draw up a new will.

Before leaving the Fort, Wallis discussed with Edward a final plan which it was hoped might keep him on the throne. Because of his huge popular appeal across the country, Wallis implored the king to broadcast a personal appeal to his people and put his case directly to them. The plan was to make the broadcast the following day, after the king had spoken with the prime minister. His plan was to then withdraw from the country for a period to allow public opinion to form on the subject of his marriage, delegating his authority to a council of state. Wallis, however, wanted the king to simply tell the people in the broadcast that he was giving her up. With help from Sir Walter Monckton and Allen, Edward drafted his "appeal to the hearth and the home." Sadly, it was never delivered. It contained the following paragraph: "Neither Mrs. Simpson nor I have ever sought to insist that she should be queen. All we desired was that our married happiness should carry with it a proper title and dignity for her, befitting my wife."[58]

Chips Channon wrote on this day: "The country and the Empire now know that their Monarch, their young King-Emperor, their adored Apollo, is in love with an American twice divorced, whom they believe to be an adventuress. The whole world recoils from the shock; but very few know that she is a woman of infinite charm, gentleness, courage and loyalty, whose influence upon the King, until now, has been highly salutary."[59]

At dusk on December 3, Lord Brownlow arrived in his Rolls-Royce, driven by his chauffeur. He found the king "rather pathetic, tired, overwrought, and evidently dreading Wallis's departure, almost like a small boy being left behind at school for the first time."[60] Wallis, the king, Aunt Bessie, Perry Brownlow and Ulick Alexander, the king's courtier who had made the arrangements for the trip to France, sat around the supper table looking desolate. Too fraught and miserable to eat, they ran over the arrangements for Wallis's departure. Brownlow recorded the scene: "Wallis deeply oppressed, the king nervous and, as ever, over-attentive to all of us, such as mixing the salad, pouring out soda-water, and lighting cigarettes for all of us."[61] After dinner, the king took Perry aside to thank him, and to entreat him to take care of his precious consignment. This, Lord Brownlow realized once they were en route, was indeed extremely precious in other ways: Wallis was traveling with part of her jewelry collection, estimated to be worth around £100,000 (£2 million today).

"Our last moments together were infinitely sad and forlorn," the king later wrote. "Nothing was said between us as to when or where we should meet again."[62] Though her last moments at the Fort were hurried, for Wallis "they were nonetheless poignant," she recalled. "I think we all had a sense of tragedy, or irretrievable finality. As for me, this was the last hour of what had been for me the enchanted years. I was sure I would never see David again."[63]

Almost as difficult as saying good-bye to Edward was Wallis's parting from Aunt Bessie. Bessie Merryman had loyally supported Wallis throughout everything, and Wallis felt that she was now leaving her behind "in the forlorn wreckage of my life."[64] They had decided that it would be best for Wallis not to take Slipper, her adored cairn. He would stay with the king. "In the bitter days that followed, I was grateful for his companionship," said Edward. "He followed me around the Fort, he slept in my bed; he was the mute witness to my meetings with the prime minister."[65]

At 7 p.m., Wallis came out of the front door of the Fort, as the chauffeur was packing away her bags. Perry discreetly moved to the far side of the car to give Wallis and Edward a last minute together. "David embraced me. His parting words were: 'I don't know how it's all going to end. It will be some time before we can be together again. You must wait for me no matter how long it takes. I shall never give you up.'"[66] Edward then "leant across to her to get one last touch of her hand," observed Brownlow. "There were tears in his eyes and on his cheeks, and his voice was shaking."[67]

Edward stood on the terrace and watched the dimmed lights of the Rolls disappear as it took the back drive down towards Virginia Water. Before Aunt Bessie left for Cumberland Terrace, she pleaded with the king not to abdicate. "Wallis will be blamed, perhaps even more than you," she told him. "She is bewildered. This terrible uproar has frightened her and not for herself alone. You can always marry someone else, but you can never again be king."[68]

Wallis, meanwhile, had left Edward one last note of instructions, written on Fort Belvedere paper. A servant delivered it to the king. "Be calm with B[aldwin]," she beseeched, "but tell the country tomorrow I am lost to you but Perry and myself can discreetly manage. We will let Bateman* know. A big big oo'oh."[69]

As Wallis was ferried to the Sussex coast, sitting in silence, trying to gather herself, the king motored to London to have his late-night meeting with the prime minister at Buckingham Palace. The king immediately "thrusted" the idea of the broadcast at Baldwin. The prime minister, who seemed startled, told the king that constitutionally he could not broadcast to the nation without the consent of his ministers. He would, however, put it to them the following morning, though again, he said it was unlikely that their consent would be forthcoming.

As the king left Buckingham Palace, a small crowd gathered to cheer him, which lifted his spirits. There was a sense that most people wanted to keep Edward VIII, "the People's King," on any terms, much to the horror of the establishment, the Church, the royal court and sections of the Tory press. The following morning, the *Daily Mail* led with the headline "The People Want Their King." A few people even expressed a liking for the fact that Wallis was not drawn from the ranks of the aristocracy. "It is character that Counts here, & in Great Britain, not a Tytle [*sic*]," a woman from south Wales wrote to the king.[70]

That night, the House of Commons was "astir as it had probably never been before," wrote the MP Chips Channon. "Baldwin rose amidst cheers

---

* William Bateman was the king's private telephone operator at Buckingham Palace, who had been instructed to give priority to all calls and messages from Mrs. Simpson.

and said that as yet there was no constitutional crisis, and that it was inexpedient to say more. Winston Churchill then got up, his voice breaking, and with tears in his eyes, said he hoped nothing irrevocable would be done before reflection, and the din of cheering was impressive."[71] Baldwin "answered noncommittally, but the sentiment in the House of Commons is pro-Government and pro-Baldwin," added Channon. "It feels that the king has no right to plunge us into this crisis and feels the Dominions would not stand Wallis as queen, even if England did."[72]

In a very uncharacteristic outburst, reflecting the high emotions of the situation, Winston Churchill shouted at Baldwin: "You won't be satisfied until you've broken him, will you?"[73]—and then left the chamber.

The exhausted king then had to go to Marlborough House to see his mother. She had written him a note at 2.30 that afternoon: "Darling David, this news in the papers is very upsetting, especially as I have not seen you for 10 days," and signing off: "Ever yr loving Mama, Mary."[74] She asked Edward to call in on her that day.

At Marlborough House, the king found the Duke and Duchess of York dining with Queen Mary. As simply as he could, Edward explained the reasons for his apparent aloofness: "I have no desire to bring you and the family into all this. This is something I must handle alone." If Queen Mary had hoped to learn that her son had changed his mind, Edward said, he was "sorry to disappoint her."[75] The Duke of York later recorded: "David said to Queen Mary that he could not live alone as King & must marry Mrs. Simpson."[76] The Countess of Shaftesbury, Queen Mary's Lady of the Bedchamber, later wrote of her mistress: "Though fond of her children she was not maternal, but she was passionately devoted to Prince David, and the way he behaved hurt her more than anything else in her life."[77]

The king did not return to the Fort until 2 a.m., accompanied by Sir Walter Monckton, who was so concerned about the king that he offered him two mild sleeping pills. In the end, it was the shattered Sir Walter who took the tablets, while the king fell asleep unaided.

Across the Channel in the early hours of December 4, Wallis and Perry had just arrived in Rouen at the Hôtel de la Poste, having booked for their small entourage under the names "Mr. and Mrs. Harris." "We found rooms in a hotel, just like ordinary tourists on the road," Perry later recalled. " 'Perry,' Wallis said to me through the door, after we'd been in our separate rooms for what seemed like an eternity, 'will you please leave the door open between your room and mine? I'm so frightened. I'm so nervous.' "[78] Soon after, Wallis called out to Lord Brownlow again, asking if he could sleep in the bed next to hers. She said that she felt too upset to be alone. He went into her room, still fully dressed, and pulled the blankets up over himself. Suddenly, Wallis started to cry: "Sounds came out of her that were absolutely without top, bottom . . . they were primeval. There was nothing I could do but lie down beside her, hold her hand, and make her *feel* that she was not alone."[79]

Later that morning, Wallis tried to call the king from the reception of the hotel. "By this time the *whole* of Rouen knew who Wallis was," said Perry. "They were standing in the hall, in the street, in the square—hundreds of them."[80] Perry, Inspector Evans, the maid and the driver tried to shield Wallis so she had a little privacy as she attempted to speak to the king.

The last leg of their journey, to Cannes, took them through endless towns and villages. Reporters lay in wait for them at every turn. Wherever they stopped, Wallis tried to speak to Edward. But the telephone lines were hopelessly bad in the 1930s, and the king could only half hear of what Wallis was trying to say to him through deafening crackling. She was forced to shout, which alarmed Perry, who feared reporters would hear. At the other end of the line at the Fort, Sir Walter Monckton, who was now living there, said that the king had to shout as well, so the entire household staff heard the attempts at conversation. The intermittent clicks on the lines, meanwhile, were the sound of Thomas Robertson at work; he was a twenty-seven-year-old MI5 intelligence officer who, standing in the undergrowth of Green Park, had tapped the telephone junction box that served Buckingham Palace. Shivering in the cold, the government spy listened in to all the king's private phone calls. He was one of the first people to learn that the king intended to abdicate.[81]

"Is *everybody* listening?" Wallis would say when the twenty clicks heralded a newcomer on the line. Nevertheless, she persevered. "*Never* leave your country! You *can not* give in! You were *born* to this, it is your *heritage*, it is demanded of you by your country," she implored Edward. "The king took absolutely no heed," said Perry Brownlow.[82]

At lunchtime, Wallis's party stopped in Évreux, a charming town in Normandy. At the Hôtel du Grand Cerf, Wallis tried to call Edward from a booth near the bar. Before she left the Fort, she and Edward had decided on some simple code words for communication: Max Beaverbrook was "Tornado," Stanley Baldwin was "Crutch," Winston Churchill was "W.S.C.," his initials, and the king was "Mr. James," after St. James's Palace.

Whilst Perry put the call through to "Mr. James," Wallis wrote down a few notes on a piece of paper: "On no account is Mr James to step down. You must get advice. You must bring in your old friends. See Duff Cooper. Talk to Lord Derby. Talk to the Aga Khan. Do nothing rash."[83] Over the abominable phone line, Wallis went over her list of points, "hoping by sheer repetition" to make herself heard and understood. "At the end I was screaming and so, too, were Perry and Inspector Evans outside the booth in an anxious attempt to drown out what I was saying."[84] In the end, with a sense of utter hopelessness, Wallis hung up.

In her distress, she realized when they were back on the road that she had left her scribbled note in the phone booth. Terrified that the press would get hold of it, the party debated turning back but decided against it. At some stage, the hotelier found it and discreetly pocketed it. In an extraordinary quirk of fate, years later, when Sir Harold Nicolson happened to be staying at the same hotel, the hotelier showed the scrap of paper to him. Harold, who knew Wallis through Sibyl Colefax, took the note and eventually returned it safely to Wallis.

The three-day journey to Cannes proved both traumatic and ill conceived. "The whole journey was mismanaged," claimed Diana Mosley, "particularly in the way Lord Brownlow dealt with the newspapermen." Lady Diana felt that "Wallis had nothing to hide" and should have spoken to the press, simply saying that she was going to stay with friends. Or Perry Brownlow should have issued a statement on her behalf. It was the biggest story of the decade and nothing was going to stop the newspapermen. Throwing a rug over Wallis in the back of the car, creeping out at three in the morning, through hotel kitchens and even escaping a restaurant in Vienne through a lavatory window into an alley to a waiting car were unedifying and humiliating for Wallis. "There was no need for them to behave like fugitives from a chain gang," concluded Diana Mosley.[85]

Back in England, during the weekend of December 5–6, rumors gripped the nation that Winston Churchill was going to form a "King's Party" in an attempt to bring down Baldwin's government. The king was now under immense strain: chain-smoking, drinking whisky, losing the thread of conversations and cradling his head in his hands. Baldwin, Archbishop Cosmo Lang, Alec Hardinge and others believed that the king was mentally ill. Tommy Lascelles overheard Clive Wigram saying, "He's mad—he's mad. We shall have to lock him up."[86]

The writer and society hostess Edith Olivier noted in her diary on December 9 that Patricia, Viscountess Hambleden, had said that the king was as "mad as George III." The viscountess had heard the bizarre assurance on good authority from the Duchess of York, to whom she was close,* that in previous years the king had been given injections "to make him able to have children and it is these which have sent him mad."[87] The courtiers were frantic that the king was so seemingly unstable; with his judgment impaired, he would be a loose cannon. Helen Hardinge, wife of Alec Hardinge, claimed that the king now slept with a loaded gun under his pillow, while Edward had been overheard on the phone telling Wallis that he would slit his own throat if she ever left him. The king was under great mental pressure, said Piers Legh, a senior member of the royal household. "His outbursts on being asked some obvious questions plainly indicated an unbalanced and thoroughly abnormal frame of mind."[88]

Winston Churchill, who dined with the king at Fort Belvedere on Friday, December 4, the day after Wallis left, was more benevolent. He

---

* Patricia, Viscountess Hambleden, became the Duchess of York's Lady of the Bedchamber in 1937. She held this position until 1994.

found that the strain Edward had been under had "exhausted him to a most painful degree," and that he was "down to the last extremity of endurance."[89] Churchill pressed the king to play for time, but Edward was emphatic that to do so would be dishonorable when his resolve never to give Wallis up was unchanged. "It was certainly this very strict point of honour which lost him the Crown," Churchill later said.[90] Churchill felt that the king was ill and urged him to see his doctor. He told Stanley Baldwin that "it would be a most cruel and wrong thing to extort a decision from him in his present state."[91]

Edward was cheered and moved by Churchill's unwavering support. During this period, Winston and his wife, Clementine, "fought like Kat and Pug"[92] over the issue of the king's abdication. Clementine felt that her husband's views were rooted in the divine right of kings and the supremacy of love. She feared that this was a near-career-ending misjudgment of the mood of the political classes, who believed the king should put duty first.[93]

The king remained at the Fort with Monckton and George Allen, both calm, utterly loyal retainers. Edward was also greatly touched by the loyalty of switchboard operator William Bateman. The private line to the Fort "was loaded with top secret calls to Downing Street, and later on with confidential conversations with Wallis at Cannes," but Bateman, who determined that there would be no leak on his watch, refused to relinquish control of the switchboard while he slept. Loyal Bateman, blithely unaware of MI5's surveillance, moved a cot bed into the room containing the Buckingham Palace switchboard and for ten days never left his post, only allowing himself catnaps between calls, such was his dedication to Edward.[94]

Although, for a moment, Edward saw the idea of a King's Party as a "rocket hung brilliantly in the sky," he did nothing to encourage or support the idea. In truth, the king had reached the stage where he wanted to go swiftly, with dignity, without further conflict and without fuss. A disappointed Beaverbrook concluded to Churchill: "Our cock won't fight."[95] Of his decision, the king later said that after sleepless nights spent pacing his bedroom, he decided that it would be best for the country if he did not challenge the prime minister any longer. "By making a stand for myself, I should have left the scars of a civil war," he wrote. "A civil war is the worst of wars. Its passions soar highest; its hatreds last longest. The price of my marriage under such circumstances would have been the infliction of a grievous wound on the social unity of my native land and the Empire. Could Wallis and I have hoped to find happiness under that condition? This was the question I answered in my soul that night. The answer was no. And so in faith and calmness, not unmixed with sorrow, I resolved to end the constitutional crisis forthwith. I decided to abdicate."[96]

Ernest Simpson, by now almost forgotten in the saga, sent a message to Clive Wigram to say how distressed he was by the course of events. He was prepared "to come forward and say that the divorce was entirely a collusion between HM, himself and Mrs. S . . . he felt that he could squash the divorce by turning the king's evidence." If Ernest admitted that he had not committed adultery, as he had testified, the divorce would not be legal. Ernest hoped that if the king thought he could not marry Wallis, he might not abdicate. Wigram, horrified that this action might further prolong the crisis, made no use of Ernest's generous offer.[97]

In the South of France, the home of Katherine and Herman Rogers was being besieged by hundreds of reporters and photographers. Lou Viei, originally a twelfth-century monastery, was situated on a stony ledge below the crest of a hill. The reporters tapped the Rogerses' telephones, tried to bribe the household staff and followed anyone who left the house; while the photographers, equipped with long-range lenses, stationed themselves on high ground, even perching in the trees. Wallis, a prisoner again, said that "in seeking to escape one trap I had run blindly into another."[98]

Immediately on her arrival, on Sunday, December 6, Wallis wrote Edward a fifteen-page letter that she hoped he would receive by airmail that evening. Muddled and barely coherent, it is evidence of her exhaustion and desperation that he heed her pleas. "Darling," she wrote, "I am so anxious for you not to *abdicate* and I think the fact that you do is going to put me in the wrong light to the entire world because they will say that I could have prevented it." She urged him to appeal to the nation but, above all, to take his time and not make any rash decisions. Echoing the advice of Churchill and Duff Cooper, she suggested that they should be separated until autumn the following year, after the coronation: "Think my sweetheart isn't it better in the long run not to be hasty or selfish but back up your people and make an 8 month sacrifice for them." Over and again she entreated him not to be silenced by Baldwin or to leave under a cloud. "I must have any action of yours understood by the world but hidden by B. we would have no happiness and I think the world would turn against me."[99]

Wallis reiterated her pleas in phone calls to the king, but to no avail. Their conversations were strained by the dire lines and the misunderstandings between them, as they adhered to their amateur conversational code. "Despite David's reassurances, it was becoming tragically clear that the balance was tipping towards abdication," Wallis recalled. "Perry was in despair."[100] Lord Brownlow urged Wallis to renounce the king, convinced that only an unequivocal statement from her would stave off abdication. Perry and Herman Rogers helped Wallis write a statement to be issued to the press:

> Mrs. Simpson throughout the last weeks has invariably wished to avoid any action or proposal which would hurt or damage His Majesty or the Throne.
>
> Today her attitude is unchanged, and she is willing, if such action would solve the problem, to withdraw from a situation that has been rendered both unhappy and untenable.[101]

On Monday afternoon, December 7, Wallis read Edward the statement over the phone. The connection, as always, was noisy and uncertain. Afterwards, there was such a long silence that Wallis thought that the king had hung up. Hurt and angry, the king's response was "Go ahead, if you wish, it won't make any difference." Indicative of the king's staggering self-absorption, he later said: "It never occurred to me that she was actually asking to be released from the claims of love. Yet that is what she meant. And others read into her statement the same meaning."[102]

Perry gave the statement to the press at seven that evening. Wallis said that "a terrible weight lifted from my mind. That night, for the first time since leaving the Fort five days before, I slept soundly."[103]

Sadly, Wallis's peace of mind was short-lived. The following morning she discovered that her divorce lawyer, Theodore Goddard, was on the way to the South of France in the prime minister's official airplane. "I don't know what his purpose is," warned the king. "All I know is that Baldwin is behind it. Don't be influenced by anything Goddard says."[104]

All day, Wallis waited in "confusion and anxiety" for Goddard. He did not appear. Just as the party were about to go to bed, at two thirty in the morning, Inspector Evans brought Perry a note signed by four British reporters. Its bombshell contents shocked Wallis to her core: "Mr. Goddard, the well-known lawyer who acts for Mrs. Simpson, has arrived at Marseilles by special plane. He brought with him Dr. Kirkwood, the well-known gynaecologist, and his anaesthetist."[105]

"Gynecologist? Anesthetist? Had the prime minister and my solicitor taken leave of their senses? Somebody had obviously gone mad,"[106] a terrified Wallis exclaimed.

Lord Brownlow exploded with rage: this was a complete affront to Wallis's dignity and the last straw. When Goddard rang on Wednesday morning to arrange his appointment, Perry "let him have it." It turned out that the press, ever ravenous for scandal, had alleged that Goddard's personal physician was a gynecologist. Goddard, it turned out, had a weak heart. The "anesthetist" was one of his law clerks.

A chastened Goddard arrived at the villa, having been instructed to walk alone in front of the press ranks, without carrying a briefcase or anything that could resemble a physician's bag. As he sat in the drawing room, he made clear the reason for his visit. He urged Wallis to withdraw her divorce action. Her decree absolute was not due for another few months. Although a rescission would be complex and take time to effect, it would prevent the king's marriage and, hopefully, the abdication.

"Mr. Goddard," Wallis replied, "any question of inconvenience is now irrelevant. I will do anything in my power to keep the king on the Throne."[107] Goddard prepared a statement that he took back to Britain, and telephoned to Stanley Baldwin:

> I have today discussed the whole position with Mrs. Simpson—her own—the position of the king, the country, the Empire. Mrs. Simpson tells me she was and still is perfectly willing to instruct me to withdraw her petition for divorce and indeed willing to do anything to prevent the king from abdicating. I am satisfied beyond doubt this is Mrs. Simpson's genuine and honest desire. I read this note over to Mrs. Simpson who in every way confirmed it.[108]

The statement was signed by Theodore Goddard and countersigned by Lord Brownlow.

That afternoon, Perry spoke frankly yet kindly to Wallis. "The hour is very late," he cautioned solemnly, "and the mills of the gods are grinding fast. You must now begin to think of the position you will find yourself in if the king does abdicate."[109]

"I who had sought no place in history would now be assured of one—an appalling one, carved out by blind prejudice,"[110] Wallis predicted.

Perry offered to go with her anywhere in the world if she were prepared to leave.

"At the end of my tether, my mind exhausted, my every fiber crying for an end of the intolerable strain, I told Perry that I was ready to leave that afternoon if he could make the arrangements."[111] They planned to travel by train to Genoa and then sail on abroad from there.

"Then came the dreadful ordeal of breaking the news to David, of burying my love for ever."[112] When Wallis was able to speak to Edward later, on a better line, she told him that she had agreed to instigate proceedings to withdraw her divorce petition. She outlined her plan to go away. After an emotive silence, the king told Wallis that George Allen would speak to her. He passed the phone to Mr. Allen, who told the stunned Wallis that it was too late. The king had made the decision to abdicate immediately and was in the process of doing so.

Edward's voice came back on the line. "The only conditions on which I can stay here are if I renounce you for all time. And this, of course, I will not do," he said firmly. "The Cabinet has met twice today, and I have given them my final word. I will be gone from England within forty-eight hours."[113]

8

The Fury

Throughout the previous week, the royal family had been tensely awaiting the decision of the king. The Duke and Duchess of York waited for news at Royal Lodge. Finally, on Monday, December 7, it came. After he had spoken to Wallis, and ignored her pleas, Edward rang Bertie and at ten minutes to seven asked him to come and see him after dinner. The Duke of York recorded: "I said, 'No, I will come and see you at once.' I was with him at seven p.m. The awful and ghastly suspense and waiting was over. I found him pacing up and down the room, and he told me his decision that he would go."[1]

The moment that George, the Duke of Kent, heard that Bertie had been summoned to the Fort, he too arrived, uninvited and unannounced. The three brothers had dinner that night, along with another unexpected guest, Stanley Baldwin, who arrived with a suitcase, intending to spend the night to help the king "wrestle with himself"—an idea that appalled Edward. Nevertheless, out of politeness, he invited the prime minister to join them. "The dinner party was, I think, his tour de force," wrote Sir Walter Monckton, present that evening with George Allen, Ulick Alexander and Major T. L. Dugdale, Baldwin's parliamentary private secretary. "In that quiet panelled room he sat at the head of the table with his boyish face and smile, with a good fresh colour while the rest of us were pale as sheets, rippling over with bright conversation, and with a careful eye to see that his guests were being looked after. . . . As the dinner went on the Duke [of York] turned to me and said: 'Look at him. We simply cannot let him go.' But we both knew that there was nothing we could do or say to stop him."[2]

When Wallis's statement was published on Tuesday, December 8, many believed it heralded the end of the crisis. Chips Channon wrote: "The press received Wallis's statement with mixed comments. Rothermere and Beaverbrook hail it with great jubilation but the *Times* and the *Telegraph* barely disguise their disappointment for they are both determined to get the king to abdicate."[3]

The process of abdication was already in motion, and the royal family, particularly Mrs. Simpson's two fiercest detractors—Queen Mary and the Duchess of York—regarded Wallis's offer to withdraw as a face-saving sham. The royal family, blind to Wallis's untenable and wholly unfair situation, rigidly adhered to the view that she had brainwashed Edward, and he had become temporarily unhinged by obsession. In their view, she had schemed to be queen and, when that looked out of her grasp, decided to settle for a morganatic marriage. When this too eluded her, she had pushed for marriage above all else, even though this would mean depriving Edward of the throne. They would never care to believe the truth: that when the king told Wallis on the telephone that he was abdicating, she ended the call, devastated and weeping. Many observers believed the royal family was wrong about Wallis. "She certainly never saw herself as queen," said Lady Diana Cooper. "I didn't sense any sheer ambition in her."[4]

Shortly after arriving at Lou Viei, Wallis wrote to her friend Sibyl Colefax of her struggle to try to prevent the abdication: "I knew him so well, I wanted them to take my advice. But no, driving on they went headed for this Tragedy. If only they had said, let's drop the idea now and in the autumn we'll discuss it again. And Sibyl darling in the autumn I would have been so very far away. I had already escaped."[5]

On December 9, as Sir Walter Monckton drove from Fort Belvedere to London with the king's royal assent to his own act of abdication, Queen

Mary was driven out of the capital to Royal Lodge. Despite thick fog, she made the journey to see Edward. In the drawing room, at around four o'clock, as twilight gathered, Queen Mary heard of her son's irrevocable decision to leave the throne. "I gave her a full account of all that had passed between Mr. Baldwin and myself during the six days since our last meeting on the Thursday before," Edward said. "She still disapproved of and was bewildered by my action, but now that it was all over her heart went out to her hard-pressed son, prompting her to say with tenderness: 'And to me, the worst thing is that you won't be able to see her for so long.' "[6]

Queen Mary headed back for London, where she dined with the Duke and Duchess of Kent. After dinner, the Duke of York arrived at Marlborough House, and they looked over the draft instrument of abdication, a document the Duke of York regarded with terror and his mother read with incredulity. "I went to see Queen Mary," the duke later wrote, "& when I told her what had happened I broke down & sobbed like a child."[7]

At breakfast the following morning, the king received the official copies of the instrument of abdication via his red dispatch box. His three brothers arrived at Belvedere by ten o'clock and assembled in the octagonal drawing room, together with Sir Edward Peacock, the king's financial advisor, Monckton, George Allen and Ulick Alexander. "As if in harmony with the lifting of the almost intolerable pressure of the last few weeks, the fog that had for some days added to the gloom had also lifted," the king later wrote. "Sitting at the desk, with my three brothers watching, I began to sign the documents."[8] After signing seven copies of one document and eight of another, formally relinquishing monarchical authority, he yielded his chair to his brothers, who signed their names as witnesses in their order of precedence.

This was the first time in British history that the Crown had been surrendered entirely voluntarily. Because the title to the Crown depends upon statute, a royal abdication can be effected only by an act of Parliament. On December 11, His Majesty's Declaration of Abdication Act 1936 was passed, giving succession to his brother George and excluding any progeny of Edward from the line of succession.

"The occasion moved me," Edward recalled. "Like a swimmer surfacing from a great depth, I left the room and stepped outside, inhaling the fresh morning air."[9] Sir Walter Monckton followed the king to the terrace to ask if there was anything the king wished the prime minister to mention in his report to Parliament. Edward had two points he wanted Baldwin to make to the house. He wrote them down on separate pieces of paper. The first was to stress his support of his brother Bertie. This the prime minister did include in his speech. ("The Duke of York. He and the king have always been on the best of terms as brothers, and the king is confident that the duke deserves and will receive the support of the whole Empire.") The other point concerned Wallis. Edward wanted the British people to know that "the other person most intimately concerned" had steadily tried "to the last" to dissuade the king from the decision he had taken. Stanley Baldwin elected to leave this second, critical point out of his speech.

Around the same time that the king's brothers arrived to sign the instrument of abdication, Edward received a generous letter from Ernest Simpson. It is a quite astonishing missive from a cuckolded husband to his usurper. "My heart is too full for utterance tonight," he wrote. "What the ordeal of the past weeks has meant to you I well know, and I want you to know that my deepest and most loyal feelings have been with you throughout! That you may find an abundance of happiness in the days that lie before you is my earnest hope and prayer. For the last time, Sir, let me subscribe myself your devoted subject, but always your loving friend and obedient servant."[10]

While the fateful documents were locked up in the official red box and taken to London by Sir Walter Monckton, Edward worked on the farewell broadcast that he proposed to make to the country. As he would no longer be king, the government would have no authority to seal his lips. Some in Westminster looked coldly on the king supplying an epilogue to the drama. Queen Mary also tried to dissuade her son, but he was determined to speak.

Edward chose to spend his last day at the Fort, and last hour as king, dining with his old friend and ally Winston Churchill. Churchill "generously supplied the final brush strokes" to the speech and made admirable suggestions including the peerless "And he [George/Bertie] has one matchless blessing, enjoyed by so many of you and not bestowed on me—a happy home with his wife and children."

"While we were thus at the table, I ceased to be King," Edward later wrote. "As I saw Mr. Churchill off, there were tears in his eyes. I can still see him standing at the door, hat in one hand, cane in the other." Tapping with his walking stick on the flagstones, Churchill began to recite the famous ode by Andrew Marvell on the beheading of King Charles I: "He nothing common did or mean / Upon that memorable scene."[11]

Two weeks later, on Christmas Day, Churchill wrote to Lloyd George: "I am profoundly grieved at what has happened. I believe the Abdication to have been altogether premature and quite unnecessary."[12]

On the evening of the abdication, the mood at Lambeth Palace was one of quiet jubilation. "Thus it came about that a King with an Empire at his feet nine months ago has gone into the wilderness as an exile from his native land for the sake of a woman who has already made a failure of two marriages!" wrote the Reverend Alan Don, Cosmo Lang's private secretary. "Here is a theme for a dozen tragedies. Here too is a demonstration for all the world to see that the British Democracy demands from those in high places an exacting standard of life and character. It is that and that alone which counts in the long run. Tonight there is a sense almost everywhere, at any rate among responsible people, a sense of relief."[13]

This "sense of relief" was not shared by all at Buckingham Palace. Of the dramatic events of December 10, Queen Mary recorded: "I saw Ld Salisbury & the PM—at 3 to Piccadilly to see Elizabeth* who was in bed

---

* The Duchess of York had come down with influenza, so was in bed while the instrument of abdication was being signed. This was an additional stress for the Duke of York, who was deprived of her comforting presence and was compelled to suffer the biggest ordeal of his life alone.

with a cold, too unlucky. The PM made his announcement in the house about David's final decision—which was received in silence & with real regret—The more one thinks about this affair the more regrettable it becomes."[14]

As the former king packed up his "most personal possessions" at the Fort, the new king came into his room, alone, to talk. Edward closed the door and pushed aside his things on the sofa to make room for his brother to sit down. "This situation seemed to cry mutely for a symbolical laying on of hands, a passing of the torch," Edward recalled. "But there is not much a former monarch can tell his successor."[15] Edward simply reassured his younger brother that he would not find the job too difficult, for he was already intimately familiar with court life. Words were not easy for Bertie in times of great emotion, but Edward "knew that he felt my going keenly."[16] They then discussed what Edward's title would be. On surrendering the Crown, King Edward VIII automatically reverted to the status of a prince of the blood royal and became His Royal Highness Prince Edward of Windsor. Bertie announced that he would create Edward a duke, and suggested the Duke of Windsor as a title. As Edward liked this idea, Bertie said that he would make it the first act of his reign, to be announced at his Accession Council meeting at St. James's Palace the following morning.[17]

As well as the former king's future status, there were many questions relating to finance which Bertie, Edward and their advisors had discussed that day. Sir Godfrey Thomas, Edward's assistant private secretary, wrote in his diary: "Will Mrs. S be prepared to face life as Mrs. Edward Windsor, or even the Duchess of Sussex, on an income of £12,000 a year, which Ulick Alexander says is all he will have if he packed up and departed as a private individual?"[18] It was of immense importance to Edward that he secure a favorable abdication settlement. Sir Walter Monckton expertly negotiated the terms on his behalf. He asked for a pension of £25,000 a year, for which the new king would ultimately be responsible, in return for surrendering his life interest in Sandringham and Balmoral. Bertie paid his brother for the two properties which had been left to Edward by his father. Edward claimed to Bertie that his fortune amounted to only

£90,000, which was less than a tenth of the true figure. This pointless lie seems to have been told in blind panic; Edward was in a despairing state, suddenly fretful for his financial future and terrified he would let Wallis down by not providing adequately for her. When this lie soon became exposed, it served to indelibly poison relations between the two brothers for the rest of their lives.[19]

That last night, however, still in no small measure of shock, the brothers dined amicably together. Edward had arranged a last supper with his family at Royal Lodge before making his final farewell broadcast from Windsor Castle at 10 p.m. Before leaving the Fort, Edward telephoned Wallis to say he would not be able to speak to her for a day or two. When she asked where he was going, he replied: to a hotel outside Zurich. She was appalled. "You can't go to a hotel. You will have no privacy. You will be hounded to death,"[20] she told him.

Edward realized that, in his overwrought state, he had not given much thought to where he would go. It was a perverse irony that it was impossible for him to be with Wallis, the drive behind his sacrifice, until after her divorce was settled in April. As Edward had made public his desire to marry her, it was essential, under the archaic laws that then existed, that they did not meet in case it jeopardized her decree absolute.

"It filled me with fury that the British Government could be so indifferent to his new vulnerability," Wallis wrote. "So ungrateful for his splendid service, as to fail to provide him with the privacy and protection he would desperately need in the first few months of readjustment. Here, at least, I could help him."[21] She telephoned their friends Baron and Baroness Eugene de Rothschild, who had a castle, Schloss Enzesfeld, near Vienna, to ask if they would invite the former king to visit them. Like the Rogerses, the Rothschilds instantly agreed.[22]

As Edward packed up the last of his belongings, the poignant moment arrived when he was due to leave the Fort. He graciously bade farewell to the staff gathered in the hall, asked Sir Walter Monckton to take Slipper to the car and stepped out onto the flagstones. Leaving the Fort—where he "had passed the happiest days" of his life—proved the greatest wrench: "in that moment I realised how heavy was the price I had paid," he said.[23]

A few minutes later, he joined his family at Royal Lodge. Here the former king dined with the new king; Queen Mary; the Duke of Gloucester; the Duke of Kent; his sister, the Princess Royal; his uncle, the Earl of Athlone; and Princess Alice, Countess of Athlone. According to Edward, "Dinner passed pleasantly enough in the circumstances. I hope I was a good guest, but I rather doubt it."[24] According to Monckton, Queen Mary "had thoughtfully left off her mourning black for the evening so as not to cast more gloom."[25]

"That last family dinner party was too awful," Elizabeth told a friend years later. "Thank goodness I had flu and couldn't go."[26] She did, however, write to her brother-in-law from her sickbed the following day—the day on which she became Queen Consort and Empress of India. "Darling David, I am so miserable that I can not come down to Royal Lodge owing to being ill in bed," she wrote, "as I wanted so much to see you before you go, and say 'God bless you' from my heart. We are all overcome with misery, and can only pray you will find happiness in your new life. I shall always mention you in my prayers, and bless you, Elizabeth."[27]

Foreshortening the dinner, Monckton arrived to take Edward to Windsor Castle to broadcast to the nation. Inside the car, on the back seat, an eager Slipper greeted his master. As they drove up the Long Walk, towards Windsor Castle, Monckton informed the former king that the Rothschilds were preparing to welcome him at Schloss Enzesfeld.

Edward was met by Lord Wigram at the castle doors. He walked up the Gothic staircase to his old rooms in the Augusta Tower, where he was received by the director of the BBC, Sir John Reith. Around his old desk, sound technicians and cameramen had set up equipment. When the moment for the broadcast came, the time signal sounded. In a deep voice, Sir John announced into the microphone: "This is Windsor Castle. His Royal Highness, Prince Edward."[28] Sir John then slipped out of the door, leaving only Edward and Monckton in the room. As Edward shifted his position in his chair, preparing to speak, he knocked his foot against the table leg, which avid listeners interpreted as a door slamming. In his inimitable voice he said: "At long last I am able to say a few words of my own . . ."[29]

In the South of France, Wallis listened intently as Edward's voice came out of the loud speaker, "calmly, movingly."[30] Everyone at Lou Viei, including the staff, had gathered around the radio in the sitting room. Wallis lay on the sofa, her hands over her eyes, trying to hide her tears. The former sovereign addressed his former subjects:

> I have never wanted to withhold anything, but until now it has been not constitutionally possible for me to speak.
>
> A few hours ago I discharged my last duty as King and Emperor, and now that I have been succeeded by my brother, the Duke of York, my first words must be to declare my allegiance to him. This I do with all my heart.
>
> You all know the reasons which have impelled me to renounce the throne. But I want you to understand that in making up my mind I did not forget the country or the Empire which as Prince of Wales, and lately as King, I have for twenty-five years tried to serve. But you must believe me when I tell you that I have found it impossible to carry the heavy burden of responsibility and to discharge my duties as King as I would wish to do without the help and support of the woman I love.
>
> And I want you to know that the decision I have made has been mine and mine alone. This was a thing I had to judge entirely for myself. The other person most nearly concerned has tried up to the last to persuade me to take a different course. I have made this, the most serious decision of my life, upon a single thought of what would in the end be the best for all.[31]

"After he had finished, the others quietly went away and left me alone," Wallis said. "I lay there a long time before I could control myself enough to walk through the house and go upstairs to my room."[32]

Wallis was not the only stunned listener to shed tears. "'The King is gone, Long Live the King.' We woke in the reign of Edward VIII and went to bed in that of George VI," Chips Channon wrote on December 11. "Edward, the beautiful boy King with his gaiety and honesty, his

American accent and nervous twitching, his flair and glamour, was part of history. At ten o'clock we turned on the wireless to hear 'His Royal Highness, Prince Edward' speak his farewell words in his unmistakably slightly Long Island voice. It was a manly, sincere farewell. . . . I wept, and I murmured a prayer for he who had once been King Edward VIII. Then we played bridge."[33]

Queen Mary recorded the event more matter-of-factly: "David made his private broadcast to the Nation which was good & dignified, he did it at the Castle, we listened to it at Royal Lodge."[34] Edward, who had included the line "during these hard days I have been comforted by my Mother and by my family," sensed that when he returned to his family after the broadcast, what he "had said had to some extent eased the tension between us."[35] As it was getting late, and fog once again shrouded the gardens and valley, Queen Mary left first. "And then came the dreadful good bye as he was leaving that evening for Austria," she wrote. "The whole thing was too pathetic for words."[36] Monckton recorded: "Queen Mary, ever magnificent, was mute and immovable and very royal. The brothers were sad and showed their emotion."[37]

After a farewell drink with his siblings and Sir Walter, Edward took his leave around midnight. "My brothers walked me to the door exactly as they would have done if I were leaving for Balmoral, Sandringham or some other familiar place," he recalled. "On this leave-taking, however, it was I who as the subject of the king bowed to Bertie; and George, watching, shook his head and cried almost fiercely, 'It isn't possible! It isn't happening!'"[38]

Monckton reported that as Edward bowed over his brother's hand, he said: " 'God bless you, Sir. I hope that you will be happier than your predecessor,' and disappeared into the night, leaving the Royal Family speechless."[39]

There was tremendous courage in the dignified way that the prince left his family, his heritage and his country. He drove with Monckton for an hour, out across the Hartford Bridge Flats, through Hampshire to Portsmouth, where a ship was being readied for him. There was, perhaps deliberately, no time for reflection as the friends chatted amiably about their time at Oxford, during which they had both been members of the Officers' Training Corps. At Portsmouth, they found the quayside dark and deserted. Eventually finding the right dock, they were met by the commander in chief, Admiral Sir William Fisher, his staff, and members of the former sovereign's household: Sir Piers Legh, Ulick Alexander and Godfrey Thomas. After brief farewells, Edward crossed the gangway with Slipper under his arm to meet the captain, Commander C. L. Howe.

At two in the morning of December 12, 1936, HMS *Fury*, an F-class destroyer, slid silently and, unusually for Edward, unescorted, out of Portsmouth harbor. Watching the shore of England recede, the former king was overcome with emotion. "If it had been hard to give up the Throne, it had been ever harder to give up Great Britain," he later wrote. "I knew now that I was irretrievably on my own. The drawbridges were going up behind me. But of one thing I am certain; so far as I was concerned love had triumphed over the exigencies of politics."[40]

From Lambeth Palace, the Reverend Alan Don observed: "A couple of hours later the poor fellow was hurrying through the darkness to Portsmouth where he boarded a ferry for an unknown destination. Will he ever set foot on these shores again? I doubt it, if he ever marries Mrs. S. Feeling has hardened against poor King Edward very noticeably. . . . His was a dual personality, a mixture of much that was good and attractive and charming with much that was rotten and unstable. His infatuation for 'the woman I love' (as he called Mrs. S in his broadcast talk) descended to something akin to madness. What will be the end thereof?"[41]

Nine hours after his brother's departure, the new King George VI, pale and haggard, addressed his Accession Council at St. James's Palace. He announced that the first act of his reign would be to confer upon his brother a dukedom. Although Windsor had been the family name of the reigning royal house of the United Kingdom since 1917, there had never been a Windsor dukedom. Edward now changed his title for the seventh time in his life. That afternoon, the new duke telegraphed King George VI via the Admiralty: "Have had good crossing. Glad to hear this morning's ceremony went off so well. Hope Elizabeth better. Best love and best of luck to you both. David."[42]

Wallis sent a letter to Kitty de Rothschild, thanking her for offering Edward a safe haven. "Dear Kitty—be kind to him," she wrote sweetly. "He is honest and good and really worthy of affection. They simply haven't understood." She also confided in her friend: "I have fallen back exhausted from the struggle to prevent this great tragedy. One felt so small not to be able to make him stay where he belonged—and then the world to turn against me—because I fought a losing battle."[43]

Wallis alone understood how harsh this period of exile would be for Edward and how impossible the transition from monarch to almost ordinary citizen. For the former king, one of the most painful aspects of his departure had been the refusal of a few of his former servants to accompany him. Fred Smith, who had been with him since 1908, had angrily and disrespectfully exclaimed, "Your name's mud. M.U.D!," to which Edward pitifully replied: "Oh, Frederick, please don't say that. We've known each other for so long."[44] Crisp, his valet, refused to come because he did not want to be parted from his wife. Edward was deeply hurt, his loneliness palpable; for four months, and for the first time in his life, he was without the security of his retinue of advisors and retainers. Only Piers Legh and Ulick Alexander accompanied him into exile. But, far more crucial to his sense of self and sanity, he did not have Wallis. Unlike Wallis, Edward did not have the inner resources of intellectual or spiritual stamina to fall back on. At Schloss Enzesfeld, there would only be golf or skiing to entertain him. In his favor, his hosts were welcoming and he could speak German.

As the official backlash against him gained momentum, Edward proved ill equipped to cope. On Sunday, December 13, the archbishop of Canterbury broadcast a sermon castigating the former king and the king's friends. "My heart aches for 'the Duke of Windsor,'" Lang wrote directly after the abdication, "remembering his childhood, his boyhood, his days at Oxford, the rich promise of his service as Prince of Wales—all ruined by his disastrous liking for vulgar society, and by his infatuation for this Mrs. Simpson."[45] Lang elected to demonstrate his aching heart via his own

BBC radio broadcast, in which he castigated the former king for his "craving for private happiness" and denounced again the "vulgar society" which had led him down this unedifying path. The duke was outraged and so were many of his former subjects; after these attacks, the archbishop received hundreds of abusive letters, many violently so. Perry Brownlow felt justifiably enraged; Chips Channon also: "I myself wrote a dignified snorter to His Grace today. I hope the old gentleman has asphyxia."[46]

Wallis was also the recipient of thousands of angry, abusive and hostile letters. The hate mail also included assassination threats. "It is no exaggeration to say that my world went to pieces every morning on my breakfast tray," she later said. "Everything that I stood for was condemned. The presumption [was] that I had somehow gained an ascendency over a beloved King."[47] She was shocked by the vocabulary of vilification in the onslaught of correspondence. Even in her darkest hour, with the world seething with "controversy and speculation" about her, with every newspaper screaming hysterical untruths, Wallis was perspicacious. "I became obsessed with the notion that, in a manner impossible for me to comprehend, a calculated and organized effort to discredit and destroy me had been set afoot."[48]

She wrote plainly to Edward: "The world is against me and me alone. Not a paper has said a kind thing for me." She was especially wounded that Queen Mary had made a "colossal denial of statements in the foreign press saying she had seen me" and felt hurt that her future mother-in-law refused to meet or publicly acknowledge her. Admirably, Wallis realized that the only answer to any peace of mind, henceforth, would be to learn to contain and control her inner world. She schooled herself to survive what would have felled the hardiest of souls: "To be accused of things that one has never done; to be judged and condemned on many sides by people ignorant of the controlling circumstances; to have one's supposed character day after day laid bare, dissected and flayed by mischievous and merciless hands."[49] She triumphed with "a kind of private arrangement with oneself—an understanding of the heart and mind—that one's life and purposes are essentially good, and that nothing from the outside must be allowed to impair that understanding."[50]

Wallis wrote a tender, warm and reassuring letter to Edward on December 12, hours after he left England:

> Darling—my heart is so full of love for you and the agony of not being able to see you after all we have been through is pathetic. At the moment we have the whole world against us and our love—so we can't afford to move about very much and must simply sit and face these dreary months ahead. . . . Your broadcast was very good my angel and it is going to be lovely. . . . Some of the papers—*Times, Telegraph, Morning Post*—have been disloyal to you and foul to me. I hope you will never forget this sacrifice and your brother will prove to the world that we still have a position and that you will be given some jobs to do. . . . I love you David and am holding so tight, Wallis.[51]

In her letter she added that Perry Brownlow's friendship with them both has been "absolutely marvelous in every way." His kindness and loyalty moved her to tears. Perry, like Wallis, realized that the duke would be lonely and disoriented in Vienna. Before returning to London, he had offered to travel via Vienna to help Edward settle in at Schloss Enzesfeld. As he was leaving Lou Viei, he turned to Wallis and said: "I shall tell them in London how you tried to stop this tragedy. They may not believe me—they may not want to believe me—but I was witness."[52]

Perry arrived at the Rothschilds' castle at around six, just as dawn was breaking. A footman took him through "this cold, lonely castle" to the duke's room. There he saw Edward, "who looked just like a little schoolboy, sound asleep, with sun coming across his blond hair. His bed was surrounded by chairs and on each chair was a picture of his beloved Wallis."[53] It struck Perry that the former monarch had no possessions at all except twenty-six suits and Slipper, his dog. The duke had placed a small yellow pillow of Wallis's on his bed. Perry, who stayed for two days with the duke, told Diana Vreeland: "It was an obsession. No greater love has ever existed."[54]

Back in London, Lord Brownlow found himself ostracized by society. Two weeks after the abdication, he wrote: "This is my life: today I walk into White's and every man leaves the bar. I walk down Seymour Street, where Kitty and I have lived all these years, and if I see a friend he crosses to the other side of the street. Nobody—but *nobody*—speaks to me in London. It's as if people really believed I was party to the abdication—to a conspiracy."[55]

Throughout their period of enforced separation, the duke and Wallis spoke almost every evening and sometimes several times a day on the telephone. This did not endear Edward to his hosts, as he ran up a phone bill of £800 in three months, which they were expected to pay. Communication via telephone was never easy: it could take up to an hour to put calls through from Cannes to Enzesfeld; and then the calls often dropped without warning. There was the constant risk of eavesdroppers, so freedom of speech was curtailed. The duke would phone Wallis every evening at seven. As the telephone at Lou Viei was in the hall, near the dining room, the butler, having laid the table, would withdraw to leave Wallis in privacy. She would bring in the phone via its long cord and sit at the dining room table, shouting to be heard, unconsciously banging her elbows on the table. Accidentally, she shattered many of the fragile coral handles on some special soup spoons that her hosts had lovingly brought back from China. Eventually, the butler decided that it would be safer to finish the table laying after her evening call to the duke.

The couple could be more open in their written correspondence, however, which was almost daily for the twenty weeks that they were apart. On December 22, Edward wrote Wallis a long, chatty letter. He detailed their joint interests, and how much Slipper was eating, exercising and missing Wallis ("He sends you millions of dog kisses"). Edward described the Rothschilds' generosity of spirit: they "are very kind and hospitable and allow me to lead my own life here by never expecting me for lunch or to sit and make conversation after tea." Parts of the duke's letters show him to be a man in the grip of manic euphoria—Perry found him "exalté to the point of madness." One minute Edward would be lamenting "how cruel and inhuman the American newspaper business is," the next, eulogizing his love for Wallis. "It's all so lovely Wallis and so dear and sweet and sacred and I'm really happy for the very first time in my life."[56]

The duke was clearly in shock and dazed by events; as ever, his moods oscillated between soaring joy at the thought of his marriage to Wallis, and seismic self-pity. He found the separation "as hard and trying as two people have had to endure." As time went on, and the biting reality of his new situation took hold—that he was an outcast from his family and his country—he was prone to outbursts of fury and bitterness. "If I ever hear another word of that old bromide 'The English are a nation of sportsmen' I'll yell the place down."[57]

Wallis described her virtual incarceration at Cannes: "So much scandal has been whispered about me even that I am a spy that I am shunned by people so until I have the protection of your name I must remain hidden."[58] Though she did manage to escape to Somerset Maugham's villa, La Mauresque, in Cap Ferrat, to join his house party for luncheon on Christmas Day.[59]

Earlier, on December 17, with endless hours of contemplation to revisit the past, Wallis had written to her estranged husband: "Ernest—none of this mess . . . is of my own making—it is the new Peter Pan plan. I miss you and worry about you—in spite of the fact that due to letters [the hate mail] I shan't live very long and in fact am a prisoner. Four detectives. I have nothing for you for Christmas because I can't move on account of threats so sit all day. Oh dear, wasn't life lovely, sweet and simple. Wallis."[60]

Ernest replied at the end of December: "I did not have the heart to write before. I have felt somewhat stunned and slightly sick over recent events. I am not, however, going into that, but I want you to believe—I do believe—that you did everything in your power to prevent the final catastrophe. My thoughts have been with you throughout your ordeal, and you may rest assured that no one has felt more deeply for you than I have. For a few pence each day I can keep *au courant* with your doings."[61] He later made a salutary point in another note: "And would your life have ever been the same if you had broken it off? I mean could you possibly have settled down in the old life and forgotten the fairyland through which you had passed? My child, I do not think so."[62]

Wallis wrote furiously to Ernest after she read the first biography about her, published in New York that December and titled *Her Name Was Wallis Warfield: The Life Story of Mrs. Ernest Simpson* by "Edwina H. Wilson." Wallis detected the heavy hand of Mary Raffray in the account. The publishers had helpfully included a foreword: "This life story is authenticated by a very close friend of Mrs. Simpson who has known her since childhood, through her school days, her debutante years and her married life in America and in London." Mary Raffray had included pointless frippery on Wallis such as: "she can complete a jigsaw puzzle in half the time the average person takes," and "a wise hostess never entertains at the same time her bridge-playing friends and those who shun the game." Nevertheless the book, which included insights such as "she does not affect dark nail polish, preferring a pale pink shade," sold out and was reprinted three times in a fortnight.[63]

"Have you read Mary's effort at literature," a wounded Wallis wrote to Ernest: ". . . It is written by Mary and one other bitch. Charming to make money out of one's friends beside sleeping with their husband. Everyone in London says the amount of stuff she has sold is the top. . . . I warned you of this ages ago but you wouldn't believe me. I am very sad."[64]

Worse for Wallis was the dreadful waxwork effigy of her in Madame Tussauds. As in life, Wallis was not grouped with the royal family but with Marie Antoinette and Joan of Arc. More offensive was the heavily jawed, fuller-figured, sour-faced depiction of Mrs. Simpson that Tussauds had created. It reflected none of Wallis's grace, style and dignity. She clearly saw it for the grotesque caricature that it was, asking her lawyers if there was any way it could be removed. "It really is too indecent and awful to be there,"[65] she lamented to Monckton.

However, Wallis generously opined that "of the two of us, it was David who had by far the worse time, although in his reticence, he rigidly held in his grief."[66] Through their telephone calls and letters, she witnessed, with increasing sadness and alarm, the fracture between him and the royal family. "It was a terrible thing to watch," she said. "David had taken leave of his family in sorrow but in a hopeful spirit, leaving many matters to be composed in what he assumed would be an equally cordial and compassionate atmosphere. Now he said to me: 'The drawbridges are going up behind me. I have taken you into a void.' "[67]

It never seemed to have occurred to Edward that abdication would mean permanent exile from Britain and virtual banishment from his family. He later said that he "never intended to renounce my native land or my right to return to it—for all time."[68] Diana Mosley recalled being told by the duke that when he abdicated, "the new king had promised that after an interval he could come back from time to time to Fort Belvedere, the house he loved so much. But this was a gentleman's agreement, there was nothing written down, no legal arrangement."[69]

Edward later said of the abdication to the royal biographer, James Pope-Hennessy: "People can say what they like for it or against it, I don't care; but one thing is certain: I *acted in good faith*. And I was treated bloody shabbily."[70]

The duke had assumed that after a suitable cooling-off period, he would be allowed to return to England and live a life with Wallis typical of genteel aristocracy. He wanted to support his brother as king and hoped that he might be given some sort of official role, alongside which he could take up a leisurely life of house parties and shooting parties, while maintaining his social status as son and brother of a sovereign. The shock for him was that his family closed ranks, forcing him to accept that he was now an outsider. His widespread popularity and the fact that most of his former subjects still adored Edward meant that George VI and his courtiers felt threatened by the prospect of the duke's return. "There appears to have been jealousy of his charm and popularity, not bestowed by fate on other members of his family," said Diana Mosley.[71] Owen Morshead, the royal librarian at Windsor Castle, spent Christmas 1936 at Sandringham with the new king and queen. He recalled that "the only topic of conversation was the new Duke of Windsor." While the queen praised his "unique talents," she was concerned that if he and Mrs. Simpson did stay together, "it would be dangerous to have such a powerful personality, so magnetic, hanging about doing nothing."[72]

"You see, you can't have two Kings," Queen Elizabeth, Bertie's wife and Edward's sister-in-law, explained years later.[73] A huge endeavor was undertaken by the palace and courtiers, aided by the government and sections of the press, to create King George VI in the image of his father: safe, dignified, old-fashioned, and a paragon of responsibility and domestic virtue. Against this was a campaign of obliteration aimed at the Duke of Windsor. Newsreel companies wiped him from cinema screens and gramophone records of the abdication broadcast were prevented from going on sale.[74]

On January 3, 1937, a perceptive Wallis wrote to Edward: "I realize that it is the politicians whose game it is to have you forgotten and to build up the puppet they have placed on the throne. And they can succeed, because just as they had for months organized a campaign to remove you—and how cleverly they worked—so have they to prove that they were right in what they did and the first step is to eliminate you from the minds of the people. I was the convenient tool in their hands to get rid of you and how they used it."[75]

Initially unaware that his exile was to be permanent, Edward bombarded his brother with telephone calls, offering unwanted advice, pestering him over money and constantly beseeching the royal family to accept Wallis into the royal circle. The real charge against Wallis came from the two queens, Queen Mary and Queen Elizabeth, who pressured the nervous Bertie. Backed by courtiers, they persuaded him that accepting Wallis would further dishonor the monarchy. Painfully, in the end, Bertie stopped accepting his brother's telephone calls. Edward was shocked to discover that the king had instructed telephone operators at Buckingham Palace not to automatically put the duke's calls through. After much wrangling back and forth, it was agreed by the king that the duke could have an annual allowance of £25,000 with the strict proviso that he would lose this should he decide to visit Britain without the king's permission. The duke fired off a furious seven-page letter to the prime minister, describing this as "tantamount to my accepting payment for remaining in exile."[76] According to John Julius Norwich: "All the duke wanted was to live in a nice country house in Hertfordshire—

he had accepted that perhaps the Fort was too close to Windsor and royal life. He just wanted somewhere suitable where he could have invited his friends, shot, played golf and he would have been happy as cricket."[77]

Chips Channon witnessed the campaign. Of Queen Mary, he wrote: "Certainly she and the Court group hate Wallis Simpson to the point of hysteria, and are taking the wrong attitude: why persecute her now that it is all over? Why not let the Duke of Windsor, who has given up so much, be happy? They would be better advised to be civil if it is beyond their courage to be cordial."[78]

In January Wallis wrote an undated letter to Edward: "something must be done to put it out of people's mind in England that your family are against us. I can't stand up against this system of trying to make me an outcast in the world."[79] Wallis, attuned to the forces against the couple, vented her despair that the government and the palace had prevented Edward's brothers from visiting him in Austria, and that "it is this Government that is trying to squash you with your country."[80] Her feeling of impotence seeps from the page, as she is aware that it is only public acceptance by the palace that would confer on them any respectability. As Edward slowly realized what was happening to him, his main reaction was one of hurt bewilderment.

A frank letter from Queen Mary to Edward eighteen months later, in July 1938, illustrated the queen's position towards her son and explained why the acceptance he craved from his family would never be forthcoming. Far from time softening the monarchy's resolve, distance had strengthened it. "You will remember how miserable I was when you informed me of your intended marriage and abdication and how I implored you not to do so for our sake and the sake of the country. You did not seem able to take in any point of view but your own," Queen Mary wrote. "I do not think you have ever realised the shock which the attitude you took up caused your family and the whole Nation. It seemed inconceivable to those who had made such sacrifices during the war that you, as their King, refused a lesser sacrifice. . . . My feelings for you as your Mother remain the same, and our being parted and the cause of it, grieve me beyond words. After all, all my life I have put my Country before everything else, and I simply can not change now."[81]

Wallis wrote to Edward on Sunday, February 7, 1937: "The *Telegraph* also adds that you are not expected back in England for some considerable time. I blame it on the wife [Elizabeth]—who hates us both. All my love and of course we will meet in March now, Wallis."[82]

By the end of February, the strain of separation and the constant pain of exclusion—not just familial but on the world stage—had, unsurprisingly, eroded Wallis's resolve. She told Edward that the previous night she had cried herself to sleep. "I really can't continue to carry on with all of England taking cracks at me and no decent society speaking to me," she wrote. "What have I done to deserve this treatment? I have never had a word said in my defense or kind word in the press. Surely your brother can protect me a bit—not to be the butt of musical comedy jokes on the radio etc. If they knew your family approved our wedding when free, things would be so different for me. I do feel utterly down. It has been a lone game against the world for me and a woman always pays the most—and you my sweet haven't been able to protect me."[83] Her last line must have stung the duke considerably, who never failed in his letters to declare his deep and everlasting love for her.

On February 18, he wrote: "Know that I love you Wallis always more and more. I know that I can make you happy for all time my sweetheart and that is a terribly big thing to stay. Still I say it."[84]

The couple decided to marry at the Château de Candé, in the Touraine region of France, which had been offered to them fully staffed and free of charge by Charles and Fern Bedaux, friends of the Rogerses. This sixteenth-century castle had been transformed by its French-born American multimillionaire owner, Charles Bedaux, with a $15,000 telephone system and state-of-the art American-style plumbing. Cecil Beaton, who stayed there, said that the modern comforts of the château would make "a Long Island millionaire envious." Overall, however, Beaton thought Candé "feudal and rather ugly, with high towers, pointed turrets and heavily embellished Gothic doorways." Outside, "tall poplars and willows grow in platoons."[85]

By 1934, Charles Bedaux had become the fifth richest man in America through the success of his Bedaux worker efficiency system, a controversial time-and-motion study that he applied to industry. During the thirties, Bedaux had begun to work closely with the Nazi government in Germany, which he believed represented "the wave of the future" and the best defense against international communism and labor unrest.[86] The Duke of Windsor, unaware that Bedaux was anxious to use his royal connections to forge closer links with the leadership in Germany, thought the château's location more suitable for his marriage than the French Riviera, with its playboy associations.

Wallis wrote to Fern Bedaux, a woman she had never met, on March 1 from Lou Viei. "Dear Mrs. Bedaux, It is frightfully difficult to convey even one tenth of what I feel about your and Mr. Bedaux's kindness and generosity to the Duke of Windsor and myself."[87] She gently warned Mrs. Bedaux about the press intrusion. "We are so used to it here that it has ceased to be upsetting—but the first encounter is a shock. Anyway the answer is always the same—'you don't know anything.'" Wallis ended her letter saying: "I am looking forward to running house once again. It is the thing I adore most, so you can feel that Candé is in interested hands. Again my most grateful thanks and appreciation. Yours Sincerely, Wallis Simpson."[88]

Soon afterwards, Wallis left Cannes for Candé, accompanied by Katherine and Herman Rogers, two personal maids, and two French detectives who had been assigned by the French government for Wallis's protection. Wallis's first view of the château—"grey walls and slim turrets in the slanting rain"[89]—was pleasing. She could not speak highly enough of Mrs. Bedaux, complimenting not only her beauty but her kind and generous spirit. Wallis was later convinced that if Charles Bedaux had another motive in loaning them the castle, his wife was "innocent of any ulterior purpose."[90]

Tactfully, without asking any questions about the wedding, Mrs. Bedaux showed Wallis around the château, only to announce that she would be leaving the following day. The bride-to-be decided that a small, pretty salon off the spacious, high-ceilinged drawing room would be perfect for the wedding ceremony. There was a guest apartment adjoining the main house that would be ideal for the duke to stay in until their wedding day. Wallis was allowed to use Fern Bedaux's suite of rooms, including a lovely bedroom with cream boiserie and expansive views of the grounds.

"At Lou Viei I had been in a state of semi-paralysis," Wallis recalled. "At Candé I gradually came alive again."[91] Despite the ever-present guard of press at the front gates, the grounds afforded some privacy. Wallis walked in the woodland and around the private golf course. She wrote to Aunt Bessie back in the States that she had "never tasted such lovely food. One eats too much, that's the trouble."[92] The chef used to work for the Duke of Alba. Amid the spacious luxury, Wallis's nerves began to settle. She wrote again to Fern Bedaux on March 15: "I can't help but write you a few lines to tell you how happy I am here. It is the first time I have been able to write that word since December."[93]

In Austria, the duke was joined by his old private secretary, Sir Godfrey Thomas. A week later, Thomas wrote to George Allen about his visit: "All well here: like those who have preceded me at Enzesfeld, I haven't for many years known my host in such good form, or so easy from every point of view. But it is tragic to see the petty activities to which he has recourse, just to fill the time. Still, whether it is counting the wine in the cellar, superintending the plucking of his dog, or examining the house books, it keeps him going till it's the hour for his next telephone connection with Tours."[94]

One evening, Edward telephoned to say that he was sending Slipper back to Wallis, to accompany her on her walks. Two days later, the cairn terrier arrived with Chief Inspector Storrier of Scotland Yard, who had been assigned to the duke in Austria. "The dog's joyous recognition was like a signal to me that, along with Slipper, David had sent a part of himself," Wallis said.[95] She wrote to Aunt Bessie that it was "divine" to have Slipper back with her.

But as ever with Wallis, her peace of mind and happiness would be fleeting. The next day, on Wallis's first walk with Slipper, he ran off into the woods, excitedly chasing a rabbit. In the undergrowth, he was bitten by a viper. Wallis found him, limp on the grass, in spasms of acute pain. He was rushed to a local veterinary surgery in Tours but died that evening. It seemed horrifically cruel and unfair. All Wallis's strength and grit were floored by the shock of this tragedy, releasing months of pent-up strain and grief. "His loss on the eve of my reunion with David seemed to me a frightful omen," she wrote later. "He had been our companion in joy and trouble; now he was gone. Was everything that I loved to be destroyed?"[96] She poured out her sorrow in a letter to Edward on April 7:

> My darling—
> I have just given Herman Mr. Loo's rug to wrap his little body in before Herman buries him. Even God seems to have forgotten WE for surely this is an unnecessary sorrow for us. He was our dog—not yours or mine but ours—and he loved us both so. Now the principal guest at the Wedding is no more. I can't stop crying and must be brave and suffer these next three weeks. You see we have had so much to bear for so many months that our resistance is low—so we must watch carefully and try and save our nerves. We are both feeling the strain—I heard it in your beloved voice—that defeated sound. . . . I love you my darling and this agony of separation is so immense.
> Wallis[97]

The duke replied that he was also heartbroken. He had not slept and had cried copiously. He suggested that rather than be buried at Candé, Slipper should be embalmed, packed into a small lead box and taken back to be buried at Fort Belvedere. Clearly, at this point, Edward still felt that they would someday be able to return to England. The whole situation was agonizing. "I feel quite stunned," wrote Edward, "and dread the remaining three weeks until I am with you never to be parted ever again my sweetheart . . . Your Sad David."[98]

Finally, on the morning of May 3, Wallis's decree absolute was granted. Edward left Austria immediately, traveling on the Orient Express, which passed through Salzburg that afternoon. The train stopped thirty miles short of Paris in order to avoid the press and the duke was taken on to Candé by car. He arrived at lunchtime on April 4, with his new equerry, Sir Dudley Forwood, who had replaced Sir Piers Legh. According to Sir Dudley, whom Edward had summoned to Schloss Enzesfeld because there were so many problems, Legh had been "horrified by the Abdication, not at all sympathetic to Mrs. Simpson and upset by the fact that he couldn't speak German."[99]

Running up the château steps two at a time, Edward's first words to Wallis were "Darling, it's been so long. I can hardly believe that this is you, and I'm here."[100]

After lunch, the couple walked through the undulating grounds. Wallis later wrote: "It was wonderful to be together again. Before, we had been alone in the face of overwhelming trouble. Now we would meet it side by side."[101]

9

Untitled

As the new king, George VI, would be crowned on May 12, Wallis and Edward decided that they would marry after this date, in June. The week before the duke's arrival at Candé, Cecil Beaton turned up to take fresh photographs of Wallis prior to her wedding. Beaton arrived to find the bride-to-be's already "incredibly narrow figure, narrower since the abdication." After "cocktails, chatter" and a lively dinner with a "superb variety of wines," followed by billiards and conversation, Katherine and Herman Rogers retired to bed at midnight, leaving Wallis and Beaton to talk "in full earnest" until dawn.[1]

Beaton was "struck by the clarity and vitality" of Wallis's mind. "I got the impression that she has been taken as much by surprise by recent events as anyone else," he later wrote. "Though her divorce proceedings had already begun, I don't believe she had any clear intentions of marriage. Of the abdication, she told me she had known less than anybody. It had been impossible to talk freely with the ex-King on the telephone as the wires were constantly tapped."[2]

"It wasn't just tactfulness, I am sure," Beaton considered, "that prevented Wallis from airing any grievance she might have against Mr. Baldwin or the so-called friends who 'welched' on her when the situation altered." Wallis told the esteemed photographer that the events had "only shown me *who* among my friends *are* my friends." She told Beaton that she had been tempted to hang herself from the antlers adorning the château walls. Cecil Beaton concluded the evening impressed that Wallis "is bitter towards no one."[3]

The following day, a manicurist and hairdresser arrived from Paris. Wallis bravely agreed to be photographed in the thick grass, even though, after Slipper's death, she was terrified of treading on a viper. In her bedroom, where she changed her clothes, "jewellery was produced in unostentatious driblets." Beaton was impressed by some of the historic stones, "including a pair of diamond pear-shaped clips the size of pigeons' eggs."[4]

The next morning, with the butler and footmen lined up to salute Mr. Beaton's departure, he concluded that: "for Mrs. Simpson, events might have been worse. If she has not been fated to wear a crown, she is still loved by an abdicated king and will soon be married to him. It won't be so bad to be called the Duchess of Windsor."[5]

Before the duke's arrival, friends from Paris regularly dropped in to see Wallis, who wrote to Edward that she was "running a hotel." Mrs. Rex Benson, an American living in London, later recalled that during a long talk, Wallis told her: "You know, I never wanted this marriage."[6] Wallis certainly did not want the abdication on which the marriage was predicated. Yet during their months of separation and isolation, Wallis, in love with Edward, made up her mind that as far as it lay in her power, she would make the duke happy.

On May 12, the day of his brother's coronation at Westminster Abbey, Edward announced that he was going to listen to the live broadcast on the BBC. A silent group gathered around the radio set in the Château de Candé. As the duke listened to the proceedings—described afterwards by the new Queen Elizabeth as "inordinately long"—he knitted a blue sweater for Wallis. "David's eyes were directed unblinkingly at the fireplace,"[7] Wallis recalled. "The words of the service rolled over me like an engulfing wave. I fought to suppress every thought, but all the while the mental image of what might have been and should have been kept forming, disintegrating and re-forming in my mind."[8]

Edward sweetly sought to allay Wallis's fears when they were alone together later. "You must have no regrets," he told her. "I have none. This much I know; what I know of happiness is forever associated with you."[9]

Wallis wrote to Ernest that day to inform him that she had decided to change her name back to Warfield. "I really felt that I had done the name of Simpson enough harm," she declared. "Now the target can be Warfield as I don't expect the world will let up on its cruelty to me for some time. . . . The publicity has practically killed me."[10] Wallis told a friend that she had aged ten years during the year of the abdication.[11] Rather oddly, when Edward sent out the handful of invitations for the June 3 wedding, he announced his bride-to-be as "Mrs. Warfield," which, of course, she never was. Edward presented Wallis with a 19.77-carat emerald engagement ring. The shank was inscribed "We are ours now."[12]

Wallis chose the American couturier Main Rousseau Bocher to create her trousseau. She had been introduced to him by her friend Elsie de Wolfe. The couture house of Mainbocher had been established in 1929 in Paris, and Wallis became a regular at his salon on Avenue George V because the designer's style was directly aligned with hers. "I like persuasive dresses that have manners," Main Bocher declared, "and I hate aggressive ill-bred concoctions."[13] Together they worked on her austere but classic wedding dress, in dyed, pale-blue crêpe satin. Its hue matched her eyes and became known as "Wallis blue." The well-known Parisian milliners Caroline Reboux made a halo-style fascinator. Constance Spry, the society florist, who was genuinely fond of Wallis and resolutely loyal to her, came from London with her assistant, Val Pirie, to create floral arrangements. Spry's close association with the Duke of Windsor (she knew about his relationship with Wallis long before others, due to the bouquets he ordered from her) meant that she missed out on the lucrative commission for the flowers for George VI's coronation. Spry was fully aware that arranging the flowers for the wedding of the Duke and Duchess of Windsor would mean years of forgoing royal commissions, yet she did not hesitate. She and Val spent two days filling the castle with Madonna lilies, white peonies, delphiniums, wild roses and wildflowers. Her outstanding floral displays were, according to Cecil Beaton, "out of all proportion to the scale of the house and the small number of people who would see them."[14]

Constance explained to Cecil: "I'm going to make the flowers as beautiful as I can. I'm so glad that they've both got what they want with this religious ceremony. I'd do anything for her. I adore her. So did all my girls when they arranged flowers for her in her Regent's Park house and didn't know who she was."[15] The flowers were Constance's personal gift to Wallis. Spry noted that, as she worked, the former king spent hours on his knees, rather pathetically scanning old and damp copies of *The Times*, which she had spread out beneath her arrangements.[16]

In the run-up to the wedding, one of Wallis's guests, Constance Coolidge, the Comtesse de Jumilhac, observed a dinner at Candé where Winston Churchill's son, Randolph, was also present. The Duke of Windsor, she said, was "like a boy let out of school . . . gay, carefree, laughing and terribly in love."[17] When Wallis asked him to fetch her handkerchief, he sprang up to go and get it. On his return, he sat close beside her on the sofa, "a little shy of her and adoring." After dinner, the duke noticed that Wallis's slipper was undone, and he knelt down to tie it up. "I caught Randolph Churchill's eye at this moment and his expression was amusing to say the least," the countess recalled.[18]

Despite the duke's tenderness towards Wallis and his caring attentiveness to her every need, he became unbalanced when his aspirations for Wallis were thwarted. As the wedding drew closer, the hammer blows from the royal family came one by one. Edward was informed that the Duke of Windsor would no longer be able to call upon the court, even for secretarial assistance; he would not be given a pension in the new civil list—and none of his family would be attending the wedding. "Right up to the last minute," Dudley Forwood recalled, "the duke hoped that his brothers would come and that somehow the royal family would relent. But they did not. He was deeply, deeply hurt."[19]

The royal family had been advised to stay away from the wedding by the king's private secretary, Lord Wigram, taking the view that their attendance "would be the final nail in the coffin of monarchy."[20] Edward later wrote to his brother: "I will never understand how you could ever have allowed yourself to be influenced by the present Government and the Church of England and their continual campaign against me."[21]

To Edward, however, cruellest of all was the news that Wallis would not be granted the title "Her Royal Highness." And neither would their children (in the unlikely event that they would have any) be entitled to address themselves as "HRH." Wallis was to be simply styled "the Duchess of Windsor." This last diktat, which the duke received in the form of a letter from the king, personally ferried to him by Monckton the day before his wedding, hit Edward like a fatal gunshot wound. "Nothing in the aftermath of the Abdication hurt David more than that gratuitous thrust,"[22] said Wallis. Monckton had warned the Home Secretary, Sir John Simon, that this move "would create an intense bitterness in the duke that should not be underestimated."[23] He was right.

On reading the letter, a shocked Edward turned to Monckton and said: "Well, this is a nice wedding present."[24] He then started shouting: "I know Bertie—I know that he couldn't have written this letter on his own. Why in god's name would they do this to me at this time?"[25] The duke believed that "this cold-blooded act" was not an idea that his brother "would have thought of himself. . . . Without question, other influences were working on him."[26] Edward considered that the letter was written by Sir John Simon but believed that the decision itself was influenced by "somebody close to him," most likely Elizabeth, the queen consort.[27] This was a view shared by Wallis, who, anticipating this move, had previously written to Edward that the Duchess of York "guided by [Queen Mary] would not give us the extra chic of creating me HRH—the only thing to bring me back in the eyes of the world."[28] This issue would become the greatest source of bitter anguish for the exiled former king.

Diana Mosley said that not according Wallis her HRH was "a clever move on the part of the politicians who devised it. They knew, none better, that the duke was loved in quite a special way in Britain and that legends do not disappear in the wave of a wand. They dreaded his return to his native land, and they reckoned, quite correctly, that he would never come back unless his wife was treated properly." Diana Mosley and others believed that "in order to ensure his continued absence they acted illegally, in the opinion of learned lawyers."[29] The editor of *Burke's Peerage* stated years later that it was the "last act of triumph of an outraged and hypocritical Establishment . . . the most flagrant act of discrimination in the whole history of our dynasty."[30]

Although Wallis had written to Edward of being denied "the extra chic of creating me HRH," her close friends claimed that she did not mind about the title for herself. "The distinction did not seem particularly important to me," Wallis wrote, but she recognized the status of acceptability that it would give her.[31] "She honestly did not care about the title," said Nicky Haslam. "She always introduced herself as: 'I am Wallis.' "[32]

Edward, however, was hurt to such a deep degree that he never recovered from this appalling slight from his family. To him, "HRH" was not just an emblem of rank but a token of the love for which he had relinquished his family. Its denial drove him to distraction and cast a permanent blight on his happiness. The two major preoccupations for the rest of his life would be, first, that he should obtain the title "HRH" for Wallis, and second, that Wallis should be received by the king and queen and the event recorded in the Court Circular. "This caused a great dissatisfaction with Edward and his family," explained John Julius Norwich. "What he wanted was for Wallis to be accepted and he wanted this so much. Not getting HRH was a deliberate snub. For the wife of an HRH not to be an HRH is totally unique. I think that the family should have given her HRH as it would have given them both so much pleasure."[33]

Although the duke was later advised that he could pursue the matter through the courts, Diana Mosley said that he would never have resorted to such action because "such a move would have injured the monarchy."[34] From that moment on, Edward would remain loyal to the Crown—but he would never forgive the brother who he considered viciously betrayed him.

Before his wedding, Edward told Herman Rogers: "I hope that you and all of Wallis's friends and mine will recognise her after tomorrow as 'Her Royal Highness' and that the ladies will curtsy to her." He instructed his equerry, Sir Dudley Forwood, to "notify the staff to address my wife as 'Your Royal Highness.' I expect you to do the same."[35] After their marriage, on the duke's orders, no one was permitted to sit down in front of the duchess without her permission. According to Sir Dudley, the abdicated monarch was never fully reconciled to his new status. "Although he was plainly a broken man, a shell, he still expected a full service, a monarch's service."[36]

Edward knew that Wallis wanted a dignified marriage ceremony, and even providing this was not without travails. The religious aspect was complicated because the Church of England forbade church marriages for those with partners still living. Initially, one Canon Andrews, from the Home Farm parish in the Duchy of Cornwall, offered to officiate; however, he swiftly withdrew his services when advised from on high that he would be acting contrary to the decisions of Convocation.[37] Thwarted at every step by the Church of England, the former king struggled to find anyone to conduct the religious ceremony. Eventually a clergyman, Reverend R. Anderson Jardine, offered to officiate. The duke was delighted. Predictably, however, the Church continued to attack and undermine the duke's wedding: Alan Don dismissed Jardine as "an entirely insignificant vicar in Darlington" acting "without any ecclesiastical authority," and added: "It is really rather tragic that the duke should demean himself by accepting the services volunteered by a poorly educated and wholly obscure cleric."[38] Later, having officiated at the wedding, Jardine was shunned by the Church. He had committed no illegality in offering a religious blessing to a couple who had just been legally married by the French mayor of Monts; yet within the month, despite receiving thousands of letters of public support, he resigned his post and left England for America.[39]

In the absence of any of his beloved brothers acting as his best man, the duke asked Lord Louis Mountbatten, who turned him down. Edward, who never forgave him, turned to his old friend and equerry Major Edward Dudley "Fruity" Metcalfe, who agreed to the duke's request. On the eve of the wedding, Cecil Beaton returned to the château to photograph the couple. The run-up to a wedding is stressful enough for any bride, but at every turn, Wallis had unendurable snubs to contend with. Beaton noticed that her face "was showing the strain. She looked far from her best."[40] In the photographs, Wallis looks utterly shell-shocked. It was impossible for her to hide the immense burden she felt or to fully digest everything that had happened. The duke, by contrast, "seemed radiant—his hair ruffled gold, his complexion clear and sunburnt, his blue eyes transparent with excitement. Marriage in Westminster Abbey should have been his birthright, yet now he beamed contentedly at the impromptu wedding arrangements set up in the music room."[41]

The music room had been converted into an Anglican chapel for the occasion—the piano removed and thirty-two chairs placed in rows, though only sixteen people would attend. The Reverend Jardine arrived, "a comic little man with a red bun face, protruding teeth and a broad grin."[42] As they shook hands, Edward said: "Thank God you've come, thank God you've come. Pardon my language, Jardine, but you are the only one who had the guts to do this for me."[43] As there was no crucifix in the château, the duke telephoned the British embassy in Paris to procure and supply one. There was a brouhaha over finding a suitable piece of furniture to use as a makeshift altar. A heavily carved chest from the hall, with a row of fat caryatids holding up a Renaissance carving, was eventually deemed suitable. "Wallis, rather harassed but not too harassed to laugh, wondered about an altar cloth," recalled Beaton. "Pointing to the caryatids, she drawled, 'We must have something to cover up that row of extra women!' "[44] She remembered that she had a coffee-colored tablecloth from Budapest in her already packed linen trunk. Wallis's cockney maid, resentful at having to unpack the trunk, declared: "If it's as much trouble as this getting married, I'm sure I'll never go through with it."[45] An amused Wallis later told the assembled guests that she "couldn't let the poor girl be put off matrimony for life," so felt duty-bound to say: "Oh, it isn't always as bad as this—only if you're marrying the ex-King of England."[46]

The wedding day, June 3, 1937, was blissfully cloud free and sunny. The only French journalist to attend the ceremony, Maurice Schumann, described how Wallis woke to a "Wallis blue sky." He praised the elegance of the duchess and her "very great dignity."[47]

"Alas! the wedding day in France of David & Mrs. Warfield. . . . We all telegraphed him," Queen Mary wrote in her diary.[48] The third of June was the date of King George V's birthday—a fact Edward would have been keenly aware of, but unlikely to have registered with Wallis. Nevertheless, Queen Mary wrote to her daughter-in-law Elizabeth that the date of the wedding hurt her deeply, blaming it on Wallis. "Of course she did it, but how can he be so weak, I suppose it is out of revenge that none of the family is going to the wedding."[49] A telegram from the king and queen read hollowly: "We are thinking of you with great affection on this your wedding day and send you every wish for future happiness and much love."[50]

Before the wedding, Beaton photographed the bridal couple, while their guests were whisked off to lunch outside the château. Afterwards, Beaton sat down with the duke, Wallis, the Rogerses and Sir Dudley on the terrace. While the duke toyed with strawberries and cream, the others ate curried eggs, kidneys and rice. When Wallis asked for more shade, despite the presence of footmen, the ever-attentive duke leapt up and lowered the large sunshade in her direction, asking: "Is this the right height? Six inches lower?" The conversation over lunch "was light and witty," Beaton recalled. "At times the duke laughed and wrinkled up his face so that it looked like last year's apple."[51]

After they had changed, the duke into a morning coat and Wallis into her wedding dress, Beaton took the official photographs in various locations in the grounds of the château, shielded from the eyes of the press. Wallis, wafer thin, wore an art deco clip of sapphires over a fan of baguette diamonds that had been made for her earlier that year by Van Cleef & Arpels.[52] When the duke saw his bride, he said: "Oh, so this is the great dress? Well, it's lovely, very pretty."

Before the wedding, Lady Alexandra "Baba" Metcalfe observed: "I have never seen HRH happier or less nervous but looking at her, and trying with all one's might and main, one is unable to register that she is the cause of the whole unbelievable story. One almost begins to think there is nothing incredible, unique or tragic about it, as they are so blind to it all. If it were not for the press, who are only allowed as far as the gate, one might be attending the wedding of an ordinary couple."[53] Of the ceremony, Baba wrote: "seven English people present at the wedding of the man who, six months ago, was King of England."[54] Ever loyal,

Aunt Bessie was Wallis's only relative at the wedding. Also there were Herman and Katherine Rogers, Kitty and Eugene de Rothschild, Fern and Charles Bedaux, Hugh Lloyd Thomas, Lady Selby (her husband, Walford Selby, had been advised not to go), Walter Monckton, George Allen and Randolph Churchill. An already ostracized Perry Brownlow backed out, which further aggrieved the duke.

Just before the ceremony began, a bouquet of red, white and blue flowers, tied with a tricolor ribbon, was delivered. It was a gift from Léon Blum, the French prime minister. In the House of Commons, the British prime minister, Neville Chamberlain—who had replaced Baldwin in May—was asked: "Has the government already decided to send, or are they considering sending a message of congratulations to the Duke of Windsor on his wedding?"[55] Chamberlain made no reply. There was no mention of the wedding in the Court Circular the following day.

Marcel Dupré, a celebrated organist from Paris, played "O Perfect Love" as Herman Rogers walked Wallis into the music room. "Wallis was in a lovely blue dress with a short, tight-fitting jacket and wore a blue straw halo-hat with feathers and tulle. On her arm was the loveliest diamond and sapphire bracelet, which was her wedding present,"[56] wrote Baba Metcalfe. "Jardine read the service simply and well: 'Do you Edward, Albert, Christian, George, Andrew, Patrick, David take . . .' etc. His responses were clear, firm and very well said. Her voice: 'I Bessie Wallis' was much lower, but very clear. It could be nothing but tragic to see an idealistic Prince of Wales and King of England buried under these circumstances, and yet, so pathetic as it was, his manner was so simple and dignified, he was so sure of himself in his happiness that it gave something to this sad little service, which is impossible to describe."[57]

During the service, "Fruity" Metcalfe used the prayer book that Queen Mary had given Edward when he was ten. Inscribed in the front were the words: "To darling David from his loving mother." Baba Metcalfe said: "It was hard not to cry. In fact I did." She was not alone. "HRH had tears running down his face as the service finished."[58] Immediately afterwards, Sir Walter Monckton gave the new Duchess of Windsor an unmistakable bow. "For my part," he said, "I never had any doubt. I always told the duke that I would treat his wife as his wife should be treated."[59]

After the wedding breakfast, the guests were received one by one by the duke and duchess. Right until the moment of their marriage, Wallis had always curtsied to the duke and addressed him as "Sir." For the first time, the awkward problem arose of who was going to bow or curtsy to the duchess. To honor the duke on his wedding day, his guests bowed and curtsied to his bride, and then to him. This issue of who would acknowledge the duchess "recurred for the rest of their lives," said Diana Mosley. "It was noticeable that everyone with the slightest pretention to good manners treated her, for the duke's sake, as he would have wished."[60] Newspapers were later full of reports that Lady Diana Cooper had committed the grave social misdemeanor of curtsying to the duchess, and subsequently the Coopers feared being ostracized from "polite society" and put on a blacklist of "friends of the Duke and Duchess of Windsor." "My mother always curtsied to the duchess, whenever she saw them both," John Julius Norwich remembered. "People said to her, 'You can't.' But she said, 'It made him so happy, so we did.' "[61] Diana Mosley commented: "Only people very anxious and unsure of themselves, hoping, perhaps, to show that they knew what was what, did otherwise."[62]

Baba Metcalfe said that although she wanted to warm to Wallis—who thanked her effusively three or four times for coming to the wedding—she was unable to because she found her attitude "so correct and hard."[63] The apparent "dearth of softness" during the wedding ceremony—the absence of a reassuring hand on the duke's arm, or a teasing glance—Baba Metcalfe interpreted as a lamentable lack of love on the bride-to-be's part. Wallis was often mistaken for being cold and austere, where in fact her rigidity was a defense against terrible nerves and abiding fear of putting a step wrong. Highly attuned to British snobbery, Wallis would have been mortified to have made a social faux pas or to have embarrassed the duke in any way—especially on his wedding day, when the critical eyes of the world were straining upon them. Having been mauled by the press, vilified by the royal family and ostracized by friends since the abdication, the new Duchess of Windsor found the wedding a tense and bittersweet occasion. Wallis, who was anything but hard, used her implacable dignity as a cover for her vulnerability. It gave her self-respect.

Before the couple left on their honeymoon, which was to be in Austria, Sir Walter Monckton took Wallis aside. He told her that "most people in England disliked her very much because the duke had married her and given up his throne, but that if she kept him happy all his days that would change, but that if he were unhappy nothing would be too bad for her." The duchess received his warning with good grace, replying: "Walter, don't you think I have thought of all that? I think I can make him happy."[64]

From England, Chips Channon wrote of the wedding day: "the Windsor wedding has taken place in a foreign country amid a blaze of publicity and rather cracked trumpets, and the photographs of him and Wallis show an animated, ecstatic pair. Reaction here, however, is setting in and people are angrily demanding why he should be so snubbed?"[65]

That afternoon, Chips was surprised to receive a telegram from the duke. "Many thanks for your good wishes. We shall write when we get the present. Edward," it read. "It must have been sent directly after the Service as it arrived at 4 o'clock and is dated Tours,"[66] Chips surmised. When still the following day there was no mention of the wedding in the Court Circular, Channon raged on the duke and duchess's behalf. "Almost every newspaper last night and again this morning has run a leader of good wishes to the Duke of Windsor. *The Times*, however, refrained. It is of course an organ of the Archbishop and he is a power behind it. I think it is disgraceful. The treatment of the Duke of Windsor by the present Government has hurt the institution of royalty far more than ever the Duke of Windsor did himself by his abdication."[67]

The day was generously referred to by Wallis afterwards as "a supremely happy moment. All I had been through, the hurts I had suffered, were forgotten."[68] For the honeymoon, the duke had arranged a stay at Schloss Wasserleonburg, a secluded castle set in the Carinthian Mountains, lent to them by Count Paul Münster, a cousin of their friend Lord Dudley, a wealthy landowner in the Black Country. Accompanied by their replacement cairns, 186 trunks and 80 additional items of luggage, the honeymoon couple stopped en route for a day in Venice, in between trains, where Mussolini's fascist government, wise to the propaganda value of the visit, greeted the newlyweds with an impressive array of flowers and gondolas.

Arriving at the castle, the duke, who had been fretful that his bride would not like the choice of honeymoon venue, was relieved when Wallis congratulated him on finding such a magnificent location with wraparound views of the snowcapped Alps. "David had indeed done well,"[69] she wrote. He had selected the Austrian staff himself, hired a chef and a butler from Vienna, and recruited a British secretary, Mrs. Bedford. "The first thing I learned about David as a husband was that he was much more thoughtful and attentive than I had expected,"[70] Wallis happily discovered.

At last, the couple found a measure of serenity. They walked, swam, played tennis and sunbathed. To sate his passion for extreme exercise, the duke would climb the Dobratsch, a rocky peak at the back of the castle, signaling to his wife below with a small mirror from the summit, while she lunched quietly on the terrace. "It was an idyllic interlude; for the moment one could almost forget the winter's pain and separation," Wallis said.[71] She wrote to her cousin Leila Barnett: "Here I am at last with my king sitting on a mountain in Austria—which is really lovely and peaceful—we hope here to gather strength for future battles. . . . Please write me and say you still love me and that we may come to Wakefield one day."[72]

However, the marital bliss was short-lived. The duke and duchess engaged in "interminable post-mortems concerning the events leading up to the Abdication," talking late into the night: "If only I had done this, if only you had done that; if only you had listened to me, if only I had known." "Endless rehashing" of "what ifs" and "if onlys" became "almost an obsession" between them.[73] But Wallis soon realized that it would be futile and unnecessarily painful to dwell on regret. Thus, a few weeks into their marriage, the couple made a pact "never to discuss the Abdication again." To preserve their relationship, they dropped the subject for good.

Later in life, the duke obliquely referred to the delicate subject of the abdication as "1936."[74]

A whisper of the loneliness felt by the duchess—adored by her husband yet reviled by the rest of the world—was apparent when she wrote to Ernest during her honeymoon. She confided in her ex-husband once more how much she missed him and their life together. "I think of us so much though I try not to. Wherever you are you can be sure that never a day goes by without some hours' thought of you & for you and again in my prayers at night."[75] She asked him for news: "I wonder so much how you are? How is the business getting on etc. I thought I'd write a few lines to say I'd love to hear from you if you feel like telling me a bit." She told Ernest that she had, at last, found peace in the mountains and was trying "to recover from all those terrible months that we all went through before starting out in the future. I have gathered up courage from that."[76] With myriad uncertainties of a future roaming in exile with the duke, it was the steadfast nature of her marriage to Ernest that Wallis now felt the loss of. She loved Edward, yet she missed the comfort and safety of her marriage to Ernest. He, better than most, knew what she was going through as he had shared her intimate knowledge of life with "Peter Pan" at the Fort.

When Sir Walter Monckton visited the duke and duchess in Austria, he was relieved to find them "both really well and happy." He urged them to find somewhere to settle, at least temporarily. "It is going to be difficult to keep his time occupied, but she is genuinely trying to help," Sir Walter recorded, "and though it is early days, I was honestly impressed and feel happier about them than I expected."[77]

Difficulties continued to ripple through the honeymoon, thanks once again to the royal family. From Austria, the duke and duchess traveled to Venice, then Vienna, Salzburg and Yugoslavia. Edward discovered that the Duke and Duchess of Kent were also holidaying in Yugoslavia. Edward exploded in rage when he was informed that only his brother George was prepared to visit them. When Edward demanded to know if Princess Marina did not want to come, or whether she had been forbidden from doing so, he was told that she did not care to meet Wallis. In the end, neither the Duke nor the Duchess of Kent visited the honeymooners; Wallis was snubbed, and the duke was shunned by his family.

After a three-month honeymoon, the couple moved to Paris, where they took a small apartment—two bedrooms and a sitting room—on the third floor of the Hôtel Meurice, overlooking the Jardin des Tuileries. This was a base while they looked for a home, which proved to be complex; the duke preferred the country, while Wallis felt more comfortable in the city. The real issue was that neither of them had envisaged living on the Continent in permanent exile. "Probably the first year was the most difficult of all their married life," said Diana Mosley, who became closer to the couple as she was then living in Paris. The duke did not want to buy a house, as he was still convinced that in time he would be allowed to go home, as part of the "gentleman's agreement" with his brother. However, "as the months went on it became obvious that this was a promise he was not going to keep."[78] As Wallis was such an exemplary hostess and took pride in creating beautiful settings, not to have a property to make her own was particularly hard for her. At the end of August, she wrote to Ernest: "It is horrid having no home & living like snails yet how difficult to decide where to live with every country quivering."[79]

While the duke was in Paris, it began to sink in that he had nothing to do. Still only in his forties, he yearned for some gainful employment. Accustomed to detailed itineraries and imposed structure, idle restlessness gave him time to nurse his many grievances against his family and dwell on injustices. While Wallis filled his life as much as she could, neither had anticipated a life of globe-trotting obscurity. Years later, she confided to the writer Gore Vidal: "I remember like yesterday the morning after we were married and I woke up and there was David standing beside the bed with this innocent smile, saying, 'and now what do we do?' My heart sank. Here was someone whose every day had been arranged for him all his life and now I was the one who was going to take the place of the entire British government, trying to think up things for him to do."[80]

The duke craved a return to the limelight, costarring with his glittering consort. It was this backdrop, in part, which compelled him to make the worst mistake of his career—a decision which was to have bitter ramifications for the Duke and Duchess of Windsor for the rest of their lives.

10

The Twilight Zone

In October 1937, the duke accepted an invitation, arranged by Charles Bedaux, to visit Hitler's Germany. The American millionaire had substantial business interests in the country which were threatened by the Third Reich. Bedaux could see that to organize a visit by the Duke of Windsor would earn him considerable credit in Berlin. The Germans could be trusted to exact the maximum propaganda from the duke's visit, as they sought to build close links with the man whom they believed could one day be of great use to them.

Edward, for his part, felt there was an urgent need for a third party that could stand aloof from the growing conflict between Germany and Britain, and that he was ideally placed to help reconcile the two countries and provide the impetus towards peace. The decision to go was, however, incredibly foolish. Floundering without his court advisors and strategists, the duke did not pause to consider that this was exactly the type of trip to attract widespread negative publicity. Subsequently, the visit would be used by the duke and duchess's detractors as evidence that they were incipient Nazis. Nominally, this was a private tour to study projects to improve workers' housing and labor conditions, subjects Edward had always shown a genuine interest in at home during his visits to the Rhondda Valley and the northeast. Less altruistic, however, was the duke's wish to return to center stage, where he could be seen as a powerful force, his new wife by his side. Dudley Forwood believed that the duke's strongest desire was to have Wallis experience a state visit. "He wanted to prove to her that he had lost nothing by abdicating," according to Sir Dudley. "And the only way such a state visit was possible was to make the arrangements with Hitler." There was also an element of pique in the duke's woefully ill-judged decision to accept the führer's invitation: "When the Foreign Office and George VI asked him not to go he felt that they'd been bloody to me, why the hell should I do what they want? They denied my wife her right."[1]

On their tours of housing projects, youth camps and hospitals in cities such as Stuttgart, Dresden and Munich, local authorities were instructed to refer to Wallis as "Her Royal Highness," affording the duchess the status of a royal on tour that she had been denied in Britain. At the historic meeting with the führer at the Berghof, his mountaintop retreat outside Salzburg, the Duke of Windsor watched proudly as, amid pomp and pageantry, Hitler leaned over to kiss the duchess's hand. This startling image and the photograph of the duke smiling shyly as he shook hands with Hitler would linger decades after the event. Edward later stated: "In spite of Hitler's phenomenal sway over the German masses, their Führer struck me as a somewhat ridiculous figure, with his theatrical posturings and bombastic pretensions."[2]

When the duke praised in glowing terms the workers' housing and the marvel of full employment, his words were retrospectively ascribed to praising the entire Nazi regime, creating an enduring picture of a man who condoned Hitler's atrocities and gave comfort to Britain's enemies. When the duke was photographed waving to the crowds, it looked like he was giving the Nazi salute. However, at the time of the duke's visit, most members of the government would have agreed with the duke that the two countries shared many aspirations, that war with Germany was not inevitable, and that Soviet communism posed the greatest danger, not least from the threat of infection with social revolution.[3]

As well as Sir Dudley, the duke and duchess's party included Winston Churchill's son, Randolph. Apparently, earlier that year, Randolph

Churchill had tried, unsuccessfully, to secure his own invitation to the Berghof via Unity Mitford. He was delighted to be able to accompany the Duke and Duchess of Windsor and to brief his father afterwards about the controversial visit.

The duke's inspection of Nazi industrial and architectural showpieces was given fulsome coverage by Goebbels's propaganda machine, which made much of Edward's pro-German sentiments and anti-communist views. Nonetheless, when the newsreels were shown to British audiences at home, the Duke of Windsor was greeted with cheers. Yet Fleet Street played down the whole visit. At court, everyone was incandescent, asserting that the duke had behaved abominably, breaking his promise not to embarrass his brother and "dropping bombshell after bombshell." His friends and advisors were written off as "semi-Nazis."[4]

Wallis, despite her critics claiming she was also a Nazi, seemed indifferent to any political dimension of their visit. She wrote to Ernest only about the domestic details: "This is a most interesting trip, though very strenuous, starting at 8 am each morning and ending at 5. Tomorrow, to vary the tour a bit, we take the train at 7.15 am. Peter Pan is determined to help working conditions. He really likes those people much better than any of us—and I'm sure they are much nicer."[5] Never before had she "been thrown in with such a strange, ill-assorted company of men," she wrote afterwards. "They both repelled and fascinated. One thing was for sure: they were a humorless lot."[6] Once, while being driven down a street in Berlin, Wallis had remarked to a Nazi official on the "charming" German custom of setting flower boxes in the windows. "That depends upon the point of view" was the solemn response. "We had those things dropped on our heads by the Communists when we entered Berlin, and I still carry a scar from that time."[7]

As ever, Wallis came across as gracious and polite to everyone she met. After a dinner with Rudolf Hess, Hitler's deputy, his wife, Ilse, described the duchess as "a lovely, charming, warm and clever woman with a heart of gold and an affection for her husband she made not the slightest attempt to conceal."[8] Dudley Forwood wrote of Wallis: "During my tours of duty with them both, she showed every kindness and understanding;

indeed often, when His Royal Highness was being somewhat difficult, she would overcome his stubbornness."[9]

On their return to Paris, the Windsors met the American ambassador to France, William Bullitt. He reported to President Roosevelt that the duke was "obviously intensely in love with his wife."[10] Of Wallis, he noted that she "behaved like a person whose insides have been taken out and replaced by an idea of what a King's wife should be like. She has lost that spontaneous wit and twinkle which used to make her very attractive; instead she is 'gracious.' I had the feeling that if one had her alone for a few minutes she would probably say: 'isn't this a hell of a mess but don't you think that I am doing it well?'"[11]

The arch anti-appeaser, Winston Churchill, congratulated the duke on his visit to Germany, which he thought had gone surprisingly well. "I was rather afraid beforehand that your tour in Germany would offend the great numbers of anti-Nazis in this country, many of whom are your friends and admirers," Winston told him, having been briefed by Randolph. "But I must admit that it does not seem to have had that effect, and I am so glad that it all passed off with so much distinction and success."[12] But the duke finally heeded Lord Beaverbrook's advice to step away from the public arena for a while, after he was mocked and scorned in the press for his German trip. A cartoon in the *New York Times* depicted him leaning on a trunk with labels saying "St. James's Palace, Honeymoon Castle, Château de Candé, Paris Hotels," with a billboard behind him blazing "Duke of Windsor to study Housing."[13] A similar trip organized by Charles Bedaux to America, which Wallis was looking forward to because a visit to the White House was on the cards, was sensibly canceled. By then Bedaux was recognized as a Fascist sympathizer and was no longer welcome in his adopted homeland. Not only did he have to cancel the Windsors' tour but officials of the American Bedaux company demanded he sever his connection to the firm he had founded.[14]

In May 1938, exactly a year after their divorce, Wallis wrote to Ernest, who was then in New York. In her valediction, she seems aware that she is at another crossroads in her life. "Ernest dear, what can I say when I am standing beside the grave of everything that was us. . . . Oh my very dear Ernest I can only cry as I say farewell and press your hand very tightly and pray to God. Wallis."[15] For Wallis, living in eternal limbo raised the specter of her peripatetic childhood. She longed for stability in the form of her own domain.

After a brief spell renting a house in Versailles, that spring the duke and duchess settled on a splendid large white-walled villa, known as La Croë, in the French Riviera. Set on the Cap d'Antibes in twelve acres of land stretching down to the sea, the villa boasted a dramatic swimming pool hewn out of rock, and a dining room that could seat twenty-four. Taking a ten-year lease on the property gave Wallis the opportunity to create the home that she and the duke yearned for. The press made a fuss about the ostentation—a bath in the shape of a swan was reputedly made of gold. The swan bath had nothing to do with Wallis, as it had been installed by Sir Pomeroy Burton, a British newspaper proprietor who had built the villa eleven years earlier.

With considerably superior taste to Sir Pomeroy's, Wallis set about transforming the property. All her belongings from Cumberland Terrace, along with the duke's prized possessions from the Fort and York House, were taken from storage at Frogmore and shipped to France. "My principal contribution to the decor," Wallis said, "was a blue and white color scheme, to harmonize with the blue of the sea and the white clouds that drift lazily across the perpetually azure sky."[16] The author Rebecca West said admiringly of the duchess: "There are not many women who can pick up the keys to a rented house, raddled by long submissions to temporary inmates, and make it look as if a family of good taste had been living there for two or three centuries."[17]

While never doubting her style, close friends felt that Wallis tried too hard to re-create the grandeur of royal palaces in the Windsors' residences. Wallis assumed that such decor would comfort the duke, whom she believed expected to be surrounded by the trappings of royal life: coronets on plates and liveried footmen. At the Fort, what Edward had valued most was the relative simplicity and cozy informality he had created there. Wallis, however, ever conscious that because of her, the duke was a royal-in-exile, built a minicourt around him. "While I could not hope to re-create on the Riviera the splendor of the life into which David had been born," she later explained, "at least he seemed happy in his new role of husband and man of the house."[18]

At La Croë, Winston Churchill was amused to find "everything extremely well done and dignified. Red liveries, and the little man himself dressed up to the nines in the Balmoral tartan with dagger and jabot etc. When you think that you could hardly get him to put on a black tie and short coat when he was P of W, one sees the change in the point of view."[19] A flag bearing the Prince of Wales's feathers flew above the property, the Garter banner of the Prince of Wales hung in the hall, while a large red-and-white tent adorned with the heraldic feathers was used for guests to undress in before bathing.

Every day, a program for the duke was put on the table in the hall. A guest at La Croë, Prince Jean-Louis de Lucinge, saw it and told his friend Diana Mosley about it. The duke liked to know who the guests, if any, were going to be, where they were dining, what time he was meeting someone for golf. "None of it was important," said Diana Mosley, "but all his life he had been accustomed to a programme, and the duchess wisely saw to it that he should have one."[20] The one thing Wallis was unable to fulfill was the "the calendar blocked out as much as a year ahead." The duke missed the daily inflow of red boxes from Whitehall bringing the never-ending news of state business. "It was devolved upon me to attempt to fill for him this perhaps unfillable gap," Wallis recalled. "I sometimes used to say to myself that today I have to be Canada, tomorrow I have to be New Zealand, and perhaps the next day the Fiji islands."[21]

The duchess did her best to cocoon the duke from the more mundane aspects of nonregal life. Like all royals, he had never carried cash in his life, so Wallis took care of all payments to tradesmen and oversaw the domestic side of their life; and she reined in his overzealous purchases of everything from tens of thermos bottles to boxes of thermometers, the former king still in the mind-set of buying in bulk for his many royal palaces. La Croë had sixteen servants, including two chauffeurs, an English butler and a French chef. According to Baron de Cabrol, "under the influence of the Windsors, the Château de la Croë was to become a cult café society venue, which it was good form to visit at least once a season and take tea served by manservants in livery and white gloves."[22]

Elsa Maxwell recalled: "I found that the duchess had an unusual flair for making a home highly attractive. Her food is superb and she knows how to make the most of furnishing and decorations. So, after dinner, she took us on a group tour of the château, which featured, among other things, a gold bath-tub." Elsa was particularly taken by the duchess's dressing table in her bedroom, which was decorated with mementoes of her courtship by the duke. "The top of the table was painted with the first formal invitation she received from the then Prince of Wales, fragments of a letter, a bouquet of flowers with the royal crest, a pair of white evening gloves, a fan and a pair of golf socks evidently worn by the duke on a weekend in the country." Downstairs in the drawing room, tables were laid out for bridge and gin rummy.[23]

"In this extremely grand seaside ambiance," wrote the Baron de Cabrol, "the Windsors received the whole world, and among them their neighbour Willy [Somerset] Maugham, the Aga Khan, Churchill and his wife Clementine"—the Churchills would later celebrate their fiftieth anniversary there—"Leopold, the ex-King of Belgium, likewise a neighbor, Noël Coward, and many other English friends, including the Dudleys, the Seftons, Sir John Aird, the Buists, and the Moncktons. From time to time they also gave dinners in the deluxe hotels round about, particularly the Hôtel de Paris in Monte Carlo, where they would go gambling at the casino and at the Hôtel du Cap d'Antibes."[24]

Harold Nicolson was staying with their neighbor Somerset Maugham when the duke and duchess came to dinner. The duke entered with his "swinging naval gait, plucking at his bow tie," recalled Nicolson. The duke explained their late appearance: " 'Her Royal Highness couldn't drag herself away.' He had said it. The three words fell into the circle like three stones into a pool. Her (gasp) Royal (shudder) Highness (and not one eye dared to meet another)."[25] When Nicolson talked at length with

Wallis, she told him that she both wished and intended to return to England, explaining: "I don't want to spend all my life in exile."[26]

Two days later, the writers Nicolson and Maugham were invited back to lunch at La Croë. Nicolson noted the elaborate food: melon filled with tomato sorbet, eggs with crab sauce, chicken with avocado pear salad, a pudding which apparently only Queen Alexandra knew how to make and fruit. The duke, who eschewed lunch, ate nothing, but waited patiently for his cup of tea at five o'clock. Nicolson considered that he looked "epileptic—a brick red face against which his fair hair and eyelashes look artificial."[27] When Nicolson told the duke that he was going back to London the next day, "his eye twitched in pain."[28] At the end of the summer, the Windsors left the Riviera for the Hôtel Meurice in Paris.

That August, the ever-loyal Sir Walter Monckton had visited George VI at Balmoral, where the prime minister, Neville Chamberlain, was one of the guests, with the aim of negotiating a return for the Duke and Duchess of Windsor. As soon as the subject of the Windsors arose, the king insisted that his wife, the queen, must participate in the discussion. Clearly, Elizabeth's influence would predominate. Chamberlain thought that the right course of action would be for the Duke of Windsor to be treated as soon as possible as a younger brother of the king, in order to take some royal functions off his brother's hands. "The King himself," Monckton recorded, "though he was not anxious for the duke to return as early as November 1938 (which was what the duke wanted) was not fundamentally against the Prime Minister's view. But I think that the queen felt quite plainly that it was undesirable to give the duke any effective sphere of work."[29] Monckton's own view was that the queen "thought that she must always be on her guard because the Duke of Windsor, to whom the other brothers had always looked up, was an attractive, vital creature who might be the rallying point for any who might be critical of the new King."[30] Monckton had the unenviable task of telling the duke, desperate to come back to England, that he must postpone his return until at least the new year.

That November, the Duke and Duchess of Gloucester, on their return from a safari in Kenya, visited the Windsors in Paris. At the Hôtel

Meurice, they were met by the British ambassador, Sir Eric Phipps, and his wife, and taken to the Windsors' suite. Princess Alice greeted her American sister-in-law with a kiss. The *Daily Mail*'s Paris correspondent, Harold G. Cardozo, reported: "There was no doubt that the Duke of Windsor was delighted at seeing his brother again and being able to discuss with him details of his own possible future journey back to England to see his mother, Queen Mary, and other members of the Royal Family. It is expected here that the visit will be in time for the Christmas festivities at Sandringham."[31]

This expectation proved wildly inaccurate and optimistic. The following day, the Court Circular noted that "the Duke and Duchess of Gloucester have arrived from abroad." It omitted to mention that they had visited the Windsors. All Princess Alice sourly ventured to Queen Elizabeth of their encounter was that she felt shown up by Wallis's elaborate purple dress and diamond clips in her hair, as she had worn a simple blue dress, the "red dust of Kenya hardly out of my hair" from the safari.[32]

When Neville Chamberlain came to Paris that month, Edward requested a meeting with him. "This seemed to David a simple and direct way for him to ascertain the feelings of the Palace and the Government on the question of his returning to Britain," Wallis recalled. "It was always in David's mind to retain his British ties; the idea of becoming an expatriate had never occurred to him."[33] Wallis was unclear as to whether the matter was for the British government or the king to decide. She was astonished that when she asked Edward, he could not give her an answer. "In fact," he said, "I doubt whether anyone can. Because there's no precedent, this is a twilight zone."[34]

Edward reported to Wallis that during his meeting with Chamberlain, the prime minister was "cordial, interested, but non-committal."[35] He proposed to discuss the matter with Parliament and the king.

"David waited hopefully," Wallis observed. But as the weeks passed, there was no word from Downing Street or the palace. When he finally made inquiries, "all he could ever find out was that the Government considered that the question of David's returning to Britain was a private matter between him and the king, and the Palace considered it a matter in which the Government should tender advice; and there things lay."[36]

"The Palace and Downing Street played a sort of game with him," said Diana Mosley, "each putting the blame for delay upon the other, turn and turn about. Perhaps neither wished to occur the odium of telling him outright that the reason was they emphatically did not want a living legend to come back to England and had hit upon this simple way of stopping him."[37] The royal embargo on the Windsors showed no signs of abating. When, earlier that year, the king and queen paid a state visit to France, the Duke of Windsor was excluded from the proceedings. Courtiers discouraged the British ambassador in Paris from inviting the duke to diplomatic functions.

With his nostalgia for Fort Belvedere, the duke must have been especially aggrieved to receive an anonymous letter, telling him that all at the Fort was desolation. The swimming pool was full of leaves; weeds were growing between the paving stones. "The King has said he is going to let the house and grounds go to ruins so bad that you will not be able to live in it again. I think this is wicked," warned the secret correspondent.[38]

A Gallup poll conducted early in 1939 showed that 61 percent of the British population wanted the Windsors to return (16 percent said they were against it, and 23 percent said they did not know).[39] Yet George VI would not relent. By this time, his relationship with his brother had been eroded over constant financial wrangles. The duke felt cheated out of some of his pension and argued over the value of Sandringham and Balmoral; most of all, his resentment burned over the Crown's attempt to link payment of his allowance from investments in his share of royal properties with his promise not to return to England without the consent of the government. In March 1939 Edward was positively blistering with rage. He had offered to pay £4,000 as half the cost towards an effigy, by Sir William Reid Dick, for his father's tomb in St. George's Chapel. Although he realized that he would not be invited to its dedication, he wanted proper acknowledgment of his financial contribution. When this was omitted in the press, he felt that the last vestiges of family loyalty and affection had been obliterated. He wrote a furious letter to his mother and from then on ceased to communicate with her, until the death of his beloved brother the Duke of Kent in 1942. "Queen Mary was actually very fond of the Duke of Windsor and was extremely upset by him," said Hugo Vickers. "From that point on, he ignored her birthday on May 26 each year, which caused her great distress. She always sent him a gift and a card for his birthday on June 23, which he never acknowledged."[40]

As the family squabbles continued, both sides were left feeling that the other had behaved disgracefully. It did not augur well for a return to Britain for the duke and duchess, far less for any form of welcome back into the family fold. At the heart of all the duke's grievances lay his family's refusal to accept Wallis. Edward simply could not accept that this was anything other than a temporary aberration which would surely change. Each time the offence was renewed, he felt the same anguished shock, then fury. Colin Davidson, a young, forthright equerry to the duke, warned Edward that "every time they heard in England that he was doing it [referring to his wife as HRH] the reconciliation and arrangements for his return were probably retarded."[41] Davidson also wrote to Monckton of the shabby treatment of Wallis: "The public must soon realise that she is making him very happy and that she must have some reward. And that the only way to manage him is to refrain from what he thinks is insulting him. If only his own family would sink their own personal disinclinations to treat her as his wife, I feel that they would be doing a National Service. She may be a little common and twice divorced but nevertheless she is the legal wife of the ex-King of England and after all he did abdicate. He was not kicked out."[42]

In the late autumn of 1938, the Windsors took another temporary lease, on a house in Paris, at 24 Boulevard Suchet. Close to the Bois de Boulogne, it was ideal for walking Pookie, Preezie and Detto, their family of adored dogs, and was not far from the golf links at Saint-Cloud. "The house was more luxurious than beautiful," Diana Mosley recalled. "It was big, with several drawing rooms, ideal for parties. The duchess took endless trouble with furnishing and decorating this house."[43] The Comtesse René de Chambrun remembered dining there, where footmen in scarlet livery lined the stairs. On the dining room table, lit by copious candles, were gold goblets filled with lilies.[44] The duke and duchess would probably have spent gentle years at the house, entertaining and dividing their time between Paris and La Croë, had war not broken out.

Both brothers, the Duke of Windsor and George VI, were united in wanting peace at any price, reflecting the views of the majority of the British public. As a veteran of the Great War who had seen the horrors of modern, industrialized conflict, the duke could not bear to contemplate another generation decimated by total war. The king fervently supported Neville Chamberlain's policy of appeasing Hitler, but the duke was more aligned with Churchill on the issue of rearmament. While the Foreign Office prevented the king from sending Hitler a direct plea for peace ("as one ex serviceman to another'), the duke sent a personal appeal on August 27, 1938. It was futile: the Nazi–Soviet pact had just been signed and Germany was poised to invade Poland. The duke, however, never ceased to claim "If I'd been King, there'd have been no war."[45]

Wallis remembered the outbreak of war vividly. The third of September 1939 was an especially hot and humid day, even for the Côte d'Azur. The Windsors were at La Croë. Fruity Metcalfe was visiting. That morning, the French footmen and assistant gardener received a postal summons to report for military duty. They wanted to personally say good-bye to the duke, who shook their hands and wished them well. Unable to reach London by telephone, as the French circuits were jammed, the duke and duchess, along with Fruity, decided to go for a swim. As the trio descended down the lane to the sea, over which hung the pool, a servant hurried out to tell the duke that the British ambassador was calling from Paris. Ten minutes later, Edward returned and said: "Great Britain has just declared war on Germany, and I'm afraid in the end this may open the way for world communism." He then dived into the swimming pool.[46]

However, the duke had no intention of idling on the French Riviera while his countrymen hurried to the colors. His primary preoccupation was how he might serve. Phone calls to London were guarded, due to eavesdropping by both British and German agents, but the duke told

Monckton to relay the message: "I want to offer my services in any capacity that my brother deems appropriate, and I must return to Britain."[47] But when the king agreed to send an aircraft to bring the duke and duchess back from the Riviera, Edward instantly reignited his campaign for Wallis, initially refusing to return home unless the duchess was received at a royal residence. Fruity Metcalfe was aghast at such a stipulation during this fearful, pivotal time. "You have just behaved as two spoiled children," he accused the Windsors. "You don't realise that there is at this moment a war going on, that women and children are being bombed and killed while *you* talk of your PRIDE."[48]

The king presented his brother with a choice of two jobs: either he could join the British military mission, attached to the French general headquarters at Vincennes, Paris; or serve as Regional Commissioner of Wales, a civil defense job that would require the couple to take up residence in Britain. "They would both stay in Wales," George VI told his mother. However, the king insisted that top-secret information must be kept from Edward due to deep-seated suspicions over the Duchess of Windsor's loyalties.[49]

Far from ferreting out official secrets, Wallis, who was terrified of flying, was anxiously negotiating a way to travel back to Britain by sea. The Duke of Windsor requested that a Royal Navy destroyer be sent. As Winston Churchill was now first lord of the Admiralty, Edward's request was sanctioned. Lord Louis Mountbatten and his destroyer, HMS *Kelly*, was dispatched to collect the Windsors from Cherbourg. Randolph Churchill, resplendent in the uniform of the 4th Hussars (marred only by his upside-down spurs), attended on behalf of his father.[50] Wallis, meanwhile, concerned that they might never see France again, frantically wrapped Edward's most valued possessions in brown butcher paper and packed them in cardboard boxes. The cairn terriers were piled into a car, along with the cardboard boxes, and she, the duke and Fruity Metcalfe drove to northern France.

The royal family awaited their return with uncharitable trepidation. On August 31, Queen Elizabeth had written to her mother-in-law from Buckingham Palace: "If David comes back here (I suppose he must if there is a war), what are we going to do about Mrs. S? Personally I do not wish to receive her at all, tho' it must depend on circumstances, what do you feel about it Mama? I am afraid that if they do return they will wriggle their way into things—tho' not come to court functions of course. It is a very difficult position & a great nuisance, with many pitfalls."[51] Baba Metcalfe may not have been Wallis's most ardent fan, but even she was incensed by the way the Windsors were treated on their return to England. "They were offered no accommodation anywhere so I invited them to stay at South Hartfield," she wrote. "Not only were no rooms made available to the Windsors during their visit but no car was made available to meet them. Walter asked the Palace but was told that nothing was going to be done from that quarter so they were our guests."[52]

Almost three years after Edward had left England in the middle of the night on one destroyer, he returned on another. As they entered Portsmouth harbor, at around 9.30 p.m., Edward turned to Wallis and said pensively: "I don't know how this will work out. War should bring families together, even a Royal Family. But I don't know."[53] After giving his wife's hand a reassuring squeeze, he walked out of the cabin.

Touchingly, Winston Churchill had given orders for the Windsors to be received with due ceremony. A guard of honor of one hundred men—wearing tin hats and gas masks—was drawn up and a strip of red carpet was laid to the gangway of HMS *Kelly*. "Even in the pitch darkness the little ceremonial was beautifully carried off, as only the British can manage such things," said Wallis. "David was stirred. He remarked later: 'Of course, I have seen hundreds of guards of honour, but I don't think I was ever prouder of inspecting one.'"[54]

"After a lot of handshaking and guard-reviewing, we went down and had dinner in Dickie [Mountbatten]'s cabin," recalled Baba Metcalfe, who was waiting with Sir Walter Monckton for the Windsors at Portsmouth. Admiral Sir William James, the new commander in chief at Portsmouth, and his wife put the duke and duchess up for the night in Admiralty House. The foursome chatted for a while before retiring to bed. "They were nice to me, almost desperately polite," Wallis remembered. "However, under the politeness, I became aware that it was I, rather than the former king, who was the object of their covert curiosity. When I was chatting with one, I could feel the sidelong glance of the other, charged with speculation, roving searchingly over me."[55] For the rest of her life, Wallis would face this oblique scrutiny, pregnant with the unasked question: Can this really be *the* Mrs. Simpson who caused it all? Is this really the woman who took our king from us?

The following morning, Baba Metcalfe collected the Windsors in her car, while her husband drove a van containing their luggage. The duke and duchess took up residence with the Metcalfes at their homes in South Hartfield, East Sussex, and at 16 Wilton Place, London. With Britain now officially at war, the duke's return attracted little excitement. The novelist and *New Yorker* columnist Mollie Panter-Downes wrote: "The Duke and Duchess of Windsor came home in a blaze of public apathy. No one seemed particularly glad or sorry, but everyone felt it was natural that yet another anxious family should want to be reunited in such times. The *Express*, always a fierce Windsor partisan, devoted space to the duke's reading on the journey, *Nazi Germany Can't Win*, and to the duchess's travelling coat—mustard-and-black tweed."[56]

On September 14, the duke met his brother at Buckingham Palace. It had been agreed with Major Hardinge that it would be "easier" if no women were present. The meeting was civil but "unbrotherly," reported the king. Edward, the king felt, "was in a very good mood, his usual swaggering one, laying down the law about everything."[57] "The Duke has slipped quietly around London," wrote Panter-Downes. He "has been photographed shaking hands with [Minister of War] Hore-Belisha at the War Office, and has taken tea with his brother at Buckingham Palace, where the sentries have put away their red coats for the duration and now mount guard, minus tourists with Kodaks, in khaki battle dress."[58] The duke had decided that he would like to accept the position in Wales, which would keep him in Britain. He had told the king this at their meeting. Suddenly his brother felt that it would be preferable for Edward to be stationed in France. He did not want to give the duke the chance to "take his wife and flaunt her before the British Army."[59] After just two weeks in Britain, the Windsors were to be sent back across the Channel.

"So far as David's family or the Court was concerned, I simply did not exist," Wallis later wrote. "The fact that our love had withstood the tests and trials of three difficult years made no difference. Neither did his desire to share, however humbly, the war time burdens of the Royal Family and the hazards that war would present to us all."[60] Typical of the English upper classes, nothing was ever said. "It was simply a case of our being confronted with a barrier of turned backs, rigid and immovable."[61] Wallis bore the hostility and malice with characteristic equanimity.

Three days before Edward and Wallis's return to France, on September 29, Queen Elizabeth wrote to her mother-in-law from Buckingham Palace. "I haven't heard a word about Mrs. Simpson—I trust that she will soon return to France and STAY THERE. I am sure that she hates this dear country, & therefore she should not be here in war time."[62] The queen kept up her delusional menace of the duchess, writing to Prince Paul of Yugoslavia in the weeks that followed:

> David's visit passed off very quietly. He and Mrs. S stayed with Baba and Fruity Metcalfe, & they have returned to France, where let us hope they will remain. I think that he at last realises that there is no niche for him here—the mass of the people do not forgive quickly the sort of thing he did to this country, and they HATE her! D came to see Bertie, and behaved as if nothing had EVER happened—too extraordinary. I had taken the precaution to send her a message before they came, saying I was sorry I could not receive her. I thought it more honest to make things quite clear. So she kept away, & nobody saw her. What a curse black sheep are in a family![63]

Before leaving England, the duke and duchess made a sentimental visit to the Fort. "The lawn was overgrown," Wallis observed. "The garden in which we had spent so many happy hours together had become a mass of weeds; and the house itself, shuttered, damp, and dark, was slowly decaying." It must have been unbearably painful for the couple. Yet Wallis, ever restrained, simply declared: "It was a sad visit."[64]

Whatever she did, it seemed, Wallis could not win. Nor could Edward. If he successfully carried out his war service, he would be perceived as upstaging his brother. If he failed, he would be chastised for letting down the monarchy. As a member of the British Expeditionary Force's military mission in Paris, liaising with the French high command, "Major General the Duke of Windsor" made a good impression. Sir Walter Monckton, who accompanied the duke to lunch at General Gamelin's headquarters at the Château de Vincennes, wrote: "HRH was wonderful. . . . He got everything going well and everyone talking and laughing etc. He really is first class at something like this."[65] However, the duke soon found himself sidelined, and his carefully compiled reports on French defenses were ignored. Many in the upper echelons of power saw his posting as pointless and contrived. The Scottish peer Lord Crawford dismissed Edward as "too irresponsible as a chatterbox to be entrusted with confidential information, which will be passed on to Wally at the dinner table."[66]

Wallis, who was staying in a hotel in Versailles, was similarly keen to do her bit for the war effort. She joined a French relief organization, the Colis de Trianon-Versailles, which had been set up by her friend Elsie de Mendl. (Lady Mendl would later be awarded the Croix de Guerre and the Légion d'Honneur for her relief work with gas-burn cases.[67]) Wallis spent long days packing comfort kits for the French troops of knitted sweaters, socks, soap, gloves, cigarettes and toiletries. Wearying of hotel life, she moved back into their house in central Paris, on the Boulevard Suchet. She lived there with the dust covers shrouding the furniture, the tall windows blacked out with heavy, dark curtains and the carpets rolled up alongside the walls. She took another job, joining the motor branch—the Section Sanitaire—of the French Red Cross. In her own car, the duchess drove to hospitals behind the Maginot Line delivering plasma, bandages and cigarettes. Wallis later acknowledged: "I was busier and perhaps more useful than I had ever been in my life."[68]

The duke and duchess spent the period later dubbed the phony war, from September 1939 to April 1940, mostly apart and often on the move. When an awkward incident broke out concerning Edward and his brother, Henry, Duke of Gloucester, Wallis wrote: "We had two wars to deal with—the big and still leisurely war—in which everybody was caught up, and the little cold war with the Palace, in which no quarter was given."[69] Both Edward and Henry, also a major general but now outranking the Duke of Windsor in precedence, had been invited to visit the headquarters of the British Expeditionary Force near Arras on October 18. Buoyed by the warmth of the reception he received from the soldiers on the ground, Edward made the mistake of instinctively taking salutes intended for the commander in chief, Lord Gort. A few days later, he was informed that he had violated military etiquette and that, from then on, his tours must be confined to the French sector. The Duke of Gloucester also felt upstaged. Edward was accused of pushing himself forward inappropriately, causing Gort's chief of staff, Henry Pownall, to rail: "If Master W. thinks he can stage a comeback he's mighty wrong."[70]

The Duke of Windsor was understandably outraged. His demand for an interview with the king, whom he accused of unbrotherly hatred, was declined. Churchill tried to smooth things over, counseling Edward to treat petty matters of precedence and protocol as beneath his dignity. Wallis astutely concluded: "David has always had a gift for dealing with the troops—the gift of the common touch and understanding. His admiration and respect for the fighting men in the ranks are deep, and its roots go back to the trenches of the First World War. It seems to me tragic, that this unique gift, humbly proffered, was never really called upon, out of fear, I judged, that it might once more shine brightly, too brightly."[71]

The duke's obsession with his family's persecution of him was given fresh impetus when he received news in February 1940 that the king had turned Fort Belvedere over to the government. This was seen as the king's preliminary thrust to reneging on his verbal agreement to reserve it for his brother. Wallis wrote to a friend: "We are both thoroughly disgusted and fed up in every way but are caught like rats in a trap until the war ends."[72]

On May 10, 1940, Hitler turned on the Low Countries and France. A week later, as the Panzers rapidly advanced, Edward drove Wallis to Biarritz. He returned to Paris briefly but, unwilling to leave Wallis alone, soon hurried south again, stuffing his car with valuables and abandoning senior staff in his desire to get to Wallis. The duke's actions drew fierce criticism from his friend and equerry Fruity Metcalfe, who told Lady Metcalfe: "I am *very* uneasy about him. He talks of doing *anything*—anything *except* the right thing. . . . W is like a magnet. It is terrible."[73] After the duke took the cars from Paris, stripping their Parisian home of its assets, Fruity resigned, forced to make his own way back to England without any transport. He wrote to Baba: "After twenty years I am through—*utterly* I despise him. . . . He deserted his job in 1936; well, he's deserted his country now. . . . It is the *end*."[74] Metcalfe believed that the duke should have remained at headquarters in Paris to help oversee the evacuation of the Dunkirk beaches, although the duke had been told to leave by his superior officer.[75] It was very difficult for outsiders to understand how desperately it mattered to the duke and duchess to be together in a world that seemed threatening and hostile on many levels; in a disintegrating Europe, the only thing it seemed they could cling to was each other. Even the appalled Fruity observed of their love: "it is *very true* and deep stuff."[76]

Before leaving Paris, the duke had managed to pause to collect his latest jewelry commission from Cartier. Several months earlier, he had visited Jeanne Toussaint, Cartier's design director, his pockets heavy with valuable stones from a necklace and four bracelets; together they created an impressive brooch: a flamingo with dazzling tail feathers of rubies, sapphires and emeralds. Thoughtfully, it even had a retractable leg, so that Wallis could wear it centrally, without the leg digging into her should she bend down. It was the duke's birthday gift to Wallis on June 19.[77]

As France collapsed, the Windsors fled to neutral Spain. On June 23, the duke's forty-sixth birthday, they arrived in Madrid, where Edward's old friend Sir Samuel Hoare had just been posted as British ambassador.

He told them that Churchill, prime minister since May following Chamberlain's resignation, was sending flying boats as part of a rescue mission to Lisbon to ensure the duke's safe return to Britain and that the Duke of Westminster had offered them Eaton Hall in Cheshire.

Yet again the duke, who was unable to think beyond his family's ill treatment of Wallis, fired off conditions, his hotheadedness persistently damaging any chance of détente with his family. He demanded a meeting with the king at which the duchess would be present, a job with royal backing, and compensation from the civil list if he lost his tax-free status. "When the world is crashing," Sir Samuel Hoare told him, "this is no time for bargaining."[78] For the past nine months, the duke had been simmering with resentment at repeated humiliations. Edward's sense of perspective had become wholly distorted and he now lashed out at every perceived slight, causing further irreparable harm. Wallis said of their time in Madrid: "In a material sense, David and I were more or less back where we were in December 1936—certainly homeless, once more adrift in a strange country, our possessions scattered, David without a post, and our prospects befogged."[79] For the first time in his life, the duke tried to exist without a valet. Although Wallis said that he "adapted himself to this refugee interlude with far more resourcefulness and good humor" than she had anticipated, he was "certainly no Admirable Crichton." It is said that no man is ever a hero to his valet; "it is almost impossible for a Prince to be a hero to his wife without a valet," Wallis quipped.[80]

While Edward continued to harass an embattled Churchill, a bizarre subplot was developing, of which the duke was entirely unaware. The Germans were weaving a web of conspiracy, poring over conversations recorded between the duke and duchess. As Hitler prepared his plans for the invasion of Britain, he became convinced that, should occupation prove necessary, he could somehow use the Duke of Windsor. Hitler and his foreign minister, Joachim von Ribbentrop, believed that Edward's rancor towards his family meant that he would agree to be installed as a puppet king of England. According to German diplomats, the duke was seen as "the logical director of England's destiny after the war."[81]

It is almost inconceivable that the duke would ever have consciously betrayed his country. He did not help his reputation by making defeatist-sounding statements about Britain's military preparedness and prospects against the Third Reich's war machine. But he undeniably loved Britain. He pined for it. His greatest wish was to return home and be treated as a royal alongside his brothers, with Wallis as consort. "I won't have them push us into a bottom drawer," he told the duchess during this time. "It must be the two of us together—man and wife with the same position. Some people will probably say that, with a war on, these trifles should be forgotten. But they are not trifles to me. Whatever I am to be I must be with you; any position I am called to fill I can only fill with you."[82]

The Windsors were oblivious to the elaborate plot, code-named Operation Willi, which entailed keeping the couple in Spain until Germany invaded Britain. Within days of the duke and duchess arriving in Madrid, German diplomats were working with their Spanish allies to try to convince the former king to remain in Spain. The couple were offered a small fortune and the mountaintop palace of Ronda, Málaga province, to sit out the war. The duke immediately notified Churchill, who insisted that the duke and duchess move to neighboring Portugal. The Foreign Office duly instructed Ambassador Hoare: "Please invite *Their Royal Highnesses* to proceed to Lisbon." The palace was furious, pointing out the breach of etiquette. At a critical moment in the war, the king's private secretary found time to chastise the Foreign Office for using the forbidden words "Their Royal Highnesses."

Meanwhile, Hitler ordered Walter Schellenberg, who was to become his spy chief in 1944, to travel to Lisbon to entice, or if necessary kidnap, the Windsors. Though Operation Willi came to nothing, when Churchill was shown the dossier after the war, he responded that the documents were "tendentious and unreliable" and should be destroyed for fear of damaging the monarchy. In 1957 the documents, known as the Marburg Papers, were published. They inspired persistent rumors that the duke was a Nazi sympathizer, yet were dismissed as self-serving misrepresentations.[83]

When the couple arrived in Lisbon, they found that the flying boats had been sent back to their bases due to the gridlock over the duke's incessant negotiations with Churchill. Wallis tried to persuade Edward that this "was a poor time to stand on a point of pride."[84] While she acknowledged that she desired recognition from her husband's family, this was not, she pointed out, a "mere desire for social status. Rather, I wanted it for the reason that I dreaded being condemned to go through the rest of our lives together as the woman who had come between David and his family."[85]

Sir Samuel Hoare pushed for the Windsors to be received by the king and queen, and for this meeting, if only for fifteen minutes, to be recorded in the Court Circular. Churchill sent a noncommittal reply, explaining that it would be sensible to consider everything when the couple had returned to England. An incensed Edward would not yield. He told the prime minister that he would not and could not return home as long as his conditions were ignored. Churchill was forced to remind the duke that he was still a serving officer in the British army and that his refusal to obey orders would have serious consequences. "I most strongly urge immediate compliance with the wishes of Government,"[86] read the angry telegram, with its veiled threat of court-martial.

After having time to stew, Edward informed Churchill that he was ready to serve anywhere the king and prime minister designated. On July 4, Churchill sent the duke a further telegram, offering him a governorship over four thousand miles away from Britain, in the Bahamas. He was also given the rather meaningless role of "Goodwill Ambassador to the Western Hemisphere." The former king and emperor accepted, telling Churchill: "I am sure that you have done your best for me in a difficult situation."[87] As governor of the Bahamas, it was hoped, the duke could be kept out of harm's way for the duration of the war.

No one viewed the appointment with any enthusiasm, apart from King George, who arranged to send Edward the accoutrements for ceremonial dress: the Garter, other orders and the Royal Victorian Chain. To the duke and duchess, it was another form of exile, while Queen Elizabeth tried to scuttle the entire plan on the basis that Wallis might be afforded a measure of official deference. Queen Mary would not even accept that the appointment had been intended. The issue, she believed, had arisen from a misunderstanding between Churchill and the duke. She wrote to the Countess of Athlone: "A great mistake to my mind on account of *her*."[88]

On August 1, 1940, at three in the afternoon, the Windsors sailed from Lisbon across the Atlantic on the American liner SS *Excalibur*. The sigh of relief from the British government, determined to diminish the duke's ongoing propaganda value to the Nazi regime, was almost audible.

11

A Shadow King

Wallis, while sad to leave Europe, was determined to shine in her first official role. "Much would be expected of David and even more of me as the wife of the Governor," she said. "I was anxious to do well for David's sake, knowing how much he wanted to make a success of his new post."[1]

Winston Churchill wrote amiably to the duke: "I am sure that Your Royal Highness and the Duchess will lend a distinction and a dignity to the Governorship."[2] Arrangements were made at Cabinet level to transport the royal couple as far as Bermuda, where they would be transferred to a Canadian ship, *Lady Somers*, bound for Nassau, the Bahamian capital. A full-scale reception ceremony had been arranged for the duke and duchess when they landed from the launch at the Royal Bermuda Yacht Club. In spite of the overwhelming heat, Wallis looked crisp in a white tailored suit, her flamingo brooch gleaming on her lapel.

"The Duke, not surprisingly, carried out his inspection and did all that was required of him in a manner made perfect by a lifetime of training," said the Government House aide-de-camp, Frank Giles. "But his brow darkened when he saw what he could not avoid seeing: the failure of [any] of the greeting wives to curtsey to the Duchess."[3] On his journey to the Bahamas, Edward had been comforted by only one thought: that the wife of a British governor had a settled status with which nothing could interfere. Immediately after the landing ceremonies, he went to complain to Giles over what he perceived as a deliberate snub to his wife. "Who ordered this?" Edward demanded angrily.

"Without saying anything I reached into a file of deciphered cables and handed him the one we had received from London, giving instructions on etiquette and modes of address," said Giles. "The Duke, it said, should be accorded a half-curtsey, but not the Duchess, who should be addressed as 'Your Grace.'" The duke read the telegram, sent from Lord Lloyd, the secretary of state for the colonies, "uttered a wordless expression of disgust and turned on his heel."[4]

And so the campaign against Wallis continued. Giles, however, developed a quiet admiration for the duchess during that first week spent with the Windsors in Bermuda. "She is a very clever woman," he noted. ". . . More than all the charm of her physical appearance, though, is her manner: she has, to an infinite degree, that really great gift of making you feel that you are the very person whom she has been waiting all her life to meet. With old and young and clever and stupid alike she exercises this charm," he continued. ". . . I never saw anyone who could resist the spell—they were all delighted and intrigued. . . . She is never anything but stately, and when she had to wave to the crowds on her arrival, and subsequently whenever we drove through [Hamilton], she did it with ease and charm and grace which suggested that she had been at it all her life."[5]

Government House stands on a hill, and from its pillared facade the view sweeps down to the sea, while from the back it looks over the gardens to the town of Nassau. As the *Lady Somers* entered the harbor and Wallis came on deck, Edward pointed out their future home. In the distance, it reminded Wallis of the southern plantation houses of her childhood, with spacious verandas, shuttered windows and swaying palms. On the morning of August 17, the Windsors, accompanied by a flotilla of bunting-covered craft sounding their horns in welcome, landed at Nassau. The royal couple walked breezily down the gangplank, Edward in his new field marshal's uniform, to be greeted by the waiting crowds, followed by their cairn terriers and fifty-seven pieces of luggage.

In 1940 the population of the Bahamas island group was around seventy thousand inhabitants, over 85 percent of whom had black African ancestry. A small colony of the British Empire, the Bahamas was physically and economically undeveloped and offered limited educational and industrial opportunities for its citizens. It openly exhibited racial discriminatory practices which, according to Sir Orville Turnquest, who became the fifth Bahamian governor general in 1995, the Duke of Windsor did nothing to address. "No black man or woman, unless as a servant or worker, was allowed to officially enter [Government House] during the duke's tenure,"[6] he said.

On the day of the duke's official reception at Government House, September 2, 1940, the summer heat was at its most intense. Both the duke and the chief justice poured with perspiration to the extent that their official signatures became two blots on the page. After the duke was sworn in, he and Wallis retired to the gardens to be interviewed by the press. When the duke was asked about the scope of his role as "goodwill ambassador to the Western Hemisphere," he replied pointedly: "I very much doubt that the British government has it in mind at present that my official activities should extend beyond the confines of the Bahama islands."[7]

Privately, the Windsors grumbled about the triviality of their roles and the challenges of being in the outpost, yet publicly, they were conscientious and enthusiastic. Wallis wrote to Aunt Bessie on August 7, 1940: "Naturally we loathe the job but it was the only way out of a difficult situation—as we did not want to return to England except under our own conditions."[8] She later described Nassau as "their Elba," likening the duke's appointment to Napoleon's island exile after he abdicated in 1814. The duke expressed equally negative sentiments about his tenure in the Bahamas; he later told Lady Diana Cooper: "It is very hard, once you've been King Emperor, to govern the Bahamas."[9] Regardless, the duke, schooled by Wallis to perfection, performed his official duties diligently with good grace. It was as if he were determined to demonstrate that if he was given a job to do, with his wife to support him, he would always excel.

"It was cruel [of the government] to send them to the Bahamas," believes Julie Le Corne, a resident of Nassau. "Government House was in a terrible state. It was not up to the standard of the duke and duchess. But the duchess surprised everyone; she wasn't sitting up on Government Hill having her nails done, she really got stuck in. There was such a negative view of her in the press, yet she was a really nice woman. My mother volunteered with her in the Services Canteen and said how kind and thoughtful she was."[10] On closer inspection, Government House, riddled with termites, was deemed uninhabitable for the royal couple. After a chunk of plaster fell from the ceiling in the drawing room where Wallis was sitting, the couple moved out. The building was renovated with a grant from the local legislature combined with the Windsors' own financial contribution. A complete internal overhaul included the installation of air-conditioning in each of the major rooms in the residence, while a new three-storey west wing (still known as the Windsor Wing) was added to house four guest suites to accommodate the duke's personal staff. While the building work was completed, Wallis and Edward were loaned the palatial home of Mr. and Mrs. Frederick Sigrist, on Prospect Ridge. Frederick Sigrist was a British aviation pioneer and millionaire who had founded the Hawker Aircraft Company. Longtime residents of the Bahamas, the Sigrists spent their summers abroad. When they returned in November, the Windsors again relocated, taking up residence at Westbourne, the country mansion of Sir Harry Oakes, a British-Canadian gold mine owner and one of the wealthiest men in the world. An unhappy Wallis disdainfully referred to his sprawling house as "a shack by the sea."[11]

At the Windsors' first social appearance on the islands, at the exclusive Emerald Beach Club in Nassau, Lady Jane Williams-Taylor, the acknowledged leader of local society, did not curtsy to Wallis. When the waiters brought the platters of food, they served the duke before the duchess. The duke, furious, instructed them to "serve the Duchess first." Their host, Sir Frederick Williams-Taylor, an elderly Canadian millionaire and president of the club, damningly omitted any reference to Wallis in his welcome speech. In his reply, the duke gave a blistering illustration of royal displeasure. He told the assembled audience that in the original text of the speech, which had been submitted to him before dinner, the welcome had included the duchess. The fact that she was not mentioned in the spoken version was, he felt sure, due to the dim lighting at the speaker's table. This, he imagined, would never happen again.[12]

Guests at Emerald Beach observed that "while the duke was having his say, it was the most magnificently embarrassing moment of their lives." As Lady Williams-Taylor remembered, when the duchess started to rise with the rest of the guests, the duke said: "You don't have to stand up for me, darling." The duchess quickly countered: "It's a pleasure to stand up for you, darling."[13]

"Wallis was incredibly popular on the island," said Ann Pleydell-Bouverie, whose parents knew the duke and duchess well. "She was well bred in an American sense and had perfect manners. My mother worked in the Red Cross with her and said she never heard anyone say a bad word about Wallis." She would bring "bags of little beads to teach local women and children to make craft."[14] The duchess became president of the Red Cross and started up two infant welfare clinics on New Providence Island. The clinics were modern and well run; Wallis bought a car for the visiting welfare nurse and attended clinic days. She organized the United Services Canteen for British and American servicemen, and arranged social events for them. She also supervised the interior decoration of Government House, lightening the heavy Victoriana with chintz and pale-green carpets. She hung her own portrait by Gerald Brockhurst over the mantelpiece and placed a rather severe photograph of Queen Mary on the duke's desk. Rumors of her extravagance were fueled when she flew in an interior designer from New York and shipped in exquisite period pieces of French furniture, some of which remain to this day.

"The duchess has always been the subject of silly stories, and it was widely believed that she went to get her hair done in Miami once a week," said Diana Mosley. "In fact, she disliked flying, and there are plenty of hairdressers in Nassau, but she did sometimes make shopping expeditions to Miami to buy garden furniture."[15]

"The duke and duchess threw wonderful parties and entertained beautifully," said Julie Le Corne. Her father, Charles Bethell, introduced the Windsors to Nassau society. The duke went duck shooting with Bethell, but it was Wallis who "intrigued" their host. "My father said that the duke was quite a bore but that the duchess was lovely. At cocktail parties the duchess would always gravitate to my father and talk to him. The duke would come and pull her away but at the next party, she would find my father again and the conversation would pick up exactly where they had left off. Wallis was very bright, captivating company and my father found her elegant and enigmatic."[16]

Wallis wrote to Sir Walter Monckton, who was working for British intelligence, running the government's information department in Cairo, in October. "There is no doubt that England carries on propaganda against us in the States in a sort of whispering campaign of the most outrageous lies against us—such as the hairdresser. There are many ways to twist things," Wallis said. "There will always be the court and the courtiers engaged in fifth column activities against us . . . it makes tears come to my eyes to see the duke doing this ridiculous job and making good speeches as though he were talking to the labouring classes of England and inspiring them to work . . . better to be in a shelter or called anything than buried alive here."[17]

In March 1941 the duke made a foolish indiscretion while being interviewed by the American novelist and broadcaster Fulton Oursler for *Liberty* magazine. The article gave the impression that the duke held no hope of a British victory in the war, and was swiftly reprinted by the *Sunday Dispatch* in London. Churchill was livid; he saw the duke's attitude as "defeatist and pro Nazi," and by implication approving of the isolationist stance of keeping America out of the war, though Edward later claimed that Oursler had put words in his mouth. Churchill instructed the duke to seek advice before making public statements of this kind. The querulous duke threatened to resign as governor, "if, as your message infers, I am more of a detriment than of assistance in these vital Anglo-American relations."[18]

Wallis made her position clear on the issue of whether America should enter the war. "I think it's all hideous and if one's in it one must pull for it," she told Monckton. "I am in complete disagreement, however, with the idea that if you mention peace, you are pro-Nazi and there is no relation between the two that I can conjure up. And when free speech is taken from us that is alarming."[19]

The duke leapt upon the court's right to free speech when an article in *Life* quoted the queen as referring to Wallis as "that woman." Edward wrote to Churchill: "I understand that articles about the Royal Family are censored in Britain before release, and this remark is a direct insult to my wife"—again using the opportunity to rage about "the chronic anomaly of my wife not having the same official status as myself."[20] Losing all patience, he snapped at Churchill: "I have both enjoyed and valued your friendship in the past but after the tone of your recent messages to me here I find it difficult to believe that you are still the friend you used to be."[21]

Churchill suggested that a "competent American publicist" instruct the duke before a proposed visit to the United States. Wallis, in favor of a press secretary, complained to Monckton that the couple had been on their own for four years when it came to dealing with the press and their endless falsifications. "The real truth, Walter, is that the government simply do not care what sort of stuff is printed and hide behind or blame us by saying 'what a pity such things are written.'"[22] She conceded it was unlikely that they would ever receive any real assistance or guidance from official sources. "It's always the same and will never change. However, if we didn't have to work for them it wouldn't be so difficult. Alas, we shall have to carry on I suppose for the duration but with victory won, we're off!!"[23]

The British embassy in Washington dispatched an experienced press officer called René MacColl to coach the duke before the Windsors' longed-for trip to America. A year earlier, the British government had prevented the royal couple from stopping in the States en route to the Bahamas, but now the duke and duchess were finally able to escape the scorching heat of the islands for the mainland. They were given permission for an extended trip, on the proviso that it did not clash with the Duke of Kent's presence in Canada and then Washington during the first week of September.

"That family of my husband's is always going to snub me," Wallis wrote to Aunt Bessie. "So one has to face the up to the fact, and face up to these humiliating situations which will forever give the American press a chance to belittle us."[24] Two weeks later, she reported: "We have been asked to stay in a hotel rather than in a private house or on Long Island. . . . There seem to be too many jealousies awakened the other way. . . . The world is funny—but not so funny as England's royal family."[25]

"MacColl arrives next Friday," Wallis informed Monckton. "I understand he's very nervous over it all. I believe he thinks HRH is for 'appeasement,' 'negotiated peace' and all the rest of the lies pinned on the duke."[26]

On September 25, the Windsors arrived in Washington. Unquestionably imprudent, they traveled with 73 pieces of luggage. (They owned 118 traveling trunks, each with a numbered lid.) The duchess, keen to flaunt her style and lavish jewels, having been confined to parochial Nassau, would have been wiser to exercise restraint at a time when Britons were being strictly rationed. The superfluity of their luggage, the splendor of their suite at the Waldorf Towers when they visited New York, Wallis's determination to make up for the previous year's deprivation with insatiable shopping, lent an unwelcome air of extravagance which the press leapt upon. Apart from this, the couple conducted themselves well and did nothing to antagonize or embarrass Anglo-American relations. Lord Halifax, the British ambassador, told Baba Metcalfe that the duke had behaved "most sensibly and ordinarily" except for their "ridiculous amount of luggage of which the papers were so critical. . . . I was a little outraged at being presented with a bill for £7.10.0 for hire of a lorry to take their luggage to and from the station."[27]

At a Washington embassy reception, both Lady Edwina Mountbatten and Lady Diana Cooper curtsied to the duchess—but Edwina d'Erlanger, wife of Baron Leo d'Erlanger, did not, on the grounds that Wallis was an American like herself. Lord Halifax, a friend of Queen Elizabeth, had met the duchess only once before. He now admitted to being "impressed with her general dignity and behaviour and . . . adroit good manners."

Bessie Wallis Warfield aged six months, with her mother, Alice, 1896.

Four generations: Edward, aged six, with his great-grandmother Queen Victoria, his grandfather Prince Edward (later King Edward VII) and his father Prince George (later King George V).

Naval cadets Edward and Bertie with their mother, Queen Mary, at Barton Manor, Isle of Wight, 1909.

The Prince of Wales, 1911.

A young Wallis, aged ten.

US Navy pilot Earl Winfield Spencer, Wallis's first husband.

Wallis with her bridesmaids and maid of honor for her marriage to Spencer, 1916.

"Adored and feted like a film star": Edward on tour, Halifax, Nova Scotia, 1919.

Edward with Winston Churchill, one of his political mentors, 1919.

Wallis and her second husband, Ernest Simpson, presented at court in June 1931.

Fort Belvedere: Edward's country retreat in Berkshire. (*Below*) Wallis relaxes at Belvedere with her favorite cairn terrier Slipper, 1935.

King George V's funeral procession, January 1936. Wallis was watching from St. James's Palace.

"A breathtaking breach of protocol," as Wallis places a hand on the king's arm during the *Nahlin* cruise along the Adriatic, August 1936.

Wallis, wearing the famous lobster dress by Schiaparelli, photographed for *Vogue* by Cecil Beaton at the Château de Candé, France, May 1937.

Three weeks after Bertie's coronation as George VI, Wallis and Edward marry, June 3, 1937, at the Château de Candé.

Never before published. An official event in Nassau, 1940. Afterwards, Wallis invited the girl who presented her with flowers to a children's party at Government House.

In Nassau during the Second World War, Wallis became local president of the Red Cross.

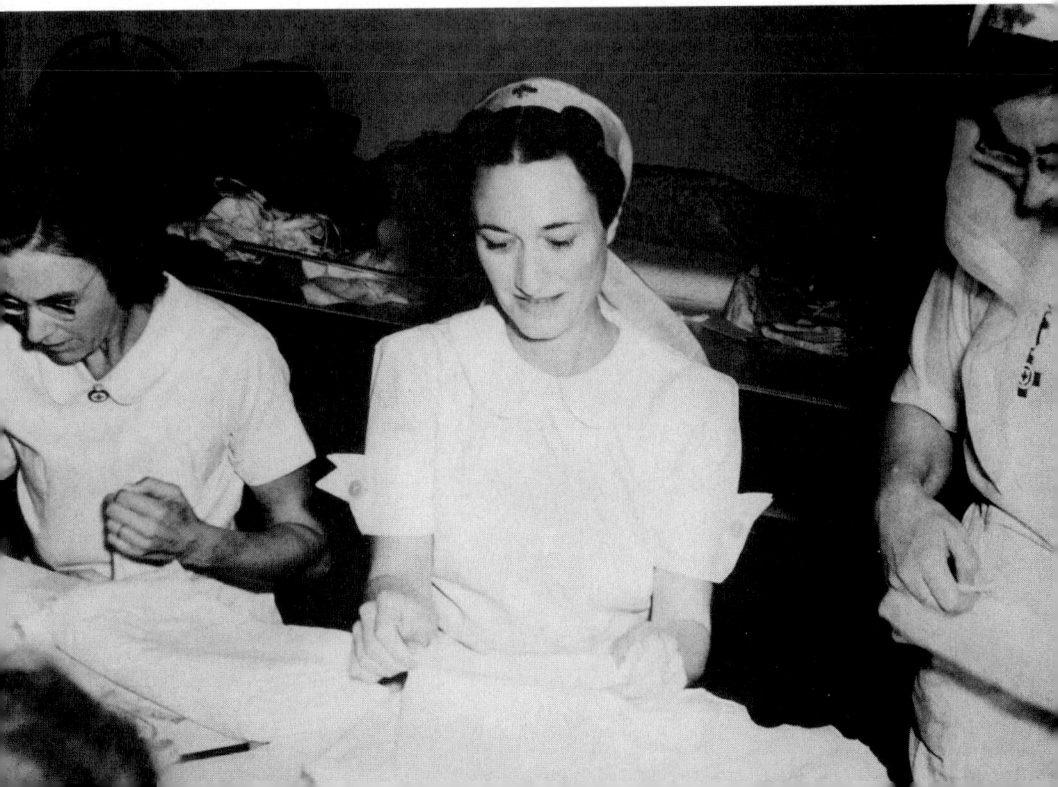

Never before published. The duke and duchess with their friend Charles Bethell, who introduced them to Nassau society, 1940.

Never before published. The duke and duchess on the steps of the Bahamian Club at a farewell party that they hosted, Nassau, 1945.

Dorothy Wilding's portrait of the duke and duchess, New York, June 1943.

"I had not seen him for nearly 9 years!" recorded Queen Mary of her son's visit to Marlborough House in October 1945. They relished their time together, but her views on his "unfortunate marriage" had not changed.

A life in exile: the duke and duchess return to France from a trip to the United States, 1955.

Never before published. Wallis dines at the Marbella Club, September 1964. Count Rudolf von Schönburg (*standing*), the Marquesa de Toreno, the Duke de Arion and the Duchess of Windsor.

The Queen, the Duke of Edinburgh and Prince Charles visit the duke and duchess in the Bois de Boulogne, in May 1972, shortly before the duke's death.

The Queen's guest: two days before Edward's funeral, Wallis watches the Trooping the Colour from Buckingham Palace, June 3, 1972. Incurably sad, it was her thirty-fifth wedding anniversary that day.

The Queen, Wallis and the Queen Mother leave St. George's Chapel after the funeral service for the Duke of Windsor.

Funeral of a duchess. Wallis's coffin is carried, watched by Prince Charles, the Queen, the Queen Mother and Princess Anne, April 20, 1986. There had been no funeral address, in accordance with the duchess's wishes. Nor any mention of her name or reference to her life.

Inside the house of the exiles: Wallis's bedroom in the villa in the Bois de Boulogne, with her glass-topped dressing table and pug cushions lined up on the sofa.

The author's bouquet of flowers: a tribute to Wallis at her grave at Frogmore, where she lies next to Edward under a wide-spreading plane tree.

Although he acknowledged that he was still puzzled as to how the king could have given up everything for her charms, he said: "she conversed quite easily and never said anything that had any east wind in it—again a mark of wisdom."[28]

On October 13, the duchess at last received her triumphant homecoming to Baltimore, where she and the duke were greeted by the mayor and a two-hundred-thousand-strong crowd, cheering and waving Union Jacks and American flags. But the highlight of their trip was lunch at the White House with the president and Mrs. Roosevelt. Lord Halifax reported to the king: "the duchess's behaviour was completely correct and in one tiny detail I thought she acted with considerable tact by making Mrs. Knox go in to luncheon in front of herself."[29] Yet the British Press Service Report of the Windsors' American visit came to the unedifying conclusion: "The general impression created was that of a rich and carefree couple, travelling with all the pre-war accoutrement of royalty and with no thought either to the suffering of their own people or the fact that the world is at war."[30]

On their way back to the Bahamas, the couple visited the duke's ranch in the hills of Alberta, Canada, which Edward had purchased over twenty years earlier. It was whilst she was there that Wallis learned of the unexpected death in England of her former best friend from school, Mary Raffray, who later married Ernest Simpson, from an aggressive form of breast cancer. She and Ernest had had a son together, Ernest Henry Child Simpson, who had been evacuated to friends in North America at the start of the war. Mary had yearned to be reunited with her child before she died. As a return flight across the Atlantic in the middle of war was not possible, Winston Churchill had come to their rescue. He arranged for a government plane for Mary, who was so frail she had to be carried on and off the aircraft on a stretcher, then taken across the runway in an ambulance. This was Churchill's tacit recognition, which could not be made public, of Ernest Simpson's exemplary behavior during his divorce from Wallis. Just before she died in October 1941, Mary wrote in her diary: "Ernest still thinks the Windsors are perfect."[31]

After Mary's death, Wallis wrote to Ernest: "God is difficult to understand at times for you deserved a well-earned happiness. If I can ever soften the blow that fate has dealt you, the duke and myself are ready to help in any way you may ask. Dear Ernest, I know you very well and all your honest and beautiful qualities, I know the depth of your sufferings—your son will be a stronghold for the future."[32]

On December 7, after the Japanese attacked Pearl Harbor, the United States formally entered the war. Back in the Bahamas, Wallis's relief work became more vital. "Wallis is very busy fixing up the RAF canteen," wrote her assistant Rosa Wood. "I really admire the way Wallis has thrown herself into all her various jobs. She really is wonderful and does work hard. I do hope that people everywhere are realising all the good she is doing. She has such charm and is always amusing to be with I really don't know what I would do without her."[33] Years afterwards, servicemen remembered the numerous plates of bacon and eggs personally served by the duchess. In 1942 Wallis compiled a book of her favorite southern recipes, donating the royalties to the British War Relief Society. Eleanor Roosevelt contributed the foreword.

The duke continued, all through the war, to hound Churchill with his endless requests: Wallis required minor medical attention in the United States; staffing arrangements were unsatisfactory at Government House. But most assiduous were his comments on Wallis's status in England. He never missed an opportunity to drive this point home. When asked by the secretary of state for the colonies to submit a list for the New Year honors, he wrote to Churchill: "I am now asking you, as Prime Minister, to submit to the king that he restores the Duchess's royal rank at the coming New Year not only as an act of justice and courtesy to his sister-in-law but also as a gesture of recognition of her two years of public service in the Bahamas. The occasion would seem opportune from all angles for correcting an unwarranted step."[34] George VI's response to Churchill on December 9 was that he was "sure it would be a mistake to reopen the matter. . . . I am quite ready to leave the question in abeyance for the time being but I must tell you quite honestly that I do not trust the Duchess's loyalty."[35]

It was easier for the royal family to believe scurrilous rumors than to consider hard and consistent evidence to the contrary. Unfortunately, the duke rarely helped matters. His meddling became tiresome and his new cohorts of friends were regularly deemed unwise. On January 14, 1942, one of the Windsors' closest friends in the Bahamas, the Swedish millionaire industrialist and founder of Electrolux, Axel Wenner-Gren, in whose yacht the duke and duchess had traveled to Miami two years earlier for the duchess to undergo dental treatment, was placed on the American State Department's Proclaimed List of Blocked Nationals. Friendship with someone suspected of being a Nazi collaborator did not make a good impression and Churchill wrote to the duke, warning him against having such individuals in his entourage. The duke was forced to sign a warrant that expelled Wenner-Gren from the Bahamas.

In June 1942, the duke was in Washington when a mass protest sparked two days of rioting in Nassau. Several people were killed and much of the Bay Street commercial district was looted and burnt. The duke flew back to the Bahamas, where he increased wages to five shillings a day, enforced a curfew, banned public meetings and censored the press. The war demanded labor and the duke secured an agreement from Washington that five thousand Bahamians should be recruited to work in the United States. The scheme, known as "the Contract," employed a sixth of all males on the island and was deemed "a momentous achievement."[36] Under the duke's tenure, a project also flourished whereby Americans were employed in the Bahamas to work side by side with local laborers at airports critical to US military strategy.

Despite these positive achievements, the Duke of Windsor's governorship was blighted by his handling of the murder of his friend Sir Harry Oakes. The millionaire was found bludgeoned to death in his bed on July 8, 1943, his corpse covered with feathers and set alight. The duke, ill suited emotionally to dealing with anything like murder, became overinvolved, creating a series of almost farcical blunders. He tried to silence the press and brought in two detectives from Miami, who fabricated fingerprint evidence and pushed for the arrest of Oakes's playboy son-in-law, Alfred de Marigny. So flimsy was the evidence presented in court that Marigny was acquitted. Rumors flared that the duke was involved with Sir Harry in illegal currency trading and thus prevented a proper murder inquiry. Oakes's killing still remains a mystery and has forever been fertile ground for sensational headlines and slander against the duke, who most likely did nothing more than act foolishly.

Sir Orville Turnquest, no fan of the duke's—he considered him "weak" and "racist"—concluded that the royal couple "set about establishing positive roles for themselves throughout their stay, which served to benefit the islands and its people."[37] Of Wallis, he declared: "For most of the duration of World War Two, the Duchess of Windsor served prominently as First Lady of the Bahama Islands, playing a leading and an outstanding role."[38]

During the Windsors' time in the Bahamas, two private matters caused the duke immense suffering. In January 1942, his beloved uncle Arthur, the Duke of Connaught, died, age ninety-two. This saddened Edward greatly. Wallis felt that "to David the passing of his Uncle Arthur represented the passing of an age—the secure and golden age of the monarchy in which his own splendid youth had been spent."[39] But nothing devastated him as much as the news that arrived by telegram late one evening that summer. His adored brother the Duke of Kent had been heading towards Iceland in a flying boat on August 25. It had crashed near Wick, in Scotland, killing Prince George, the pilot and all others on board. Edward was consumed with grief. Wallis watched his agonies, feeling helpless: "These two deaths brought home to me the essential inner loneliness of every human being."[40] On each occasion, the duke insisted that a memorial be held in the Nassau cathedral. At the second service, at Edward's request, his servant and piper, Fletcher, joined by the piper of the Cameron Highlanders, played the moving lament "The Flowers of the Forest." It must have been a truly desolate period for the duke, exiled from his family, excluded from the small comforts of shared grief, mourning his dear brother alone in the baking heat. "I had hoped that under the impact of these two blows so close together there would have been a drawing together of the family," Wallis recalled. "A softening of all hearts. But even these shared sorrows proved not enough."[41]

It was poignant that a few months earlier, in April 1942, Wallis had tried, without her husband's knowledge, to make "one last try to reach his mother and to heal the breach between them."[42] Wallis, who had been so close to her own mother, was genuinely pained by her husband's estrangement from Queen Mary. The bishop of Nassau and chaplain to the Royal Navy, the Right Reverend John Dauglish, had been recalled to Britain by the archbishop of Canterbury. Aware that Queen Mary might receive him, Wallis wrote a generous-spirited letter to her mother-in-law:

> Madam,
> I hope that you will forgive my intrusion on your time as well as my boldness in addressing Your Majesty. My motive for this letter is a simple one. It has always been a source of sorrow and regret to me that I have been the cause of any separation that exists between Mother and Son and I can't help feeling that there must be moments perhaps, however fleeting they may be, when you wonder how David is.[43]

Wallis gently suggested that if Queen Mary wished to hear news of her son, she might like to send for Bishop Dauglish, who could fill her in with "the little details of his daily life," before concluding:

> The horrors of war and endless separations of family have in my mind stressed the importance of family ties. I hope that by the end of the summer, we will be nearer to the victory for which we are all working so hard and for which England has so bravely lighted the way.
> I beg to remain,
> Your Majesty's most humble and obedient servant, Wallis Windsor[44]

"It is a nice letter," admitted the king, before adding uncharitably: "I wonder what is the real motive behind her having written. I must say I do feel a bit suspicious of it!!"[45]

Queen Mary did receive the bishop, who wrote to Wallis, describing his audience with the monarch's mother. She asked about her son with interest and the work he was doing. When Bishop Dauglish approvingly mentioned the duchess, he met "a stone wall of disinterest." However, when Queen Mary wrote to Edward about the Duke of Kent's funeral, she added the line: "Please give a kind message from me to your wife. She will help you to bear the sorrow."[46]

"David was astonished," Wallis said. "Now what do you suppose," he asked in genuine bewilderment, "has come over Mama?"[47] Wallis did not reply, and it was only thirteen years later, when she wrote her memoirs, that the duke found out the truth.

Typically, Edward leapt on his mother's tiny gesture of goodwill, hoping to force a more concrete reconciliation. His obsessive and pushy tendencies regularly undid whatever minuscule steps forward had been made. A more restrained and strategic approach could have resulted in a very different outcome for the duke and duchess. "If you gave the Duke of Windsor an inch, he took a mile," explained Hugo Vickers. "He could be hugely whiney, especially to Queen Mary and Queen Elizabeth."[48] Edward immediately wrote to his mother, detailing the love and comfort Wallis had given him, explaining that their long silence had been as painful for him as he was sure it was for her. He ended saying that he hoped he would have "the intense pride and pleasure of bringing Wallis to see you."[49]

As ever, on that, Queen Mary would not yield.

In May 1943, Churchill addressed Congress; the Windsors, who were in Washington, went to hear his speech, seated in the diplomatic gallery. Churchill's physician, Lord Moran, noted that "as the duke descended to his seat in the front row, he got as much clapping as Winston, or more, by which we were surprised."[50] Chips Channon noted: "The newspapers gave a vivid account of Winston's speech to Congress, and report that the Windsors were cheered on their arrival and departure: never before have they had an ovation in the USA. This is Winston's doing, and his attentions to them have obviously affected American opinion: people here [at Westminster] are a touch annoyed."[51]

On June 2, the duke and duchess visited the Fifth Avenue studio of the celebrated photographer Dorothy Wilding. They were first photographed separately, then together. As the duke sat for his solo portrait, his expression was melancholy. When Wilding asked what would prompt a smile, "he turned his head and looked across to the dressing room where his wife was receiving the expert attentions of Charles of the Ritz to her hair. 'You just wait till the Duchess comes out,' he said simply. 'She's the one who'll make me smile.'"[52]

Despite their ever-strengthening union, by the spring of 1944, the Windsors as a couple were becoming increasingly disconsolate. Desperate to leave the Bahamas, they began to agitate over their postwar future. The duke was keen for a roving commission in America, cooperating with the British ambassador but acting independently. Despite his popularity, given his notoriety and capacity for faux pas, it was more likely that the government would consider him a rogue diplomat than a safe pair of hands. But the duke never stopped badgering Churchill for a suitable role. Wallis believed that Edward "had been dumped here solely by family jealousy."[53] To a friend she wrote: "They murdered Sir Harry Oakes once. They will *never* stop murdering the Duke of Windsor. . . . It is his own family who are against him."[54]

In May 1944 the question of what the duke might do after the war was raised in court circles. Tommy Lascelles, by then King George VI's private secretary, did not want Edward in England. He said that the duke's presence would be "a constant agony (I use the word advisedly) to the present king, which might have really serious consequences."[55]

Winston Churchill, though, did not abandon the Windsors and made several more attempts to heal the rift within the royal family. The duke, who met with Churchill in September 1944, knew that it was court protocol and the right of every colonial governor and his wife to be received at Buckingham Palace, following an official posting. He pleaded with Churchill that he and the duchess be received by the king and queen, which would have "the merit of silencing, once and for all, those malicious circles who delight in keeping open an eight-year-old wound that should have been healed officially, if not privately, ages ago." Would Churchill not try to persuade the king and queen to "swallow 'the

Windsor pill' just once, however bitter they may think it is going to taste?"[56]

Typically, the king and queen did not relent. They made the case that in wartime the diplomatic rulers of Britain's colonies could not expect to be received by the royal family as in times of peace. Churchill delayed replying for three months, as the "King sent a most cold reply" to his request for a fraternal greeting to the duke. The queen told Tommy Lascelles that she and Queen Mary had drawn up a signed statement to clarify that "they were not prepared to receive the Duchess, now, or at any time, for the same reasons they would not do so in 1936."[57] Churchill passed this bitter missive on to the duke, who was understandably outraged. To preserve his pride, he responded that if that was the state of things, he and the duchess would never return to Britain. Faced with the utter hopelessness of the situation, the duke pointedly resigned from the governorship of the Bahamas ten weeks before his term officially expired. His resignation was announced on March 15, 1945.

The Windsors set sail on the short voyage from Nassau to Florida on May 3. Five days later, VE Day, the king and queen stood triumphantly on either side of Winston Churchill on the balcony at Buckingham Palace, taking in the jubilation of the London crowds. Edward and Wallis lay aimlessly in the sun in Palm Beach wondering what to do and where to go next. The duke still hankered after some official position but, as one by one the possibilities for him, which had included governorships in Madras and Ceylon, were extinguished from London, it would seem that his public life was over. He was fifty years old.

12

Son Altesse Royale

The Windsors spent the rest of the summer in the United States, pondering their future. They could have settled in America, or at the duke's ranch in Alberta, but Edward, who was worried about money, having lost $100,000 drilling for nonexistent oil in Canada, did not want to pay taxes on his fortune. Wallis had infected him with her deep-seated sense of lack and constant anxieties over financial stability. "I hear all these stories that he has become so mean with money," said Freda Dudley Ward, "that he never tips his servants. He didn't used to be like that. She must have made him like that."[1]

The duke and duchess decided to return to France, where Edward enjoyed immunity from taxation (the French government having generously bestowed this benefaction on the former king). But it was Wallis, more than the duke, who favored France; she loved its couture, its cuisine, its ineffable chic. She was also astute enough to realize that the British were never going to offer Edward the recognition or role he craved, nor would his family cease their hostility towards the couple. For seven years after the war, the duke refused to settle and buy a house in France, still nursing hopes of returning to England or obtaining a suitable post representing his country abroad. On October 4, 1945, after spending a couple of weeks with his wife, Edward deposited Wallis in

France and flew to London. He had asked his mother if he could stay with her at Marlborough House. Without Wallis by his side, he was welcomed. "I need scarcely assure you what a joy it will be to me to see you once again after all these years," Queen Mary said, "for I have missed you very much indeed."[2]

The king had telegraphed from Balmoral to say that he would come down specially to see his brother. Queen Mary recorded on Friday, October 5: "Lunched with Bertie who arrived this morning from Balmoral. At 4 *David* arrived by plane from Paris on a visit to me—I had not seen him for nearly 9 years! It was a great joy meeting him, he looked very well—Bertie came to dinner to meet him."[3]

Mother and son both relished their time together; it was probably the longest they had spent, just the two of them, in their lives. Queen Mary delighted in "those nice talks on so many subjects in which both of us are interested."[4] She later wrote to Edward: "I have felt so much being cut off from you for such ages."[5] Yet she was on her mettle for any mention of Wallis, writing to the Countess of Athlone during this time: "I hope he does not bother me too much about receiving her—as nothing has happened since to alter my views about that unfortunate marriage."[6] The duke was uncharacteristically restrained. His last words to his mother were simple yet firm as to the limits to their reconciliation: "I can only ask that you remember that I am no longer a bachelor."[7]

In spite of conversations with the king and Tommy Lascelles, who told him "most frankly" that there could be no return to court life in England if he was with Wallis, Edward did not jettison his wish to spend part of the year in England with his wife. In March 1946 he wrote to Ulick Alexander, requesting that if Fort Belvedere was ever sold by the Crown, could he please be informed. The Fort was never offered to him. It languished, falling into further disrepair, until finally, in 1955, a ninety-nine-year lease was sold to the Honorable Gerald Lascelles, a distant relation of Tommy Lascelles. The building most loved by the former king passed from royal hands.

It is a mark of Edward's devotion to Britain that, even if he could not live there, he still wanted to return home in the event of his death. In

August 1946 he obtained the king's permission to erect a mausoleum in the grounds of Fort Belvedere, where he and the duchess could be laid to rest. An architect was summoned to the Fort to draw up plans but was informed that, for fear of vandalism, the site would be changed to Frogmore. As the Fort (and Frogmore) are on private royal lands, vandalism seemed unlikely. More likely, the move to Frogmore was calculated to allow the sale of the Fort, ensuring that the duke and duchess never came back there.

The duke tried once again to harness the possibility of some official role in the United States, which the king was keen for his brother to have. Bertie was disappointed that it could not be arranged. It was the court, driven by Tommy Lascelles, now the king's private secretary and keeper of the Royal Archives, who determined that there could be no place for the Duke of Windsor under the British Crown. Lascelles repeated to both the king and the duke that the British Empire was like a clock which had to be kept ticking. He and others had tried to take it to pieces a hundred times to fit in an extra wheel—the wheel of a former king. They had never found a way of doing so without damaging the works. When the duke remonstrated that the extra wheel had worked perfectly well in the Bahamas, Lascelles replied: "Ah, yes, but that was in wartime. The experiment had worked once but could not be safely repeated."[8] When Roger Sherfield, the British ambassador to the United States, was later asked by the duke if he and the duchess could come and stay at the Washington embassy, Sherfield agreed. Lord Sherfield soon heard from an angry Foreign Office that although British embassies were permitted to entertain the Windsors to meals, they should never be invited to stay.[9]

"It was not King George who denied his brother, it was the government," claimed Count Rudi von Schönburg. "The government had such an influence over the royal family. Everything that happened to the duke was political. The only government that behaved well towards them was the French government."[10]

The Duke and Duchess of Windsor found on their return to Paris that the freehold of their house on the Boulevard Suchet had been sold. They could negotiate an extension only until April 1946. Later, they took another house, 85 Rue de la Faisanderie, a palatial yet rather gloomy residence that neither of them really liked but was suitable for grand-scale entertaining. Owned by the industrialist and philanthropist Paul-Louis Weiller, it was loaned rent free to the royal couple.[11] Paris, that first winter after the war, was a grim city; the electricity was often cut off, restaurants were either closed or subsisted on black-market supplies, and ordinary citizens struggled for basic food and housing. It was good fortune for the Windsors that their close friend Duff Cooper was the first postwar British ambassador to Paris.

On October 17, 1945, Duff wrote: "We dined with the Windsors. The electric light was out when we arrived. The house was beautifully lit with candles but the dinner could not be brought up except by electric lift so we had to wait for it until the electricity came on again. I hadn't seen the Windsors since 1940. They have both got extraordinarily thin, but otherwise look very well and he seems as devoted as ever."[12]

Noël Coward met the couple for dinner at the British embassy, an elegant eighteenth-century building on the Rue du Faubourg Saint-Honoré. "He loves her so much, and at long last I am beginning to think she loves him," he confided to his diary. A few months later he wrote again: "The Windsors were charming. I like her, and I think she is now genuinely fond of him."[13] (Coward famously once said that "a statue should be erected to Mrs. Simpson in every town in England for the blessing she had bestowed upon the country." He was referring to the removal of Edward VIII from the throne.)

The real problem for the duke in France was his interminable boredom. "The duke used to bore my father stiff when he was ambassador," said John Julius Norwich. "He would call to see him, plop down on the sofa and talk for two hours about his own asinine views on the world. He had nothing to amuse him apart from the duchess and nothing to fall back on."[14]

"The dinner parties they gave or to which they were invited were impossibly tedious," recalled Fred de Cabrol. "The duke had little to say, having few centres of interest outside golf and card games, and, if he did make a political remark, it was seldom to the advantage of the discussion."[15] After spending two successive Christmas Eves with the Windsors and other friends, Gore Vidal declared: "I like Wallis. She had a flapper's wisecracking charm. David, as Wallis called him, always had something of such riveting stupidity to say on any subject that I clung to his words like the most avid courtier of the ancien regime."[16]

The duke's empty existence consisted of trawling around Paris after the duchess, who was fully able to amuse herself with appointments at hairdressers, couturiers and beauty salons. She especially liked the Elizabeth Arden salon, where she rarely paid and had her own robe with the initials SAR (Son Altesse Royale—the French version of HRH) embroidered on the pocket.[17] Then she would return home for her early-evening French lessons. The duke whined that when the duchess had her French lesson, "he had no one to talk to."[18]

Lady Monckton recalled visiting the Windsors in Paris, only to find Wallis had gone to the hairdressers. "The Duke had got himself into the most frantic state. He was pacing round and he couldn't stop looking at his watch. 'Why isn't Wallis back? Why isn't she back?' he kept asking me. I tried to explain that it takes quite a time to have your hair set. One always had to explain that things took time to the duke. He always got so upset when Wallis was late coming back from fittings and things like that."[19]

For Wallis, Paris was the perfect city in which to indulge her obsession with fashion. According to Fred de Cabrol: "After a period wearing some of Schiaparelli's cult outfits, such as the lobster dress, she went through the hands of Hubert de Givenchy, Christian Dior and Yves Saint Laurent."[20] Wallis charmed everyone in the designers' ateliers. "People who worked for the duchess nearly always became fond of her and Hubert de Givenchy is no exception," said Diana Mosley. "Givenchy says that when it was rumoured that he was to make her dresses he was told [by people who did not know her] that the duchess never paid her bills; in fact, he found that she paid them on the dot."[21]

For thirty years the duchess employed the same hairdresser, Alexandre de Paris, born Louis Alexandre de Raimon. Wallis discovered him as a twenty-two-year-old stylist in Saint Tropez, catapulting him to become one of the most famous hairdressers in the world. The first time she called him, "she gave a thousand explanations as to what she wanted, and then I did her hair,"[22] Alexandre remembered. "The next day I got another call. 'What did you do to my hair?' she asked. 'I disobeyed you and did the exact opposite of what you requested,' I admitted. 'It's wonderful!' she said. 'For the first time in my life, I woke up with my hair exactly as it was when I went to sleep. From now on, you will stay by my side.'"[23]

Alexandre did Wallis's hair daily after her return from the Bahamas. The elegant but severe style, which Alexandre said he had "knitted" for the duchess, became her postwar trademark. The duchess introduced him to hundreds of high-profile clients. Later, propelled to New York, Alexandre, who created the chignon in the late fifties, became Hollywood's most coveted hairdresser. His clients included Princess Grace, Elizabeth Taylor and Sophia Loren. He adored the Windsors. "They were like parents to me," he said.[24]

Wallis also established her famed jewelry collection. As well as an icon for Cartier, she was a client of Fulco di Verdura, Harry Winston and Van Cleef & Arpels. Wallis loved bold statement jewelry, such as the two gem-set bib necklaces made by Cartier, one in 1945 with rubies and emeralds, the other in 1947 with amethyst and turquoise. After the war, the duke continued to work with Cartier on many pieces for the duchess, including the "Great Cat" series of jewels, which became legendary. The most magnificent, perhaps, was a sapphire and diamond panther lolling across an enormous Kashmir sapphire.

In April 1946, when the lease expired on their house in Paris, they moved back south to Antibes. The duke preferred being at La Croë, which was more of a home to him than anywhere else since the Fort. Damage during the war, when Italians and Germans inhabited the house, was negligible; the resourceful duchess soon got the house pulsing with light and life again. By the end of the month, twenty-two staff had been recruited, in addition to the duke's personal valet, Sydney Johnson, a young Bahamian man who had been with them since Nassau, and who would stay until the duke's death in 1972.

Of La Croë, Wallis proudly told Aunt Bessie: "I imagine outside the embassies it is the only house run in this fashion in France and probably England today."[25] As a major general, the duke was able to draw rations from the British army depot at Marseilles, which allowed them to entertain their friends with their inimitable prewar style. "You can't imagine the sense of luxury at La Croë after the war," said Daisy de Cabrol. "It was a really good villa and to amuse us, the duchess arranged to serve a dinner in a different room each night the ten days we stayed there."[26]

That autumn, the duke returned to England with Wallis. He made no attempt to ask for an invitation to a royal residence or even to contact his family. The Windsors stayed with their friends the Earl and Countess of Dudley at Ednam Lodge in Sunningdale. Laura Dudley, who became the Duchess of Marlborough on her fourth marriage and chatelaine of Blenheim Palace, referred to Ednam Lodge as their "suburban villa." The Windsors hoped that their visit would be relatively low profile. Unfortunately, their stay created front-page headlines.

The Windsors arrived with a huge caravan of luggage in three army lorries under the command of an officer of the Royal Army Service Corps. The duchess always traveled with a series of identical suitcases, in order not to draw attention to the one that contained her jewel box. Only her maid knew which suitcase it was in. The royal couple were given rooms on the first floor of Ednam Lodge, overlooking the front of the house. On Wednesday October 16, the hosts and their guests went to dine in London. The servants had their communal supper at 5.30 p.m. When the duchess's maid, Joan Martin, returned from supper over an hour later, thieves had entered by an open upstairs window. The jewel box was open, its inner case full of treasures stolen. The following morning, the case was found discarded outside the boundary of Ednam Lodge on the golf course. Eleven significant pieces of jewelry had been taken, including Wallis's latest acquisition, a vast sapphire converted into a bird of paradise by Van Cleef & Arpels. Further pieces were found left in the bottom drawers of the case, while other valuable jewels, along with Fabergé boxes, were discovered tossed in the long grass, including a string of pearls which had belonged to Edward's grandmother, Queen Alexandra.[27]

According to Lady Dudley, Wallis had earlier rejected their butler's suggestion that the valuables be locked away in the Dudleys' safe, in favor of stashing the jewel box under her maid's bed, as she always did. (This habit apparently stemmed from Wallis's southern roots. In the American South, it was common practice for rich families to hide their treasures under the mattresses in the servants' quarters, where thieves were unlikely to look.) Wallis took the theft extremely badly; her response to the incident did not show her in a good light. The jewelry collection probably had a powerful and complex emotional resonance for her. Edward had lavished these wildly extravagant gems upon her since the first days of their courtship, consistently demonstrating his unwavering and obsessive love for her. Subconsciously, perhaps, the jewels were Wallis's reward for being forced into marriage, and then exile, with him. Edward created for Wallis his own form of crown jewels. The exquisite adornments affirmed her femininity and her status and, as importantly, represented financial security.

"The duchess was in a bad way," reported Laura Dudley. "The detectives found something like eighteen odd earrings scattered over the Sunningdale Golf Course but, much to her fury, not one pair. She wanted all the servants put through a kind of third degree, but I would have none of this, all of them except for one kitchen maid being old and devoted staff of long standing."[28]

The next day, according to Lady Dudley, "the duke was demented with worry and near to tears."[29] Wallis wore the only brooch she had left. Before the party went out for a stroll, she asked the duke to put it somewhere safe for her. On their return, he could not remember where he had put it. He thought that he had put it in the room where he was sorting papers that he had collected from Windsor. But to no avail. Wallis and Lord Dudley retired for the evening but the duke could not rest until the brooch had been found. Lady Dudley felt "desperately sorry for him" as he looked "grey with worry and exhaustion." She stayed up most of the night with the former king, searching for the jewel to which "the Duchess appeared attached."[30]

"He obviously feared to go to bed empty-handed," said Lady Dudley. "I made endless cups of black coffee while the duke went through his papers. At about 5 a.m. by some miracle we found it, under a china ornament. Never have I seen a man so relieved. He was still ashen in the face, but he rushed upstairs."[31]

It was claimed that uncut emeralds belonging to Queen Alexandra, part of the crown jewels, had been taken in the burglary. The haul was never recovered so the duke used the sizable insurance money to rebuild his wife's precious pieces. Later in her life, Laura, Duchess of Marlborough, confirmed that Wallis had definitely owned Queen Alexandra's jewels. "All those jewels were replaced by the duke," she said. "The replacements may not be royal but they are madly valuable jewels."[32*]

The Windsors left England thoroughly downcast, the duke concluding that "old values have disappeared and been replaced by strange tendencies, and one senses an unfamiliar atmosphere throughout the country."[33]

The following summer, 1947, the king's elder daughter, Princess Elizabeth, became engaged to Prince Philip of Greece. A delighted Queen Mary wrote on July 10: "Heard with great pleasure of darling Lilibet's engagement to Philip Mountbatten. They both came to see me after lunch looking radiant."[34]

Instantly, the press were abuzz and the question was asked: Would the Duke and Duchess of Windsor be invited to the wedding of the duke's niece? Astonishingly, given the decade of snubs that he had received, Edward still held out hope that he and his wife would be included on the guest list. When he was told that no invitation would be forthcoming, he wrote to Ulick Alexander. "Believe me, Ulick, this form of publicity is as distasteful to the duchess and myself as it is no doubt to the king. But so long as the royal family do not feel disposed to change the attitude they have adopted for more than ten years, these unpleasant exposés of a cheap and undignified family situation will inevitably flare up each time some relevant error occurs to ignite them, until all concerned are in their graves."[35]

To his mother, Edward wrote plaintively: "I am always hoping that one day you will tell me to bring Wallis to see you, as it makes me very sad to think that you and she have never really met . . . it would indeed be tragic

* After the Duchess of Windsor's death, her jewels were sold at Sotheby's in Geneva for prices vastly exceeding the estimates: the sale total was $50,281,887.

if you, my mother, had never known the girl I married and who has made me blissfully happy."[36]

Riled, the duke renewed his battle over the duchess's right to be restyled Her Royal Highness. In 1937, when the duke had consulted the esteemed lawyer Sir William Jowitt on the question, Jowitt had replied that the duke had never ceased to be a Royal Highness himself, so technically, there was no question of his wife not being entitled to the distinction. Jowitt maintained that the letters patent issued by King George VI, which had granted the title to the duke but denied it to his wife, should never have been issued. Twelve years later, Jowitt was now Lord Chancellor in Attlee's Labour government. The duke called on him to convince the king of the justice of the duchess's case.

This time Jowitt would not be tied to a definite answer. A fresh letters patent, he considered, could not be issued by the king alone but on the advice of his ministers, who would probably feel it necessary to consult all the Commonwealth governments. Tommy Lascelles, who had been informed of the conversation by Jowitt, told the king: "It was the best example I have ever seen of a clever lawyer trying to eat his own words without giving himself indigestion."[37] The matter did not sit lightly with Jowitt, however, who wrote to Lascelles the following week after his conversation with the duke. He said that he still felt a legal mistake had been made: "In reality he remained HRH notwithstanding the Abdication and the attribute to which he was entitled would automatically pass to his wife."[38]

Although he knew nothing of this letter, Edward began to press his case with the prime minister. The king warned Attlee: "You will not encourage him to think that any alteration can be made at this time."[39] When the duke arranged to meet with Attlee to discuss the matter, Queen Mary wrote to the king: "I cannot tell you how grieved I am at your brother being so tiresome about HRH. Giving *her* this title would be fatal, and after all these years I fear lest people think that we condoned this dreadful marriage which has been such a blow to us all in every way."[40] She encouraged the king to be "very firm and refuse to do anything about it," insisting that the government back him up. Queen Mary continued, giving no quarter: "I was grieved that Leopold of the Belgians and his wife saw quite a lot of her in the South of France lately, but she is so pushing and she leaves no stone unturned to remain a thorn in our sides and advertise herself whenever she can."[41]

The king sent his brother a stern letter, making it absolutely clear that there was no chance of Wallis's title being reconsidered. He concluded: "I made your wife a Duchess despite what happened in 1936. You should be grateful to me for this. But you are not."[42] Edward replied succinctly to his brother's letter. He merely corrected the king's statement that his life would not be worth living under these conditions. "On the contrary I could not conceive greater happiness than Wallis has given me in these thirteen years of our married life," he wrote.[43]

The queen wrote to her daughter Princess Elizabeth about another badgering visit from the Duke of Windsor: "Papa seems well, but gets a bit tired with all the worries—Uncle David came & had one of his violent yelling conversations, stamping up & down the room, & very unfairly saying that because Papa wouldn't (and couldn't) do a certain thing that Papa must hate him. So unfair, because Papa is so scrupulously fair & thoughtful & honest about all that has happened. It's so much easier to yell & pull down & criticise, than to restrain, & build, & think right, isn't it."[44]

In 1948, the lease expired on La Croë and the couple were on the move again. Wallis wrote to her friend Elsie Mendl, saying that she hoped that they might visit her for the weekend at her house in Versailles, on their way to Paris. Between the lines, Wallis was weary of their peripatetic lifestyle and unpredictable future. (Duff Cooper noted that summer that the Windsors looked "faded and worn."[45]) Wallis detailed to Elsie their "traveling army," her responsibilities for packing up a home again and the difficulties of maneuvering their staff, which included two maids, two chauffeurs, a secretary and a valet, plus the Windsors' two dogs. There is a sense of despondency about Wallis, who confided in her friend: "I wish that I could come on ahead of the duke and stay with you first but alas it is that I know the things here. Do let me know if you can have us then—but not if we are an effort. I am very sad to give up La Croë and to have to go to a rented house with store houses full of my possessions. I do not think it very intelligent and long to talk to you about everything—you are so very wise and yet is this the time to buy in France? And not being able to move capital out of England—America becomes beyond us—such a messy world, isn't it darling?"[46]

The Windsors always seemed to be traveling but never arriving anywhere meaningful. They stayed in France from April until after Christmas 1948, when they went to America, where they stayed in their six-room apartment on the twenty-eighth floor of the Waldorf Towers in New York, or in their friends' magnificent mansions in Palm Beach. The novelist Cecil Roberts said of their apartment in the Waldorf Towers: "this did not look like exile"; there were full-length portraits of George III and George IV in their coronation robes, other royal portraits, two footmen in livery and napkins embroidered with the royal coat of arms.[47]

David Maude-Roxby-Montalto di Fragnito met the duke and duchess at a party in Palm Beach. "It was at a big house on a beautiful estate with lavish gardens and a large swimming pool. There was a wonderful dinner, then dancing. I was seated across from the Duke of Windsor, who knew the daughter of our hostess," he remembered. "The duke was so polite and put everyone at their ease. He was charming, laughing with the younger guests. The duchess was sitting at another table. To my great surprise, after dinner, a servant came across and told the duke that the duchess wanted to leave and was waiting in the car. I was shocked when the servant told the duke that he must come immediately or the duchess was leaving without him. When he got the message, he jumped up and said good-bye and took his leave. He was like a little boy, almost running off."[48]

The duchess had various medical treatments in middle age. When they were living at Nassau, she had traveled to Miami to have an operation to help ease her stomach problems. In 1951, she fell ill in New York and had a hysterectomy. Whenever she was unwell, the duke was beside himself. Queen Mary wrote to him at this time: "I feel sorry for your great anxiety about your wife, and am thankful that so far you are able to send a fair account."[49] The duchess joked: "At the moment I am going through the repair shop—every day a doctor for some 'part.'"[50]

A few years before, *Life* magazine had encouraged the duke to write a series of articles about his reign. Although the duke had always considered that a dignified silence was the sine qua non of royal life, as others involved began to make their versions of the abdication crisis known—stirring him to successful litigation in some cases—he decided to put his own side across. An American writer Charles Murphy helped him with his memoirs, which became *A King's Story*, published in 1951. The title alone caused resentment amid palace courtiers. It would earn the duke over £300,000.

Murphy confided in Cecil Beaton about the Windsors: "The Prince is happy in his relationship with her. He depends on her utterly. It is a mother-mistress relationship. She looked after him like a child, & yet makes entertainment for him as she did in the days when he was the prince coming to her home for relaxation at the end of a long day. She now gives him the antidote to hard work but he has none of the hard work. He has nothing to do. She is nearly driven mad trying to find ways of amusing him. He has no intellect. He has no interests. Steam baths & brandy have made him very weak."[51]

Beaton, who photographed the duke in Paris, reported: "His face now begins to show the emptiness of life. It is too impertinent to be tragic. . . . He looks like a mad terrier, haunted one moment, and then with a flick of the hand he is laughing fecklessly."[52]

The only time that Wallis let herself down in her thirty-five-year marriage to the duke was in the early 1950s, when she became infatuated with American Jimmy Donahue, a flamboyant playboy nineteen years her junior and gay. His mother was a Woolworth heir; he was a cousin of the socialite Barbara Hutton. Wallis's flirtation with this spoilt hedonist, who once bought her a jeroboam of perfume at a Paris nightclub, was her visible rebellion against the pressured constraints of her marriage and the cloying, overattentive affections of the duke. Donahue shared Wallis's taste in witty retorts, nightclubs and dancing until dawn. Sadly, though, Wallis hurt her husband with this liaison and, uncharacteristically, behaved recklessly, generating ugly rumors. In three successive summers, Donahue and the Windsors went on Mediterranean cruises together, paid for by Woolworth money.

Wallis's friends were stunned by her behavior, especially when she was usually so "violently fastidious" in her conduct. At a tense and excruciating dinner party in Paris, Wallis mopped up a spilt glass of champagne using a fan representing the Prince of Wales's feathers.[53] The party moved on to the Monseigneur nightclub, where Wallis danced endlessly with Donahue to "La Vie en Rose" and "C'est Si Bon." As the duke watched, he became increasingly distraught, close to tears. When the couple returned to the "Windsors' special table," Wallis asked the waiter for a vase for the red roses Jimmy had bought her. She shoved her soggy ostrich fan and the roses into the vase, inexplicably announcing: "Look, everybody! The Prince of Wales plumes and Jimmy Donahue's roses."[54]

"The whole evening was ghastly," said Lady Diana Cooper. "Once it was over, I ended up in a car alone with Donahue. I couldn't bear him. He was so pleased with himself. He lolled around on the car cushions looking as puffed up as a toad because he had proved he had the power to cause distress. I thought he was seriously cruel and common."[55]

Donahue kept saying to Lady Diana: " 'Don't you love "our Duchess"?' " 'Don't you think "our Duchess" is fantastic?' " She turned to him and retorted coldly: "I happen to be the daughter of a duchess, so Wallis can't ever be 'our Duchess' to me."[56]

"None of us could understand it," said Laura, Duchess of Marlborough. "Jimmy Donahue was the most dreadful creature. . . . [Wallis] tormented the duke. I remember taking the duke home one night from a Paris nightclub and he was in floods of tears because the duchess had vanished somewhere with Donahue."[57]

According to a friend of Wallis's, Cordelia Biddle Robertson, the duchess told her exactly why this strange, unsuitable friendship ended. "It didn't end as we all thought it would with a terrible scandal on the front pages. It just ended one night when Wallis had a date with Jimmy."[58] Wallis went downstairs to wait for Donahue, who was due to arrive in his car at midnight. He was ten minutes late, which annoyed her. But she became incensed when he turned up smelling of garlic, which she loathed. They had a row and never spoke again, which must have been the sweetest relief to the duke. Friends felt that once Wallis had this uncharacteristic rebellion out of her system, she settled comfortably into middle age with the duke. Possibly guilty about her weird infatuation, after that, her watchful maternal devotion to her husband never wavered.

Shortly after Wallis dropped Donahue, a friend of Lady Diana Mosley's was dining with the Windsors. "This is our wedding day," the duke announced out of nowhere. "We've been married eighteen years. There *may* be a happier couple somewhere but I doubt it."[59]

The couple moved again; they accepted an offer from the French government to live for a peppercorn rent on a fifty-year lease in a nineteenth-century mansion in the Bois de Boulogne once owned by the Renault family. The French government had sequestered the property after the Second World War and Charles de Gaulle occupied the house in the late forties. According to Elsa Maxwell: "It is perhaps the most beautiful house in Paris. You have the impression of being in the midst of the country as you look through the spacious windows in the drawing room on to the smooth, green lawn and the trees around. The drawing room in white and silver is entirely lit by candlelight from exquisite silver sconces that rise like silver trees upon paneled walls."[60]

Here the duke and duchess entertained in their customary lavish style. "We visited the Windsors often for dinner at their Paris home," recalled Rudi von Schönburg. "The duchess gave parties that were elegant, formal but not stiff. She was not vulgar as people said. Their home was like being in a small royal principality: lovely furniture and paintings, exquisite flowers."[61]

John Julius Norwich remembered going to dinner there as a young man. "Wallis was fun," he recalled. "If you found yourself sitting next to her, the ball came back over the net and she made the party go. She was very good with people my age. She wasn't remotely flirtatious, she just talked to me as if I was a contemporary, which is enormously flattering when you are eighteen. She was a wonderful hostess, perhaps slightly overdoing the splendor, though. There were always too many golden ashtrays."[62]

With the duke finally resigned to settling in France, the Windsors looked to buy their first home. Edward managed to persuade the Chancellor of the Exchequer, Rab Butler, to release £30,000 from his capital in England, which was still blocked by currency control.[63] Edward wanted somewhere in the country, but close enough to Paris to keep the duchess happy. They found an enchanting eighteenth-century water mill at the mouth of the Chevreuse valley, twenty miles from the capital. Moulin de la Tuilerie, known as the Mill, gave the duchess another renovation and decoration project; there were a cobbled courtyard, outhouses and a large barn. Wallis transformed this collection of buildings into entertaining areas and guest cottages. In the barn, one wall was covered with a map of the duke's world travels when he was Prince of Wales. The large first-floor sitting room opened onto a terrace where the couple and their many and frequent houseguests—who included Maria Callas, Marlene Dietrich, Elizabeth Taylor, Richard Burton and Cecil Beaton—played canasta. Wallis's decorator, Stéphane Boudin, created her jeu d'esprit in imposing letters on the wall of the sitting room: "I'm not the miller's daughter, but I have been through the mill." This frescoed trompe l'oeil depicted a ribbon running through a mill wheel.

The duke was delighted to have another garden to develop. He commissioned English designer Russell Page to design the grounds. They were fashioned like a traditional English country garden, with two herbaceous borders filled with the flowers—delphiniums, phlox and asters—he loved at the Fort. He created a rock garden with alpine blooms and water splashing from a small, steep hill, exactly as he had done at the Fort. The head gardener, Edouard Kruch, was Alsatian. As the duke was still not fluent in French, he could speak to the gardener in German, which he relished. Endearingly, the duke would come and read comics with Kruch's sons in the Indian tepee in the garden which he had bought for them.

Wallis and Edward loved the Mill, the first house that had belonged to them in all their married life. "It was the prettiest, most cheerful place imaginable," remembered frequent guest Diana Mosley. "With crackling wood fires in winter and in summer the bright flowers."[64] Her good friend the fashion editor Diana Vreeland recalled being called upstairs into the duke's bathroom by the duchess. "The tub was covered with a wooden board which he'd obviously had one of the men on the property make—a kind of table. It was piled with papers, papers . . . pa-pers, PAPERS! Bills, little things to do with golf."[65] Wallis affectionately remonstrated about the chaos. "What was so odd was that this mess was in the house of the best housekeeper in the world, where naturally everything, between dozens of housemaids, was perpetually organized every day," said Vreeland. The two women were helpless with giggles at this messy male domain when the duke appeared. "What are you two doing in here?! May I ask you two ladies to get the hell *out*! This happens to be *my* bathroom and that happens to be *my* table."[66]

"By this time, the couple were absolutely devoted to each other," recalled Rudi von Schönburg. "They had been through so much together and you could see that just as the duchess was an influence on the duke, he was on her too. He calmed her down. They shared a mutual respect and dedication towards each other."[67]

James Pope-Hennessy, who spent a weekend with the couple at the Mill, was touched by their "very great kindness." He wrote in his diary that "Every conceivable luxury and creature-comfort is bought, called-on, conscripted, to produce a perfection of sybaritic living. The Queen Mother at Clarence House is leading a lodging house existence compared to this." The whole atmosphere was "intensely unstrained and unshy, owing, I should say to the duchess and the job she has done on the duke." Pope-Hennessy concluded that the duke was "one of the most considerate men I have ever met of his generation. Like the duchess, he is perhaps too open and trusting towards others."[68]

Miss Jean Drewes, who worked for the Windsors for four years as their private secretary at Government House in Nassau, had concluded that there was "a lonesomeness about the couple—a lonesomeness they shared, and because of it, I felt that there was a selfish devotion to each other."[69] Sadly, the duke never felt truly at home in France. "He never bothered to conceal the fact that he hated living in France," said John Julius Norwich. "His French was execrable and he made no attempt to improve it."[70]

Diana Vreeland agreed that the duke's love of his home country was "overpowering." When she arrived for a grand dinner at the Windsors' Parisian property in the Bois de Boulogne, there was torrential rain. She was wearing white satin slippers. "The Duke was at the door, which I thought was terribly charming . . . and he was just roaring with laughter as I was struggling out of the car. And I got in soaking, absolutely soaking, and I said: 'Your country, sir!' meaning that it rained too much there in France . . . and his whole countenance changed. '*My* country?!' He . . . was . . . furious . . . at my suggesting that *France* was his country. Oh, he wasn't joking at all! Of course, immediately he recovered himself and was charming. But I had hit on something that was just about the . . . *end*."[71]

During the autumn of 1951, the Windsors were again in London. The king's health was deteriorating; a malignant growth had been found in his left lung. The queen, furious that the king was aggravated by the publicity in the British press concerning his brother's memoirs, wrote to Tommy Lascelles: "You can imagine that I do not want to see the Duke of Windsor—the part author of the king's troubles."[72]

Yet one of the king's last acts before undergoing an operation to remove the entire left lung was a touching gesture of affection towards his older brother. In his own hand, he gave written instructions for the master of the household to deliver three brace of grouse to the house in Upper Brook Street, where the duke and duchess were staying. "I understand he is fond of grouse," he said, thoughtfully.[73]

King George VI died peacefully in his sleep on February 6, 1952. The Duke and Duchess of Windsor were in New York at the time and received the news by telephone. The following day, on board the Cunard liner *Queen Mary* bound for England, the duke, a black mourning band on his sleeve, read a prepared statement to the gathered press: "This voyage, upon which I am embarking aboard the *Queen Mary* tonight, is indeed sad—and it is all the sadder for me because I am undertaking it alone. The duchess is remaining here to await my return."[74] The duke had been bluntly informed by Buckingham Palace that there could be no question of Wallis accompanying him to his brother's funeral.

Wallis, present for the press statement before the ship sailed, regarded her husband in watchful silence. Wearing a black suit with a sealskin bolero jacket, the press reported that she "repeatedly glanced at the duke in compassion."[75] As the duke continued his statement, offering his comfort and support to "Her Majesty, my mother," he omitted to refer to the one person who would feel the king's loss most keenly: his widow, Elizabeth.[76]

Wallis sent the duke off to England with the sage advice "Do not mention or ask for *anything* regarding recognition of me."[77] The duke stayed with his mother at Marlborough House for the funeral. Four days after her son's death, Queen Mary sent a letter to the king's widow (who would become the queen mother) with the request that she and "the girls" see the duke "& bury the hatchet after 15 whole years." Queen Elizabeth, the heir apparent, Princess Elizabeth, and her sister, Princess Margaret, did meet the Duke of Windsor for tea at Buckingham Palace but any attempt at true reconciliation was perfunctory. Edward noted: "Cookie [the Windsors' nickname for Queen Elizabeth] listened without comment and closed on the note that it was nice to be able to talk about Bertie with somebody who had known him so well."[78] Queen Mary was overoptimistic about the meeting. "So that feud is over, I hope, a great relief to me."[79]

Queen Elizabeth was blind in her conviction that Wallis was accountable for her husband's death. "She felt that the loss of her husband could be laid firmly at the door of Wallis Simpson, blaming her for his early death," reported her former equerry, Major Colin Burgess.[80] Convinced that the strain of being king—the "intolerable honour"[81] as Elizabeth called it—caused Bertie's failing health and cancer, she perhaps never paused to consider that if Edward had been allowed to help shoulder his brother's duties as king, his royal burdens would have been eased, especially though the war years.

The duke, who found his mother "hard as nails but failing," left with a doomed feeling that his wife would never be welcomed in Britain. The new monarch held no fresh promise, he believed, as the young Queen Elizabeth II could not help but be indoctrinated by her mother and grandmother against Wallis. "It's hell to be even this much dependent on those ice-veined bitches," he wrote to his wife.[82] Worse, he discovered that the £10,000-a-year allowance that he received from George VI was lost on his brother's death. This was especially inopportune as he and Wallis were in the middle of renovating the Mill.

The following year, when the duke and duchess were in New York, Edward heard that his mother was gravely ill. He and his sister, the Princess Royal, travelled from America together. Queen Mary died at Marlborough House on March 24, 1953. The duke arrived at her bedside a few minutes too late. At the sight of his deceased mother, all his hopes of her ever accepting or even meeting his wife extinguished, bitter fury welled up with his undeniable grief. Edward told Wallis: "My sadness was mixed with incredulity that any mother could have been so hard and cruel towards her eldest son for so many years and yet so demanding at the end without relenting a scrap. I'm afraid that the fluids in her veins have always been as icy cold as they now are in death."[83]

Five years later, James Pope-Hennessy asked the duke if perhaps one of Queen Mary's difficulties in understanding her son's dilemma was that she had never been in love herself. The duke replied: "No, I don't think she had. You're right. My mother was a cold woman, a cold woman. And I, you see, I suppose I had never really been in love before. No, I hadn't, I thought I had, but I hadn't ever been in love."[84]

Edward stayed with the Gloucesters at York House for the funeral, which must have been difficult, as the brothers never got on. He refused to stay at his mother's home, declaring of Marlborough House: "I'm not going to sleep in this mortuary."[85] Throughout the stay Edward remained "boiling mad" that the duchess was not at her rightful place by his side, telling Wallis: "What a smug stinking lot my relations are and you've never seen such a seedy worn-out bunch of old hags most of them have become."[86] In person, however, he was charming. The Duchess of Gloucester remarked: "It was particularly moving listening to the duke, because he was obviously pleased to be talking within his own family again."[87]

The tragedy is that Edward never gave up his longing to be reconciled with his family. Nor did he ever let go of his deepest desire that they acknowledge his wife, the woman he loved and the person who made him happiest in the world. All it would have taken was the smallest gesture of recognition from the royal family towards Wallis, and his resentments would have melted. Grief, an unruly emotion, causes hair-trigger reactions to the tiniest of slights. There were so many opportunities to have healed this wretched familial rift. Ever naive, he still clung to the hope that he and the duchess would be invited to the coronation of Queen Elizabeth II in June that year. But, with Tommy Lascelles installed as private secretary to the new monarch, that was clearly fanciful. The duke wrote to Winston Churchill that he was "disappointed and depressed that you foresee no change in my family's attitude towards the duchess or to her rightful official status as my wife."[88]

The Windsors watched the coronation in Paris, on their black-and-white television, with friends gathered around. In days preceding, when Wallis was asked if the duke would attend his niece's coronation, she gave the quick-fire reply: "Why should he go to her coronation? He didn't go to his own."[89]

13

My David

The problem for the Duke and Duchess of Windsor was that they now had little to give weight to their lives. After the abdication, they lived with a laminated form of grief as it became increasingly clear that their previous existence was unrecoverable. The duchess decided that the best revenge against her harsh and flinty in-laws was a life lived well. The couple became major players amid a dazzling, but ultimately unfulfilling, café society, attending exotic balls and charity functions. "They are like people after a cataclysm or a revolution, valiantly making the best of infinite luxury," said the writer James Pope-Hennessy. "I am much taken by both of them."[1] The glittering hue of celebrity had a tawdry underbelly: the wealthy, unsophisticated hangers-on. Prince Charles described some of the Windsors' circle as "the most dreadful American guests I have ever seen."[2]

Wallis had a series of cosmetic surgeries to lift her face, yet nothing could conceal the tragic lack of purpose eating into the fabric of their day-to-day existence. Both she and Edward began to drink too much and eat even less than before. A bitter loss for her was the death in November 1958 of Ernest Simpson, who passed away following an operation for throat cancer in London. Ten years earlier, he had been married for a fourth time, to Avril Mullens. Wallis, who had never met Avril, wondered if she should send flowers or a telegram to his widow. The duke advised her to write a kind, handwritten note. *The Times* obituary commended Ernest Simpson for having maintained "the highest standard of personal conduct. In an age of commercialisation he refused all offers to write his reminiscences or to give interviews to the Press. He shunned any form of publicity, preferring dignified silence. The courage with which he faced his last illness," it said, was "typical of the man."[3] The death of Ernest affected Wallis deeply. "She missed him and mourned him like a brother," observed Rudi von Schönburg.[4]

In June 1962, the Windsors celebrated their silver wedding anniversary. Wallis wrote to Baba Metcalfe: "It is as you say almost impossible to believe the scene at Candé was 25 years ago—I sometimes wonder how the duke and I have survived the trying years that followed—but now they too are forgotten and life is as serene as it can be living as we all do—with costs mounting and running a house a trial instead of a pleasure."[5] Wallis poignantly admitted that her "one continuing regret" was never knowing "the joy of having children of my own." She lamented: "Perhaps no woman can say her life has been completely fulfilled unless she has been part of the miracle of creation."[6] The couple's four pug dogs, like the cairn terriers before them, were totally spoilt and almost like surrogate babies.

Lacking her own progeny, perpetually shunned by her husband's family, without "My Romance,"[7] as Wallis had started to refer to the duke, she faced a desolate slide into old age. Edward had a fresh preoccupation: How could he protect and provide for his wife when he died? What would happen to her, reviled by the world, when he, her emotional bulwark and most ardent defender, was gone? "The duke harboured this terrible fear that they didn't treat Wallis well when I was alive, how will they treat her when I am dead?" said Rudi von Schönburg. "He confided in me that he was very worried that the duchess would end up in poverty and be badly treated." The duke's fears were completely groundless, as Wallis would, by any standards, be a very wealthy woman. Years later, when his health was in rapid decline, Edward appealed to the queen to continue the £10,000-a-year allowance that his brother Bertie had authorized for him for the duchess's lifetime. She agreed to carry on paying £5,000 a year.[8]

Every September, for three consecutive years in the early sixties, the duke and duchess stayed at Rudi von Schönburg's Marbella Club on the Andalusian coast. They had first visited the club with Sir Walter and Lady Monckton, and struck Count Rudi and his wife, Princess Marie Louise of Prussia, as delightfully low key. The Windsors booked a bungalow as normal paying guests, brought only a maid and a valet with them, and never expected royal treatment. However, Count Rudi felt aggrieved that they were not officially entitled to royal treatment. Unlike other members of the British and European royal families, the British government had informed the Spanish Guardia Civil that the Duke and Duchess of Windsor could not have official protection.

"They fitted in perfectly," said Count Rudi. "The duchess felt very happy here because the duke was happy. She was immediately accepted, whereas in other places, this was not always the case as her husband's relations turned people against her."[9] This understated yet suave club, founded by Prince Alfonso of Hohenlohe-Langenburg in 1954, offered tropical gardens, swaying palms and a lively clientele: a heady mix of aristocrats and Hollywood stars. Regular guests included most of the crowned heads of Europe, as well as Ava Gardner, Audrey Hepburn, Laurence Olivier and Cary Grant. The duke played golf daily, then every evening created his own ceremonial ritual. At seven o'clock on the dot, he would pick a fresh lime from the tree in the garden and squeeze it into his dry martini. The Windsors always had the same discreet corner table in the restaurant at dinner. Every evening, when they rose to retire after dinner, such was Edward's popularity among his countrymen that every single British man in the restaurant got up and bowed to him, then to her.[10]

Each September, the club held a gala evening to celebrate the end of summer. Prince Alfonso recalled asking "sixty really good friends" to dinner at the Beach Club. He told them that the evening was in honor of the Duke of Windsor. The guests were to arrive at 9 p.m. and Prince Alfonso said that he would collect the duke and duchess from their bungalow in the grounds at 9:15. When the duke was informed that the dress was casual, the duchess was concerned that he would not come, as he had nothing suitable to wear. Later that afternoon, she found Count Rudi and said: "I'm so pleased; I have finally convinced the duke to come. He has found a Hawaiian shirt to wear."[11] However, because of the duke's presence, everybody ignored the casual dress code and "dressed up in blue suits with ties, looking like lawyers," recalled Prince Alfonso. "I collected the duke and duchess and we went to the balcony overlooking the pool; the duke was wearing a red and white Hawaiian shirt. So he said, 'Alfonso, I have to go quickly back to the bungalow' and he dressed in a dark suit. We came over the terrace and everybody had seen the Duke of Windsor with a colourful Hawaiian shirt, so had taken off their jackets and ties. The duke was so funny," the prince continued, "because he took his tie and threw it into the pool and he took off his suit jacket and there was big applause. That was what made him come back again and again, because he felt at home. The people respected him but at the same time made him feel comfortable."[12]

At the Marbella Club, "the duchess was also respected and we honored her, calling her HRH, because she made the duke so happy," said Count Rudi, who cohosted the gala dinner. "But she was never trying to act as a deposed queen. The duke suffered very much from the way people, especially his family, treated her."[13]

In June 1964, the Duke of Windsor turned seventy. Queen Elizabeth II sent a telegram of congratulation. To mark the milestone, James Pope-Hennessy wrote a profile for the *Sunday Times* in which he suggested that the queen and the royal family should relax their rigid disdain and invite the Windsors for lunch. The article caused an uproar in certain quarters. The life peer and former MP for Hemel Hempstead, Viscountess Joan Davidson, was apoplectic. She wrote a public rebuke to the article, thundering that it was "essential to keep the duchess away from England & how dangerous it would be even now after all these years to reverse the original decision." Tommy Lascelles, retired from royal service in 1953 yet still keen to influence the narrative, put his poisonous point of view of Pope-Hennessy across: "Who the hell does he think he is, to dictate to the queen or to anybody else, whether or not they should invite their aunts to luncheon?"[14]

It was a torrid time for Wallis. In November 1964, her lifelong stalwart Aunt Bessie died, having reached the plucky age of a hundred. Edward attended her funeral, while Wallis remained in New York recovering from foot surgery. But it was the duke's health that was of greatest concern. In December he underwent an operation to remove a grapefruit-sized "blister" from his aorta. After notifying the duchess, who was waiting in a side room, that the surgery had been a success, the surgeon and British consul general sent a telegram to the queen, who "had asked the consul for periodic reports on the duke's condition and a report on the operation as soon as it was finished."[15] The queen also sent flowers. Months later, when Edward underwent an operation for a detached retina in a clinic in London, the queen visited him in person. Afterwards, the eye surgeon, a Mr. Hudson, commented to the Windsors' American doctor, Dr. Arthur Antenucci, that he was "absolutely enchanted with the duchess and her devotion during the duke's time in hospital." She took a room next to the duke's in the clinic and sat with him all day, reading him the newspapers.[16]

In June 1967, the queen made a startlingly kind gesture towards Wallis. She invited both the duke and the duchess to the dedication of a plaque outside Marlborough House in memory of Queen Mary. It had been the queen's original intention to hold the unveiling ceremony on Friday, May 26—the centenary of Queen Mary's birth—but the duke and duchess were in America and unable to attend on that date. Signaling that their presence was important, the queen postponed the occasion until Wednesday, June 7.

The Windsors arrived in Southampton on June 5, on a liner from New York. As the ship docked, the royal couple could be seen waving from the deck rail, the duchess dressed in a summery blue-and-white-striped coat, the duke sporting a matching blue cornflower in his buttonhole. As they came down the gangplank hand in hand, Lord Mountbatten greeted them as a crowd of Southampton dockers gave a loud cheer, yelling: "Good old Teddy!"[17]

Probed by the press and asked if he was surprised to receive an official invitation to the unveiling, the duke replied smoothly: "Not at all. It is only natural that her eldest son should be invited to this purely private family ceremony, and that the duchess should be with me." Asked if the couple might make their home in England again, the duke replied: "No." When questioned how he would like to spend the remaining years of his life, the duke turned towards the duchess. Smiling, he answered: "Together."[18]

The following day, the Court Circular made no mention of the couple's arrival in Britain. The Windsors spent their first night at Broadlands, the Mountbatten family home in Hampshire, where Queen Elizabeth and Prince Philip had stayed for part of their honeymoon. They were invited to plant a tree in the grounds to commemorate their visit, receiving an address of welcome from the mayor of Romsey. At one point, the mayor mistakenly addressed the duchess as "Your Royal Highness," before hastily correcting himself to "Your Grace."[19]

The following day, when the couple arrived to stay at Claridge's, a crowd had gathered on the pavement. "Welcome home, sir," someone called out. The duke raised his trilby in acknowledgment. An even larger crowd gathered the next day to watch the Windsors leave for St. James's Palace, where the royal family was to assemble prior to the unveiling. "There were no formal processions that day in case there were unseemly demonstrations of loyalty to the duke,"[20] said Hugo Vickers.

The Windsors received the loudest cheer as their car drew up outside Marlborough House. A crowd estimated at five thousand had gathered to witness the historic encounter between two women: Wallis and the queen mother, who had been her bitter adversary for a third of a century. The duchess was elegance personified in a dark-blue shantung coat and white stole, her magnificent Cartier panther and Kashmir sapphire broach a dazzling addition. The sixty-six-year-old queen mother was dressed in pale lilac, with a matching hat covered in elaborate berries, which seemed to fascinate (or appal) Wallis. Elizabeth had not seen Edward since Queen Mary's funeral, fourteen years before. When the duke, with courtly grace, bowed to kiss his sister-in-law's hand, she leaned across and kissed him on the cheek. The queen mother then turned to the duchess and extended her hand. The duchess stood her ground. Wallis did not curtsy. She later explained to a surprised girlfriend: "She stopped people from curtsying to me. Why should I curtsy to her?"[21]

When the queen arrived and walked past the royal lineup, the duke bowed his head deeply and the duchess bobbed a brief but unmistakable curtsy. The Windsors were not invited to join the queen's luncheon party at the Derby that afternoon. After a small lunch hosted for them at Kensington Palace by Princess Marina, they were flown back to Paris, as a special concession from the sovereign, in the queen's aircraft. The following day, the Court Circular noted the presence of every royal at the unveiling. There was no mention of the Duke and Duchess of Windsor. For the first time in thirty years, the duchess had publicly taken her rightful place with her husband's family; but to the court and its senior officials, the former king and his wife remained personae non gratae.

Old age fast encroached on the duke. He was Peter Pan no more. Where once he had been hyperactive, now he was lethargic and despondent. After a hip operation in 1968, he could no longer work with pleasure in his garden. When he had lumbago and could not comfortably bend over, Wallis bought him a wooden milking stool to sit on for weeding the borders. This soon held little enjoyment, as his sight was so impaired. Friends noted Wallis's tender solicitude to her ailing husband. He once fell off a chair playing cards after dinner in Paris, briefly losing consciousness. Immediately after she had helped him to a sofa, she whipped the doctor's telephone number out of her handbag, alerting the American Hospital of Paris. Shortly afterwards, he recovered consciousness, and they were able to go home, the duke leaning heavily on the duchess's arm.

In November 1969, royal biographer Kenneth Rose was invited to a dinner party to meet the Windsors by Baron Bentinck, the Netherlands ambassador to France. "I notice that most of the guests greet the Duchess of Windsor as if she were Royal. It seems only polite to do so,"[22] recorded Rose. Wallis looked "quite remarkable for her years. She is smaller than I should have expected, but very trimmed and plucked and pressed, more like a woman of forty. She is dressed simply in pale blue, with no jewels except one huge sapphire round her neck. She has a harsh voice, but great vivacity and friendliness."[23] According to Rose, the couple departed "very regally, with much bowing and scraping all the way to the door. Thirty-three years after his Abdication, he is still very much King in manner, and nobody takes the slightest liberty with him."[24]

Prince Charles, now in his early twenties, had learned all about his "Great-uncle David" from his adored confidant Lord Louis Mountbatten. Mountbatten had for some time been angling for the duke and duchess to be able to return to Britain and finally heal the family rift. In 1971, Prince Charles wrote to Mountbatten: "I, personally, feel it would be wonderful if Uncle David and his wife could come over and spend a weekend. Now that he is getting old he must long to come back and it is pointless to continue the feud."[25] He raised the matter with his grandmother, the queen mother, who made it quite clear that she brooked no reconciliation. Later that year, Prince Charles made a private visit to France, where the British ambassador, Sir Christopher Soames, arranged for him to visit the Duke of Windsor. Prince Charles recorded his stay at the Windsors' home overlooking the Bois de Boulogne, describing how the footmen and pages wore identical "scarlet and black uniforms to the ones ours wear at home." He considered that "rather pathetic," and noted the red box with "The King" on it, placed in the front hall.[26]

Prince Charles was relieved to be able to escape the throng of guests, whom he deemed frightful, to a small sitting room, where he could speak to his great-uncle alone. The duke told the prince that he had had a very difficult time with his father, and Queen Mary (whom Prince Charles nicknamed "Gan-Gan") was "a hard woman." "While we were talking the duchess kept flitting to and fro like a strange bat. She looks incredible for her age and obviously has her face lifted every day," wrote Charles. "Uncle David then talked about how difficult my family had made it for him for the past 33 years. I asked him frankly if he would like to return to England for the last years of his life, and he hesitated to ask Wallis if he should give me 'the works.' It sounded as though he would have liked to have returned but no one would have recognised him. I assured him that would not be the case. The whole thing seemed so tragic—the existence, the people and the atmosphere—I was relieved to escape it after 45 minutes and drive round Paris by night."[27]

On June 3, 1971, the Windsors celebrated their thirty-fourth—and final—wedding anniversary together. The duchess, almost seventy-five, cut a gutsy dash, appearing at a party in a floor-length slit skirt over brown floral hot pants by Givenchy. Both knew, however, that the party was over. When the duke's old friend Lord Sefton fell ill, the duchess had written a note of sympathy to his wife. She told Lady Sefton: "Dearest Foxie, we are not well. I have a flood of nerves and the duke is having X-ray for this throat. I too from worry have a painful time with my old friend the ulcer." She concluded: "There is nothing to be said for growing old."[28]

While Wallis had never smoked, believing the habit dangerous and foul, the duke had smoked all his life; cigarettes, cigars and pipes. He was diagnosed with throat cancer that autumn. At the age of seventy-seven, his life was slipping away and his worst fear was realized: he was certain to leave Wallis alone.

After a period in the American Hospital of Paris in February 1972, when the duke was admitted under the pseudonym of Mr. Smith, the tumor in his throat was deemed inoperable. Edward insisted on returning home. An Irish nurse from the hospital, Oonagh Shanley, accompanied him to look after him. Nurse Shanley was touched that the duke's first question each morning was "Is the duchess awake?" If she was, he would go through to her room in his dressing gown. Later, they would have brunch together in the sitting room between their two suites, eating scrambled eggs and thin slices of bacon with slivers of toast. By early May, the duke's decline was rapid. "He underwent coughing spasms and suffered from fever," said Oonagh Shanley, "but all he ever wanted to know was if he would be well enough to dine with the duchess."[29]

The queen had a state visit to France on May 18. Throughout May daily bulletins concerning the duke's health were sent to Buckingham Palace. The duke's doctor was summoned by the British ambassador and instructed that the state visit was of tremendous political importance. Sir Christopher Soames told Dr. Jean Thin that "it would be politically disastrous" if the duke died during the visit.[30] Implicit was the message:

let him die before the queen arrives or keep him alive and let him die after the visit. It was not admitted to the press corps the extent to which the duke's life was in peril. Sir Martin Charteris, the queen's private secretary, told a journalist who inquired after the duke's health: "I know he's dying, you know he's dying but *we don't know* he's dying."[31]

On May 18, the queen went to the races at Longchamps. Afterwards, at 4.45 p.m., she arrived at the Windsors' house in the Bois. With her were the Duke of Edinburgh, Prince Charles, the Duchess of Grafton and Charteris. Wallis had filled the house with orchids. She received her visitors wearing a blue crêpe Dior dress, before personally serving them tea in the library. After fifteen minutes, she took the queen upstairs to have a private audience with Edward. The duke had insisted on getting dressed to receive his niece, a Herculean effort considering how ill he was. His blue blazer hung off his emaciated frame; he weighed less than six stone (84 pounds). He was still on an intravenous drip, but Dr. Thin had managed to conceal the medical apparatus behind a yellow chair in which the former king was seated. When the queen entered the room, Edward rose slowly from his chair, summoning every last bit of energy, to bow to his sovereign. With his unbreakable dignity, he then kissed her on each cheek. Typical of his English restraint, when she asked how he was, clearly drained from the immense strain of rising to greet her, he replied: "Not so bad."

That night, the duke's pug, Black Diamond, who always slept on his bed, was restless, which upset the duke. On 27 May, when Dr. Thin came as usual early that evening to check on the duke, he found that Black Diamond was sitting by himself on the floor, "thus letting me know that the end was near."[32] During the day, Wallis had stayed with Edward almost constantly. She struggled to remain composed; it was the duke, his voice a feeble whisper, who strove, as always, to comfort *her*. Sensing death was near, Wallis wanted to stay up all night but Edward, devoted to the end, insisted: "No, darling. I shall soon be asleep, get some rest, please."[33]

On Sunday morning, May 28, at 2.30 a.m., the duke passed away peacefully. The duchess was woken immediately and came to her husband's bedside. She took his hand and kissed his forehead, whispering "My David." Nurse Shanley later said: "Her quietness was much sadder than tears."[34] When Wallis was led back to her room, the duke's Bahamian valet, Sydney Johnson, insisted on maintaining a solitary vigil by his master's body for the rest of the night.

When the news broke, with each bulletin the BBC broadcast the abdication speech. "It made the same impact as it had thirty-five years before,"[35] said Diana Mosley, who had dined with Wallis in the library the night before the queen's visit, the duke too ill to join them. The queen ordered nine days of court mourning. She honored the duke's final wishes, which they had agreed over a decade before in 1961, in every respect. The RAF would fly the former monarch home to Britain. He would lie in state for two days at St. George's Chapel, Windsor. Then, after a private funeral service, he would be interred at Frogmore, waiting for the duchess to one day lie beside him for eternity.

The queen invited Wallis to stay at Buckingham Palace ahead of the funeral, rather than the Claridge's suite that she and the duke had lately frequented. "How ironic it is," pointed out the London *Evening News*, "that the first occasion since the abdication on which she will have been welcomed to the palace will be for her husband's burial. Would this visit not be an appropriate time for her to be accorded the courtesy title of Her Royal Highness on which the duke had set his heart?"[36]

Despite the fact that the queen permitted her first cousin Prince Michael of Kent to remain a Royal Highness after he forfeited his place in the line of succession to marry a Roman Catholic, only six years later—also conferring the royal status of HRH on his divorced wife—there was no question of her reversing her father's decision and upsetting the queen mother by allowing Wallis the royal status that she was legitimately entitled to.

The finality of death, while close and anticipated, came as a biting shock to Wallis, desolate and alone. After weeks of strain and anxiety, terrified for the future, she suffered a nervous collapse. Dr. Antenucci could see that she was in no fit state to accompany the duke's body when it was flown across the Channel to England forty-eight hours later. While the duchess rested, her friend Hubert de Givenchy made her a black mourning coat and matching dress, with a waist-length chiffon veil, overnight.

The duke's lying in state at Windsor attracted over sixty thousand visitors, many queuing for hours in lines that stretched over a mile long down Castle Hill and beyond. "My abiding memory of this is the atmosphere of solemnity and sadness," said Hugo Vickers, who acted as lay steward of St. George's Chapel. "It was clear that for those who came to pay their respects, their affection was undimmed. During those two days at Windsor, it was the young, charming Prince of Wales who was being remembered, not the Duke of Windsor who had deserted his subjects to take the supposed path of happiness."[37]

Wallis arrived in Britain on the second day of the duke's lying in state. She flew in on one of the queen's aircraft. "She no longer feared flying," explained Diana Mosley, "she felt her life was over."[38] Her arrival in England finally brought Wallis the first recognition she had received in the Court Circular during thirty-five years of marriage to the former king: "Buckingham Palace, June 2. By command of The Queen, Admiral of the Fleet the Earl Mountbatten of Burma was present at Heathrow Airport—London this morning and, on behalf of Her Majesty, greeted the Duchess of Windsor upon arrival in an aircraft of The Queen's Flight."[39]

The queen had sensitively ordered that all cross-traffic along the duchess's route into London be blocked off until her four-car procession had passed, to spare her gawping stares while the cars were stopped at intersections. Described by palace officials on her arrival as "unwell, tired and distressed," Wallis was shown to the suite of rooms on the first floor of Buckingham Palace, overlooking the Mall.[40]

The following morning, the queen had hoped that the duchess would join the other members of the royal family for the traditional ceremony of Trooping the Colour. She would have traveled in an open carriage with the queen mother, the most public and striking means of proclaiming reconciliation between the two women. For Wallis, the acceptance her husband had so desperately craved for her his entire married life, and unsuccessfully fought for, had come too late. She did not have the energy nor the inclination to be publicly recognized in his absence, nor paraded as the grieving widow. Her pain of loss was too intense—it was Wallis and Edward's thirty-fifth wedding anniversary on that very day—and her in-laws' urgent desire to honor her bittersweet. The only man in the world who would have been ecstatic to have witnessed this was no longer here by her side. To Wallis, it now seemed pointless.

On Saturday, June 3, the queen rode out on horseback at the head of the parade, a black armband adorning the left arm of her scarlet tunic. In honor of the duke, there was a roll of drums followed by a minute's silence, a further roll of drums, then Edward's favorite lament, the haunting "Flowers of the Forest," was played by the pipers of the Scots Guards. Photographers captured the duchess as she pulled aside the curtains of the state suite to watch the procession return. Her face is the image of stunned grief. Her eyes stare in bewildered shock. She looks afraid, vulnerable and incurably sad.

That evening, Prince Charles took the duchess to see the duke after all the visiting crowds had gone, accompanied by Lord Mountbatten. "I shall never forget the scene," the prince wrote.

> The Chapel was silent, almost dark except for the huge candles round the catafalque, which cast a flickering peaceful glow on the great pillars and the statuesque figures of the Guards Officers who stood vigil round the coffin. With great bearskinned heads bowed they stood absolutely motionless and silent. The duchess did not seem to be well. Uncle Dickie supported her all the time and at one point she moved away from us and stood alone, a frail, tiny, black figure, gazing at the coffin and finally bowing briefly. . . . As we stood she kept saying "he gave up so much for so little." . . .
>
> After she had gone back to B.P. [Buckingham Palace] Uncle Dickie and I waited until the Welsh Guards Bearer Party had removed the coffin to the Albert Memorial Chapel. . . . The whole evening was full of grandeur, simplicity, beauty and mystery and I shall never forget it. I only wish I had known Uncle David better.[41]

The funeral, two days later, on Monday, June 5, was described by Cecil Beaton as "short and entirely noble." During the service, in which she sat between the queen and Prince Philip, Wallis appeared lost and distraught. Lady Avon, seated behind the duchess, told Beaton that throughout the service, "the Queen showed a motherly and nanny-like tenderness and kept putting her hand on the Duchess's arm and glove."[42]

The most stirring and historic moment in the funeral came when the Garter King of Arms called out the styles and titles of the late duke: Knight of the Garter, of the Thistle, of St. King Edward VIII of Great Britain, Ireland, the British Dominions beyond the Seas, Emperor of India, Defender of the Faith . . . and uncle of the Most High, Most Mighty and Most Excellent Monarch, Queen Elizabeth—the roll call of heraldic honors and imperial birth a stark reminder to the congregation of just how much Edward had given up.

The weight of his decision was resting on the fragile shoulders of the duchess, bereft and confused in her pew. "During these days of death, she has behaved with extreme dignity. She has by the simplicity of her silhouette made the rest of the Royal Family appear dowdier than ever, but she made me marvel once again that she should ever become a figure in such a drama," wrote Cecil Beaton. "Wallis has been a good friend to me, I like her. She is a good friend to all her friends. There is no malice in her. There is nothing dislikeable."[43]

After the funeral, at a lunch at Windsor Castle, the duchess was seated between the Duke of Edinburgh and Lord Mountbatten. She later told the duke's old friend Walter Lees, a Scottish diplomat who lived in Paris, that Prince Philip had asked her what her plans were and if she was going back to America. She replied: "I won't be coming back to England if that's what you're afraid of, except to visit the grave."[44]

A private burial followed at Frogmore. The original intention was that the queen mother would not go to the committal, but, at the last minute, she decided she would. Undoubtedly her motives were more to do with public opinion than a genuine sense of remorse. At 2.25 p.m., the queen stood next to the duchess as the duke's body was lowered into the grave on the site he had chosen. Beneath a wide-spreading plane tree, surrounded by hawthorns, rhododendrons, wild azaleas and flowering cherries, it was close to where he had played as a child. As the body was lowered, the queen asked the duchess where she would like to be eventually laid to rest: to the right side of Edward's grave, or to the left? The duchess—who commented that she did not anticipate flowers would be placed on her grave—said she would like to be buried to the left, beneath the plane tree. She loved the leaves of plane trees, often collecting them from the garden for her dressing table, and liked the idea of their falling onto her grave in the autumn.[45]

Shortly afterwards, the duchess flew back from Heathrow to Paris on an aircraft of the Queen's Flight. As she left the tarmac, press lenses trained on her, she painted a forlorn picture. Her minute figure in her black Givenchy mourning coat, walking up the aircraft steps alone, underlined the fearful loneliness that lay ahead for her. She did not turn and look back.

She would return to England only once again in her life: a year later on July 11, when she visited Frogmore to put flowers on the duke's grave, by then covered by a plain white stone of Portland marble.

At 5:20 on the afternoon of her husband's funeral, the duchess's plane landed at Villacoublay air base, from which she was driven to her Paris home. "To get back to the empty house; never more to be greeted by the duke's call: 'Darling, darling, I'm here!' was unbearable for Wallis," said Diana Mosley. "He had cherished, adored and protected her for nearly four decades with his extraordinary devotion. There can hardly be a widow with quite so much to miss."[46]

With the duke's death, Wallis's raison d'être was extinguished. Her visceral emptiness was tangible. She had created her own version of a fairytale castle with the duke; now it became a mocking fortress. Everything was a reminder that the sovereign of their gilded kingdom was gone. The royal portraits, coats of arms and grand images of the Prince of Wales's feathers remained; but what did it matter any more if the staff addressed her as "*Votre Altesse Royale*" or bowed and curtsied to her? Terrified of penury, she swiftly reduced the Paris staff from twenty-five to fourteen and sold the Mill for £320,000 to a Swiss millionaire. Her lifelong terror of destitution was still not quelled when she received £3 million in the duke's will. However, her fears that the French government would evict her from the Bois de Boulogne mansion were allayed when the French foreign minister reassured her that his government would not be imposing death duties on the former king's estate and that she would continue to remain immune from taxation for her lifetime. Furthermore, she was welcome to stay on as tenant of the villa in the Bois de Boulogne.

On Lord Mountbatten's advice, delivered in person, the duchess returned the duke's Garter robes, uniforms, orders and decorations to the queen. However, the repeated presence of Dickie in her home, picking over precious objets d'art, insisting that they should be returned to the royal family as they belonged to the Royal Collection, unsurprisingly put her back up. According to Mountbatten's daughter Lady Pamela Hicks her father was adamant that some gold and kettledrums belonged back in London, not with the duchess in Paris.[47] Even royals, or especially royals, fight over the family silver. Lady Gillian Tomkins, wife of the new British ambassador in Paris, Sir Edward Tomkins, said: "I have to say that the behaviour of the royal family was quite tactless at this point. They had snubbed the duchess for years and then once the duke was gone, they started making friendly overtures toward her because they wanted her jewels and possessions. The duchess was much too clever not to see through that. She always hid the royal swords before Mountbatten visited her."[48]

"The duchess had no relations but many friends, and her friends tried to help," said Diana Mosley. "After the first shock of grief she saw them often, but she was often tired and depressed, unhappy and lonely."[49] Diana Vreeland recalled arriving in Paris shortly after the duke had died. "The duchess called me on the telephone and said: 'Oh, Diana. I know you've just arrived, but come out here and have dinner with me. I'm all alone.' I went out to the house in Neuilly [in the Bois de Boulogne]. The duchess looked too beautiful, standing in the garden, dressed in a turquoise djellaba embroidered in black pearls and white pearls—marvelous—and wearing all her sapphires."[50] After dinner, the two women talked and reminisced. "Suddenly Wallis took hold of my wrist, gazed off into the distance, and said: 'Diana, I keep telling him not to abdicate. *He must not abdicate.* No, no, no! No, no, no, I say!' Then suddenly, after this little mental journey back more than thirty-five years, her mind snapped back to the present; she looked at me, and we went on talking as we had been before."[51]

Without the duke to live for, Wallis's health swiftly deteriorated. She barely ate, preferring to drink vodka from an iced silver mug. She drank too much, irritating her sensitive stomach. She developed a gastric ulcer, which perforated, and she was rushed to the American Hospital of Paris, where she remained for six months. She began to suffer falls, fracturing her hip over Christmas 1972. Disorientated and enfeebled, she became morbid, longing for death. In one of her more lucid moments, she confided to Gore Vidal: "My life's not important. But I think [the duke's] was. Such a waste, really, for everyone."[52]

With lapses into senility, Wallis made a decision that would ensure her last years were a horrific nightmare. In January 1973, she terminated the services of the duke's long-standing lawyer, Sir Godfrey Morley, of Allen & Overy, London. Vulnerable and fearing for her future, she hired Maître Suzanne Blum, who had been the Windsors' Paris lawyer since 1946, to take over all her legal affairs. This Machiavellian woman, only two years Wallis's junior, but robust in health, fueled Wallis's worst fears that others were taking advantage of her. Although Blum had, in her heyday, acted for Charlie Chaplin, Walt Disney, 20th Century Fox and Rita Hayworth, and remained a formidable legal opponent, she developed a macabre obsession with Wallis. Cleverly and carefully, she dismissed the duchess's loyal retainers, including Sir John Utter, a retired American diplomat who had been the duke's private secretary. She seized power of attorney over the duchess and was soon running her entire life, suing newspapers and authors for considerable damages. Under the guise of championing the duchess's causes, she imprisoned her. Wallis's friends were soon banned from seeing her as Blum kept Wallis under her perverse, steely control.

"When I met Maître Blum, she couldn't have been more charming but in a sinister way," said Hugo Vickers. "This Satanic figure wore the mantle of good intention to disguise her inner malevolence."[53] The Irish society hostess Aileen Plunket, who was friends with the Windsors, said that Wallis becoming "Blumed" was "just one of those horrible mistakes people make."[54] Before the duke died, Suzanne Blum had no influence. "The woman came zooming in the moment she heard the duke was dead and tried to make the duchess think that all her staff were cheating her. Poor Wallis was in a terrible state after his death. Her health was getting worse and worse. She became really paranoid and she thought the whole world was against her. Obviously that clever old beast Blum knew exactly how to work on her paranoia. She did a sort of purge and she tried to get rid of everyone who'd ever been fond of the duchess. She wanted Wallis to herself."[55]

The last time that Diana Mosley saw Wallis, she was deeply upset. "The poor little thing was lying there on her side. Her big blue eyes were open and she was staring desperately in front of her. She never said a word. And something had gone horribly wrong with her sad little hands."[56]

When Aileen Plunket tried to visit Wallis, she was turned away by Maître Blum, saying that she might endanger the duchess's life. This made Mrs. Plunket, an elegant octogenarian, incandescent. "If the duchess was too ill to want to talk, I only wanted to peek my head through her bedroom door. I wanted to wave to her. . . . I wanted to blow her a kiss and maybe put some flowers by her bed. . . . I only wanted Wallis to know that I hadn't forgotten her."[57] It was heartbreaking for Wallis's friends to think that Wallis was lying alone in her Parisian mansion, caged by the despotic Blum, thinking they had all abandoned her. "We all accepted her marvellous hospitality in the old days," said Diana Mosley. "It's too dreadful if poor Wallis thinks that now she is old, and ill, and widowed, we have all deserted her."[58]

"Wallis was a very nice woman and she didn't deserve that awful end," said Laura, Duchess of Marlborough. "Poor little thing, locked up by her servants. The duke knew something awful would happen to Wallis if she survived him. He loved her so much that he was always worried as to what would become of her once he had gone."[59]

Gore Vidal lunched with the duchess during her last visit to New York in 1974, when, going against medical advice, Wallis underwent another face-lift. Vidal believed that her subsequent lapses into non compos mentis were the result of too many anesthetics; by this time she had had four or five face-lifts. Of her last operation, he wrote: "The result was splendid, but of course, she died on the operating table for several minutes, quite long enough to scramble her oxygen-denied brain."[60]

During the last years of her life, the emaciated duchess was cared for by a rota of nurses. Lying in a narrow hospital bed in her Wallis-pale-blue bedroom, fed by a tube through her nose, she alternated between coherence and fantasy. One of her nurses, Elvire Gozin, was distraught that Wallis's visitors were turned away, while the mansion fell into a state of disrepair. To the dying duchess, the consummate housekeeper, any knowledge of this would have been another unbearable indignity. The gardens were no longer tended, the house was decaying, her priceless paintings and furniture gathering dust. It had the brooding stillness of a mausoleum, waiting for her final demise. "She was alive, and yet not alive," said Diana Mosley. "Doctors had become very clever at keeping the heart beating. Who knows what she suffered?"[61]

Meanwhile, Maître Blum was ensuring her own future was well furnished. She squirreled valuable possessions away and in 1982 sold twenty-one snuffboxes from the duke's collection at Christie's Geneva.

At last, Wallis's longed-for release came. Fourteen desperate years after the duke passed away, the Duchess of Windsor died, aged eighty-nine, on April 24, 1986. The duke was able, once again, to protect her in death. As the royal machine clicked into action, any plans that Maître Blum might have concocted for her funeral or her burial place held no sway. The Lord Chamberlain's Office interceded. The duchess's body was flown to Britain in an aircraft of the Queen's Flight, then driven to Windsor Castle, where it remained overnight in the Albert Memorial Chapel. Fittingly, her coffin rested on the same spot that had been occupied by the duke, and the kings and queens of England before that.

At the duke's funeral, the wreaths and flowers had covered the whole hill in front of St. George's Chapel. For the duchess's death, there were only two rows of wreaths in the cloisters. The entire royal family attended the duchess's funeral. "No one could really be said to be in a funeral mood—except perhaps Granny,"[62] said Prince Charles. "I am flabbergasted that they all attended," said John Julius Norwich. "This was not in very good taste, after the way they had treated her. But it would have been the courtiers who suggested that to ensure favourable publicity for the royal family."[63]

In death, the duchess was afforded the dignity of a royal funeral. The court pulled out all the stops in terms of pomp and pageantry. "There was the queen and the royal family, and the chapel beautifully lit and the choir singing. It was everything the duke would have wanted for the duchess,"[64] observed Princess Ghislaine de Polignac, a close friend of the Windsors in Paris. Diana Mosley noted how "The queen in her clever way gave the best seats to George and Ofelia," the duchess's long-standing servants.[65]

"The atmosphere in the chapel was charged with a moving stillness," remembered Hugo Vickers. "The sentences were sung and the short service was beautifully conducted, especially the anthem. The only thing that they got wrong was that there was absolutely no mention of the duchess by name. They never commended the spirit of 'our sister Wallis'. . . . [The courtiers] thought that they would have offended the queen by mentioning the duchess by name. They should have asked the queen, instead of presuming not to mention Wallis. Apart from that, it was everything that the duke would have wanted for her; the flowers on the coffin, the choir, the entire royal family there."[66]

At the private committal at Frogmore afterwards, the Duchess of Windsor was finally mentioned by name. As her body was lowered beneath the wide-spreading plane tree, next to the man who had loved her so deeply that he had renounced everything for her, the queen wept.[67]

Years before, Edward had copied out lines from a Tennyson poem, in his own hand on royal stationery, for Wallis. It stood, framed, on her glass-topped dressing table, amid photographs of the duke, the man who had adored her like no other.[68]

My friend, with thee to
live alone
Methinks were better than
To own
A crown, a sceptre, and
A throne.[69]

EPILOGUE

The Cedar Walk

In her memoirs, Wallis wrote that she loved the Fort so much that she planned to haunt the Cedar Walk. "A part of me remains in the vicinity of the Fort, and history is herewith given fair warning that one day a pale and anonymous phantom may be observed in the shadows along the Cedar Walk that is such a distinctive feature of the property."[1]

I was honored to be allowed by the present custodians to visit Fort Belvedere while researching this book. To Wallis, the Fort was "the most romantic house I have ever known,"[2] a sentiment easy to accept. Like a turreted folly, with its distinctive crisscross markings—flint chips embedded in render—it is unique, quirky and intimate. It was shrouded in mist on the day of my visit, the gentle rain heightening the undeniable nostalgia of the building and its undulating grounds. There were the flint-green ceremonial cannons that the Prince of Wales had installed, twenty of which line the battlements overlooking the vista of the famed Cedar Walk, planted in 1780. I imagined Wallis strolling with her beloved cairn, Slipper, through the grassy sweep of parkland.

I stood outside the drawing room, on the historic paving stones where Edward told Wallis that he was going to abdicate that foggy night in December 1936. The rock garden, with its stream gushing through and the special lumps of stone that he had had hewn and delivered from

Yorkshire, is incomplete; the king had to discard his plans for it when he abdicated. He created an exact replica twenty years later at the Mill. This idyllic home, with its private, peaceful grounds, according to Wallis, "meant more to David than anything else in the world save honour, the honour with which he was so rashly, yet so gallantly, to invest the love he came to have for me."[3]

A private photograph album at Fort Belvedere contains images of a summer lunch captured in 1935; the couple's ease and carefree bonhomie radiate off the page. Wallis and Edward are entertaining friends. The king larks around in the circular drive in a bearskin, pipe in hand, Wallis oversees lunch on the terrace; they play croquet on the lawn. The most moving image is of the couple walking together in the distance, their heads tilted towards each other, deep in conversation. Of course, this was in the halcyon days before the abdication and the devastation that this decision unleashed.

I left the Fort, which has a compelling magic, hoping that Wallis—and Edward—haunt the Cedar Walk together, the spirits of their canine companions dancing at their heels. The Duke of Windsor would be enchanted by the love, care and attention that the present owners have lavished on the grounds. It brought tears to my eyes: every bank of snowdrops, every wildflower meadow, every rose trained up a trellis feels in rightful memory of Edward and the garden he adored.

That afternoon, I was further blessed to be invited to Royal Lodge, also tucked away in Windsor Great Park. The drawing room is imposing with its pale-green paneling, soaring ceilings, vast oils depicting the surrounding park and acres of Persian carpet. I tried to envisage the awkward tea that Wallis endured with the Duke and Duchess of York in the spring of 1936, the judgmental loathing of the late queen mother silently upon her. The present Queen Elizabeth, the only member of the royal family to soften towards Wallis, was then a little girl, playing with her sister, Margaret.

I considered how history hangs like an invisible mist in these legendary rooms. Here the king had met Queen Mary for the last time before abdicating. He had sat with his mother, sister and three brothers in the formal drawing room before dinner. I imagined them stunned yet scrupulously polite, each nursing abject fear of what the future would hold when their beloved David left England that night. Only he was unwavering in his resolve.

The greatest surprise to me writing this book was how much I warmed to the Duke of Windsor. I already knew that I liked and related to Wallis. No one forced her to begin a relationship with the Prince of Wales but when she could not extricate herself, she must have felt devastatingly alone prior to the abdication. Most of the time she was viewed by the world as hard as granite, and the severe look she cultivated did not help. But it is too easy to write her off as manipulative and domineering, when inside she often felt vulnerable and afraid. She was powerful—in her effect on Edward—but powerless, in her inability to prevent events from spiraling out of control.

I felt disappointed in Wallis when she embarrassed the duke with her foolish flirtation with Jimmy Donahue and wished that she had not belittled him in an overly domineering way in public. But I could see that it was hard for her to live with that kind of obsessive, suffocating devotion. After his death, it was even harder to live without it. Wallis's loyalty to Edward was unquestionable. Before he abdicated, she genuinely wanted him to reign as a successful and fulfilled sovereign. Once she was entrapped in marriage to him, she determined to do her best by him because she had grown to love him. In this endeavor, against the backdrop of psychological assassination from the rest of the world, she triumphed.

The deeper I got into researching his story, the more I felt for Edward; I liked him, despite his wild inconsistencies of character. He was both public hero and private coward; ostentatious and wincingly mean, overindulged and emotionally neglected; weak, rash and infuriatingly stubborn. He knew that royalty promises a palace but delivers a cage. His endless torment was that he caged Wallis without any of the expected gilded trappings. However, he deserves respect for never giving up on his quest to have his wife accepted by his family. His love for Wallis was as selfish and as crucial to his survival as a child's; it would have been the more loving act to have relinquished her. However, he remained true to his principle, determined to show the world that Wallis was worthy of marriage, as opposed to relegating her to the diminished role of mistress. Wallis had to suffer the rejection of not being honored by her husband's family on an international scale. She contained her private agonies with laudable dignity.

The love affair between Edward and Wallis was both an iconic story of sheer devotion and a heartrending chronicle of the consequences of sacrifice. I believe that Wallis never wanted to marry the king of England. She was enthralled by the glitter and prestige of his position, yet later maintained that she would have preferred to have stayed in the shadows of history with Ernest Simpson. Whether, as Ernest doubted, this would have sustained her after the excitement of royal favor is questionable. However, once trapped into marriage to Edward, burdened by his almost choking adoration, she did her best to make their life together as perfect as possible. No matter who was in the room, "the duke only had eyes for her," Diana Mosley said of Edward's love for Wallis. "I think that it is something quite unique for middle-aged and old people who have been married for over thirty years to be so completely in love as he was. She was devoted to him and did her utmost to make him happy and that's where she succeeded."[4]

Count Rudi von Schönburg observed: "In over fifty years of running a hotel, I have seen thousands of couples together. I have seldom seen a couple as integrated as they were. They had been married for thirty-five years by this point and had a deep confidence in each other and mutual respect. It was an extraordinary love."[5]

I wanted to honor this love by placing flowers on Wallis's grave, to pay tribute to the woman I had come to respect and feel great affection for. It pained me that the duchess had commented that she did not expect anyone to visit her in death. I was deeply fortunate to be allowed to go to Frogmore, situated in the Home Park at Windsor, to visit the Royal Burial Ground. I chose my bouquet with care; it contained her wedding flowers: white peonies, delphiniums the color of her Mainbocher blue wedding dress, larkspur and sprigs of wild grasses. For the duke, I took a smaller posy of white carnations, a reminder of his wedding day boutonnière, mixed with forget-me-nots.

The duke's and duchess's graves are together but set apart from the other royal graves, separated by the vast, protecting boughs of the plane tree. As I placed my bouquet, I felt relieved; they were together at last, accepted into the royal fold. It would have given the duke tremendous pleasure that they had finally taken their rightful place in history. His brothers' graves are to the right; opposite stands the Royal Mausoleum, the resting place of Queen Victoria and Prince Albert. Tranquillity radiates; the quiet power of monarchy and manicured privilege.

The sacred ground is surrounded by the lovely, almost informal gardens of Frogmore House, with its lake and paths mown through wildflowers. A month earlier, Meghan Markle celebrated her marriage to Prince Harry here. The plane tree by Wallis's grave lies in the distance.

As I stood over the Duke and Duchess of Windsor's final resting places, it struck me as ironic that, in death, Wallis and Edward were back in this unique realm, when they had been driven from it in life. The duke's smooth Portland stone grave is adorned with his heraldic roll call of names and his regal title. The duchess's grave, of rougher-hewn stone, simply says: "Wallis, Duchess of Windsor, 19th June 1896–24th April 1986." Her lack of HRH remains jarring.

Wallis wrote to Edward after the abdication, astutely aware of the fact that receiving the title Her Royal Highness would be "the only thing to bring me back in the eyes of the world." Given everything that she went through and the propriety with which she endured her suffering, this is the title she should have had, was legally entitled to and deserved. It has been my intention to bring Wallis Simpson favorably back in the eyes of the world, and this book is dedicated posthumously to HRH the Duchess of Windsor.

I reject the notion put forward by some that, faced with a choice between love and duty, I chose love. I certainly married because I chose the path of love. But I abdicated because I chose the path of duty. I did not value the Crown so lightly that I gave it away hastily. I valued it so deeply that I surrendered it, rather than risk any impairment of its prestige.

—Edward, Duke of Windsor, 1947[1]

ACKNOWLEDGMENTS AND NOTE ON SOURCES

My interest in the love affair between the Duke and Duchess of Windsor began early. Aged eleven, I watched the 1978 television series *Edward and Mrs. Simpson* with my parents. Edward Fox, as the charismatic yet petulant Prince of Wales, stands out in my mind to this day. My mother gave me Michael Bloch's *Wallis and Edward: Letters 1931–1937* when the collection was first published in 1986; I read them when I was at university, and felt moved and haunted by this tragic love affair. Bloch's book contains the most romantic documents of the era, charting Edward's obsessive and overwhelming passion for Wallis, and the struggle that she endured trying to stave off the abdication.

When it was announced in November 2017 that Prince Harry was to marry American divorcée Meghan Markle I felt a profound sense of injustice flare up for poor Wallis. While I was relieved that the royal family has modernized to the extent that they allowed Ms. Markle to become the Duchess of Sussex and accord her the title Her Royal Highness, I still feel a burning sense of prejudice on Wallis's behalf. While I was delighted that the popular Prince Harry would remain a legitimate member of the royal family on his marriage, I felt sadness for his great-great-uncle Edward, who was exiled not just from the country but also from the inner sanctum of his own family on his marriage to Wallis.

It was Prince Harry and Meghan Markle's engagement that precipitated my interest in writing about Wallis Simpson, fuelling my desire to rehabilitate her in history. Interest in the abdication story will doubtless reignite when Prince Charles ascends to the throne. Current debate simmers over whether Camilla, Duchess of Cornwall, can ever become queen as opposed to princess consort. As Camilla is also a divorcée, this uncertainty echoes some of the battles Edward and Wallis endured. Will we see Queen Camilla or will this become a morganatic marriage, the solution Edward was denied? Though Edward and Wallis lived in different times, monarchy is about continuity and the use of titles is a powerful element of that; it therefore seems bitingly unfair that Camilla was granted the coveted title HRH, a title that the British royal family cruelly denied Wallis (and even any future children).

In my quest to rehabilitate Wallis, I have been touched and surprised by friends who have introduced me to their friends who knew the royal couple. I decided that fate was on my side when I went to stay with the Duke and Duchess of Fragnito, in Gstaad, just as the idea for this book was percolating. I had not realized that my host, David, had spent time with the Duke and Duchess of Windsor in Palm Beach in the sixties. During our visit, David and his wife, Patricia, held a dinner party for us. One of the guests, Ann Pleydell-Bouverie, from a prominent Nassau family, mentioned that her parents had known the duke and duchess well in the Bahamas. She introduced me to Julie, whose father, Charles Bethell, was the duke's closest friend during his time in the Bahamas and was able to provide many insights. Julie Le Corne also showed me photographs never seen before of the royal couple. By now it truly felt like fate, and as the praise for Wallis from a wide, unrelated circle began to accumulate, I knew that this was an important book for me to write.

Anne Sebba wrote the last definitive biography of Wallis, *That Woman*, in 2011. I decided to seek her counsel while writing my book. Her excellent portrayal of Wallis and her situation highlights Wallis's entrapment by the prince and reveals Wallis's enduring love for Ernest. When I asked Sebba: "Did you like Wallis?" she replied, "What's to like?" I, however, have taken a completely contrary view: my response would be "What's not to like?" I am grateful to Anne for encouraging me to pursue a book about Wallis in which I hope that the reader feels the same sympathy and tenderness for the female protagonist that I do.

Other friends of the duke and duchess, I was delighted to discover, were happy to contribute to a book that celebrated rather than condemned Wallis. Georgia Coleridge introduced me to Nicky Haslam, whom I cannot thank enough for his kindness and generosity towards me and the extent to which he has championed this book. He let me quote from never-before-seen correspondence and has been a constant source of inspiration, steering me towards the memoirs of Elsa Maxwell, Diana Vreeland, Mollie Panter-Downes, Edith Olivier and the glamorous scrapbooks of Baron de Cabrol.

Rachel Kelly introduced me to Lord Norwich, who was equally kind, generous and supportive. My time spent with him was especially meaningful as, sadly, John Julius Norwich died on June 1, 2018, while I was completing this book. I treasure a postcard he sent to me after our meeting. "I too greatly enjoyed our talk," he wrote. "You probably know what Wallis is said to have said to him in November '36: 'You must understand, darling, that you can't abdicate and eat it.' "

I am grateful to Sarah O'Brien, who introduced me via her father, the Honorable Michael O'Brien, to historian and writer Hugo Vickers. Vickers's *Behind Closed Doors: The Tragic, Untold Story of the Duchess of Windsor* is a gripping portrayal of the end of the duchess's life and her captivity by the despotic Maître Blum. Vickers's later book, the edited diaries of James Pope-Hennessy, *The Quest for Queen Mary*, is funny, riveting and insightful. I thoroughly recommend this to anyone interested in the royal family and was grateful to be able to quote from it, as well as to interview Hugo, who was at both the Duke and the Duchess of Windsor's funerals.

I am indebted to Count Rudi von Schönburg, with whom I had a fascinating, long lunch at the Marbella Club. He could not have been more generous with his recollections. Thank you also to Alejandra García at the club, who sourced the archives for a wonderful, previously unpublished photograph of Wallis.

I am profoundly grateful for and touched by the generosity of Mrs. Galen Weston, the current owner of Fort Belvedere, who allowed me to visit this fascinating property as part of my research. My thanks, too, go to Dean Peckett, who gave us a memorable tour of the gardens that Edward loved so much. He was patient with my desire to touch the trees along the Cedar Walk and allowed me time to soak up the atmosphere. I am equally indebted to Sarah, Duchess of York, and HRH the Duke of York for allowing me to visit Royal Lodge and, the most special of all, to place flowers on Wallis's grave at Frogmore. This was the most moving and fitting end to my journey with Wallis.

I am incredibly appreciative of everyone above who has given me so much time, help, wisdom, expertise and support during the research and writing of this book. My immense gratitude also goes to Audrey Pasternak, Daisy Pasternak, Eugenie Furniss, Arabella Pike, Trish Todd, Kate Johnson, Katherine Patrick, Linda Mathews-Denham, Charles Spicer, Monika Barton, Richard Furgerson, Yvonne Williams and Judith Osborne. Also, my thanks go to Julie, April and May from Bluebells Florist, Henley, who each week prepared a spectacular bouquet of flowers, which I had on my desk while writing to inspire me, as Wallis adored flowers so much.

Finally, but most important, this book could not have been written without the love, patience, kindness, generosity, wizardry and magnificent support of my husband, Andrew. To him I am the most grateful. A huge and wholehearted thank-you.

NOTES

PROLOGUE: THE HEART HAS ITS REASONS

1. Elsa Maxwell, *I Married the World* (London: William Heinemann, 1955), 243.
2. Diana Vreeland, *DV*, ed. George Plimpton and Christopher Hemphill (New York: Alfred A. Knopf, 1984), 70.
3. Hugo Vickers, *Behind Closed Doors: The Tragic Untold Story of the Duchess of Windsor* (London: Hutchinson, 2011), 280.
4. Philip Ziegler, *King Edward VIII: The Official Biography* (Glasgow: William Collins and Sons, 1990), 74.
5. Duchess of Windsor, *The Heart Has Its Reasons: The Memoirs of the Duchess of Windsor* (London: Michael Joseph, 1956; London: Tandem, 1969), 305. Citations refer to the Tandem edition.
6. Caroline Blackwood, *The Last of the Duchess: The Strange and Sinister Story of the Final Years of Wallis Simpson, Duchess of Windsor* (New York: Vintage Books, 2012), 245.
7. Duchess of Windsor, *Heart Has Its Reasons*, 215.
8. Ibid., 215–16.
9. Michael Bloch, ed., *Wallis and Edward: Letters 1931–1937: The Intimate Correspondence of the Duke and Duchess of Windsor* (New York: Summit Books, 1986), 174.
10. Hugo Vickers, interview with author, London, November 2017.
11. Vreeland, *DV*, 68.
12. Henry Channon, *Chips: The Diaries of Sir Henry Channon*, ed. Robert Rhodes James (London: Weidenfeld and Nicolson, 1967), 51.
13. Duchess of Windsor, *Heart Has Its Reasons*, 305.
14. Count Rudolf Graf von Schönburg, interview with author, Marbella, Spain, September 2017.
15. Ibid.
16. David Maude-Roxby, interview with author, Gstaad, Switzerland, March 2017.
17. Vreeland, *DV*, 73.
18. Vickers, interview.
19. Nicholas Haslam, interview with author, London, August 2017.
20. Ibid.
21. Duchess of Windsor, *Heart Has Its Reasons*, 150.
22. Duchess of Windsor to Elsie

Mendl, September 24, 1948, private collection of Nicholas Haslam.

23. Ibid.
24. Vickers, interview.
25. Duke and Duchess of Windsor, interview by Kenneth Harris, broadcast on the BBC, October 1970.
26. Duchess of Windsor, *Heart Has Its Reasons*, 398.

1: THE PRINCE'S GIRL

1. Gloria Vanderbilt and Thelma Lady Furness, *Double Exposure: A Twin Autobiography* (London: Frederick Muller, 1959), 274.
2. Ibid.
3. Sara Wheeler, Too Close to the Sun: The Audacious Life and Times of Denys Finch Hatton (London: Jonathan Cape 2006), 215.
4. Siân Evans, *Queen Bees: Six Brilliant and Extraordinary Society Hostesses Between the Wars* (London: Two Roads, 2016), 197.
5. Duchess of Windsor, *Heart Has Its Reasons*, 177.
6. Ibid., 178.
7. Ibid., 180.
8. Ibid.
9. Ibid., 181.
10. Duke of Windsor, *A King's Story: The Memoirs of H.R.H. the Duke of Windsor* (New York: G. P. Putnam's Sons, 1947; London: Cassell, 1951, 256). Citations refer to the Cassell edition.
11. Ibid.
12. Diana Mosley, *The Duchess of Windsor: A Memoir* (London: Gibson Square Books, 2012), 89.
13. Sebba, Anne, *That Woman: The Life of Wallis Simpson, Duchess of Windsor* (London: Weidenfeld & Nicolson, 2011), 64.
14. Duchess of Windsor, *Heart Has Its Reasons*, 130.
15. Mosley, *Duchess of Windsor*, 12.
16. Haslam, interview.
17. Channon, *Chips*, 51.
18. Mosley, *Duchess of Windsor*, 27.
19. Duchess of Windsor, *Heart Has Its Reasons*, 8.
20. Ibid., 160.
21. Ibid., 56.
22. Ibid., 27.
23. Ibid., 160.
24. Ibid., 8.
25. Ibid., 13.
26. Ibid.
27. Ibid., 14.
28. Ibid., 45.
29. Ibid., 50.
30. Ibid.
31. Ibid.
32. Ibid.
33. Ibid., 52.
34. Ibid., 7.
35. Fleur Cowles, "The Duchess of Windsor Talk's Clothes with Fleur Cowles, *Harper's Bazaar*, May 1966.
36. Suzy Menkes, "The Duchess of Windsor's Royal Style," *Harper's Bazaar*, October 15, 2010, www.harpersbazaar.com/culture/features/a592/duchess-of-windsor-style-1010.
37. Maxwell, *I Married*, 249.
38. Vreeland, *DV*, 69.
39. Maxwell, *I Married*, 249.
40. Haslam, interview.

41. Nicholas Haslam, *Redeeming Features* (New York: Vintage, 2010), 192.
42. Duchess of Windsor, *Heart Has Its Reasons*, 178.
43. Sebba, *That Woman*, 88.
44. Bloch, *Wallis and Edward: Letters*, 51.
45. Duchess of Windsor, *Heart Has Its Reasons*, 186.
46. Duke of Windsor, *King's Story*, 257.
47. Duchess of Windsor, *Heart Has Its Reasons*, 187.
48. Duke of Windsor, *King's Story*, 258.
49. Ibid.
50. Ibid., 4.
51. James Pope-Hennessy, *The Quest for Queen Mary*, ed. Hugo Vickers (London: Zuleika, 2018), 182.
52. Duke of Windsor, *King's Story*, 27.
53. Ibid., 8.
54. Ibid., 43.
55. Ibid., 52.
56. Pope-Hennessy, *Quest for Queen Mary*, 96.
57. Ibid., 115.
58. Blackwood, *Last of the Duchess*, 267–68.
59. Michael Turner, *Osborne House* (Bristol, UK: English Heritage, 2016), 51.
60. Duke of Windsor, *King's Story*, 28.
61. Ibid., 41.
62. Ibid., 74.
63. Piers Brendon, *Edward VIII: The Uncrowned King* (London: Allen Lane, 2016), 11.
64. Duke of Windsor, *King's Story*, 95.
65. Ibid.
66. *New York Times*, June 1, 1913, cited in L. W. B. Brockliss, *The University of Oxford: A History* (Oxford: Oxford University Press, 2016), 458.
67. Duke of Windsor, *King's Story*, 84.
68. John Julius Norwich, interview in documentary *Wallis Simpson: The Secret Letters*, Channel 4, August 2011.
69. Maude-Roxby, interview.
70. Duke of Windsor, *King's Story*, 98–99.
71. Schönburg, interview.
72. John Julius Norwich, interview with author, London, October 2017.
73. Duke of Windsor, *King's Story*, 97.
74. Mosley, *Duchess of Windsor*, 63.
75. Pope-Hennessy, *Quest for Queen Mary*, 144.
76. Duke of Windsor, *King's Story*, 78.
77. Channon, *Chips*, 51.
78. Ibid., 50.
79. Duke of Windsor, *King's Story*, 111.
80. Brendon, *Edward VIII*, 15.
81. Duke of Windsor, *King's Story*, 119.
82. Ibid., 120.
83. Brendon, *Edward VIII*, 17.
84. Ibid., 25.
85. Ibid., 32.
86. Ziegler, *Edward VIII*, 222.
87. Ibid., 163.
88. Vickers, *Behind Closed Doors*, 276.
89. Cited in *Chartwell Bulletin*,

Winston Churchill Centre, retrieved September 21, 2015.

90. Haslam, interview.
91. Norwich, interview.
92. Channon, *Chips*, 23.
93. Pope-Hennessy, *Quest for Queen Mary*, 200.
94. Blackwood, *Last of the Duchess*, 265.
95. Vickers, *Behind Closed Doors*, 277.
96. Duchess of Windsor, *Heart Has Its Reasons*, 59.
97. Ibid., 68.
98. Mosley, *Duchess of Windsor*, 24.
99. Duchess of Windsor, *Heart Has Its Reasons*, 91.
100. Mosley, *Duchess of Windsor*, 27.
101. John Julius Norwich, ed., *The Duff Cooper Diaries* (London: Weidenfeld & Nicolson, 2005), 403.
102. Duchess of Windsor, *Heart Has Its Reasons*, 398.
103. Sebba, *That Woman*, 27–28.
104. Mosley, *Duchess of Windsor*, 27.
105. Maxwell, *I Married*, 259.
106. Sebba, *That Woman*, 35.
107. Ibid.
108. Vickers, *Behind Closed Doors*, 310.
109. Haslam, interview.
110. Norwich, interview.
111. Martin Gilbert and Randolph Churchill, *Winston S. Churchill: The Official Biography*, Vol. 5 (Heinemann, 1976), 810.
112. Susan Williams, "The Vilification of Wallis Simpson," *BBC History Magazine*, December 2006.
113. Evans, *Queen Bees*, 198.
114. Duchess of Windsor, *Heart Has Its Reasons*, 21.
115. Ibid., 145.
116. Ibid.
117. Alex Kerr-Smiley, interview in *Wallis Simpson: The Secret Letters*.

118 Duchess of Windsor, *Heart Has Its Reasons*, 145.

2: *ICH DIEN*

1. Duchess of Windsor, *Heart Has Its Reasons*, 151.
2. Ibid., 161.
3. Ibid., 168.
4. Edwina H. Wilson, *Her Name Was Wallis Warfield* (New York: E. P. Dutton, 1935), 17.
5. Ruth Franklin, quoting Elsie de Wolfe in *New Yorker* magazine, September 27, 2004.
6. Duke of Windsor, *King's Story*, 257.
7. Maxwell, *I Married*, 249.
8. James Reginato, "The Raj Duet," *Vanity Fair* online, October 2013.
9. Duchess of Windsor, *Heart Has Its Reasons*, 202.
10. Bloch, *Wallis and Edward: Letters*, 67–68.
11. Duke of Windsor, *King's Story*, 238.
12. Diana Cooper, *Autobiography: The Rainbow Comes and Goes, The Light of Common Day, Trumpets from the Steep* (London: Faber and Faber, 2008), 397–98.
13. Vanderbilt and Furness, *Double Exposure*, 269.
14. Duke of Windsor, *King's Story*, 239.

15. Ibid., 188.
16. Cooper, *Autobiography*, 397.
17. Duchess of Windsor, *Heart Has Its Reasons*, 192.
18. Duke of Windsor, *King's Story*, 27.
19. Duchess of Windsor, *Heart Has Its Reasons*, 195.
20. Ibid., 196.
21. Ibid., 199.
22. Bloch, *Wallis and Edward: Letters*, 76.
23. Ziegler, *Edward VIII*, 216.
24. *Daily Sketch*, January 30, 1929.
25. Duke of Windsor, *King's Story*, 256.
26. Vickers, interview.
27. Ziegler, *Edward VIII*, 199.
28. Pope-Hennessy, *Quest for Queen Mary*, 199.
29. Ziegler, *Edward VIII*, 199.
30. Vickers, *Behind Closed Doors*, 281.
31. Ziegler, *Edward VIII*, 199.
32. Pope-Hennessy, *Quest for Queen Mary*, 171.
33. Duke and Duchess of Windsor, interview by Harris.
34. Dr. Charles Spicer, interview with author; Charles Spicer, "Ambulant Amateurs: The Rise and Fade of the Anglo-German Fellowship" (PhD thesis).
35. Sebba, *That Woman*, 183.
36. Evans, *Queen Bees*, 197.
37. Duchess of Windsor, *Heart Has Its Reasons*, 200.
38. Bloch, *Wallis and Edward: Letters*, 65.
39. Sebba, *That Woman*, 93.
40. Ibid., 93–94.
41. Vanderbilt and Furness, *Double Exposure*, 279.
42. Bloch, *Wallis and Edward: Letters*, 82–83.
43. Duchess of Windsor, *Heart Has Its Reasons*, 201.
44. Bloch, *Wallis and Edward: Letters*, 91.
45. Ibid., 93.
46. Kerr-Smiley, interview in *Wallis Simpson: The Secret Letters*.
47. Sebba, *That Woman*, 98.
48. Norwich, interview.
49. Duchess of Windsor, *Heart Has Its Reasons*, 203.
50. Ibid., 200.
51. Ziegler, *Edward VIII*, 200.
52. Ibid., 201.
53. Duke of Windsor, *King's Story*, 258.
54. Ibid., 257–58.
55. Bloch, *Wallis and Edward: Letters*, 96.
56. William Shawcross, ed., *Counting One's Blessings: The Selected Letters of Queen Elizabeth, the Queen Mother* (Macmillan, 2012), 198–99.
57. Ibid., 198.
58. Michael Thornton, *Royal Feud: The Queen Mother and the Duchess of Windsor* (London: Michael Joseph, 1985), 74.
59. Bloch, *Wallis and Edward: Letters*, 108.
60. Duchess of Windsor, *Heart Has Its Reasons*, 204.
61. Bloch, *Wallis and Edward: Letters*, 110.
62. Ibid., 114.
63. Ibid., 110.
64. Duchess of Windsor, *Heart Has Its Reasons*, 205.
65. Ibid., 258–59.

66. Ibid., 206.
67. Bloch, *Wallis and Edward: Letters*, 116.
68. Ibid., 117.
69. Ibid., 120.
70. Ibid.
71. Vanderbilt and Furness, *Double Exposure*, 236.
72. Ibid., 297–98.
73. Ibid.
74. Ibid.
75. Ibid.
76. Bloch, *Wallis and Edward: Letters*, 119.
77. Duchess of Windsor, *Heart Has Its Reasons*, 207.
78. Bloch, *Wallis and Edward: Letters*, 122.
79. Ibid., 120.
80. Sebba, *That Woman*, 98.

3: ONE AND ONLY

1. Duchess of Windsor, *Heart Has Its Reasons*, 207.
2. Ibid.
3. Ziegler, *Edward VIII*, 230.
4. Ibid.
5. Duchess of Windsor, *Heart Has Its Reasons*, 209.
6. Ibid.
7. Ziegler, *Edward VIII*, 230.
8. Duchess of Windsor, *Heart Has Its Reasons*, 210.
9. Ziegler, *Edward VIII*, 231.
10. Ibid.
11. Ibid., 214–15.
12. Mosley, *Duchess of Windsor*, 79.
13. Bloch, *Wallis and Edward: Letters*, 120–30.
14. Duchess of Windsor, *Heart Has Its Reasons*, 218.
15. Ibid.
16. Ibid., 219.
17. Thornton, *Royal Feud*, 73.
18. Duchess of Windsor, *Heart Has Its Reasons*, 219.
19. Bloch, *Wallis and Edward: Letters*, 134.
20. Thornton, *Royal Feud*, 73.
21. Ziegler, *Edward VIII*, 231.
22. Ibid.
23. Thornton, *Royal Feud*, 74.
24. Major Colin Burgess with Paul Carter, *Behind Palace Doors: My Service as the Queen Mother's Equerry* (London: John Blake, 2006), 78.
25. Vickers, interview.
26. Ibid.
27. Duchess of Windsor, *Heart Has Its Reasons*, 220.
28. Ibid.
29. Ibid., 256.
30. Duke and Duchess of Windsor, interview by Harris.
31. Ibid.
32. Ibid.
33. Bloch, *Wallis and Edward: Letters*, 132–33.
34. Ziegler, *Edward VIII*, 238.
35. "How His Majesty's Secret Service Spied on His Majesty." *Sunday Telegraph*, April 2, 2017.
36. Ibid.
37. Haslam, inteveiw.
38. Norwich, interview.
39. Duchess of Windsor, *Heart Has Its Reasons*, 134.
40. Mosley, *Duchess of Windsor*, 78.
41. Diary entry: autumn 1935, Richard Buckle, ed., *Self-Portrait with Friends: The Selected Diaries of Cecil Beaton 1926–74* (London: Weidenfeld & Nicolson, 1979), 47.

42. Evans, *Queen Bees*, 199.
43. Mosley, *Duchess of Windsor*, 78.
44. Channon, *Chips*, 23.
45. Duchess of Windsor, *Heart Has Its Reasons*, 215.
46. Ibid., 223.
47. Ibid.
48. Ibid., 225.
49. Ibid.
50. Ibid., 226.
51. Ibid.
52. Ibid.
53. Ziegler, *Edward VIII*, 232.
54. Ibid.
55. Ibid.
56. Ibid., 233.
57. Ibid.
58. Ibid.
58. *Wallis Simpson: The Secret Letters.*
60. Duchess of Windsor, *Heart Has Its Reasons*, 231.
61. Bloch, *Wallis and Edward: Letters*, 147.
62. Ibid., 149–50.
63. Channon, *Chips*, 45.
64. Ibid.
65. Duchess of Windsor, *Heart Has Its Reasons*, 233.
66. Bloch, *Wallis and Edward: Letters*, 151.
67. Ibid.
68. Duke of Windsor, *King's Story*, 259.
69. Channon, *Chips*, 33.
70. Cooper, *Autobiography*, 397–98.
71. Bloch, *Wallis and Edward: Letters*, 153–54.
72. Evans, *Queen Bees*, 208–9.
73. Channon, *Chips*, 48.
74. Bloch, *Wallis and Edward: Letters*, 158.
75. Maureen Emerson, *Riviera Dreaming: Love and War on the Côte d'Azur* (London: I. B. Tauris, 2018), 94.
76. Bloch, *Wallis and Edward: Letters*, 160.
77. Ziegler, *Edward VIII*, 234.
78. Bloch, *Wallis and Edward: Letters*, 162–63.
79. Vickers, interview.
80. Williams, "Vilification of Wallis Simpson."
81. Brendon, *Edward VIII*, 47.
82. Duke of Windsor, *King's Story*, 260.
83. Bloch, *Wallis and Edward: Letters*, 170–71.
84. Ibid.

4: GOD BLESS WE

1. James Pope-Hennessy, *Queen Mary, 1867–1953* (London: George Allen and Unwin, 1959), 556.
2. Ziegler, *Edward VIII*, 199.
3. Duke of Windsor, *King's Story*, 261.
4. Ibid., 262.
5. Bloch, *Wallis and Edward: Letters*, 177–78.
6. Norwich, *Duff Cooper Diaries*, 225.
7. Bloch, *Wallis and Edward: Letters*, 181.
8. Channon, *Chips*, 70.
9. Duke of Windsor, *King's Story*, 264.
10. Pope-Hennessy, *Queen Mary*, 558.
11. Duke of Windsor, *King's Story*, 265.
12. Ziegler, *Edward VIII*, 240–41.
13. Ibid., 240.
14. Lelyveld, Joseph, "1936 Secret Is Out—Doctor Sped George V's

Death," *New York Times*, November 28, 1986.
15. Duke of Windsor, *King's Story*, 266.
16. Ziegler, *Edward VIII*, 241.
17. Duchess of Windsor, *Heart Has Its Reasons*, 236.
18. Ziegler, *Edward VIII*, 241.
19. Duke of Windsor, *King's Story*, 268.
20. Ibid., 267–68.
21. Channon, *Chips*, 71.
22. Ibid., 71–72.
23. Norwich, *Duff Cooper Diaries*, 226.
24. Norwich, interview.
25. Norwich, *Duff Cooper Diaries*, 226.
26. Bloch, *Wallis and Edward: Letters*, 189.
27. Ibid., 190.
28. Brendon, *Edward VIII*, 48.
29. Frances Donaldson, *Edward VIII: The Road to Abdication* (London: Weidenfeld & Nicolson, 1974), 97.
30. Channon, *Chips*, 74.
31. Evans, *Queen Bees*, 232.
32. Ziegler, *Edward VIII*, 247.
33. Ibid.
34. Norwich, *Duff Cooper Diaries*, 227.
35. Ibid., 228.
36. Vickers, *Behind Closed Doors*, 297.
37. Bloch, *Wallis and Edward: Letters*, 190.
38. Channon, *Chips*, 78.
39. Brendon, *Edward VIII*, 49.
40. Lord Beaverbrook, *The Abdication of King Edward VIII*, ed. A. J. P. Taylor (London: Hamish Hamilton, 1966), 20.
41. Duke and Duchess of Windsor, interview by Harris.
42. Lord Beaverbrook, *Abdication of Edward VIII*, 14.
43. Duchess of Windsor, *Heart Has Its Reasons*, 239.
44. Norwich, interview.
45. Duke of Windsor, *King's Story*, 275–76.
46. Ibid., 276.
47. Ziegler, *Edward VIII*, 250.
48. Ibid.
49. Brendon, *Edward VIII*, 53.
50. Donaldson, *Road to Abdication*, 98.
51. Bloch, *Wallis and Edward: Letters*, 187.
52. Ibid.
53. Ibid.
54. Ibid., 191.
55. Ibid., 76.
56. Ibid., 189.
57. Ibid., 192.
58. Duchess of Windsor, *Heart Has Its Reasons*, 239–40.
59. Sebba, *That Woman*, 128.
60. Ibid.
61. Ibid.
62. Donaldson, *Road to Abdication*, 103.
63. Bloch, *Wallis and Edward: Letters*, 216.
64. Sebba, *That Woman*, 182.
65. Ibid., 125.
66. Ziegler, *Edward VIII*, 274.
67. Philip Ziegler, *Diana Cooper* (London: Hamish Hamilton, 1981), 176.
68. Ziegler, *Edward VIII*, 274.
69. Bloch, *Wallis and Edward: Letters*, 211.
70. Ibid., 213.
71. Ibid., 212.

72. Duchess of Windsor, *Heart Has Its Reasons*, 243.
73. Bloch, *Wallis and Edward: Letters*, 243.
74. Ibid.
75. Duchess of Windsor, *Heart Has Its Reasons*, 244.
76. Mosley, *Duchess of Windsor*, 89.
77. Duchess of Windsor, *Heart Has Its Reasons*, 242.
78. Ibid.
79. Thornton, *Royal Feud*, 95.
80. Ibid.
81. Duchess of Windsor, *Heart Has Its Reasons*, 242–43.
82. Thornton, *Royal Feud*, 95.
83. Mosley, *Duchess of Windsor*, 85–86.
84. Ibid., 86.
85. Ibid.
86. Bloch, *Wallis and Edward: Letters*, 214.
87. Ibid.
88. Vickers, *Behind Closed Doors*, 297.
89. Bloch, *Wallis and Edward: Letters*, 221.
90. Ziegler, *Edward VIII*, 281.
91. Channon, *Chips*, 89.

5: DOWN WITH THE AMERICAN HARLOT

1. Ziegler, *Edward VIII*, 263.
2. Pope-Hennessy, *Queen Mary*, 565.
3. Ziegler, *Edward VIII*, 263–64.
4. Brendon, *Edward VIII*, 56–57.
5. "Edward VIII's Coronation Portrait Uncovered," *Daily Telegraph*, December 9, 2011.
6. Pope-Hennessy, *Queen Mary*, 566.
7. Ibid., 567.
8. Duke of Windsor, *King's Story*, 309.
9. Emerson, *Riviera Dreaming*, 72.
10. Sebba, *That Woman*, 135.
11. Bloch, *Wallis and Edward: Letters*, 229.
12. Ziegler, *Edward VIII*, 282.
13. Norwich, interview.
14. Duchess of Windsor, *Heart Has Its Reasons*, 248.
15. Cooper, *Autobiography*, 411.
16. Ziegler, *Edward VIII*, 283.
17. Norwich, interview.
18. Cooper, *Autobiography*, 411.
19. Ibid., 421.
20. Ibid., 420.
21. Ibid.
22. Ziegler, *Diana Cooper*, 177.
23. Ibid., 177–78.
24. Duchess of Windsor, *Heart Has Its Reasons*, 251.
25. Maxwell, *I Married*, 244–45.
26. Ziegler, *Edward VIII*, 286.
27. Pope-Hennessy, *Queen Mary*, 568.
28. Duke of Windsor, *King's Story*, 314.
29. Duchess of Windsor, *Heart Has Its Reasons*, 253.
30. Bloch, *Wallis and Edward: Letters*, 234–35.
31. Vickers, interview.
32. Bloch, *Wallis and Edward: Letters*, 233.
33. Ibid., 236.
34. Duke of Windsor, *King's Story*, 315.
35. Ibid.
36. Shawcross, *Counting One's Blessings*, 220.
37. Ziegler, *Edward VIII*, 288.

38. Thornton, *Royal Feud*, 99.
39. Bloch, *Wallis and Edward: Letters*, 239.
40. Ibid.
41. Ziegler, *Edward VIII*, 288.
42. Thornton, *Royal Feud*, 113.
43. Ziegler, *Edward VIII*, 288.
44. Buckle, *Self-Portrait*, 54.
45. Ibid., 48.
46. Ibid.
47. Duke of Windsor, *King's Story*, 316.
48. Shawcross, *Counting One's Blessings*, 221–22.
49. Ibid., 223.
50. Bloch, *Wallis and Edward: Letters*, 241.
51. Ibid., 240.
52. Duke of Windsor, *King's Story*, 317.
53. Ibid.
54. Lord Beaverbrook, *Abdication of King Edward VIII*, 30–31.
55. Brendon, *Edward VIII*, 59.
56. Lord Beaverbrook, *Abdication of King Edward VIII*, 33.
57. Bloch, *Wallis and Edward: Letters*, 243.
58. Ibid., 236.
59. Donaldson, *Road to Abdication*, 116.
60. Ibid.
61. Ziegler, *Edward VIII*, 293.
62. Donaldson, *Road to Abdication*, 117.
63. Lord Beaverbrook, *Abdication of King Edward VIII*, 14.
64. Ibid., 26.
65. Duke of Windsor, *King's Story*, 320.
66. Ibid., 320–21.
67. Ziegler, *Edward VIII*, 293.
68. Thornton, *Royal Feud*, 116.

6: OCEANS OF AGONY

1. Thornton, *Royal Feud*, 116.
2. Duchess of Windsor, *Heart Has Its Reasons*, 258.
3. Duke of Windsor, *King's Story*, 321.
4. Duchess of Windsor, *Heart Has Its Reasons*, 260.
5. Channon, *Chips*, 99.
6. Buckle, *Self-Portrait*, 48–50.
7. Ibid.
8. Ibid.
9. Vreeland, *DV*, 69.
10 Duke of Windsor, *King's Story*, 322.
11. Ibid., 326.
12. Donaldson, *Road to Abdication*, 119.
13. Channon, *Chips*, 101.
14. Duchess of Windsor, *Heart Has Its Reasons*, 270.
15. Donaldson, *Road to Abdication*, 119.
16. Ibid., 119–21.
17. Maude-Roxby, interview.
18. Duke of Windsor, *King's Story*, 326.
19. Evans, *Queen Bees*, 249.
20. Bloch, *Wallis and Edward: Letters*, 248–49.
21. Duchess of Windsor, *Heart Has Its Reasons*, 260.
22. Duke of Windsor, *King's Story*, 327.
23. Ibid.
24. Ibid., 327–28.
25. Ibid., 328.
26. Ibid., 329.
27. Duchess of Windsor, *Heart Has Its Reasons*, 261.
28. Duke of Windsor, *King's Story*, 329.

29. Ibid., 330.
30. Ibid.
31. Ibid.
32. Duchess of Windsor, *Heart Has Its Reasons*, 263–64.
33. Ibid., 264.
34. Ibid.
35. Ibid.
36. Ibid.
37. Ibid., 265.
38. Ibid.
39. Ibid.
40. Duke of Windsor, *King's Story*, 331.
41. Ibid.
42. Donaldson, *Road to Abdication*, 129.
43. Duke of Windsor, *King's Story*, 332.
44. Ibid., 332–33.
45. Ibid., 332.
46. Ibid., 204.
47. Ibid., 205.
48. Ibid., 332.
49. Kenneth Rose, *Who's In, Who's Out: The Journals of Kenneth Rose:* vol. one, *1944–1979*, Ed. D. R. Thorpe (London: Weidenfeld & Nicolson, 2018), 383.
50. Duke of Windsor, *King's Story*, 332.
51. Sebba, *That Woman*, 156.
52. Donaldson, *Road to Abdication*, 130.
53. Norwich, *Duff Cooper Diaries*, 229.
54. Duchess of Windsor, *Heart Has Its Reasons*, 266.
55. Duke of Windsor, *King's Story*, 333.
56. Thornton, *Royal Feud*, 120.
57. Duke of Windsor, *King's Story*, 333.
58. Thornton, *Royal Feud*, 120.
59. Duke of Windsor, *King's Story*, 334.
60. Pope-Hennessy, *Quest for Queen Mary*, 306.
61. Duke of Windsor, *King's Story*, 334.
62. Ibid., 334–35.
63. Mosley, *Duchess of Windsor*, 103.
64. Pope-Hennessy, *Queen Mary*, 576.
65. Duke of Windsor, *King's Story*, 335–36.
66. Shawcross, *Counting One's Blessings*, 224–25.
67. Ziegler, *Edward VIII*, 300.
68. Norwich, *Duff Cooper Diaries*, 230.
69. Ibid.
70. Norwich, interview.
71. Norwich, *Duff Cooper Diaries*, 230.
72. Ibid.
73. Norwich, interview.
74. Duke of Windsor, *King's Story*, 340.
75. Ibid.
76. Norwich, *Duff Cooper Diaries*, 231.
77. Mosley, *Duchess of Windsor*, 576.
78. Channon, *Chips*, 103.
79. Ibid., 104.
80. Duke of Windsor, *King's Story*, 336.

7: THE LAST HOUR

1. See "The King in South Wales," 1936, historical video clip, 3:30, British Pathé online, www.britishpathe.com/video/the-king-in-south-wales.
2. Duke of Windsor, *King's Story*, 338.
3. Duke and Duchess of Windsor, interview by Harris.
4. Ziegler, *Edward VIII*, 301.
5. Ibid., 302.

6. Mosley, *Duchess of Windsor*, 105–6.
7. Duchess of Windsor, *Heart Has Its Reasons*, 267.
8. Ibid.
9. Ibid.
10. Williams, "Vilification of Wallis Simpson."
11. Thornton, *Royal Feud*, 121.
12. Channon, *Chips*, 105.
13. Ibid.
14. Ibid., 106.
15. Norwich, *Duff Cooper Diaries*, 232.
16. Shawcross, *Counting One's Blessings*, 225.
17. Duchess of Windsor, *Heart Has Its Reasons*, 268.
18. Duke of Windsor, *King's Story*, 341–42.
19. Ibid., 342.
20. Channon, *Chips*, 108.
21. Ziegler, *Edward VIII*, 302.
22. Duchess of Windsor, *Heart Has Its Reasons*, 269.
23. Ziegler, *Edward VIII*, 303.
24. Duke of Windsor, *King's Story*, 344.
25. Ziegler, *Edward VIII*, 304.
26. Ibid.
27. Duke of Windsor, *King's Story*, 346.
28. Lord Beaverbrook, *Abdication of King Edward VIII*, 61.
29. Ibid.
30. Ibid.
31. Duchess of Windsor, *Heart Has Its Reasons*, 270.
32. Ibid.
33. Shawcross, *Counting One's Blessings*, 226.
34. Duchess of Windsor, *Heart Has Its Reasons*, 271.
35. Ibid., 270–71.
36. Pope-Hennessy, *Quest for Queen Mary*, 200.
37. Duchess of Windsor, *Heart Has Its Reasons*, 273.
38. Channon, *Chips*, 111.
39. Bloch, *Wallis and Edward: Letters*, 254–55.
40. Ibid.
41. Donaldson, *Road to Abdication*, 142.
42. Duke of Windsor, *King's Story*, 355.
43. Ibid., 354.
44. Ibid., 355.
45. Ibid.
46. Duchess of Windsor, *Heart Has Its Reasons*, 273.
47. Ibid., 273–74.
48. Duke of Windsor, *King's Story*, 356.
49. Ibid., 355.
50. Lord Beaverbrook, *Abdication of King Edward VIII*, 67.
51. Ibid., 68.
52. Duchess of Windsor, *Heart Has Its Reasons*, 274.
53. Duke of Windsor, *King's Story*, 358.
54. Duchess of Windsor, *Heart Has Its Reasons*, 274.
55. Ibid., 275.
56. Vreeland, *DV*, 72.
57. Ziegler, *Edward VIII*, 308.
58. Duke of Windsor, *King's Story*, 361.
59. Channon, *Chips*, 114.
60. Ziegler, *Edward VIII*, 310.
61. Ibid.
62. Duke of Windsor, *King's Story*, 362.
63. Duchess of Windsor, *Heart Has Its Reasons*, 276.

64. Ibid.
65. Duke of Windsor, *King's Story*, 362.
66. Duchess of Windsor, *Heart Has Its Reasons*, 276.
67. Ziegler, *Edward VIII*, 310.
68. Duke of Windsor, *King's Story*, 364.
69. Bloch, *Wallis and Edward: Letters*, 257.
70. Williams, "Vilification of Wallis Simpson."
71. Channon, *Chips*, 115.
72. Ibid., 114–15.
73. Mosley, *Duchess of Windsor*, 115.
74. Pope-Hennessy, *Queen Mary*, 578.
75. Duke of Windsor, *King's Story*, 365.
76. Pope-Hennessy, *Queen Mary*, 578.
77. Ibid., 128.
78. Vreeland, *DV*, 73.
79. Ibid.
80. Ibid., 74.
81. "How His Majesty's Secret Service Spied."
82. Vreeland, *DV*, 74
83. Duchess of Windsor, *Heart Has Its Reasons*, 283.
84. Ibid., 284.
85. Mosley, *Duchess of Windsor*, 113–14.
86. Brendon, *Edward VIII*, 61.
87. Penelope Middleboe, ed., *Edith Olivier: From Her Journals 1924–48* (London: Weidenfeld & Nicolson, 1989), 187.
88. Ziegler, *Edward VIII*, 315.
89. Ibid., 317.
90. Ibid.
91. Ibid.
92. Sonia Purnell, *First Lady: The Life and Wars of Clementine Churchill* (London: Aurum Press, 2015), 194.
93. Ibid., 194.
94. Duke of Windsor, *King's Story*, 371.
95. Brendon, *Edward VIII*, 64.
96. Duke of Windsor, *King's Story*, 384.
97. Ziegler, *Edward VIII*, 330.
98. Duchess of Windsor, *Heart Has Its Reasons*, 293.
99. Bloch, *Wallis and Edward: Letters*, 262.
100. Duchess of Windsor, *Heart Has Its Reasons*, 294.
101. Ibid., 295.
102. Ziegler, *Edward VIII*, 395.
103. Duchess of Windsor, *Heart Has Its Reasons*, 296.
104. Ibid.
105. Ibid., 297.
106. Ibid.
107. Ibid., 298.
108. Donaldson, *Road to Abdication*, 156.
109. Duchess of Windsor, *Heart Has Its Reasons*, 300.
110. Ibid.
111. Ibid.
112. Ibid., 301.
113. Ibid.

8: THE FURY

1. Duke of Windsor, *King's Story*, 398.
2. Donaldson, *Road to Abdication*, 156.
3. Channon, *Chips*, 122.
4. Vickers, *Behind Closed Doors*, 190.
5. Bloch, *Wallis and Edward: Letters*, 264.

6. Duke of Windsor, *King's Story*, 402.
7. Pope-Hennessy, *Queen Mary*, 579.
8. Duke of Windsor, *King's Story*, 405.
9. Ibid.
10. Sebba, *That Woman*, 185.
11. Duke of Windsor, *King's Story*, 406–7.
12. Williams, "Vilification of Wallis Simpson."
13. Vickers, *Behind Closed Doors*, 304.
14. Pope-Hennessy, *Queen Mary*, 580.
15. Duke of Windsor, *King's Story*, 408.
16. Ibid.
17. Ibid.
18. Ziegler, *Edward VIII*, 325.
19. Duke of Windsor, *King's Story*, 65.
20. Ibid., 409.
21. Duchess of Windsor, *Heart Has Its Reasons*, 302.
22. Ibid.
23. Duke of Windsor, *King's Story*, 410.
24. Ibid.
25. Channon, *Chips*, 131.
26. Thornton, *Royal Feud*, 130.
27. Shawcross, *Counting One's Blessings*, 231.
28. Duke of Windsor, *King's Story*, 410.
29. Ibid., 411.
30. Duchess of Windsor, *Heart Has Its Reasons*, 302.
31. Duke of Windsor, *King's Story*, 411.
32. Duchess of Windsor, *Heart Has Its Reasons*, 302.
33. Channon, *Chips*, 126–27.
34. Pope-Hennessy, *Queen Mary*, 581.
35. Duke of Windsor, *King's Story*, 412.
36. Pope-Hennessy, *Queen Mary*, 581.
37. Channon, *Chips*, 131.
38. Duke of Windsor, *King's Story*, 412.
39. Channon, *Chips*, 131.
40. Duke of Windsor, *King's Story*, 413.
41. Vickers, *Behind Closed Doors*, 304–5.
42. Thornton, *Royal Feud*, 131.
43. Ziegler, *Edward VIII*, 338.
44. Ibid., 333.
45. Ibid., 338.
46. Channon, *Chips*, 129.
47. Duchess of Windsor, *Heart Has Its Reasons*, 304.
48. Ibid., 305.
49. Ibid., 306.
50. Ibid.
51. Bloch, *Wallis and Edward: Letters*, 274–75.
52. Duchess of Windsor, *Heart Has Its Reasons*, 303.
53. Vreeland, *DV*, 75.
54. Ibid., 74–75.
55. Ibid., 73.
56. Bloch, *Wallis and Edward: Letters*, 278–79.
57. Ibid., 270–71.
58. Ibid., 277.
59. Emerson, *Riviera Dreaming*, 27.
60. Sebba, *That Woman*, 185.
61. Duchess of Windsor, *Heart Has Its Reasons*, 307.
62. Ibid.
63. Wilson, *Her Name Was Wallis Warfield*, 89.

64. Sebba, *That Woman*, 192.
65. Ziegler, *Edward VIII*, 352.
66. Duchess of Windsor, *Heart Has Its Reasons*, 312.
67. Ibid., 313.
68. Norwich, interview.
69. Mosley, *Duchess of Windsor*, 8.
70. Pope-Hennessy, *Quest for Queen Mary*, 289.
71. Mosley, *Duchess of Windsor*, 8.
72. Shawcross, *Counting One's Blessings*, 234.
73. Philip Ziegler, *George VI: The Dutiful King* (London: Allen Lane, 2014), 43.
74. Brendon, *Edward VIII*, 69.
75. Bloch, *Wallis and Edward: Letters*, 288.
76. Ziegler, *Edward VIII*, 377.
77. Norwich, interview.
78. Channon, *Chips*, 158.
79. Bloch, *Wallis and Edward: Letters*, 291.
80. Ibid.
81. Pope-Hennessy, *Queen Mary*, 575.
82. Bloch, *Wallis and Edward: Letters*, 306.
83. Ibid., 312.
84. Ibid., 311.
85. Buckle, *Self-Portrait*, 51.
86. David Nasaw, *New York Times*, March 11, 1996.
87. Bloch, *Wallis and Edward: Letters*, 314.
88. Ibid., 314–15.
89. Duchess of Windsor, *Heart Has Its Reasons*, 315.
90. Ibid.
91. Duchess of Windsor, *Heart Has Its Reasons*, 318.
92. Bloch, *Wallis and Edward: Letters*, 325.
93. Ibid., 326.
94. Ibid., 327.
95. Duchess of Windsor, *Heart Has Its Reasons*, 319.
96. Ibid., 319–20.
97. Ibid., 336.
98. Bloch, *Wallis and Edward: Letters*, 337.
99. Obituary, *Daily Telegraph*, January 27, 2001.
100. Duchess of Windsor, *Heart Has Its Reasons*, 321.
101. Ibid.

9: UNTITLED

1. Buckle, *Self-Portrait*, 51–54.
2. Ibid.
3. Ibid.
4. Ibid.
5. Ibid.
6. Mosley, *Duchess of Windsor*, 129.
7. Duchess of Windsor, *Heart Has Its Reasons*, 321.
8. Ibid., 322–23.
9. Ibid., 322.
10. Sebba, *That Woman*, 200.
11. Vickers, *Behind Closed Doors*, 42.
12. *The Jewels of the Duchess of Windsor* (Geneva: Sotheby's, 1987), 80.
13. Mainbocher by Main Bocher, *Harper's Bazaar*, January 1938, 102–3.
14. Buckle, *Self-Portrait*, 56.
15. Ibid.
16. Sebba, *That Woman*, 206.
17. Vickers, *Behind Closed Doors*, 314.
18. Ibid.
19. Obituary, *Daily Telegraph*, January 27, 2001.
20. Shawcross, *Counting One's Blessings*, 243.
21. Ziegler, *Edward VIII*, 355.
22. Duchess of Windsor, *Heart Has Its Reasons*, 324.

23. Thornton, *Royal Feud*, 165.
24. Ibid.
25. Duchess of Windsor, *Heart Has Its Reasons*, 324.
26. Thornton, *Royal Feud*, 165.
27. Ibid.
28. Bloch, *Wallis and Edward: Letters*, 276.
29. Mosley, *Duchess of Windsor*, 138.
30. Ibid.
31. Duchess of Windsor, *Heart Has Its Reasons*, 324.
32. Haslam, interview.
33. Norwich, interview.
34. Mosley, *Duchess of Windsor*, 8.
35. Thornton, *Royal Feud*, 165–66.
36. Obituary, *Daily Telegraph*, January 27, 2001.
37. Vickers, *Behind Closed Doors*, 315.
38. Ibid.
39. Sebba, *That Woman*, 210.
40. Buckle, *Self-Portrait*, 55.
41. Ibid.
42. Sebba, *That Woman*, 206.
43. Ibid.
44. Buckle, *Self-Portrait*, 55.
45. Ibid.
46. Ibid.
47. Mosley, *Duchess of Windsor*, 136.
48. Pope-Hennessy, *Queen Mary*, 586.
49. Shawcross, *Counting One's Blessings*, 243.
50. Thornton, *Royal Feud*, 167.
51. Buckle, *Self-Portrait*, 56.
52. Sebba, *That Woman*, 207.
53. Vickers, *Behind Closed Doors*, 317–18.
54. Ibid., 318.
55. Thornton, *Royal Feud*, 167.
56. Vickers, *Behind Closed Doors*, 318.
57. Ibid.
58. Ibid., 318–19.
59. Thornton, *Royal Feud*, 166.
60. Mosley, *Duchess of Windsor*, 139.
61. Norwich, interview.
62. Mosley, *Duchess of Windsor*, 139.
63. Sebba, *That Woman*, 210.
64. Ziegler, *Edward VIII*, 364–65.
65. Channon, *Chips*, 163–64.
66. Ibid., 164.
67. Ibid., 163–64.
68. Duchess of Windsor, *Heart Has Its Reasons*, 324.
69. Ibid.
70. Ibid.
71. Ibid., 325.
72. Vickers, *Behind Closed Doors*, 320.
73. Duchess of Windsor, *Heart Has Its Reasons*, 325.
74. Pope-Hennessy, *Quest for Queen Mary*, 284.
75. Sebba, *That Woman*, 213.
76. Ibid., 212.
77. Ziegler, *Edward VIII*, 367.
78. Sebba, *That Woman*, 213.
79. Ibid.
80. Gore Vidal, *Palimpsest: A Memoir* (New York: Random House, 1995), 206.

10: THE TWILIGHT ZONE

1. Sebba, *That Woman*, 215–16.
2. Duke of Windsor, *King's Story*, 279.
3. Ziegler, *Edward VIII*, 386.
4. Brendon, *Edward VIII*, 72–73.
5. Sebba, *That Woman*, 216–17.
6. Duchess of Windsor, *Heart Has Its Reasons*, 333.
7. Ibid.
8. Ziegler, *Edward VIII*, 391.
9. Mosley, *Duchess of Windsor*, 140.

10. Vickers, *Behind Closed Doors*, 323.
11. Ibid.
12. Ziegler, *Edward VIII*, 393.
13. *New York Times*, November 7, 1937, and October 10, 1937.
14. Nasaw, *New York Times*, March 11, 1996.
15. Sebba, *That Woman*, 219.
16. Duchess of Windsor, *Heart Has Its Reasons*, 337.
17. Michael Bloch, *The Duke of Windsor's War* (London: Little Brown, 2012), 97.
18. Duchess of Windsor, *Heart Has Its Reasons*, 339.
19. Ziegler, *Edward VIII*, 386.
20. Mosley, *Duchess of Windsor*, 153.
21. Duchess of Windsor, *Heart Has Its Reasons*, 343.
22. Thierry Coudert, *Beautiful People of the Café Society: Scrapbooks by the Baron de Cabrol* (Paris: Flammarion, 2016), 215.
23. Maxwell, *I Married*, 249.
24. Coudert, *Beautiful People*, 222–23.
25. Ziegler, *Edward VIII*, 369.
26. Ibid.
27. Ibid., 369–70.
28. Ibid.
29. Thornton, *Royal Feud*, 182.
30. Ibid.
31. Ibid.
32. Ibid., 210.
33. Duchess of Windsor, *Heart Has Its Reasons*, 340.
34. Ibid.
35. Ibid., 341.
36. Ibid.
37. Mosley, *Duchess of Windsor*, 142–43.
38. Ziegler, *Edward VIII*, 371.
39. Ibid., 375.
40. Vickers, interview.
41. Sebba, *That Woman*, 223.
42. Ibid., 224.
43. Mosley, *Duchess of Windsor*, 153.
44. Ibid.
45. Brendon, *Edward VIII*, 76.
46. Duchess of Windsor. *Heart Has Its Reasons*, 345–46.
47. Shawcross, *Counting One's Blessings*, 346.
48. Ziegler, *Edward VIII*, 402.
49. Ibid., 403.
50. Ibid.
51. Shawcross, *Counting One's Blessings*, 275.
52. Sebba, *That Woman*, 226.
53. Duchess of Windsor, *Heart Has Its Reasons*, 350.
54. Ibid., 351.
55. Ibid.
56. Mollie Panter-Downes, *London War Notes*, ed. William Shawn (London: Longman, 1972), 11.
57. Ziegler, *Edward VIII*, 404.
58. Panter-Downes, *London War Notes*, 11.
59. Ziegler, *Edward VIII*, 405.
60. Duchess of Windsor, *Heart Has Its Reasons*, 352.
61. Ibid.
62. Shawcross, *Counting One's Blessings*, 279.
63. Ibid., 280.
64. Duchess of Windsor, *Heart Has Its Reasons*, 352.
65. Ziegler, *Edward VIII*, 408.
66. Brendon, *Edward VIII*, 77.
67. Anne Sebba, *Les Parisiennes: How the Women of Paris Lived, Loved and Died in the 1940s*

(London: Weidenfeld & Nicolson, 2016), 5.

68. Duchess of Windsor, *Heart Has Its Reasons*, 228.
69. Ibid., 357.
70. Ziegler, *Edward VIII*, 411.
71. Duchess of Windsor, *Heart Has Its Reasons*, 357.
72. Brendon, *Edward VIII*, 78.
73. Ziegler, *Edward VIII*, 416.
74. Ibid., 417.
75. Ibid.
76. Ibid., 418.
77. Sebba, *Les Parisiennes*, 41.
78. Brendon, *Edward VIII*, 79.
79. Duchess of Windsor, *Heart Has Its Reasons*, 365.
80. Ibid., 365–66.
81. Norwich, interview.
82. Duchess of Windsor, *Heart Has Its Reasons*, 370.
83. Hugo Vickers, "*The Crown*: What to Believe and What Is Make-Believe," *Times (*UK), December 11, 2017.
84. Duchess of Windsor, *Heart Has Its Reasons*, 370.
85. Ibid.
86. Vickers, *Behind Closed Doors*, 330.
87. Ibid.
88. Ziegler, *Edward VIII*, 427.

11: A SHADOW KING

1. Duchess of Windsor, *Heart Has Its Reasons*, 374.
2. Ziegler, *Edward VIII*, 429.
3. "The Duke of Windsor's 1940 Bermuda Detour," Bernews.com, May 2013.
4. Ibid.
5. Ibid.
6. Sir Orville Turnquest, *What Manner of Man Is This? The Duke of Windsor's Years in the Bahamas* (Nassau, the Bahamas: Grant's Town Press, 2016), xx.
7. See "Duke of Windsor Takes the Oath," 1940, historical video clip, 1:29, British Pathé online, www.britishpathe.com/video/duke-of-windsor-takes-the-the-oath.
8. Turnquest, *What Manner of Man*, 136.
9. Norwich, interview.
10. Julie Le Corne, interview with author, London, August 2017.
11. Turnquest, *What Manner of Man*, 54.
12. Thornton, *Royal Feud*, 215.
13. Ibid.
14. Ann Pleydell-Bouverie, interview with author, Gstaad, Switzerland, February 2017.
15. Mosley, *Duchess of Windsor*, 165.
16. Le Corne interview.
17. Sebba, *That Woman*, 238.
18. Ziegler, *Edward VIII*, 460.
19. Sebba, *That Woman*, 240.
20. Brendon, *Edward VIII*, 87.
21. Ziegler, *Edward VIII*, 461.
22. Sebba, *That Woman*, 241.
23. Ibid.
24. Ibid.
25. Thornton, *Royal Feud*, 220.
26. Ziegler, *Edward VIII*, 466.
27. Ibid., 467.
28. Thornton, *Royal Feud*, 221.
29. Ziegler, *Edward VIII*, 468.
30. Thornton, *Royal Feud*, 221.
31. Sebba, *That Woman*, 243.
32. Ibid.
33. Ibid., 245.
34. Ibid., 249.
35. Ibid.
36. Brendon, *Edward VIII*, 89.

37. Turnquest, *What Manner of Man*, 133.
38. Ibid.
39. Duchess of Windsor, *Heart Has Its Reasons*, 382.
40. Ibid., 383.
41. Ibid., 382.
42. Ibid., 387.
43. Ibid., 387–88.
44. Ibid., 388.
45. Ziegler, *Edward VIII*, 487.
46. Vickers, *Behind Closed Doors*, 335.
47. Duchess of Windsor, *Heart Has Its Reasons*, 388.
48. Vickers, interview.
49. Ziegler, *Edward VIII*, 485.
50. Thornton, *Royal Feud*, 225.
51. Channon, *Chips*, 438.
52. Dorothy Wilding, *The Pursuit of Perfection* (London: National Portrait Gallery, 1991), 24–25.
53. Thornton, *Royal Feud*, 226.
54. Ibid., 226–27.
55. Vickers, *Behind Closed Doors*, 337.
56. Thornton, *Royal Feud*, 227.
57. Ziegler, *Edward VIII*, 488.

12: *SON ALTESSE ROYALE*

1. Blackwood, *Last of the Duchess*, 270.
2. Ziegler, *Edward VIII*, 500.
3. Pope-Hennessy, *Queen Mary*, 614.
4. Ziegler, *Edward VIII*, 501.
5. Ibid.
6. Ibid., 500.
7. Ibid., 501.
8. Ibid., 507.
9. Rose, *Who's In, Who's Out*, 558.
10. Schönburg, interview.
11. Emerson, *Riviera Dreaming*, 85.
12. Norwich, *Duff Cooper Diaries*, 390.
13. Ziegler, *Edward VIII*, 509.
14. Norwich, interview.
15. Coudert, *Beautiful People*, 63.
16. Vidal, *Palimpsest*, 205–6.
17. Sebba, *Les Parisiennes*, 384.
18. Blackwood, *Last of the Duchess*, 246.
19. Ibid.
20. Coudert, *Beautiful People*, 222.
21. Mosley, *Duchess of Windsor*, 188.
22. "A Cut Above: Stylist to the Stars Dies," *Independent* (UK), January 14, 2008, www.independent.co.uk/news/world/europe/a-cut-above-stylist-to-the-stars-dies-769905.html.
23. Ibid.
24. Ibid.
25. Ziegler, *Edward VIII*, 511.
26. Coudert, *Beautiful People*, 222.
27. Vickers, *Behind Closed Doors*, 339.
28. Blackwood, *Last of the Duchess*, 100.
29. Ibid.
30. Ibid., 101.
31. Ibid.
32. Ibid., 258.
33. Ziegler, *Edward VIII*, 513.
34. Pope-Hennessy, *Queen Mary*, 615.
35. Ziegler, *Edward VIII*, 529.
36. Ibid.
37. Ibid., 529–30.
38. Ibid., 530.
39. Ibid.
40. Ibid., 531.
41. Ibid.
42. Ibid., 532.
43. Ibid.

44. Shawcross, *Counting One's Blessings*, 420–21.
45. Norwich, *Duff Cooper Diaries*, 467.
46. Duchess of Windsor to Lady Mendl, September 24, 1948.
47. Ziegler, *Edward VIII*, 518.
48. Maud-Roxby, interview.
49. Ziegler, *Edward VIII*, 533.
50. Vickers, *Behind Closed Doors*, 341.
51. Ibid., 343.
52. Ziegler, *Edward VIII*, 519.
53. Blackwood, *Last of the Duchess*, 251.
54. Ibid., 252
55. Ibid.
56. Ibid., 252–53.
57. Ibid., 261.
58. Vickers, *Behind Closed Doors*, 350.
59. Mosley, *Duchess of Windsor*, 187.
60. Maxwell, *I Married*, 259.
61. Schönburg, interview.
62. Norwich, interview.
63. Ziegler, *Edward VIII*, 534.
64. Mosley, *Duchess of Windsor*, 175.
65. Vreeland, *DV*, 68.
66. Ibid.
67. Schönburg, interview.
68. Pope-Hennessy, *Quest for Queen Mary*, 278–79.
69. Vickers, *Behind Closed Doors*, 333.
70. Norwich, interview.
71. Vreeland, *DV*, 72
72. Shawcross, *Counting One's Blessings*, 439.
73. Thornton, *Royal Feud*, 250.
74. Ibid., 256.
75. Ibid.
76. Ibid., 250.
77. Ziegler, *Edward VIII*, 537.
78. Ibid.
79. Vickers, *Behind Closed Doors*, 345.
80. Burgess, *Behind Palace Doors*, 80.
81. Blackwood, *Last of the Duchess*, 249.
82. Brendon, *Edward VIII*, 98.
83. Ziegler, *Edward VIII*, 538.
84. Pope-Hennessy, *Quest for Queen Mary*, 290.
85. Ibid., 199.
86. Ziegler, *Edward VIII*, 539.
87. Ibid.
88. Ibid., 540.
89. Norwich, interview.

13: MY DAVID

1. Vickers, *Behind Closed Doors*, 355.
2. Jonathan Dimbleby, *The Prince of Wales: A Biography* (New York: William Morrow, 1994), 178.
3. *Times* (UK), December 1, 1958.
4. Schönburg, interview.
5. Vickers, *Behind Closed Doors*, 357–58.
6. Duchess of Windsor, *Heart Has Its Reasons*, 398.
7. Diana Cooper, *Darling Monster: The Letters of Lady Diana Cooper to Her Son John Julius Norwich 1939–1952* (New York: Overlook Press, 2014), 442.
8. Ziegler, *Edward VIII*, 555.
9. Schönburg, interview.
10. Ibid.
11. Ibid.
12. Nicolas Foulkes, *The Marbella Club* (London: Random House, 2014), 129.
13. Schönburg, interview.
14. Vickers, *Behind Closed Doors*, 359.

15. "Windsor in 'Excellent' Condition After Surgery Lasting One Hour," *New York Times*, December 17, 1964.
16. Mosley, *Duchess of Windsor*, 198.
17. Thornton, *Royal Feud*, 299.
18. Ibid., 300.
19. Ibid.
20. Vickers, interview.
21. Thornton, *Royal Feud*, 302–3.
22. Rose, *Who's In, Who's Out*, 382.
23. Ibid., 383.
24. Ibid., 384.
25. Dimbleby, *Prince of Wales*, 178.
26. Ibid., 178–79.
27. Ibid.
28. Mosley, *Duchess of Windsor*, 201.
29. Vickers, *Behind Closed Doors*, 19.
30. Ibid.
31. Thornton, *Royal Feud*, 316.
32. Vickers, *Behind Closed Doors*, 22.
33. Thornton, *Royal Feud*, 319.
34. Ibid.
35. Mosley, *Duchess of Windsor*, 201.
36. *Evening News* London, May 29, 1972.
37. Vickers, interview.
38. Mosley, *Duchess of Windsor*, 207.
39. *Times* (UK) and *Daily Telegraph*, June 3, 1972.
40. Thornton, *Royal Feud*, 325.
41. Dimbleby, *Prince of Wales*, 180.
42. Vickers, *Behind Closed Doors*, 30.
43. Ibid.
44. Ibid., 32.
45. Ibid., 33.
46. Mosley, *Duchess of Windsor*, 207.
47. Email to author from Lady Pamela Hicks, August 21, 2017.
48. Blackwood, *Last of the Duchess*, 30.
49. Mosley, *Duchess of Windsor*, 207.
50. Vreeland, *DV*, 68.
51. Ibid.
52. Vidal, *Palimpsest*, 206–7.
53. Vickers, interview.
54. Blackwood, *Last of the Duchess*, 38.
55. Ibid.
56. Ibid., 19.
57. Ibid., 38–39.
58. Ibid., 18–19.
59. Ibid., 258.
60. Vidal, *Palimpsest*, 207.
61. Vickers, *Behind Closed Doors*, 190.
62. Dimbleby, *Prince of Wales*, 180.
63. Norwich, interview.
64. Vickers, *Behind Closed Doors*, 192.
65. Ibid., 193.
66. Vickers, interview.
67. Vickers, *Behind Closed Doors*, 198.
68. Michael Thornton, "Did Mrs. Simpson Ever Truly Love the King Who Gave Up His Throne for Her?," *London Daily Mail*, April 8, 2017.
69. Alfred Lord Tennyson, "Ode to Memory," 1830.

EPILOGUE: THE CEDAR WALK

1. Duchess of Windsor, *Heart Has Its Reasons*, 190.
2. Ibid.
3. Ibid.
4. Diana Mosley, interview by Russell Harty, *All About Books*, BBC 1, June 26, 1980, www.bbc.co.uk/archive/edward_viii/12928.shtml.
5. Schönburg, interview.

POSTSCRIPT

1. Duke of Windsor, *King's Story*, 385.

SELECT BIBLIOGRAPHY

Beaton, Cecil. *Self-Portrait with Friends: The Selected Diaries of Cecil Beaton, 1926–1974*. Edited by Richard Buckle. London: Weidenfeld & Nicolson, 1979.

Beaverbrook, Lord. *The Abdication of King Edward VIII*. Edited by A. J. P. Taylor. London: Hamish Hamilton, 1966.

Blackwood, Caroline. *The Last of the Duchess: The Strange and Sinister Story of the Final Years of Wallis Simpson, Duchess of Windsor*. New York: Vintage Books, 2012.

Bloch, Michael. *The Duke of Windsor's War*. London: Little, Brown, 2012.

———, ed. *Wallis and Edward, Letters, 1931–1937: The Intimate Correspondence of the Duke and Duchess of Windsor*. New York: Summit Books, 1986.

Brendon, Piers. *Edward VIII: The Uncrowned King*. London: Allen Lane, 2016.

Burgess, Major Colin, with Paul Carter. *Behind Palace Doors: My Service as the Queen Mother's Equerry*. London: John Blake, 2006.

Channon, Henry. *Chips: The Diaries of Sir Henry Channon*. Edited by Robert Rhodes James. London: Weidenfeld & Nicolson, 1967.

Cooper, Diana. *Autobiography: "The Rainbow Comes and Goes," "The Light of Common Day," and "Trumpets from the Steep."* London: Faber & Faber, 2008.

———. *Darling Monster: The Letters of Lady Diana Cooper to Her Son John Julius Norwich, 1939–1952*. Edited by John Julius Norwich. New York: Overlook Press, 2014.

Coudert, Thierry. *Beautiful People of the Café Society: Scrapbooks by the Baron de Cabrol*. Paris: Flammarion, 2016.

Dimbleby, Jonathan. *The Prince of Wales: A Biography*. New York: William Morrow, 1994.

Donaldson, Frances. *Edward VIII: The Road to Abdication*. London: Weidenfeld & Nicolson, 1974.

Evans, Siân. *Queen Bees: Six Brilliant and Extraordinary Society Hostesses Between the Wars*. London: Two Roads, 2016.

Foulkes, Nicholas. *The Marbella Club*. London: Random House, 2014.

Haslam, Nicholas. *Redeeming Features: A Memoir*. New York: Vintage Books, 2010.

The Jewels of the Duchess of Windsor. Geneva: Sotheby's, 1987. Auction catalog.

Maxwell, Elsa. I Married the World. London: William Heinemann, 1955.

Middleboe, Penelope, ed. *Edith Olivier: From Her Journals, 1924–48*. London: Weidenfeld & Nicolson, 1989.

Mosley, Diana. *The Duchess of Windsor: A Memoir*. London: Gibson Square Books, 2012.

Norwich, John Julius, ed. *The Duff Cooper Diaries*. London: Weidenfeld & Nicolson, 2005.

Panter-Downes, Mollie. *London War Notes*. Edited by William Shawn. London: Longman, 1972.

Pope-Hennessy, James. *The Quest for Queen Mary*. Edited by Hugo Vickers. London: Zuleika, 2018.

———. *Queen Mary, 1867–1953*. London: George Allen and Unwin, 1959.

Purnell, Sonia. *First Lady: The Life and Wars of Clementine Churchill*. London: Aurum Press, 2015.

Sebba, Anne. *Les Parisiennes: How the Women of Paris Lived, Loved and Died in the 1940s*. London: Weidenfeld & Nicolson, 2016.

———. *That Woman: The Life of Wallis Simpson, Duchess of Windsor*. London: Weidenfeld & Nicolson, 2011.

Shawcross, William, ed. *Counting One's Blessings: The Selected Letters of Queen Elizabeth, the Queen Mother*. London: Macmillan, 2012.

Sparke, Penny. *Elsie de Wolfe: The Birth of Modern Interior Decoration*. Edited by Mitchell Owen. New York: Acanthus Press, 2005.

Thornton, Michael. *Royal Feud: The Queen Mother and the Duchess of Windsor*. London: Michael Joseph, 1985.

Turnquest, Sir Orville. *What Manner of Man Is This? The Duke of Windsor's Years in the Bahamas*. Nassau, the Bahamas: Grant's Town Press, 2016.

Vanderbilt, Gloria, and Thelma Lady Furness. *Double Exposure: A Twin Autobiography*. London: Frederick Muller, 1959.

Vickers, Hugo. *Behind Closed Doors: The Tragic Untold Story of the Duchess of Windsor*. London: Hutchinson, 2011.

Vidal, Gore. *Palimpsest: A Memoir*. New York: Random House, 1995.

Vreeland, Diana. *DV*. Edited by George Plimpton and Christopher Hemphill. New York: Alfred A. Knopf, 1984.

Wheeler, Sara. *Too Close to the Sun: The Audacious Life and Times of Denys Finch Hatton*. London: Jonathan Cape, 2006.

Wilding, Dorothy. *The Pursuit of Perfection*. London: National Portrait Gallery, 1991.

Wilson, Edwina H. *Her Name Was Wallis Warfield: The Life Story of Mrs. Ernest Simpson*. New York: E. P. Dutton, 1936.

Windsor, Duchess of. *The Heart Has Its Reasons*. London: Tandem, 1969. First published 1956 by Michael Joseph (London).

Windsor, Duke of. *A King's Story: The Memoirs of H.R.H. the Duke of Windsor*. London: Cassell, 1951. First published 1947 by G. P. Putnam's Sons (New York).

Ziegler, Philip. *Diana Cooper*. London: Hamish Hamilton, 1981.

———. *George VI: The Dutiful King*. London: Allen Lane, 2014.

———. *King Edward VIII: The Official Biography*. Glasgow: William Collins and Sons, 1990.

IMAGE CREDITS

Bessie Wallis Warfield aged six months, with her mother, Alice, 1896: Keystone-France/Gamma-Keystone via Getty Images

Four generations: Edward, aged six, with his great-grandmother Queen Victoria, his grandfather Prince Edward (later King Edward VII) and his father Prince George (later King George V): Keystone/Getty Images

Naval cadets Edward and Bertie with their mother, Queen Mary, at Barton Manor, Isle of Wight, 1909: Kirk and Sons of Cowes/Heritage Images/Getty Images

The Prince of Wales, 1911: Universal History Archive/UIG via Getty Images

A young Wallis, aged ten: Bettmann/Getty Images

Wallis's first husband, US Navy pilot Earl Winfield Spencer: Wikipedia

Wallis with her bridesmaids and maid of honor for her marriage to Spencer, 1916: TopFoto.co.uk

Edward on tour, Halifax, Nova Scotia, 1919: Ernest Brooks/Central Press/Getty Images

Edward with Winston Churchill, one of his political mentors, 1919: Keystone/Getty Images

Wallis and her second husband, Ernest Simpson, presented at court in June 1931: Granger/Bridgeman Images

Fort Belvedere: Courtesy of the author

Wallis relaxes at Belvedere with her cairn terrier Slipper, 1935: Granger/Bridgeman Images

King George V's funeral procession, January 1936: Print Collector/Getty Images

Wallis places a hand on the king's arm during the *Nahlin* cruise along the

Adriatic, August 1936: © Hulton-Deutsch Collection/CORBIS/Corbis via Getty Images

Wallis photographed for *Vogue* by Cecil Beaton at the Château de Candé, France, May 1937: Cecil Beaton/Condé Nast via Getty Images

Three weeks after Bertie's coronation as George VI, Wallis and Edward marry, June 3, 1937, at the Château de Candé: Bettmann/Getty Images

An official event in Nassau, 1940: Courtesy of the author

In Nassau during the Second World War, Wallis became local president of the Red Cross: Keystone/Hulton Archive/Getty Images

The duke and duchess with their friend Charles Bethell, who introduced them to Nassau society, 1940: Courtesy of the author

The duke and duchess on the steps of the Bahamian Club at a farewell party that they hosted, Nassau, 1945: Courtesy of the author

Dorothy Wilding's portrait of the duke and duchess, New York, June 1943: Courtesy of the author

Queen Mary and Edward, Marlborough House, October 1945: Reg Speller/Fox Photos/Getty Images

The duke and duchess return to France from a trip to the United States, 1955: Bettmann/Getty Images

Wallis dines at the Marbella Club, September 1964: Courtesy of the author

The Queen, the Duke of Edinburgh and Prince Charles visit the duke and duchess in the Bois de Boulogne, May 1972, shortly before the duke's death: Keystone Pictures USA/Alamy Stock Photo

Two days before Edward's funeral, Wallis watches the Trooping the Colour from Buckingham Palace, June 3, 1972: Bettmann/Getty Images

The Queen, Wallis and the Queen Mother leave St. George's Chapel after the funeral service for the Duke of Windsor: Central Press/Getty Images

Funeral of a duchess: Wallis's coffin is carried, watched by Prince Charles, the Queen, the Queen Mother and Princess Anne, April 20, 1986: Popperfoto/Getty Images

Wallis's bedroom in the villa in the Bois de Boulogne, with her glass-topped dressing table and pug cushions lined up on the sofa: Manuel Litran/*Paris Match* via Getty Images

The author's bouquet of flowers: a tribute to Wallis at her grave at Frogmore: Courtesy of the author

Every effort has been made to contact copyright holders and obtain permission to reproduce material in this book. The publisher would be pleased to rectify any omissions in subsequent editions of the book.

INDEX

ABOUT THE AUTHOR

Anna Pasternak is the author of *Princess in Love* and *Lara*, which revealed the true story of the love affair behind her great-uncle Boris Pasternak's *Doctor Zhivago*. Her work has appeared in *Vanity Fair, Vogue, Harper's Bazaar, Town & Country, Tatler*, and every major British newspaper. She lives in England.